TIME'S UP!

TIME'S UP!

THE SUBSCRIPTION BUSINESS MODEL
FOR PROFESSIONAL FIRMS

PAUL DUNN

RONALD J. BAKER

WILEY

Published by John Wiley & Sons, Inc., Hoboken, New Jersey.
Published simultaneously in Canada.

For general information on our other products and services or for technical support,
please contact our Customer Care Department within the United States at (800) 762-
2974, outside the United States at (317) 572-3993 or fax (317) 572-4002.

Wiley also publishes its books in a variety of electronic formats. Some content that
appears in print may not be available in electronic formats. For more information about
Wiley products, visit our website at www.wiley.com.

Library of Congress Cataloging-in-Publication Data is Available:

ISBN 9781119893523 (Hardback)
ISBN 9781119893530 (ePDF)
ISBN 9781119893547 (ePUB)

COVER ART & DESIGN: PAUL MCCARTHY

SKY10036806_101222

PAUL: To David Hartley and Ric Payne, both of whom helped me see that working with accountants, their teams, and their customers was such a noble calling. Both continue to do that, too—David with his work on Triple Entry Accounting using the blockchain and Ric with stunning insights (and Radar Charts) that open up new ways for accountants to add enormous value to their customers.

RON: For Ken Baker, who we lost far too soon. A Persian proverb teaches, "He that hath no brother hath weak legs." I now understand.

For what it's worth: it's never too late or, in my case, too early to be whoever you want to be. There's no time limit, stop whenever you want. You can change or stay the same, there are no rules to this thing. We can make the best or the worst of it. I hope you make the best of it. And I hope you see things that startle you. I hope you feel things you never felt before. I hope you meet people with a different point of view. I hope you live a life you're proud of. If you find that you're not, I hope you have the courage to start all over again.

—F. Scott Fitzgerald

CONTENTS

Foreword   xi

Preface   xv

Acknowledgments   xxiii

About the Authors   xxix

The Keynote and the Workshop:
How to Read This Book   xxxiii

I   The Keynote   1

1   What Got You Here Won't Get You There . . .
      Thank Goodness!   3

2   We All Have a Story—Here's a New One for You   11

3   Time-Driven Sucks . . . Impact-Driven Matters   27

4   How Aretha Got It Right   41

5   This Could Be the Most Important Business
      Question Ever   47

6   Thank Goodness—A New Definition for ESG
      That Really Does Make a Difference   79

7   The Ongoing Upward Spiral—Perhaps a
      Different Kind of Legacy   87

II   The Workshop   97

8   A Renaissance: The Subscription Economy   99

9   The Direct Primary Care Disrupters   107

10   Business Model Evolution   119

11   Purpose, Strategy, and Positioning   137

12   Marketing, Innovation, and Risk   151

13   Customer Transformations   167

14   Two Timeless Truths and Two Theories   179

15   Pricing the Relationship   189

16   Customer Segmentation and Pricing Tiers   205

17   Pricing the Portfolio   217

18   Measurements and Moral Hazards   239

19   Subscription Business Income Statement and KPIs 257

**20   Knowledge Worker KPIs and the After-Action
       Review (AAR)   279**

21   From Zero Defects to Zero Defections   297

22   Adoption Models   311

23   What's Next?   327

References   335

Index   349

FOREWORD

Is it sacrilegious to call this book a revelation? Because that's what *Time's Up! The Subscription Business Model for Professional Firms* is.

This book reveals a whole new way of thinking about economics, business, and even accounting. And this way of thinking—this relatively new business model—is the solution to many of the problems that plague professional firms.

Let me explain. But first, let's go back over a decade, to the last time I had this feeling about one of Ron's books.

I'd just finished reading Ron's book *Implementing Value Pricing: A Radical Business Model for Professional Firms*. I was immediately sold on the theory. I implemented Ron's ideas in my own firm, dropping hourly billing and cost-plus pricing in favor of fixed monthly prices determined not by my own costs, but rather by the value created in the mind of the customer. The result was a great success.

I observed my colleagues and the broader accounting profession struggle to do the same. They seemed inexorably fixated on billable hours and job costing, even in the face of so much evidence that these methods are far from ideal.

I wondered, why? Why do accountants resist dropping their timesheets?

I sold my firm and went to work for a large accounting firm. My coworkers there struggled the most. I realized within a year that implementing value pricing at that firm was a lost cause.

Disillusioned, I abandoned public accounting to work for a startup company that made SaaS (Software-as-a-Service). We sold cloud-based software to businesses on subscription. Like many SaaS start-ups, we were growing like crazy.

What surprised me is that hardly anyone in SaaS cares about financial accounting. Especially GAAP. We did it because we had to, but we never looked at the financials.

Instead, what we used to run the business was a whole host of alternative SaaS metrics, an alphabet soup of acronyms that included MRR, ARR, ACV, LTV, CAC, CRR, NPS®, and Churn.

At the time, I was so excited to be working in tech that I didn't think too much of it. But it never sat right with me.

As a CPA, it felt somehow wrong that the fastest-growing technology companies in the world don't care about accounting. I asked myself, what's the deal with all these non-GAAP metrics proliferating across financial statements? It seemed irresponsible.

There was a disconnect in my mind between the excitement of contributing to the growth of a tech startup and the general disdain for the outputs of my chosen profession. But I didn't know how to articulate it.

Then I read this book, and it all clicked.

The accounting profession struggles to change because it doesn't understand the subscription economy.

And the reason the profession doesn't understand it is because our accounting theory can't handle it. Our accounting theory taught in universities and applied in public accounting firms is still rooted in the Industrial Age of railroads and assembly lines. It is transactional. It is focused on tangible assets. It's a system that developed over a hundred years ago and was perfected in the Gilded Age. But it hasn't changed much since then.

Our generally accepted accounting principles don't know how to value intellectual capital, intangible assets, and customer relationships. These are what drive value creation in subscription businesses, not equipment or inventory.

Ironically, the transactional mindset of accounting itself is what is holding back our profession from embracing a business model that has the potential to bring us closer to our customers, give greater meaning to our work, and make us wealthier, too.

It's time to unlearn the accounting of the Industrial Age and invent a new accounting for the knowledge economy. We need to go back to putting relationships at the center, not just with our rhetoric, but with our business model.

But that takes a significant mind shift. That's where *Time's Up! The Subscription Business Model for Professional Firms* comes in. This book is about replacing a transactional mindset with a relationship mindset through the lens of the subscription economy.

There is so much opportunity. Many professional firms are a perfect fit for subscriptions. The firms that have embraced subscriptions are growing the fastest and are achieving valuations at multiple times their annual revenue. But the best part is, you'll have better relationships with your customers and your team.

So dig into this book. And perhaps you'll have a revelation, too.

Blake Oliver, CPA
Email: blake@blakeoliver.com
Website: https://blakeoliver.com
Twitter: @BlakeTOliver

PREFACE

An idea starts to be interesting when you get scared of taking it to its logical conclusion.

—Nassim Nicholas Taleb, essayist, scholar, mathematical statistician, risk analyst

[Ron] It has been nearly two decades since Paul and I published *The Firm of the Future: A Guide for Accountants, Lawyers, and Other Professional Services*. Readers would always ask us what we would change if we were to update it, and my reply was always, "Not much." As one author put it, "Writing a book is more risky than having a child. After all, you can always disown a child." We still take responsibility for the ideas laid out in the book, and believe it's held up quite well, especially since most business books don't have a long shelf life. The book did change the lexicon in the professions, introducing such terms as *intellectual capital, human capital, social capital, value pricing,* and *effectiveness over efficiency.*

Yet times change. New business models arise that disrupt industries, including the professions. You've experienced it with the rapid pace of technology now being deployed across professional firms, from cloud accounting and artificial intelligence, to Robotic Process Automation and the blockchain. These technologies are important, allowing professional firms to do more work in less time, which is why the "we sell time" business model was obsolete even in 2003, when *The Firm of the Future* was first published.

The COVID-19 pandemic illustrated for us another hinge point in history: The importance of relationships. Sure, professional firms have always been relational, to the point of paying lip service to the importance of being so. But look at what we have the customers pay for: transactions, scope of work, and efforts. Would it not be more optimal if we aligned our business and revenue models with our values, both as professionals and businesspeople? To restore the original reason, and purpose, of why we entered our profession in the first place? The reason certainly wasn't billing the most hours, or processing the most tax returns, but rather to help people and make a lasting impact on the lives of the customers we are privileged to serve.

Historian Will Durant wrote, "Education is a progressive discovery of our own ignorance." The hardest part of learning something new is unlearning so much of what one already thinks one knows. Another question I am constantly asked: "Aren't you worried about people stealing your ideas?" When it comes to intellectual capital, this is misguided thinking. As I learned from Howard Hathaway Aiken, who was a pioneer in computing, being the original conceptual designer behind IBM's Harvard Mark I computer: "Don't worry about people stealing your ideas. If your ideas are any good, you'll have to ram them down people's throats." Besides, if I give away all my intellectual capital, it compels me to replenish it, which in turn forces me to unlearn and adjust to creative destruction.

There are essentially two ways to change a mind. Change your thoughts, or change your behavior. The Jewish tradition of attaching *tefillin* insists you bind your arm *before* you bind your head, stressing changing behavior as a way of changing your thoughts and mind rather than the reverse.

However, in a book, it is nearly impossible to accomplish this type of behavioral change, since we can only make you think *with* us, and that is a process of the mind. But both methods are effective, and if you begin to challenge why your firm exists, including what you monetize and measure, you will be able to alter people's behavior as well as their thoughts.

I cannot speak for Paul, but I experienced a wide range of emotions researching and writing this book—from optimism and pessimism, to incomprehensible and unknowable thoughts and challenges, and plenty of cognitive dissonance in between—and no doubt you will do the same as you read it. I do not consider this a disadvantage, or a sign of unclear expression. On the contrary, it is the indisputable consequence of dealing with the most significant aspects of the professions. You simply must struggle with them if you are to seek the truth of a changing marketplace. As I continue to learn I am constantly taking one step closer to that truth while knowing I will never arrive.

We want you to subject everything we write to your own belief system, challenging and discarding what you think is wrong, while acknowledging what may be right. We do not want you to think *like* us, but *with* us. But think you must. This book is a conversation between us; but you, dear reader, have the last word.

Ronald J. Baker
Petaluma, California
June 30, 2022

[Paul] This is a very different book than you might expect.

Typically, when two people are shown on the cover as "authors," you're never really sure who wrote what—their thoughts are (mostly) combined as one voice.

That's not the case here. And there's a very good reason for that.

Every time Ron and I speak at conferences, it's always me going first, setting some frameworks in place, putting some stakes in the ground. And then Ron follows and pounds those stakes firmly and deeply into the ground.

And that's what we've decided to do here with the added benefit that we know ahead of time what the other one is going to say (sometimes we surprise ourselves and say things on stage that neither me nor Ron have ever said before!).

So, in a way, continuing with that rural "stakes in the ground" metaphor, I'm tilling the ground, ready for Ron to create a harvest for you.

And I'm thrilled to be doing that because, in a funny kind of way, it gives me more scope—scope to share my passions, my purpose, my insights, and so on.

You'll learn later on how Ron and I first met in 1996. Every single meeting continues to be amazing as we explore ideas together.

And that process of exploration and discovery took a deep dive in 2002.

That's when Ron and I "sat down" (him in California, me mostly in France at the time) to write our first book together, *The Firm of the Future*. That was a very different time.

Even though at the time it seemed very fast, looking back now it was so slow. As someone put it once, "Things will never be slower than they are today."

There was no Zoom, people still faxed things. And we had face-to-face meetings with time to spare in between.

And here we are at the beginning of 2022 as I write this, having experienced a two-year plus period on our planet unlike any other.

Of course, it's easy to focus on COVID-19 and the havoc it created. Yet so many great things happened in 2021 alone that we could not have imagined (including Ron and I getting together for this book).

Here's a list of just 10 of those great things, sourced from the *New York Times*, "2021 Year in Review" list:

1. An African woman led the World Trade Organization.

2. A purely digital artwork sold at auction for $64 million.

3. A human brain was wirelessly connected to a computer via a transmitter device.

4. Mexico elected its first transgender lawmakers.

5. The world's first 3D-printed school opened in Malawi.

6. El Salvador became the first country to make Bitcoin a national currency.

7. NASA's *Perseverance* rover made oxygen on Mars, and the James Webb Space Telescope was launched to look back so much farther than Hubble.

8. *National Geographic* cartographers recognized the Southern Ocean as the world's fifth ocean.

9. *SpaceX* launched the first all-civilian crew into space.

10. Sales of zero-emission vehicles surpassed diesel sales in Europe.

And things were happening that would not make the *Times*' list.

For example, the pandemic meant that some professional knowledge firms got hammered in so many ways. Yet many grew in more ways, too.

Significantly, perhaps, business owners were (for the very first time that I've seen) literally begging their external advisors (accountants and lawyers in particular) to help with all the "advisory" things governments required them to do so that their businesses could get their hands on stimulus payments during lockdowns.

And, sticking with accountants for a moment, here's what Tom Hood (now the EVP Business Engagement & Growth at the

Association of International Certified Professional Accountants) had to say three months into the pandemic:

This presents an amazing opportunity for our profession to play an important role to shape the future with insight and integrity. A new world is upon us. Those who conquer it will be those who reimagine, redefine, and reinvent themselves and their businesses. This is our opportunity to make this our defining moment.

And then in July 2021, long-time AICPA president Barry Melancon said this:

We are now in a world reimagined, a world forever different from the profession prior to COVID.

We won't recognize the profession in five years. The change is going to be phenomenal going forward.

In 1996, Andy Grove, the late CEO of Intel, famously wrote:

The point in the life of a business [or an industry] when its fundamentals are about to change. The change can mean an opportunity to rise to new heights. But it may just as likely signal the beginning of the end.

Strategic inflection points can be caused by technological change but they are more than technological change. They can be caused by competitors but they are more than just competition. They are full-scale changes in the way business is conducted, so that simply adopting new technology or fighting competition as you used to is no longer sufficient. They build up force so insidiously that you may have a hard time even putting a finger on what has changed, yet you know something has.

[It's that time] when something is changing in a big way, when something is different, yet when you're so busy trying to survive that the signals of change only become clear in retrospect.
—Andrew S. Grove, *Only the Paranoid Survive*, 1996.

And what Barry Melancon referred to as this "world forever different" is now magnified further by the Russian invasion of Ukraine and the rippling down impact on refugees, food supplies, value-chains, and so on.

If you had an offshoot in Russia or were doing work for the owners of large-scale yachts, you've no doubt stopped that already. And, like us, you've been appalled by the images we've seen in real time.

Even without that, the shift is tectonic in so many ways. Just as importantly, the shift is speeding up at an unprecedented rate.

For example, a quick visit to internetlivestats.com will show you some staggering numbers. On May 4, the site showed the following things happening EVERY SINGLE SECOND:

9,978 Tweets

101,694 Google searches

148,886 GBytes of internet traffic

3,140,164 emails and

95,267 YouTube videos watched.

Again. Every. Single. Second.

You'll also see interesting things like the number of websites hacked today too!

Strategic infection points at speed!

And that is precisely why this book is so important.

Because here we set out the context, the framework, the mindset, and the skill sets you need to be at the forefront of this phenomenal and positive change going forward.

And it really does matter. Let me explain why.

In 2017, 14 years after *The Firm of the Future published,* I did a whole series of events around the world. I began each event by saying that, "Looking back, I wish we had titled *The Firm of the Future* as *The Firm of Now*. That's because all of, yes all of, the points we made on the pages of that book are relevant now."

And of course, that's still true.

That's why so many people referred to the 2003 *The Firm of the Future* book as a breakthrough book.

And because tens of thousands of firms around the world have implemented the ideas, here we want to (rather naturally) encourage you to go further.

The title of this book says it well: *Time's Up!* (actually, here it's better to get rid of the apostrophe for real emphasis) TIME IS UP.

There are no more excuses for holding on to old, outdated, UN-professional (and unnecessary) ways of doing things.

Time really is up!

So here we go all in to give you a powerful way of doing things, building on the foundations we set back in 2003. Here we take it to the max with you.

We pull you (as opposed to pushing you) much more now to establish different relationships with your team, your *customers*—yes, we still use that word instead of "clients" —your community, and our world.

And we do all of this bearing in mind a key message from Tamsin Woolley-Barker in her book *Teeming: How Superorganisms Work Together to Build Infinite Wealth on a Finite Planet* (and your company can, too): "Nature" she recently said in a conversation, "doesn't look for problems, it looks for potential."

We really do like that idea.

Problems demand solutions—fix this, fix that. Potential goes way beyond.

Potential is looking beyond what you see in front of you. Potential is looking not for outPUTS but for better outCOMES. Potential is next level. That's true for your firm *and* the customers you're privileged to serve.

When you start thinking about potential rather than problems, you see things you may never have seen. I like what a friend of mine (Roger James Hamilton) told me a long time ago. "Perspective," he said, "is looking at things from a place where you're not." We're going to pull you to that place here.

And as is often the case, people outside the professions may see those things so much more than you—the so-called Can't see the woods for the trees syndrome.

Our Canadian friend Ryan Lazanis, the Founder of futurefirm.com, put it like this in a recent conversation:

> Venture-backed accounting firm models are currently hitting the streets where their goals are to entirely disrupt the accounting profession along with completely revamping the customer experience. Clients hate their accounting. They find it incredibly painful. And the accounting profession has not done enough to remove this pain. That's where these venture-backed firms are smelling opportunity—

*that's where they're seeing the potential. Just look at what Uber did
to the taxi industry. It's possibly the exact same thing that is playing
out in the accounting profession right now with these new venture-
backed models.*

But we think it goes way beyond that, too. Uber made the transactions less painful. But it's doubtful you had a relationship with Uber. When someone else comes along with a slightly better speed or coverage you'll instantly switch.

Here, what we're suggesting is you go way beyond reducing the pain in the transaction (the problem) and look directly at the relationship (the potential).

Let's give you just one example of that. When you're putting the ideas here to good use, you might well remember the "duty of care" you have as an advisor to your customers in every field. Bearing that duty of care in mind, you may recognize you have a responsibility to share with your customers the business models and the insights we're urging you to apply here. The same ideas apply to them, too. And that's just part of the real potential here.

So we want you to develop processes and new revenue streams and then share the ideas with them. As you move forward with them in what is essentially a partnership mode, both of us would like you to realize you really do have a deep responsibility to do that. And you can only do that when you have a real relationship (as opposed to a transactional relationship) with your customers.

Let's put that last sentence another way which is perhaps more profound. You can only do that when your customers have a real relationship with *your firm,* not just with the services you sell.

The change is indeed going to be phenomenal going forward. Our goal here is to put you and your firm at the forefront of it.

Again, time really is *Up!*

There's a lot to do.

So . . . . let's get started . . . .

ACKNOWLEDGMENTS

The great teacher tells. The good teacher explains. The superior teacher demonstrates. The great teacher inspires.

—William Arthur Ward, author, educator

[PAUL] Every major work you undertake is rarely, if ever, the result solely of your own efforts.

Time's Up! is a classic case of that. It's also a classic case of taking care to assimilate a lot of ideas.

I'm indebted to so many people. To every single organization and person I've served since 1981 when the "Results" concepts started to form for me, thank you. Thank you for having the faith. And thank you for sharing with me all the ideas you've implemented so that I can excitedly share them with others.

More recently, I think of people who've helped me really "get" why I'm here and what I need to do about that. Of course, Ron Baker is major in that, as are Ric Payne, Steve Pipe, Simon Bowen, Aynsley Damery, and Stephen Briginshaw at Clarity; as well as Heather Yelland, Wayne and Sally Schmidt, Harvee Pene, Maya Shahani, Sarah McCrum, Deborah and Jeremy Harris, Tim Wade, Kylie Anderson, James Lizars, Stephen Kelly, Paul Polman, Barry Melancon, Brody Lee, Adam Houlahan, Yves Daccord, Jennie McLaughlin, Mick Hase, Gabriela Styf Sjöman, Calvin Ng, David Dugan, Dan Priestley, Glen Carlson, Consolata Norbert, Casandra Treadwell, Fred Mito, and Rob O'Byrne.

Countless others played and continue to play significant parts in the learning environment for me. These people continue to enrich my life.

The "chief enricher," though, is my wife, Masami Sato, who does more than anyone else to keep me grounded, focused, and on purpose (as well as fed and watered).

My incredible good fortune has been to be a part of the learning and to be able to present it to others to change the way they enrich lives, too. That remains—above all—a special privilege.

[RON] We are the composite of our connections. This book is the product of an astounding collection of human and social capital. As always, I have stood on the shoulders of giants who have helped me see the world as it is, not as I believe it should be. Please do not condemn the prophets for the ineptitude and errors of the disciple. I take full responsibility for any and all faults that remain.

Many economists have contributed to my education: Milton and Rose Friedman and their son, David Friedman, Friedrich Hayek, Steven Landsburg, Deirdre McCloskey, Ludwig von Mises, Michael Munger, Russ Roberts and his magnificent podcast, *EconTalk*, Julian Simon, Mark Skousen, Thomas Sowell, and Walter Williams.

Even though I am not Jewish, I am proud to have my very own rabbi—Daniel Lapin. His grasp of human behavior is astounding, his book *Thou Shall Prosper* is profound, and he was the inspiration for the distinction between that which is *spiritual* and that which is *material*. Thank you, Rabbi.

Thank you, Dr. Paul Thomas, founder of Plum Health DPC, for evangelizing the DPC movement, for your books (the first from which I borrowed the epigraph), and for appearing on *The Soul of Enterprise* four times (so far), and sharing your wisdom, passion, challenges, and successes. I wish you were my doctor.

Four leading authors profoundly affected me through their books and through interviews we were able to do with each of them on *The Soul of Enterprise*—I thank you all for writing, and contributing your immense tacit knowledge to my understanding of the subscription economy: Tien Tzuo (who coined the term), Robbie Kellman Baxter, Anne Janzer, and John Warrillow.

B. Joseph Pine II and James H. Gilmore, for your wonderful books on *The Experience Economy*, which introduced me to the timeless idea of guiding customer transformations. I cannot thank you enough for this insight.

Peter Drucker, who consistently contributed real insight and wisdom to the discipline of management thinking. In one way or another, everyone who writes on business stands on his shoulders. His legacy is large, and it will endure for the ages. He should have been awarded a Nobel Prize.

Indescribable gratitude must go to my 41-year mentor, George Gilder, for conducting an interview with *Playboy* that a barber read and was so inspired by, he purchased your book for his stubborn son, changing the boy's life forever after. His book *Wealth and Poverty* created the desire in me to write my own. His subsequent books are equally profound, from *The Spirit of Enterprise* and *Life after Google,* to *Life after Capitalism*, just to mention three (there's more). Gilder is the Adam Smith of the twentieth and twenty-first centuries.

Elbert Hubbard wisecracked in 1923 that the job of an editor is to "separate the wheat from the chaff, and to see that the chaff is printed," which is the exact opposite of the results the talented team at John Wiley & Sons, Inc. produced. Thank you, Sheck Cho, Susan Cerra, Julie Kerr, Cheryl Ferguson, Samantha Wu, and Natasha Wolfe for giving birth to our thoughts that will endure on the page.

To my friend and colleague Tim Williams, who has taught me everything I know about purpose, strategy, positioning, marketing, and branding. Tim is largely the inspiration for Chapter 11, and many other points throughout the book. I am eternally grateful for his wisdom.

Ric Payne is another mentor to me and one who has taught me an inordinate amount about strategy, disruption, and accounting firms pivoting to advisory work. I may have never convinced him of the uselessness of timesheets, over which we have engaged in a friendly debate for two decades, but there is one salutary effect. If it were not for this disagreement, I would agree with Ric on everything else relating to the profession, thereby rendering one of us superfluous— me, I'm afraid. Thanks, Ric, I cherish our friendship.

The Talmud says, "I have learned much from my teachers, more from my colleagues, and most of all from my students." It is my good fortune that my students are also my colleagues, from our amazing, worldwide audience of listeners to *The Soul of Enterprise* and our phenomenal Patreon members, to the beloved Black Swans—including Melissa Michalski, who read the early manuscript and provided valuable feedback—my VeraSage Institute colleagues, and all the professionals who have read my prior works. You have all contributed tremendously to my knowledge while providing epistemic humility given that the world is complex and the future unknowable.

Thank you, Hector Garcia, Ed Kless, Melissa Michalski, Blake Oliver, Ric Payne, Ethan Williams, and Mark Wickersham for reviewing the rather chaotic manuscript and contributing your insights, wisdom, and tacit knowledge. A special thank you to Dan Morris for doing a deep read and providing detailed feedback; and to Ethan Williams, I look forward to seeing how you use these concepts to future-proof your pricing.

An enormous thank you to Blake Oliver, host of *Cloud Accounting* and *Earmark Accounting* podcasts, for reading the first draft, providing invaluable feedback, and being bold enough to write the Foreword to a book destined to cause some controversy and cognitive dissonance in our chosen profession.

Ralph Waldo Emerson wrote in *Character*: "A chief event of life is the day in which we have encountered a mind that startled us." This perfectly describes my dear friend, colleague, and fellow Cognitor, Dan Morris. Thank you, Dan, you are like a brother to me.

Novelist Edna Buchanan wrote, "Friends are the family we choose for ourselves." In that spirit, I am honored to call Ed Kless a treasured brother. Our 20+-year collaboration has been epic, and *The Soul of Enterprise*—that I cannot imagine hosting without you—is one of my proudest contributions. Aristotle described his idea of the "perfect friendship" as based on willing each other's well-being and shared love for something good and virtuous that is outside either of you. Liberty and human flourishing come to mind.

Having the opportunity to work closely with Paul Dunn since our first meeting in 1996 has been nirvana—especially since I learned that in Zen, *nirvana* literally means a complete sense of timelessness. In the Acknowledgments to Paul in *The Firm of the Future*, I wrote, ". . . and if I know Paul, the next book will be even better." Let us learn together if that is so. You are a *great teacher*, my friend.

A wise rabbi said, "Pay attention to the ways in which your relationship continues," in reference to those loved ones who have departed. This means more to me each passing day as I fondly remember my brother, Ken Baker. Robert Browning expresses it beautifully in *A Blot on the 'Scutcheon, II, 1843*:

I think, am sure, a brother's love exceeds

All the world's loves in its unworldliness.

To my mother and father for genetically encoding me to challenge the conventional wisdom, and providing the most immeasurable of all blessings: their love and unwavering support in all I do.

And to you, Dear Reader, we now await your final verdict of value.

ABOUT THE AUTHORS

Paul Dunn is a four-time TEDx speaker.

He holds a Lifetime Service Award to the Accounting Profession in the United Kingdom. He was honored as a Social Innovation Fellow in his home of Singapore, something he shares with film star and philanthropist Jet Li and former Walmart Chairman Rob Walton.

He was one of the first 10 people in Hewlett-Packard in Australia. He then co-created one of Australia's first computer companies, developing groundbreaking software specifically for the accounting profession.

He followed that with the creation of The Results Corporation, where he helped develop and grow 23,000 small- and medium-scale business enterprises.

He then created Results Accountants' Systems, developing the radical Accountants' Boot Camp training process, enabling over 17,000 accountants worldwide to work with their clients in new ways.

Paul continues to push the boundaries. He was featured in *Forbes* magazine alongside Sir Richard Branson in a global piece on "disrupters" in business.

The profession continues to honor Paul—he was the Inaugural Recipient of the "Outstanding Contribution to the Profession" Award made by AccountingWeb in the United Kingdom. Paul remains the first non-accountant to be honored in this way.

He now works with thousands of accountants and leading-edge business owners around the world, inspiring them, cajoling them, and helping them build companies that people want to buy from, work for, and rave about.

Paul is the co-founder of the revolutionary B1G1: Business for Good, a company that's already enabled businesses to connect in new ways and create over 293 million giving impacts around the world.

Ronald J. Baker started his CPA career in 1984 with KPMG's Private Business Advisory Services in San Francisco. Today, he is the founder of VeraSage Institute—the leading think tank dedicated to educating professionals internationally—and radio talk-show host on the www.VoiceAmerica.com show: *The Soul of Enterprise: Business in the Knowledge Economy*.

As a frequent speaker, writer, and educator, his work takes him around the world. He has been an instructor with the California CPA Education Foundation since 1995 and has authored over 20 courses for them, including *You Are What You Charge For: Success in Today's Emerging Experience Economy (with Daniel Morris); Alternatives to the Federal Income Tax*; *Trashing the Timesheet: A Declaration of Independence*; *Everyday Economics*; *Everyday Ethics: Doing Well by Doing Good*; and *The Best Business Books You Should Read*.

He is the author of seven best-selling books, including *Professional's Guide to Value Pricing*; *The Firm of the Future: A Guide for Accountants, Lawyers, and Other Professional Services*, co-authored with Paul Dunn; *Pricing on Purpose: Creating and Capturing Value*; *Measure What Matters to Customers: Using Key Predictive Indicators*; *Mind Over Matter: Why Intellectual Capital Is the Chief Source of Wealth*; *Implementing Value Pricing: A Radical Business Model for Professional Firms*; and *The Soul of Enterprise: Dialogues on Business in the Knowledge Economy*, co-authored with Ed Kless.

Ron has toured the world, spreading his value-pricing message to over 275,000 professionals. He has been named on *Accounting Today's* 2001 to 2007, and 2011 to 2021, Top 100 Most Influential People in the profession; voted among the Top Ten Most Influential People in the profession in 2012–2021; selected as one of LinkedIn's Influencers; inducted into the CPA Practice Advisor Hall of Fame in 2018; and received the 2003 Award for Instructor Excellence from the California CPA Education Foundation. He graduated in 1984 from San Francisco State University, with a Bachelor of Science in accounting and a minor in economics. He is a graduate of Disney University and Cato University, and is a faculty member of the Professional Pricing Society. He resides in Petaluma, California.

To contact Ron Baker:

VeraSage Institute
E-mail: Ron@verasage.com
Website/Blog: www.verasage.com and
www.thesoulofenterprise.com
LinkedIn: linkedin.com/in/ronbaker1
Twitter@ronaldbaker
www.thesoulofenterprise.com/timesupbook (for updated information on the subscription model for professional firms).

The Keynote and the Workshop: How to Read This Book

[Ron] Meeting Paul on April 30, 1996, was a pivotal event in my life, even though I did not realize it at the time. It is interesting how paths cross. C. G. Jung's classic book, *Synchronicity: An Acausal Connecting Principle*, defines synchronicity as "a meaningful coincidence of two or more events, where something other than the probability of chance is involved." I believe this describes my relationship with Paul—fate brought us together.

I will never forget the second time Paul and I met in person. It was in San Diego, and we were both speaking at an event for CPAs. Here is a priceless bit of wisdom you can take to the bank: Never, never, ever, follow a Paul Dunn presentation. He is the most dynamic and inspiring speaker you will ever have the pleasure of seeing.

Unfortunately, I was not in charge of that day's agenda, and I had to speak after Paul. I survived, just barely. Little did I know, this speaking order would continue for the next several years as Paul and I traveled around the world speaking about the revolutionary Boot Camp his company was conducting. It was the highlight of my speaking career being able to work with a true master.

Paul and I are different. Yogi Berra said about George Steinbrenner, "We agree different," and that is an apt portrayal. Because of this, we decided for this book that we would make it comparable to the reader attending a conference. Paul will perform the keynote presentation in the first part of the book, then I will present the workshop in the second part, both in our own voice. We hope you find this approach effective.

We need to mention one other point: The words we use in this book. Words have meaning, and we use them to label and help us comprehend the world around us. Yet, many of them are distorting lenses that can make us misperceive and misjudge what we are observing. The great nineteenth-century English jurist Sir James Fitzjames Stephen put it aptly, "Men have an all but incurable propensity to prejudge all the great questions which interest them by stamping their prejudices upon their language."

Throughout this book, for example, we use the words customer, price, invoice, and team member in lieu of client, fee, bill, and staff (except when we are quoting from other sources). We do this because we believe these words convey better images of what they are attempting to describe. The welfare state has *clients*, while businesses have *customers* (we will let you decide if *members* is an even better word for customers). A *fee* is negatively associated with a tax or some other charge, while *price* is a benign term most customers easily comprehend, conjuring up no positive or negative images.

It is not our objective to change your vocabulary; we simply are far more comfortable using words we believe elicit superior images and feelings in others. See if you agree.

[Paul] If you've ever played or watched tennis, you'll have heard this phrase before: "the secret of playing great doubles is to select the right partner."

That is SO true here.

You already know from reading that opening that Ron is incredibly generous in his praise. What you're about to discover as well is that Ron is one of the deepest thinkers, brilliant researchers, and compelling writers you'll ever get access to.

He just doesn't "feel" things are right, he knows they are. And he knows that at the deepest level.

That's partly what makes Ron so compelling.

I remember commenting once that if "billing by the hour" was in the judicial dock with Ron as the prosecuting barrister or attorney, the case would be quickly over. Any jury anywhere in the world would return a verdict of "guilty as charged." And I think the judge would comment that "the evidence of guilt is overwhelming."

Of course, here we're not in a judicial setting.

Being here requires a different analogy. Perhaps as Ron suggests, a Conference is the most appropriate one.

Consider me as the person who opens your mind, the person who introduces you to some brand-new concepts in a powerful and passionate way.

We do that quickly at rapid speed. And you like what you hear—the examples make your head buzz with possibilities.

But you're not yet quite sure—you have this "what if" question followed by another.

But now your mind is really open to the possibilities (or as we touch on frequently in the book—the "potential").

What you need right now is someone equally passionate (that's the other part that makes Ron so compelling), someone who takes you deeper than you've ever been before. Someone who doesn't want you to think like him but who wants you to think *with* him.

So you end up (just like that jury) being totally, utterly, and unwaveringly convinced.

So much so that you know (deeply too) that you can move forward positively, powerfully, and passionately to create a brand-new future for your firm—one that truly does enrich lives.

That's a journey worth taking.

Congratulations on letting us in on that journey with you.

1

THE KEYNOTE

1

WHAT GOT YOU HERE WON'T GET YOU THERE . . . THANK GOODNESS!

It's true—what got you here won't get you there.

In fact, in so many instances, it's amazing that we got "here" at all.

That's because for so many, the "baggage" they've been carrying has more than weighed them down; the wonderful dreams they had when they started their firms simply have not materialized. In fact, their dreams have become nightmares.

The dreams they had of creating a business that people *love* to buy from, *love* to work for, really *respect,* and love to *refer* others to just evaporated. Not in the proverbial "puff of smoke" but in a whole lot of practices that locked them into becoming so much less than they could have been.

A business that they set up to bring them joy now brings them stress. A business they dreamed of as great for the family many times destroys the family. A business where they thought they'd love every customer has turned into one where the customer is a number and an interruption to their day as opposed to the reason for their day. A business they dreamed of where they had teams of people truly energized and connected turned into a nightmare where people have more (not less) mental pressures.

And in some businesses, that pressure of forcing people to account for every minute of their time in six-minute units is (at last!) recognized as a source of harm, not of life. I remember well the CEO of a mental health organization commenting on the rapid increase in people coming to them from professional firms. "We need to realize that forcing people to account for their time in six-minute units is actually coming close to killing them," she said.

3

Once we get that, as in really "get" it, surely all we need to say is, "Enough is enough." That alone surely trumps any argument you could muster to defend the process.

As you'll discover moving forward, the goal—some would say the only goal—is to enrich lives. And our goal here really is to do just that.

Here we bring together all the insights and passion we can muster to reverse those outdated and unnecessary processes for you by giving you new ways of seeing and thinking about things. Behaviors, we're told, always follow thoughts. So here we're investing time together to change up thoughts first before we get to behaviors.

But, it's not just about the words and thoughts in this book. To put it nicely, coming on this journey with us takes courage. To put it less nicely, it takes guts.

It takes the guts to come out and be bold. And guts are what the owners of the Vancouver, Canada–based law firm of Miller Titerle have a lot of. I first came across them in 2017 when I was speaking at a professional firm's conference in Tokyo.

In preparing to speak, I checked out the names of firms that were coming. And, rather naturally, I went to their websites to see how they were positioning themselves. I could not believe what I was seeing (and still am!) at www.millertiterle.com.

Take a look Figure 1.1.

FIGURE 1.1

FIGURE 1.2

And focus, if you will, on the pure guts of the statement underneath the surfboard: "The practice of law is broken.'

And at the risk of taking you away from the pages of this book for a moment, take a look at what happens when you click on that statement. Studying the picture below saves you a click. Here's where you get to Figure 1.2.

We could spend an entire chapter on this site alone (do this later, click on the "Meet the Team" link and get some real surprises as you scroll down)—make sure you note "Norman the Dog"—but for now just look at this sequence on that page above:

Why brag about things that everyone does?

Browse most firms' websites and they'll tell you that they provide quality legal advice and practical solutions. They may also claim to be client-focused, accessible, and responsible.

Like any good lawyer or law firm, we do these things. But unlike most firms, we don't think they're anything to brag about—they are the things that should be expected from your law firm.

Put all of that another way, those things they mention here are just table stakes.

Like MT+, this book is more than just being about "table stakes."

This is very much a "looking forward" book in the sense that the pictures we paint, the examples we give you, the stories we sculpt for you lead to great outcomes for you and the customers you're privileged to serve.

That's partly because we see professional knowledge firms in all their shapes and sizes as central to businesses of all shapes and sizes. And for "central" read "absolute necessities."

Let's just take two prime examples: accounting firms and legal firms.

First let's look at accounting firms. Here's a simple truth—most (and it's most by a huge margin) businesses simply do not understand numbers, financial numbers, in the way they need to grow their businesses in both revenue and profit. So the knowledge and the skill sets you have quite literally change lives. Be very clear—that is the potential you have. It's the potential you can (we would say "must") realize.

And with legal firms in mind, in this ever-more-regulated world, errors and omissions in things like privacy laws can (and do) put businesses out of business. Stopping that changes lives. Again, that's the potential you have.

To repeat a phrase we coined in 1994, firms need to move beyond reporting on history to helping their selected customers create history. Be very clear on that—that is precisely what you can do.

Doing it requires you to be at the forefront of innovation, pushing performance in every aspect, all the way from hiring to firing and everything in between. And increasingly, "everything in between" refers to the way your firm uses (and indeed develops) technology.

Ryan Lazanis, who we quoted in the Preface, put it like this in a conversation recently:

> Up until now, accountants have been using existing technology to automate their firms and automate work for their clients. But now, we're seeing accountants getting into the software development game, where they're actually building custom automation tools for their clients and they're either up-skilling or hiring developers in-house. It's the next frontier, which will certainly intensify.

Add to that the truly fascinating and game-changing possibilities of Web 3.0 and you see how Barry Melancon's comments from the Preface are so right on point.

Do note this though—it's not technology to "replace" you—it's technology to enhance the human-to-human relationships you have—to allow your firm to bring humanity back to the very core of your business model. We really do need humanity to be the focus.

Companies really are getting that at last. Take the technology firm Sage as one example. They've now changed their brand focus from the classic B2B (the acronym for business-to-business) to "human-to-human."

One of the technology firms I mentor has recently moved its classification from the normal SaaS—(Software as a Service) phrasing—to the much more powerful TaaS. And we love what that acronym stands for: "Transformation as a Service."

Just consider that oh-so-subtle shift for a moment. When you're branded as a "Software as a Service" company, you and your team members could easily consider that your job is done when you deliver the software.

But when you really understand the shift to "Transformation as a Service," your job is effectively never done. You develop a powerful partnership-type relationship that clearly focuses on outCOMES—the transformation of your customers' business through an ongoing relationship.

That transition is the central theme of this book.

Let's be clear here, too—our role here is *not* to focus on technology per se—that's a way to very quickly date a book.

Our role is to impact you, to move you and to add process and structure to the way you think, the way you frame challenges and the way you partner with others in finding not just solutions but new potentials.

Part of my role in that "shifting-thinking" piece has been to convince firms that they need to do two critical things in a standout way:

1. They need to build companies that matter—as in *really* matter—to the customers they're privileged to serve.

2. They need to build companies that those self-same customers feel that they "belong" to as well.

One way to do that is to think about companies who start by thinking about how they can eliminate the "pain points" of doing business within a particular sector. They seek to disrupt by focusing on the "pain" of doing business with the "standard" way of doing things.

In his *Atomic Habits* book, author James Clear gives us a great example of that thinking in a downloadable Addendum to his widely read book. He asks us to think about the first ride-sharing services like Uber or Lyft:

Just imagine if you were in the room as they were planning the launch.

Together you could have mapped out the chain of behaviors a customer had to perform to get a ride across town: walk outside, wait for a taxi to pass on the street, get in, ride across town, arrive at destination, pull out a credit card or cash, pay for the ride, put the credit card (or any change) back in their purse or wallet, get out of the car, etc. (Clear 2018)

And then together with your colleagues you could look at each stage and ask yourselves how you could reduce the friction (the pain) associated with the task (or eliminate that step entirely).

Here's how James Clear explains the process by posing a series of questions and possible answers:

How can we make it easier to walk outside? What if users could download an app that would summon a car from their phone and didn't have to walk outside at all?

How can we make it easier to wait for the ride? What if we told users how long it would be until a ride arrived? Then they could just walk outside at the right moment.

How can we make it easier to get in the car? No change.

How can we make it easier to ride across town? Rather than leave it up to the driver's memory, we could display the route on the users phone and the driver's phone. Now the user can make suggestions if they want to go a different way, and the driver can rely on the GPS for up-to-date information and routing.

How can we make it easier to pay for the ride? We already have an app on the user's phone. What if we asked users to upload their credit card information? Then, they could pay automatically and just exit the car once they arrive. (Clear 2018)

Simple. It's a great example of the truth of this phrase: "Questions change the future before the answers even arrive."

Jonas Salk, the discoverer of the first successful polio vaccine, put the same thought this way, "What people think of at the moment of discovery is really the discovery of the question."

We wonder what questions you'd pose to do that. Actually, we'll be doing a lot of "question-posing" moving forward, too.

And as Clear writes in Chapter 12 of *Atomic Habits,* "Business is a never-ending quest to deliver the same result in an easier fashion."

That's true. But, as we've said, there's so much more to it than that. Or, as we put it in this chapter heading: "What got you here won't get you there."

And it was with that spirit in mind when (in April 2019) I met with Ron in Chicago. I remember Ron being so excited, inasmuch as it was the first time he was going to present his ideas on the *subscription economy* to a group of people who knew him well.

It was amazing to be a part of it. And it was the first time I'd heard Ron use this phrase:

> *Moving to the subscription economy means we have to learn not to monetize the transaction but rather to monetize the relationship.*

Such a powerful thought.

You see, you may think that moving to the subscription economy requires simply a pricing decision.

It is much, much more. It's a complete re-look at (and in some cases, a complete re-do of) your current business model.

Let's look at Ron's phrase once again to emphasize the point:

> *Moving to the subscription economy means we have to learn not to monetize the transaction but rather to monetize the relationship.*

Here's the key: You can only do that when (notice *when* as opposed to *if*) you do several key things:

- Do stuff that really matters to the people you're privileged to serve.
- Do it in a way where it becomes "sticky"—where the relationship is so locked into the customers' well-being they're simply not going to go anywhere else—they feel "this is the place I really belong" or, as Seth Godin so beautifully puts it, "People like us do things like this."

- Do it in a way that underscores that you and your team care deeply—very deeply—about the customer.
- Have a vision (what Stephen Covey famously described as a "North Star") that is valuable enough to your customers that they can easily justify a recurring payment commitment to you.
- Have clear criteria on what customers you want and, perhaps even more importantly, customers you will not accept.

And if you'd like to take that caring piece even further (why not?), consider what loyalty-guru Fred Reichheld had to say in an interview with John Abraham of Medallia in March 2022: "Every company should be looking at Customer LOVE as their purpose. Not just because it's good for customers but it seems like it's the only way to provide a wonderful job, a meaningful career for employees and it's the only way to deliver outstanding long-term value to investors."

Then he added this seriously powerful point: "If you don't exist to make a customer's life better, I don't think as a business that you have a legitimate reason to exist."

Be clear on this—the subscription model we're outlining here specifically does that—it focuses you on making the lives of your customers better. Indeed, it forces you to do that. It really is potential realized.

It's no longer about transactions. It's about a deep relationship that enriches you, your team, AND the lives of your customers and their teams.

Be aware of this too—this is NOT some Pollyanna "customer-is-always-right" philosophy. Far from it. You need to bear in mind that a profitable relationship with your customer comes from challenging them and not just having what might be called a cozy relationship with them.

The relationship here is more like us having the friend who tells us things we need to hear rather than the things we want to hear. It's you seeing a greater potential in your customers' businesses than even they do. And it's you working together with them to make sure that happens—to make sure that is, in fact, the outcome. Just consider what you need to do to make that the reality.

One way to do that is to realize that it needs you and your team to create (not just to tell, but to create) a brand-new story.

We begin that story over the page . . ..

2

WE ALL HAVE A STORY—HERE'S A NEW ONE FOR YOU

On June 2, 2021, I received an email from a friend of mine, Bernadette Jiwa. That single email was to forever change the way I connect and communicate with the people I serve and know.

This single email was one of those moments in time that changes outcomes.

Moments really are extremely critical. As a friend of mine puts it, "Where you are in your life and your business today is simply the result of your reaction to the key moments in your life that brought you here right now."

Bernadette's email to me was absolutely one of those moments. It was a *call to action*. (We hope that's precisely how you'll see this book—a moment in time that changes outcomes for you, for your team members and for the customers you serve.)

The email had this simple subject line:

"The most powerful person in the world is the storyteller."

Of course, we all know about the power of stories. We know that our ancestors communicated life-lessons and much more by passing on stories. Anthropologists tell us that, as a direct result, the power of stories is in our DNA.

It's as if when we hear the words "I want to tell you a story," or even as kids, "Once upon a time . . ." our ears prick up. We lean in. The storyteller has our full attention. Great films, great speeches, great books all have brilliantly crafted story "arcs."

So, when I saw that "The most powerful person in the world is the storyteller" subject line, I naturally opened the email.

And I learned that it was Steve Jobs who said those words in 1994 when he was CEO of Pixar (he'd been fired from —or perhaps we should say "he left"—Apple in 1985).

Then I read by far the most powerful part of the quote: "The storyteller," said Jobs, "sets the vision, the values and the agenda for an entire generation yet to come."

Think about that just for a moment. "The storyteller sets the vision, the values and the agenda for an entire generation yet to come."

Here's what that means: just by virtue of what you do and how you do it, you—yes, you—are setting the vision, the values, and the agenda for an entire generation yet to come. Things are rippling or radiating out from you and they're having a profoundly important outcome.

The stories you create and tell are changing and enriching lives.

And here's a critically important point. This book is so important not because we're going to tell you how to tell stories in a better way. Here we're going to co-create brand-new stories for you to tell. We're going to give you new stories to live and to create.

You see, Steve Jobs wasn't just a great storyteller (and he certainly was that); he was a great story creator. And as it turned out, he created tools to allow us to create even better stories more simply *and* to let those stories spread wider and last longer too.

You can be (and we would argue "must be") the story creator. It's you leading your firm by creating a brand-new story of what a professional firm is, what it does, how it does it, and how it innovates across all areas to set the vision, the values, and the agenda for an entire generation yet to come.

That's you. That's you creating amazing moments. That's you changing outcomes. That's you changing, enriching, and enhancing lives. That's you changing up other people's stories.

When you think of stories, you'll recognize that all great stories essentially have just four main characters—the hero, the guide, the victim, and the villain.

And when your firm fully embraces the subscription model and gets it really working, you see that your role becomes that of the guide, the guide who makes the customer the hero. (Importantly too, your customers learn to make their customers the hero, too.)

To do that, you're going to have to change up your story to make it happen. Here's a story arc that illustrates that for you:

From history ... to ... Your current story ... to ... Your brand-new story

Again, what we're doing here in this book is, in effect, co-creating that brand-new story together with you. Actually, with "potential" in mind, I'd prefer us to be thinking of co-ELEVATING the new story together with you. And we're doing that so that you can create more impact in your business, in your customers' businesses, in your community, and on our world than you previously imagined possible.

For now, let's ignore the history part in our story arc above (that's just another word for the baggage that has weighed firms down, mentioned in Chapter 1) and let's focus on your current story.

Because speed of change is not what most professional knowledge firms are famous for, it's more than likely that your current story mostly reflects the pre-COVID world. Certainly, you've moved to accommodate work-from-home and it's ever more likely that you've done some great work on mental health programs for your team and so on. Even so, it's likely that a lot of your core beliefs from history still remain firmly anchored in place in your firm.

It's highly likely that your core business model, that rock upon which you stand, is still essentially the same as it was pre-COVID. And although you'd reasonably argue that it has served you well, we want to strongly suggest that it no longer is or will.

Let's come face-to-face with perhaps the biggest understatement of this book to illustrate why: Our world has changed.

And that change accelerated BIG TIME in the two years of us coming to terms with COVID. And as we said earlier, it continues to change: Russia invaded the Ukraine in early 2022, disrupting both food and energy production. Inflation is giving families concern over how they will pay their bills.

In some ways, we should not be surprised by the changes. The changes were already getting under way ahead of the so-called *global financial crisis* of 2008.

We'd endured years of the *Wolf of Wall Street* "Greed is good" mentality, and it came crashing down around us.

We emerged with new understandings—with a new realization that things must change.

COVID accelerated that.

It taught us lessons far more quickly than in "normal" times. And of course, that's because every single one of us was impacted. It was not happening "over there" where we could have ignored it and/or hoped that it would go away. It didn't. It happened to almost every single one of us in deeply personal ways.

On May 5, 2022, the World Health Organization reported that "an additional 14.9 million lives had been lost between January 2020 and December 2022 directly and indirectly because of Covid" (World Health Organization 2022).

As a result of that personal impact, we see things now that we simply didn't see before. And it's not just "you" who sees things you didn't see. It's your team. They have different priorities now—sometimes vastly different priorities.

And then there are your customers. They, too, are seeing things differently both from a business perspective and from a family perspective as well.

Interestingly, the family no longer "owns" the things it used to—the family subscribes to streaming services, to cars, to software, to medical services, to wardrobes to . . . . fill in the blanks. The once-common phrase "There's an App for that" increasingly means ". . . . and you can subscribe to it." Buying something and then owning it is less often the go-to model.

So yes, your customers are seeing things vastly differently. And most importantly, they are seeing businesses differently. They are understanding more and more that business plays a critical and crucial part in shaping our world . . . and they no longer universally like what business has created by serving only itself.

That plays out—it aggregates out—to your community. It too sees things differently.

And now, because of our enhanced interconnectivity and the global nature of everything we do, our world sees it, too. Our world has changed BIG TIME.

And again, we—specifically the "we" who create, operate, and advise businesses—are the primary cause of that change. Governments haven't done it. They enabled it (or made it more difficult).

It's taken a while for some of us to recognize and accept that. All of us readily accept the positive consequences of businesses. But for a long time, we've missed or ignored those outcomes, those consequences, that are not so good.

As my friend Carolyn Butler-Madden points out in her April 2022 *Cause Effect* newsletter:

We all know we're living in extraordinary times. We face serious challenges in our society that are begging for action and solutions. The problem is we have a crisis in trust in all of our major institutions and this is threatening societal stability.

The good news (and the opportunity) is that societal leadership is now considered by the majority of people to be a core business function. This reflects two simple truths:

- Business does not exist in a vacuum.
- Business has the resources, the capital, the capacity for innovation, and the means to effect significant positive change.

Yet how many businesses continue to operate as if they are oblivious to all of this? In a vacuum. Or worst, head in the sand.

We are living in times that call for courageous leadership.

I hope you got that—"Societal leadership is now a core business function." It's not added on as an afterthought. Now, it must be built right into the structure and fabric of your business. And it's not some short-term thing.

Most significantly, many short-term focused leaders have missed the flow-on effect, that crucial point we raised earlier about setting the vision, the values, and the agenda for an entire generation yet to come.

So . . . when we stand back with a new perspective and see some negative impacts of the way we've done business until now, we see that we can (and indeed must) play a part in changing it up again. We can and must create a positive feedback loop.

Crucial to that is to understand that to do that, it can no longer be about me . . . it has to become about *we*. That is precisely what *relationship* means. It implies "together."

That's just one of the important shifts. There are many others that build on from "me to we."

Take "belonging" as an example.

I remember three years ago listening to a recording of Jeff Bezos being interviewed at a large gathering in the United States—it could have been a South By Southwest conference.

The interviewer said, "Jeff, when you talk to and advise your marketing department about how to do things today, how different is it now from when you started?"

To the great surprise of the interviewer, Mr. Bezos answered, "It hasn't changed at all."

"Really . . .. how do you mean?" said the interviewer.

Bezos's reply is a classic: "I tell them there's one human trait that we must always remember—people want to belong."

And in a private group meeting in 2022, Seth Godin riffed on *belonging* like this:

> All the humans I know, care about (once you have a roof over your head and enough to eat, once your family is taken care of) all the humans I know of care about one of two things, sometimes both, sometimes at the same time: status and affiliation.
>
> So what do I mean by that? Affiliation means who is next to me? Who's to my left? And who's to my right. It's Groucho Marx saying, "I don't want to belong to any club that would have me as a member."
>
> It's you showing up and seeing people on Zoom who you recognize from the last time and it makes you feel safe, even though you've never met in real life, right? Affiliation drives culture, being part of stuff, people like us do things like this. It's a key reason that people take action.
>
> And then there's the second reason which often runs counter to this first one. It is status. Who is up? Who is down? Who is defeating my enemies? Who am I defeating?
>
> If you want to understand politics in the modern world, you don't have to look very far. You will see status. Whether it's the way world leaders struggled to beat each other with a handshake, or people causing horrible things to happen. It's just about status, who's winning and who's losing, whereas affiliation is, "Oh, he didn't come to the services this week. I wonder where he is?" Who's in and who's out.

So whether you call it belonging or affiliation, it's a key component of building your subscription business model.

Figure 2.1 illustrates the principal shifts that we believe are required (and it contains a huge hint on why shifting to the power of the subscription model is indeed so powerful).

So let's start at the bottom and move up.

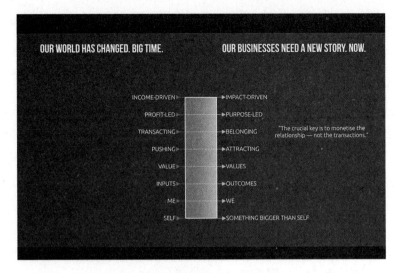

FIGURE 2.1   The shifts we need to make.

FROM ME TO WE AND FROM SELF TO BIGGER THAN SELF

The first two are really intertwined—From Me to We and From Self to Something Bigger Than Self.

One is rather cute and catchy: "From Me to We." Yet it's so powerful to contemplate *and* implement the power of that thought.

But expressing it as moving from Self to Something Bigger Than Self gives it real clout—and, as you'll see, it gives us a neat measuring stick, too.

We'll delve deeper into this in later chapters. For now, though, let's just say this: People, be they customers or team members, are not attracted to you per se—they are attracted to who they become as a result of dealing with you. They are attracted by *affiliation*—they're asking, "Who else are you working with?" And they're attracted by status. They too are attracted to potential!

FROM INPUTS TO OUTCOMES (IN OUR CASE, TRANSFORMATIONS)

We all value testimonials.

Most often, testimonials come instantly as in "I just read this book and it was GREAT!" or "The food at the restaurant was the best I've ever eaten," or "This course changed my life."

But here's one that didn't come instantly. In fact, it came 27 years *after*—yes, years *after*—the triggering event.

That event was a process in which Ron and I were both involved. Ron mentioned it in the "How to Read This Book" segment. It was called the Accountants Boot Camp. All told, globally some 17,700 accountants experienced it (and it was an "experience" in every sense of that word) from 1992 to 2000.

The testimonial we're referring to here came in the form of a video—a video sent 27 years after the initial moment. Here's the transcript for you:

> *Hello, My name is Paul Kennedy. I'm an accountant. I'm an accountant in practice in England just north of London.*
>
> *And I'm here to tell you about something—an event—that happened many years ago—but something that was to change my life—change my life quite radically.*
>
> *And that something, that event, was the Accountants Boot Camp. And I think it also radically changed the way we saw our own business and indeed how we saw business generally.*
>
> *I think, probably for the first time—and how I didn't think about this before I'm not sure—but for the first time, I saw that wealth or profits, your own profits, was a direct byproduct of the value that you create for other people.*

Summary: We all must move from a focus on inputs to a focus on outcomes, specifically the outcomes we produce for others.

Please notice how those last six words in that sentence are perfectly in sync with "something bigger than self."

And . . . spoiler alert . . . that's going to get even bigger soon as well.

Of course, that's the total opposite of what so many people in your profession have been taught—that somehow the value of what you produce has to do with the time it took you to do something—it never has, and it never will. (That's why our upcoming chapter has the title "Time-Driven Sucks." We'll get there soon.)

For now, let's go back to the fourth line from the bottom on our diagram.

FROM VALUE TO VALUES

Value is something you must deliver (remembering, too, that value is, just like beauty, always in the eye of the beholder).

So the concept of value will always be with us. But now there's something else that is proving to be much more important to the buyer than value alone. And that's ValueS. Yes, what you *stand for* is now even more important than the value you deliver. After all, how can you "belong" to something where there is no match of values, no alignment?

It's always been partly that way—for example, I might choose to deal with a printer who happens to support a favorite charity of mine or support the same football team. Or someone might NOT choose to deal with someone because they're on what the buyer believes to be the "wrong" side of the vaccine divide.

And, in this currently polarized world we're in, questions about what you stand for are being asked more and more.

Most recently (as you may have read), Patagonia withdrew its multimillion dollar ad campaigns from Facebook. Not only that, as this CNN piece reveals, they stepped up their campaign to ask other advertisers to do the same.

> In the wake of the revelations in the Facebook Papers, Patagonia CEO Ryan Gellert on Thursday called for companies to join the brand in pressuring Facebook to fix its platforms.
>
> We believe Facebook has a responsibility to make sure its products do no harm, and until they do, Patagonia will continue to withhold its advertising, Gellert said in a statement to CNN. "We encourage other businesses to join us in pushing Facebook to prioritize people and planet over profit."
>
> In the summer of 2020, Patagonia joined a growing list of companies pulling ads from Facebook (FB) platforms as part of an advertiser boycott.
>
> "Patagonia stopped all paid advertising on Facebook platforms in June 2020 because they spread hate speech and misinformation about climate change and our democracy. We continue to stand by that boycott 16 months later," Gellert said.
>
> "Facebook's executives know what steps it can take to mitigate such harm—yet they have repeatedly failed to reform."

That's "From Value to ValueS" powerfully expressed.

And it's not only Patagonia. Hundreds of millions of dollars have been cut from Facebook's revenue as companies like Microsoft, HP, Verizon, Reebok, Adidas, Lululemon, Levi's, Ben & Jerry's, Hershey's, Honda, Unilever, Volkswagen, and Pfizer found a "values mismatch."

And in the UK, a bank not happy with Meta's (the holding company of Facebook and other brands) values reported it like this:

> Starling Bank has stopped all paid advertising on Facebook and Instagram, and says it will not return to the platforms until Meta can guarantee cyber scammers are not able to advertise.
>
> The bank's CEO Anne Boden says she has "repeatedly called out" social media giants for allowing financial fraudsters to advertise and post content on their platforms, which results in "people being scammed out of their savings" every day. (Tesseras 2022)

In January 2022, Bruce Simpson, senior adviser to McKinsey on ESG and Purpose, wrote that, "Almost 40 percent of consumers today are boycotting a product or service, not because they are unhappy with the performance but because of that company's social stance. The forces are moving very strongly in this direction, and CEOs tell us that they are spending half of their time on this topic right now" (Hunt 2022).

Of course, all of this raises the critically important question: What is it that you stand for?

And once you've sorted out that deep, soul-searching question, how do you express it so that it attracts as opposed to repel? Or even, should you express it at all? You'll find much more on these interesting questions later.

FROM PUSHING TO ATTRACTING

It's a nice segue to this next in line of our list of eight "from–to's."

Let's put it in the form of a question: Should you be pushing ads or should you be doing something that powerfully attracts your chosen market to you?

The answer should be obvious—building something attractive is the way to go.

Building a subscription-based service and business model is part of doing that. And that's partly because when you really commit to doing it well, you'll automatically be closer to the people you want most to serve.

They'll feel as though they belong when you do it well.

And that leads us nicely up the ladder to this . . .

FROM TRANSACTIONS AND TRANSACTING TO BELONGING

This is one of the most crucial parts of the shift we're strongly suggesting you make. Remember earlier how Ron told me this:

> *Moving to the subscription economy means we have to learn not to monetize the transaction but rather monetize the relationship.*

That is what belonging is all about. It's when people feel so connected to you, they "belong."

In an "all-is-covered-for-you" subscription model, you're there for the customer whenever they want or need you to be (within the limits of the model).

In this ever-more-connected world, we somehow feel less "connected." That's precisely why we believe so strongly that people are craving connection.

It's also coupled with what we call *mattering.* Seth Godin, who we quoted earlier on belonging (or *affiliation,* as he called it), expressed it well when he said:

The challenge is not to be successful, the challenge is to matter.

As you build your subscription model, you really will matter even more to the people you seek to serve. Maybe we should make a one-word change to that last sentence so that you realize just how important it is:

> As you build your subscription model, you really *must* matter even more to the people you seek to serve.

As Robbie Kellman Baxter put it when commenting on Taco Bell's move to a subscription model: "As opposed to transactional pricing where the sale is the finish line, in a membership (subscription) model, the sale is the starting line."

Such a powerful sentence. And while we might celebrate (or indeed reward others) for getting to that starting line, it's what lies ahead that we really should be celebrating.

And that thought leads us nicely to this next rung on our ladder . . .

FROM PROFIT-LED TO PURPOSE-LED

This sounds perverse.

Yet it's anything but. It's central to your new story.

Larry Fink, CEO of the world's largest investment house, BlackRock, put it this way in his annual letter to Wall Street in 2018: "To prosper over time, every company must not only deliver financial performance, but also show how it makes a positive contribution to society."

And in 2019 he went further: "Without a sense of purpose no company (either public or private) can achieve its full potential. It will ultimately lose the license to operate from key stakeholders."

And then this in 2020:

> *Profits are in no way inconsistent with purpose—in fact, profits and purpose are inextricably linked. Purpose unifies management, employees, and communities. It drives ethical behavior and creates an essential check on actions that go against the best interests of stakeholders. Purpose guides culture, provides a framework for consistent decision-making, and, ultimately, helps sustain long-term financial returns for the shareholders of your company.*

Taking Mr. Fink's point one step further about purpose guiding culture is Jeffrey Hollender, co-founder of Seventh Generation (the maker of sustainable cleaning products): "Everything a company does is an expression of its culture."

Note that . . . everything.

Corrie Barrie, Best Buy CEO, clarifies that beautifully like this: "The purpose of this company is not to make money. It is imperative to make money, but it is not the purpose. Our purpose is to enrich lives through technology."

What's seriously fascinating (though perhaps not so surprising) is this truth: Purpose-led companies outperform others—and they do it massively, too.

Consider this 2021 report from Monitor Deloitte as just one example, illustrated in Figure 2.2 (Schoenwaelder et al. 2021).

Let's take just five highlights:

1. In terms of brand and reputation, you're 78% more likely to be remembered (or in our terms—to *stand out*) when you're seriously on purpose.

2. And take a look at those Sales and Innovation numbers—a near 40% premium is possible according to the study.

3. And it's not just sales you attract—you attract the large number of people who would prefer to work with an on-purpose company—you become a magnet for talent as well once you're seriously *on purpose*.

4. Oh and did you notice that a significant number of those people you attract will work for less, too?

FIGURE 2.2   Monitor Deliotte's eye-opening report.

5. Right now, as the owner of your company, you may not be looking to exit your company. But did your scan of those numbers go down to the bottom left? If it did, you'll see that your company is likely to have a four times larger valuation number too when you make purpose the North Star of your model.

6. Pretty interesting numbers, aren't they?

It's so critical for us all to get these numbers and build them into your new model.

But . . . and it is a big *but* . . . bear in mind what *Start with Why* author Simon Sinek wrote in his April 22 newsletter: "Purpose does not need to involve calculations or numbers. Purpose is about the quality of life. Purpose is human, not economic."

Realizing that can sometimes make it seem as though purpose is "the soft stuff." For example, it's easy to dismiss this quote from Fred Reichheld's *Winning on Purpose* book:

> Today we can establish that business success begins with leaders who embrace a fundamental proposition that their firm's primary purpose is to treat customers with loving care.
>
> That approach begets loyalty, which powers sustainable, profitable growth. (Reichheld 2021, p. 25)

And in the *Winning on Purpose* book, Reichheld shows how revered books like Jim Collins's *Good to Great* fall short.

In a series of graphs (Reichheld 2021, pp. 30–32), Reichheld shows companies referenced in Collins's work, first published in October 2001, have actually not done very well as compared with companies who've embraced Reichheld's Net Promoter Score.

Reichheld points out that the reason for that is the massive shift of focus that's occurred. He observes:

> (Companies) gauged their success using the metrics of financial capitalism—primarily profits. When profits become purpose, it becomes too easy for companies to boost their financial performance by short-changing customers. This is value extraction not value creation, and since value extraction doesn't show up in audited financial statements, this kind of abuse can go undetected for months or even years, at least by the investor community. (Reichheld 2021, p. 28)

Here's the point: The world has seriously shifted. And regulations (never our favorite way of forcing change) are catching up with the shift. Sean Brown, global director of communications for McKinsey's Strategy & Corporate Finance Practice, put it this way in a piece early in 2022:

> Regulators are also getting very interested in ESG (Environmental, Social, and Governance) and purpose. The European Union has already implemented the Non-Financial Reporting Directive [requiring companies to report how they manage social and environmental challenges], and the Securities and Exchange Commission [SEC] has started to evaluate ESG measures in the United States. (Hunt 2022)

And in the United Kingdom right now, you cannot submit bids for certain government agency contracts unless you have a measurable track record of enabling positive social change.

Again, regulations are never our favorite way of forcing change. But it is as well to note how our world is shifting.

Interestingly though, it's been shifting for eons—it's just that we've been slow to see it. As Tamsin Wooley-Barker points out in *Teeming*: "Purpose is the glue that integrates the work of one into the work of many, and it's what gets us up in the morning."

And then she adds, "The bolder and more ambitious our collective goals, the greater our potential in the world."

The larger point is this: Being seriously on purpose (and that means more than just nice-sounding words in your mission and vision statements) adds value in so many ways. But perhaps we should say that this way: being on purpose can add value in so many ways.

Since we just used their name, let's take Deloitte as an example:

Deloitte's Purpose

Making a positive, enduring impact that matters.

It's good. But how much better does it read with the addition of just one more word:

> Making a positive, enduring impact that really matters.

Much better, we think. Here's the reality. Purpose powers you. When you're *really* clear on your purpose, when it's what you stand for, when it's front and center of everything, when everyone on your team lives and breathes it, then in that moment, what you do becomes profoundly more attractive and compelling *and* you're on the path to what we define later as STANDOUT.

In a conversation with *Start with Why* author Simon Sinek, he made these crucial points:

> **True purpose is always human. True purpose is the idea of knowing why your business exists in terms beyond your products and services.**

He followed up with this:

> *It's knowing that the infinite goal that you set is something that will leave this world, this place and the people in it in better shape than we found them.*

You'll find that Ron digs down even deeper into this later. But there could still be an issue. Again, let's put it this way: Being on purpose *can* add value in so many ways.

Why the emphasis on *can*? You'll see precisely why in your next chapter.

It's the final step on our ladder: From *income*-driven to *impact*-driven.

3

TIME-DRIVEN SUCKS . . . IMPACT-DRIVEN MATTERS

I well remember meeting Ron for the first time at a seminar I was presenting to the Californian State CPA Society in San Francisco in 1996. As Ron mentioned earlier, it was April 30 that year (and yes, we still celebrate that anniversary).

Ron was sitting in the middle of the room on an aisle right of center.

And at one point, it was almost as if he was cheering me on in a room of otherwise furrowed brows as I got very passionate about what I saw then (and still do) as the indefensible practice of keeping timesheets and charging things based on time.

When the session ended, Ron enthusiastically introduced himself (thank goodness). "My mission," he said, "is to bury the billable hour. I want it inscribed on my tombstone that that is precisely what I achieved in my life."

Now, just 26 years later, Ron can consider it largely done.

He's championed that cause so well. And it's done. He of course claims it's not just him . . . but it is. No one has so eloquently buried the billable hour as Ron.

All of us who have played a small part in it acknowledge that. Ron really is a giant. As Sir Isaac Newton put it in 1675: "If I have seen further, it is by standing on the shoulders of giants." Thank goodness Ron has broad shoulders, too.

And we all acknowledge that being time-driven sucks. In a March 2022 piece reporting on Gravity, CEO Dan Price, put it very simply like this:

> Give employees what they need to do a job well; then, focus on outcomes, not hours. Because an employee should be rewarded for doing their work well. Not for taking more time to do it. (Bariso 2022)

It's so obvious and almost basic, isn't it?

IMPACT-DRIVEN PURPOSE

Being impact-driven takes you way beyond basic. It gives you and your team the potential to soar.

That's because, despite what you've just read in the previous chapter, being purpose-driven is not the end point. It's the beginning of an even more important journey—the journey toward being impact-driven.

Significantly, the phrase *social impact* is being searched for more and more—at last count 17,000 hits in LinkedIn's job tab as just one example.

And firms are increasingly expected to speak out on social issues. There are, of course, no surprises there. Public concerns mount over the pandemic, climate change, labor rights, racial justice, diversity, and so on.

We're seeing job titles change—chief purpose officer titles (yes, there are already such titles in, for example, the so-called Big 4 accounting firms) are now changing to become CIOs—chief impact officers. And some famous names are lining up for those jobs. Prince Harry is now the CIO of BetterUp, Lil Nas X became CIO of Taco Bell, and John Legend styles himself CIO at his NFT company, OurSong.

Perhaps more "impactfully" (no pun intended), we're seeing more and more companies and firms joining in movements like BCorp Certification, www.bcorporation.net and/or membership of organizations like B1G1, Business for Good, www.b1g1.com.

At the time of writing, BCorp is rapidly approaching 5,000 member organizations and B1G1 is sprinting past 3,000. Significantly, many professional knowledge firms—particularly legal and accounting firms—are members of both groups.

And we like what you find writ large on the BCorp site: "We won't stop until all business is a force for good."

And, like B1G1, as you'll see in this grab from the BCorp website, they're serious about it, too.

Notice that the website doesn't just tell you what is required for certification. It tells you how companies benefit from it.

To understand why all of this is happening—and why it's happening now—let's take a quick look at the trajectory to go deeper. We'll start from 2009.

Measuring a company's entire social and environmental impact.

B Corp Certification is a designation that a business is meeting high standards of verified performance, accountability, and transparency on factors from employee benefits and charitable giving to supply chain practices and input materials. In order to achieve certification, a company must:

- Demonstrate **high social and environmental performance** by achieving a B Impact Assessment score of 80 or above and passing our risk review. Multinational corporations must also meet baseline requirement standards.
- Make a **legal commitment** by changing their corporate governance structure to be accountable to all stakeholders, not just shareholders, and achieve benefit corporation status if available in their jurisdiction.
- Exhibit **transparency** by allowing information about their performance measured against B Lab's standards to be publicly available on their B Corp profile on B Lab's website.

As leaders in the movement for economic systems change, B Corps reap remarkable benefits. They build trust with consumers, communities, and suppliers; attract and retain employees; and draw mission-aligned investors.

Source: BLab, https://www.bcorporation.net/en-us.

In that year, Simon Sinek burst onto the scene (and is still doing precisely that) with his *Start with Why* book and his October 2009 TEDx talk. It is now the third-most watched TED talk of all time (57 million people had watched it as of March 2022).

And in the early 2000s, this quote (incorrectly attributed to Mark Twain) went viral in various ways: "The two most important days of your life are the day you're born and the day you find out why."

Since then, purpose has become one of the most used terms in business. More than 500 books have been written on it, and there are thousands of articles touting the wisdom of "finding your purpose." For example, Rick Warren's 2002 book *The Purpose-Driven Life* became a bestseller, eventually selling 50 million copies in 85 languages. Company owners and leaders have extensive retreats to "find our purpose."

And then they (largely) struggle to articulate it or overly think it so that the resulting document is something that hangs on walls in toilets in an endeavor to make the document (or perhaps more accurately, the spirit of the document) ubiquitous.

And therein is the challenge—in spite of the data in the Monitor Deloitte report (and many similar reports), for many, purpose can and does become just a set of words.

FROM STANDARD TO STANDOUT

As important as words are, in the end it's the *doing* that matters, not the writing. And that leads us to adding impact-driven on top of purpose-led (Figure 3.1).

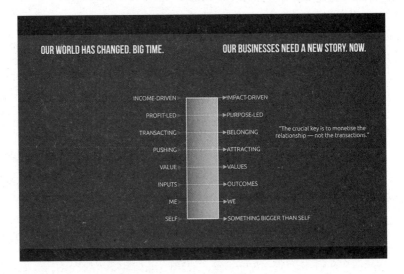

FIGURE 3.1 The shifts we need to make.

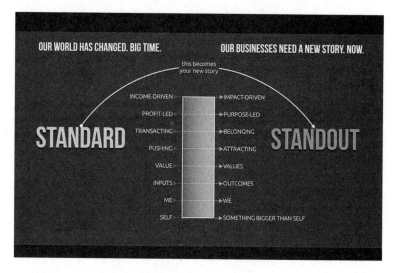

FIGURE 3.2   Moving from standard to standout.

Let's begin the process by referring again to the diagram we introduced in Chapter 2 (Figure 2.1).

When you look at the words alone, you can see the significant shift we're suggesting you make. The left-hand side is essentially all about transacting, the right-hand side is all about connecting or, as we've put it, belonging.

Let's look deeper. The left-hand side is all about self, the right-hand side, we'd suggest, is all about humanity.

When you take that further, you get to something more related to outcomes and position in the marketplace.

As you can see in Figure 3.2, we think of it as a move from standard (think ordinary) to standout (think outstanding).

And bearing in mind the starting point on the ladder (moving from "self" to "something bigger than self") you get this rather useful alliteration in Figure 3.3.

The mere mention of standing for something bigger than yourself leads to the concept of mission.

Here are some example mission, positioning, or WHY statements (expressed in landing pages for accounting firms) that reflect what we're suggesting:

Sample mission statements from accounting firms

We help you build the kind of business that you've always dreamed of by helping you achieve more time, better cash flow, less stress, and more impact (oh and less tax, too). Joining us helps you make a great contribution to our community and to our world as well.

We help you build, protect, and retain your assets through optimal planning, structuring, wealth creation, and tax minimization strategies. We help you live life on your terms by enjoying your retirement, transferring wealth as desired, giving back, and positively impacting others.

We believe you were put on this planet to do more than simply break even. So . . . if you think it's about getting your tax done, you've missed the point. It's about helping you create a business that gives you the freedom to put your family first and make a difference in our world.

You may think the statement from Assured is overly long . . . . but it does get read! And it makes the point about "something bigger than us" really neatly:

Assured mission statement

When we do business together at Assured, we change lives. Simple as that.

And your life—yes, you reading this if you're an existing or future client—is one of them that we'll significantly enrich.

That's because we help you create a business and a legacy that you're proud of, one that brings you joy as opposed to stress and one that also does good in our world too.

We help you create a business and lifestyle that really works so that you don't have to work quite as much. And we make sure the impact on you, your family, our community, and our world is inherently positive, inherently good.

That's why people refer to us as "Accountants for Good."

We're not for everyone—we don't try to be. But we could be just right for you.

A call is all it takes to find out.

We're looking forward to connecting with you.

FIGURE 3.3   Moving to standing for something bigger.

FIGURE 3.4   The website of an accounting firm in a town of 21,400 people — collinshume.com.

If you'd like to see a really simple expression of what we're getting at here, just click through to this site—it says what they stand for very well: www.collinshume.com. To save you a click, what you'll see is Figure 3.4.

It has the interesting (and in our view, totally correct) twist on *story*. "You.

That's all we focus on.

You, you're family your wealth, your business and the legacy you (and we) leave.

That's it.

Join us on this amazing journey."

Note that this firm is based in a community of just 21,400 people. Yet they work globally. And right now, there's a waiting list to join them!

They perfectly capture the point we made earlier about story. And that's this: that your story is all about helping your customers create a much better story for them and then their customers in turn.

Now, it's highly possible that these examples may not express your feelings your way. And that's OK.

What we want you to see here is the common thread of "bigger than yourself." And in the cases we've introduced you to so far, it's all about customer-centered outcomes.

Here's one more example of that for you from Novus Global. As you'll see from its website (https://novus.global) they focus very firmly on potential and on impact.

Following Tamsin Wooley-Barker's beautiful point about potential, let's look at that first. Here's how Novus express it:

> Most coaching firms help you get what you want. We help you explore what you're capable of. We work with teams and individuals— from Fortune 500 executives to professional artists, athletes, and more—all of whom consider themselves high-performing. We strategically partner to elevate their thinking, actions, and culture to move beyond high-performance into what we call Meta Performance™. We have a proven track record of success with world-class leaders who are now seeing results they never imagined reaching for before.

We hope you noted that lovely *potential* line: "We help you explore what you're capable of."

And then they back that up with a rolling information-graphic that in static form on May 6, 2022, looked like Figure 3.5.

You can see where that's reached right now by going to the Novus Global website and scrolling down: www.novus.global.

It's great stuff. And notice that, because it's *impact* as opposed to simply "purpose," it's measurable.

Because of that, it's possible to go even bigger—it's possible to amplify your impact significantly. You can go even bigger to community and even "world" outcomes.

And when you really get the magic of being impact-driven and being able to actually measure those impacts, you can share them with your team and, what's perhaps even more important, you can

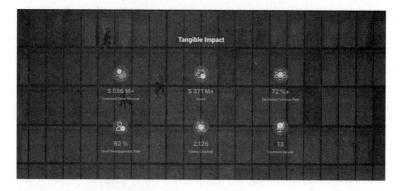

FIGURE 3.5   Novus.global getting it right.

FIGURE 3.6   A stunning example of "standing for."

share them with your customers in helping you (and them) achieve even more impacts . . . together.

Here's a great example of what we mean—going way beyond to community and world impact. *Really* going for something much bigger than yourself.

When you click on the OUR IMPACT tab of Master Coach and Event Producer Brody Lee's site (www.beyondimpact.com), you'll see the company's mission described numerically, as shown in Figure 3.6.

Clearly, the most important words there are these: SO THAT WE CAN . . .

GIVE 10 MILLION MEALS

PROVIDE 100,000 YEARS
OF CLEAN WATER

PLANT 100,000
NEW TREES

and

Save 1000 CHILDREN
FROM SEX TRAFFICKING

FIGURE 3.7   This really is "bigger than self."

Pause for a moment about how great those four words are: "We do this SO THAT WE CAN do some great things in our world too." Categorically bigger than self, isn't it?

And as you scroll down (Figure 3.7), you'll see what that leads to

And then, as you scroll down farther, you see how well they're going with that—you'll see the map (Figure 3.8) with the location of the specific impacts being made and you'll see how that all relates to the Sustainable Development Goals (SDG).

Now I should pause at this moment because what you've just seen (the SDG or Global Goals numbers) may not be very familiar to you.

And I do that because of something that happened to me in 2018.

I was in Silicon Valley speaking at the San Jose Convention Center for a program with 5,236 attendees run by Intuit.

About 20 minutes into my session I showed the slide in Figure 3.9.

I asked the audience—mostly accountants in public practice—to raise their hands if they knew what "these" (meaning the global goals displayed on the slide) were.

Staggeringly, even though they were a very engaged audience at that point, only an approximate 4% raised their hands. (That perhaps illustrates the reality of what one of my colleagues told me afterwards. "Paul," he said, "now you know that the SDGs were not developed by a bunch of great marketers!")

TOTAL *impacts*
3,461,851

FIGURE 3.8   More great reporting on progress.

FIGURE 3.9   The Sustainable Development Goals.

So . . . . just in case you're not familiar with the goals, when you search for them on Wikipedia this is the opening paragraph:

> The Sustainable Development Goals (SDGs) or Global Goals are a collection of 17 interlinked global goals designed to be a "blueprint to achieve a better and more sustainable future for all". The SDGs were set up in 2015 by the United Nations General Assembly (UN-GA) and are intended to be achieved by 2030. They are included in a UN-GA Resolution called the 2030 Agenda or what is colloquially known as Agenda 2030. The SDGs were developed in the Post-2015 Development Agenda as the future global development framework to succeed the Millennium Development Goals which ended in 2015. (Wikipedia n.d.)

In September 2015 when they were introduced, the then–secretary general opened the session with this never-before heard opening at the UN, "Governments do not change our world."

What followed culminated in this important sentence: "Businesses must become a force for good in our world."

There's much more we could say (and much, much more you could search for) on these goals.

For an increasing number of companies around the world now, they serve as North Stars. And later on, we'll show you how you can make them yours, too.

To illustrate the depth (or perhaps we should say the impact) of what's going on here, let's revisit "belonging" again and bring into play a word that you frequently hear in marketing when people talk about customer loyalty.

In his 2021 book, *Quantum Marketing: Mastering the New Marketing Mindset for Tomorrow's Consumers,* MasterCard Chief Marketing Officer, Raja Rajamannar makes us think differently about loyalty.

He begins that by referencing a study reported by the BBC, which found that 75% of men and 68% of women admitted to cheating at some point in a relationship.

Rajamannar points out if we can't expect people to be loyal when they know there'll be HUGE consequences for a lack of loyalty, how on earth can you expect them to be loyal to you when they're hit with many "come-and-join-us" messages from your competitors every day?

He suggests that loyalty is a continuum with four layers (what he calls manifestations; see Figure 3.10).

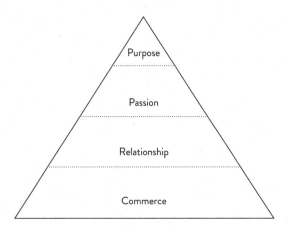

FIGURE 3.10   Raja Rajamannar's Purpose Triangle.

Raja has this to say about purpose: "This is the highest order of commitment. When customers can support a cause such as climate change, education, income equality or medical research they will do so with efforts that transcend any selfish motive or any expectation of something in return. They care about something deeply and they support it fully. And they remain committed to that cause or purpose."

Again, "Purpose is the highest form of commitment." We would add this to that, "Purpose as measured by the Impact being created is the highest form of commitment."

However you say it, Raja's point remains—when your company has a "bigger than yourself" purpose that either matches that of your customer or inspires them, the chances of them staying loyal are significantly amplified and multiplied.

Speaking at the World Federation of Advertisers (WFA)'s Global Marketer Week (April 7, 2022), Raja added these thoughts:

> It is critical that businesses are purpose driven, and profits will follow when brands pursue this passionately. We are leveraging the power of our network. We have 80 million merchants and 60,000 banks whose power we can bring to the table. This is a very significant effort.
>
> Profits will follow when you really passionately go through the purpose. You want to follow your North Star, identify the right causes, and then actually pursue that.

And Raja is passionate about it. He concluded his remarks by adding that in his 36 years in the field of marketing, now is "by far the most exciting and inspiring moment."

But let's pick up more on his point about leveraging the power of our network.

You've always had the power to do that, too. But the focus on transactions has limited that power. Your subscription model makes it even more powerful.

Think of it this way: in the absence of a strong commitment in their lives before subscribing to you, your customers can and will pick up on your purpose and be loyal to it. That's belonging to the max. Just reflect on it—you're not simply enriching their lives. Together you're enriching the lives of people you may not ever get to meet.

And even better than that, it's now possible to match your impact easily with that of the customer. We talk more about that in Chapter 7. In Chapter 4 we'll give you more on the outcomes—this time, the outcomes are for you.

4

HOW ARETHA GOT IT RIGHT

I hope mentioning Aretha Franklin is not showing my age.

R.E.S.P.E.C.T. is such a classic song (stunningly reprised by Jennifer Hudson in the 2021 film, *Aretha*).

Yet respect is not something that's common when we think of professional knowledge firms. Consider a large dinner function where people are mulling around before the doors to the dinner are opened.

You find yourself in a group of people you don't know. And someone acknowledges you with a welcome handshake and then asks, "And what do you do?"

"Oh, I'm an accountant," you say.

And then they turn to the person next to you with the same question.

"Oh I'm a corporate lawyer," she says.

And then the final person responds, "I'm a heart surgeon."

It's more than likely that the heart surgeon automatically gets the respect. And that's because we connect with the impact and meaning of what she does: saving lives.

So let's reset. Same conversation, different answers.

"And what do you do?"

"Well, I'm an accountant and, together with my team, I create better, wealthier, and more fulfilling lives for the 127 business owners we're privileged to work with right now."

Even the heart surgeon might find it difficult to top that. (True, she could say, "I'm a heart surgeon and I saved three lives today." But many of us would see that as bragging, not as earning greater respect.)

You'll instantly see here the connection to story—one of the major themes of this book.

We all have a story. Yet we mostly don't tell it well.

You can change that up AND simultaneously change the level of respect by considering the triangle in Figure 4.1. (By the way, triangles make fantastic models because they have just three sides. And that means they fall into this wonderful feature of our language and our brains—we simply love things in threes. As Nikola Tesla once

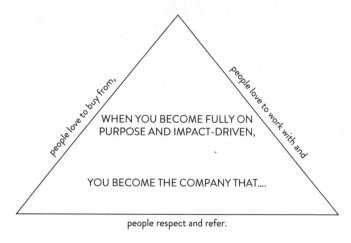

FIGURE 4.1   The Impact-Driven Results triangle.

said: "If only you knew the magic of 3, 6, and 9 then you would have the keys to the universe.")

So . . . Figure 4.1 shows the triangle.

And in spoken form, "When you become fully on purpose and impact-driven, you become the company that people love to buy from, that people love to work with, and (the company that) people respect and refer."

That triangle has such powerful implications for you as you build your subscription model.

Let's consider each aspect one-by-one for a moment.

When *people love to buy from you*, you can say "no" to those that don't fit your criteria. More than that, you can "fire" those existing customers that may not fit your new criteria.

Let's add to that. When you do those things, you'll attract GREAT customers. (As we said in the original *The Firm of the Future*, "Bad customers drive out good ones.")

Our great friend and colleague Ric Payne had a magnificent way of illustrating that. He called it not the 80/20 rule but the 80/225 rule. Figure 4.2 illustrates the point.

It's simple to understand. The "A" customers create 225% of your end profit. The D customers (the ones you don't like, the ones you should have said no too early on) are sucking from that super profit. It doesn't have to be that way. And of course, your

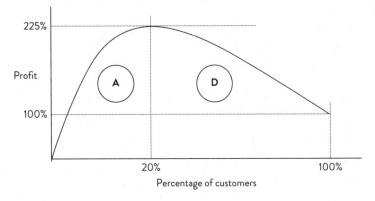

FIGURE 4.2 The 80/225 rule.

subscription model creates the super-profits for you when it's correctly implemented.

In fact, just look back at that earlier triangle. Recognize that when you're attracting great customers, you automatically move from chasing customers to choosing customers. Clearly, that's part of the move from "Pushing to Attracting" that we highlighted in Chapter 3.

Let's go to the right-hand leg of the triangle. When *people love to work with you*, you effectively become a magnet for talent (word spreads). And because you're now attracting better talent, you can let those people create what we call "Teams of Income."

This is so critical. Your job as the owner does not become the "doing"; your job becomes the visioning, the inspiring, and the "master of flow" (see Chapter 5 for more).

Your teams form themselves (well, you do give them some direction on that) into "pods"—each pod consisting of, let's say, five people—five people with appropriate skill sets—to enrich the lives of the customers they're working with.

Crucially, you are *not* doing the work. As you'll see later in this book, there's an important "reversal of flow" to make sure you really do build the firm you've always wanted—to connect with and belong to.

As you traverse these first two "legs" of the triangle, you move from (just in case you haven't done this step already) being time-driven to being outcome-driven and impact-driven. Your KPIs shift to making certain you're enriching the lives BOTH of your team members and your customers. You're moving from being time-driven to being outcome-driven and impact-driven.

Your morning huddles (more on them later) become much more focused on customer-centric tasks, and your weekly retro get-togethers focus very deliberately on your customers' wins—just how well are you enriching their lives.

Those things taken together form the wonderful virtuous circle of your subscription model—it just keeps growing.

You move from the traditional marketing funnel to a customer-centric flywheel. Hubspot explains it very well in this post (https://www.hubspot.com/flywheel). Figure 4.3 is a diagram that explains it.

Let's look at the three key areas of the flywheel:

ATTRACT:

> Here you're earning people's attention as opposed to forcing it. Of course, you're attracting the attention of visitors to your website and/or your LinkedIn posts with useful content, and you're making it very easy for them to connect with you—you're making sure that the first contact is truly outstanding in every way—that each moment really does matter.

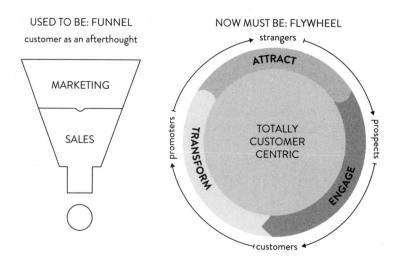

FIGURE 4.3   **From funnel to flywheel.**

Interestingly though, and to jump ahead on the flywheel for a moment, it's your customers who've turned into promoters who are introducing most people to your firm. They want others, others who are in so many ways just like them, to connect to you. Seth Godin puts it beautifully this way: "People like us do things like this."

ENGAGE:

Here your focus is to open relationships as opposed to closing deals. You're making sure there's a fit between you and the prospective customer (prospects)—you're making sure they fit your criteria—you're making sure you really can enrich their lives. And, not surprisingly, you're doing that mostly by listening, *not* by presenting. And uppermost in your mind as you're listening is that lovely quote from Tamsin Wooley-Barker: "Nature doesn't look for problems, it looks for potential."

You're also making sure potential customers are engaging with you on their preferred timeline and channels. And your people, *not you,* are leading that entire engaging process.

And when these prospects become customers, you're making sure that any incentives you have for your conversion process are not tied to the conversion per se; if there are incentives they are tied to the pod, and they're tied to customer success, not just the customer acquisition itself.

TRANSFORM:

You'll notice that (if you've looked at the HubSpot website we referenced above) this piece of the flywheel is called DELIGHT in the HubSpot model.

Certainly, you do have to delight your customers. You make sure your team is fully equipped (and expected) to do that. You know already they've got the basics right—the basics of fast-response, the basics of respect and kindness, the basics of caring, the basics of being on-time for meetings (actually, always ahead of time is best), the basics of an "enriching lives" at every interaction. And, like Apple, you're checking that with things like NPS® (net promoter score) and so on.

And in addition to those basics, they know that their key KPI is to transform your customers' businesses.

Those transformed customers then become your (in NPS® terms) promoters, introducing you and your team to the businesses those customers work with, and so on.

And at long last, perhaps, you can charge what you're really worth.

You transform so that your customers transform. And if Mastercard were your marketing department, they would certainly describe those outcomes as "Priceless."

In our next chapter, we take you even further on that journey.

5

THIS COULD BE THE MOST IMPORTANT BUSINESS QUESTION EVER

I can't remember who first mentioned this quote to me (one we used early in the book).

I think it could have been Jon Berghoff at XCHANGE. Here it is again:

Questions change the future before the answers even arrive.

Just ponder for a moment how profound and powerful that is. Consider this: On October 5, 2021, Paul Polman and Andrew Winston released their first book together, *Net Positive: How Courageous Companies Thrive by Giving More Than They Take*. Right at the start of the book, they pose this question:

Is the world better off because your business is in it?

Is it?

Does it matter? Of course it does.

We want you to be able to enthusiastically answer that with a pumped-fist "Yes!"

Just as importantly, we believe it's a question you might want to pose to your customers. In fact, you may well want to include it in a series of "criteria" questions to determine whether there's a good fit between you and the potential client.

Such a series of questions on this particular issue might go like this:

- On a 1–10 scale, where 1 represents a "Definitely not" and a 10 represents an "Absolutely yes," how would you

---

> answer this question: Is the world better off because your
> business is in it?
>
> - Could you explain why you've answered the way you
>   have, please?
> - If our firm could help move that number up the scale,
>   would that be something in which you'd be interested?

Those three simple questions alone could open up a whole plethora of possibilities and potential. Now let's put that idea aside for a
while and focus back on you and your team.

To do that, we've created a series of stepping stones for you in
Figure 5.1 below. Here are the steps moving upward:

Looking at the steps from the bottom up . . . .

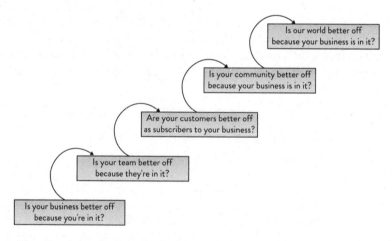

FIGURE 5.1   Some critically important stepping stones.

IS YOUR BUSINESS BETTER OFF BECAUSE YOU'RE IN IT?

There are many models for how businesses should (and do) function
and grow. Figure 5.2 is one of the simplest—it is also one of the
most powerful.

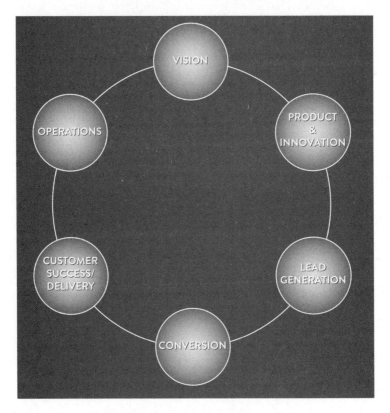

FIGURE 5.2 The six engine rooms of a business—part 1.

You see just six areas. And of course, the key question is, which bubble are you in. Depending on the size of your business right now, a better question might be, "How many bubbles are you in?"

And of course, your answer to that question depends on whether your business is starting, static, or scaling. Figure 5.3 shows how that looks.

You're in every box—like Figure 5.4.

And everything depends on you, too. As my colleague, Dr. David Dugan, points out, you're following these steps in a clockwise direction:

- You're developing, defining, and refining the product or service.
- Then you get some lead generation going—it could be advertisements, calling people you know, calling people you don't

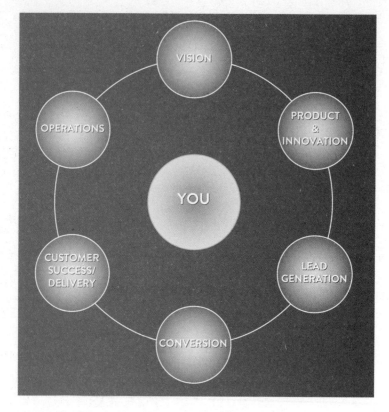

FIGURE 5.3   The six engine rooms of a business—part 2.

yet know, it could be web events (everyone has "webinars"—
you'll have *web events*. So much more "presence" AND so
many more people turning up, too!).

- Then you convert those leads. If you're really good at it, you
  follow a defined flow (almost a script), and you refine that as
  you go, too.
- Then you "deliver the goods" so to speak.
- And lastly, you make sure all the bills are being paid and all the
  processes are running correctly.

As the owner, your task is always to represent the vision, the values, and the value proposition of your organization in a way that is
authentic, congruent, and meaningful.

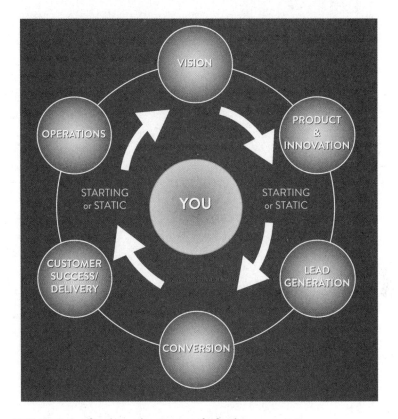

FIGURE 5.4 The six engine rooms of a business—part 3.

But clearly, unless you're a freelancer selling your time and expertise for money, you're going to struggle if you're in every box.

What we recommend you do now is counterintuitive. Figure 5.5 shows the idea in action.

You go counterclockwise now, letting others head operations/customer success and so on. Your job is to become the master of flow—leading the business instead of running it.

It's effectively run by what David Dugan refers to as your ELT—your executive leadership team—the leads in each of the circles.

First, you hire (even if it's part-time) in operations, then you get someone to do (and/or help you with) the delivery, then you get someone to handle the sales and you get a marketing person to get the leads flowing.

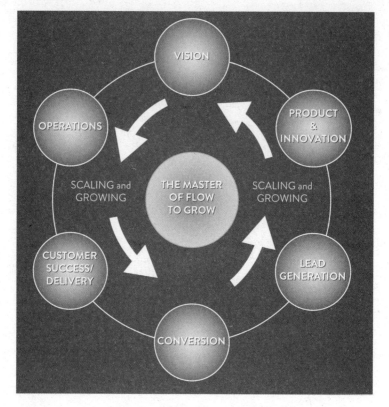

FIGURE 5.5   The six engine rooms of a business—part 4.

You need people who can focus on management so the business flows beautifully and meets its performance goals. The key as your business grows is not to become stuck as a manager. And this process of flow continues with you at the center like this and everything else almost bursting at the seams (Figure 5.6).

Again, when you start the business, it might be you and you alone. And here are some keys to make sure it doesn't stay that way—some keys to make sure you enrich more lives.

Monitor Your Value Score

Each month, monitor what we'll call your Value Score (a.k.a. Value Creation Score).

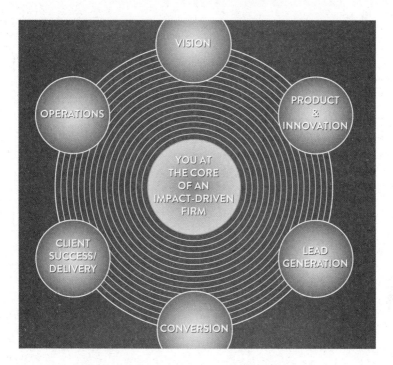

FIGURE 5.6   The six engine rooms of a business—part 5.

Your Value Score is simply the total revenue of the firm divided by the hours you're working. This becomes a critical marker for you. Clearly it needs to become high, very very high (by the way, this is not an hourly rate that you charge—it is simply an internal measure looking at how effective and valuable you are at growing the business. Nor are we suggesting you track time spent on a timesheet. Simply guesstimate the hours you worked the past month, or year. After all, it can't be higher than 8,760).

You always make sure you're NOT doing tasks that could be easily done by you paying someone less than your Value Score.

The Value Score is really a measure of your opportunity cost. You should spend your time on those areas where you have a comparative advantage, not an absolute advantage. You may be able to type faster than your executive assistant, but that does not mean you should do the typing. The Value Score allows your opportunity cost to grow as your firm does, and gives you a mental shortcut to determine what activities you should not be performing. We do not want surgeons piercing ears.

If you haven't done so already, be sure to get an executive assistant (I prefer to call them a DJ, a director of joy—joy for you AND for your customers) to at least handle your inbox and your calendar.

Use a three-step process that Master Coach Dan Martel calls ATF:

1. Audit—you simply check that a particular task can, in fact, be handled by you paying someone less than your Value Score.

2. Transfer—you transfer that task to someone to whom you're paying less than your Value Score.

3. Fill—now that you've freed up that task (e.g., handling your calendar), define how you're going to fill the new time you have to do things that really matter.

Establish a Cadence

And talking of calendars, if you haven't done it already, immediately set up what some people call a "default diary" so that you establish as repeatable a rhythm or cadence for the business and your part in it as quickly as you can.

Of course, that cadence can change trimester by trimester or quarter by quarter (depending on how you set the overall business rhythm).

For example, in very broad detail, my cadence in one of the businesses I own is like this:

-   Mentoring and Marketing Monday—early on, marketing checks and processes, then high-value customers
-   Touch-base Tuesdays—prospective high-value customer contacts and Partnership opportunities
-   Web-event Wednesdays—speaking
-   Touch-base Thursdays—internal connections principally led by 2-IC (your second-in-charge)
-   Financials and Fantastic Fridays—hopefully self-explanatory

Right now, though, there's an additional cadence item every day for three hours max (and some days it's two of them). Yes, you're right, it's writing this book!

If you're an owner of the business, your focus—some would say your only focus—must be on making sure the business is delighting existing customers, transforming their businesses, and attracting new ones.

It is incredibly easy for you not to do that. It's incredibly easy for you to focus all of your time on dealing with internal team problems, issues, challenges, systems, glitches, lack of communication, etc.

So it's absolutely critical to make sure that as you grow, you don't get stuck "running" the business. Your job is to lead your business.

Think of it as a simple case of supply and demand. Your job is primarily to create demand, to be out front capturing the attention of the market.

The team's job is to manufacture supply. Running the business is the task of the CEO or 2-IC.

What we see so often is where owners fall into the trap of applying themselves to the manufacture of supply and, as a result, they put themselves in a position where no matter how hard they work, or how great the work they do is, they're simply not going to be profitable. And that's clearly because no amount of referrals will exceed the amount of demand required to make that system profitable.

Your team's job (not yours) is to be able to help manufacture supply. Sadly, this is where the vast majority of business owners spend way too much time—manufacturing supply.

Now of course, manufacturing supply also means delivering great value. That's why it's such an easy trap to fall into, because you want to delight your customers. You want to build better systems and processes. You want to innovate—you want to build better products and services to help your customers transform.

But let's just step back a little to look at the fundamentals of supply and demand. Whenever there's more demand than supply, prices go up. Whenever there's more supply than demand, prices go down.

Just grabbing that simple point is enough to transform a struggling business into a thriving business.

Most small- to medium-sized business owners—your very customers—are most likely applying themselves to the manufacturer of supply and as a result, they're putting themselves in a position where no matter how hard they work, or how great the work they do is, they're simply not going to be profitable, because no amount of referrals will exceed the amount of demand required to make that system profitable.

You can help them stop that.

Once again, that's why we want you to share your insights from this book and your implementation of it with them.

This simple point about supply and demand can transform businesses quickly—very quickly indeed.

So, that's the foundational rung of this ladder hopefully nailed for you. And please don't make it complex—as a friend of mine put it recently: simple scales; complex fails.

Let's now move to the question on the second rung . . . .

IS YOUR TEAM BETTER OFF BECAUSE THEY'RE IN YOUR BUSINESS?

You probably know of Gallup for the surveys they regularly (and globally) conduct with the aim of letting us know how things are.

One such study is their ongoing global study of engagement in businesses.

Engagement is one of those things that we tend to think of in binary terms: Engaged/DisEngaged.

Gallup suggests it's not binary—in fact, is provides three categories: Engaged, Not Engaged, and Actively Disengaged. And in its 2021 update to the ongoing Employee Engagement story, Gallup reports that globally just 20% of employees are fully engaged. Just 20%. (In the United States, that number is closer to 35% fully engaged.)

CompanyFounders.com show the numbers graphically for us in Figure 5.7.

FIGURE 5.7   Rowing the boat the wrong way.

Think of that graphic as a shot of a rowing boat heading from the left of the page to the right of the page. What you've got is 30 out of 100 rowing the right way (in every sense of the word right), 50 with their oars just dangling in the water and 20 actively rowing the wrong way—from right to left!

It's not a very good look!

For comparison purposes, the latest (January 2022) update to the Gallup surveys gives these stats and commentary from Gallup:

In the first half of 2021, Gallup reported that 36% of workers were engaged, matching the 2020 composite result. But the second half of 2021 saw a drop, resulting in the annual figure of 34% engaged workers in 2021. This may not be surprising given the many challenges leadership faced in recent months, including record increases in employee quit rates, implementing vaccine mandates, and planning for various combinations of remote and on-site work while trying to match worker preferences with leadership expectations.

The ratio of engaged to actively disengaged workers in the U.S. is 2.1 to 1, down from 2.6 to 1 in 2020. (Harter 2022)

And in April 2022, Gallup updated the numbers again like this:

This pattern has continued into early 2022, as 32% of full- and part-time employees working for organizations are now engaged, while 17% are actively disengaged, an increase of one percentage point from last year.

These three standout numbers provide good examples of the negative consequences.

FACT:

Companies with disengaged employees experience 18% less productivity and 60% more workplace errors than those with an engaged workforce.

Source: Seppälä and Cameron 2015.

FACT:

Unengaged employees account for almost $7 trillion in lost productivity the world over every year! The bad news doesn't stop there. The actual cost of replacing employees can be twice their base salaries, depending on their wage, role, and experience.

Source: Misra 2018.

FACT:

Team members were 12 times more likely to leave their job if the company wasn't helping them grow in their careers.

Source: Misra 2018.

So let's take a look at how we can get the boat moving faster AND in the right direction.

To do that let's first go back to that Monitor Deloitte Report we looked at in Chapter 2. To save you flipping pages, we put it this way back there:

> And it's not just sales you attract—you attract the large number of people who would prefer to work with an on-purpose company—you become a magnet for talent as well once you're seriously *on purpose*. Oh and did you notice a significant number of those people you attract will work for less too?

When you look in-depth at that Deloitte report, you start to get a handle on moving the boat the right way AND speeding it up— moving it forward faster.

Specifically, the report said fully 78% of people—that's a HUGE number—would prefer to work for an "on-purpose" company and three-quarters of the millennials questioned said they'd take a pay cut to do it!

Such is the power of purpose fully expressed as *impact*.

The question is, of course, now that we've got more of the "right" people in the boat, how do we keep them all rowing in right direction all the time?

Huddles are part of the answer. *Huddles* are daily time-limited get-togethers designed to inspire, to catch potential issues early, and, of course, to make sure we're all rowing in unison the right way.

Here's a great example taken from the culture document of InspireCA, an accounting firm in Brisbane, Australia:

Own the day.

To help you create space for personal or family success, we do an "early start, early finish" with office hours between 7:20 and 3:50. Daily at 7:47 sharp we assemble in a circle for a Standing Team Huddle, where we each share three things:

What am I grateful for?

What are my top three priorities for today?

Am I ahead, on track, or behind with my measures of success?

Think of "747" as everyone standing around a campfire and the goal is to get everyone warmed up. What you say and how you say it can be like either throwing cold water or fuel on the fire. Please be brief, inspirational, and to the point.

That was pre-pandemic. The exact same process applied during lockdowns, work-from-homes, and so on—the only difference was that they "stood around Zoom" as opposed to huddling together.

Critically, huddles are quick—we find 15 minutes to be the absolute maximum. Everyone has to get their three things out in less than a minute. So that means huddles are *not* "all-hands"—they can be project groups, leadership groups. They are tight-knit groups that are all focused on keeping that boat moving.

Let's be clear—huddles are *crucial*, not optional. And if you need more help to get you started, you can check this piece from a Huddle champion, Verne Harnish: https://blog.growthinstitute.com/scale-up-blueprint/daily-huddle.

Retros help enormously, too.

The Retro

We highly recommend that you have regular "retro" (it's short for retrospective) rituals. Ron is a real champion of them (as you'll discover soon), even though he gives them a different name: AAR, or After Action Reviews.

Whatever you choose to call them, do them.

Perform them at least monthly if not weekly, and, of course, have them whenever a project completes. Think of them as a check-up—a check of the pulse of your organization.

And it's important to note that the retro is not just a review—you'll get some tasks handed out as a result of the check-up so you and your team can constantly learn and constantly improve.

Like so many other things in Leadership, the secret is to ask great questions. People WANT to be listened to . . . questions (and then actions) are the way to make sure your team know they're listened to—it's part of the culture you're creating.

Here are three questions that get you started:

- What's working? As your team members answer this, encourage them to express their gratitude and recognize the people, the efforts, and the inputs that they appreciate as well as what the impact was on you, the team, the customer, and/or the business.
- What's not working, what could we be doing better? Make sure this is a "no blame" discussion. Here you need to focus people on systems and processes, *not* people.
- What could be missing? This is where you look for new insights and ideas to make the boat go faster and smoother—to make things flow. And of course, it could well be a time where you identify a skill set that might be missing from the team.

One great way to make retros work really well is to use an old "technology"—Post-it Notes.

As you ask the questions, get your team to write their answers on Post-it Notes. Then (in the office situation) stick them on a board so you can group similar issues together. Of course, on Zoom-type sessions, the chat is the place with someone monitoring the chat to do the grouping.

And of course, you address the issues with the most Post-it Notes in the groupings first.

Let's say it again: Huddles and retros are really essential.

At the end of the chapter, you'll see a full example of the InspireCA culture document. As you look at it, you may find some things incongruent with the way you'd like to work. That's fine—just change those specific things. And use the document as a "boat-rowing" framework for you to create a real one for your business.

Culture really is key. I'll always remember an example of it that I saw in the back corridors of Intuit in Silicon Valley in 2018 when Brad Smith headed the company. It happened at Intuit's QB CONNECT Conference in San Jose. I was with a tiny group with my dear friend from England, Steve Pipe.

Here's the story as Steve told it in his blog later that day:

> A very proud Intuit team member (thank you Kim) had offered to give a small group of us a tour of the campus where 2,000 of their 9,000 global employees work.
>
> Perhaps inevitably it is an incredibly cool workplace (let your imagination run riot, think automated R2-D2 type robots delivering food for example, and you'll begin to get the picture).
>
> But then we turned a corner from one corridor into another, and were confronted with something unexpected: a production line.
>
> But it wasn't software they were assembling, it was food parcels for the needy. And they were doing it joyfully, with visible love and compassion in their hearts, and glowing smiles on their faces.
>
> Suddenly someone rang a gong and the corridor burst into applause.
>
> They were celebrating assembling their 2,000th food parcel of the day. 2,000 quiet acts of kindness.
>
> That moment told me everything I needed to know. And earned my admiration and loyalty, FOR EVER.
>
> It is what businesses do when no one is looking that tells you who they really are and what they really stand for.

That's what culture does for you. The boat gets rowed even when you're not there to see it.

No timesheets. No one standing over your shoulder. But a bell being rung so cheerfully when the milestone is hit.

Bells ringing when great things happen should be a part of your business, too.

It's all part of your team members being truly connected to your business—it's a central tenet of your subscription business.

When that connection fails, Shift the Work gives us these staggering numbers. When employees feel less connected to their workplace, culture, and purpose . . .

- The likelihood of producing great work falls 90%.
- The probability of burnout increases 11x.
- The odds that employees will leave within three years surge 6x (Shift 2022).

Friend, fellow writer, and consultant Ryan Lazanis added this important dimension to those numbers in a discussion we were having early in 2022:

> We're seeing work-life balance as a central theme emerge in terms of work culture. Working at a firm traditionally came with a "suck-it-up" mentality. Push through the busy seasons. Push through the stress. The ones that can do that will make it to the top.
>
> We're now seeing the deterioration of this kind of mentality and attitude with the emergence of Gen Z. They'll just quit to find somewhere else that provides the balance, meaning, and flexibility they crave.

Remember, too, that quote from Jeffrey Hollender we mentioned earlier: "Everything a company does is an expression of its culture."

More simply, everything springs from culture.

That being said, maybe it's time for a check on yours.

In her book *The Forever Transaction*, Robbie Kellman Baxter offers us this table to gauge your firm's movement toward a true subscription business model.

Subscription	No	Testing	YES
Leadership support	Leader focused quarterly	Strong project manager and light CEO support	CEO fully engaged on culture
Team lead	None	Dedicated low-level manager	Senior strategist with tenure

Subscription	No	Testing	YES
Ongoing relationship with customer	No	Track all metrics with customer lifetime value as key	Customer is at the center of everything, and recurring subscriptions prove it
Target customers	Everyone	Tracking by cohort	Well defined by behavior demographics and referrals
Technology	Old and transactional	Ready to invest in tech	Sophisticated tech stack in place and ready for customization
Culture	Product-centric	Someone on the team responsible for customer voice	Totally customer-centric

Let's hope you were able to tick off everything in that right-hand column.

And just to add one important piece to the "Ongoing relationship" line, at an April 2022 conference in the UK, *The Financial Times'* managing director of consumer revenue, Fiona Spooner, made the crucial point that the company's focus has shifted away from acquisition and even retention. She said,

> *Now, our North Star is around lifetime value; the way we think about our business in relation to customer needs. From editorial to finance, we need to think about increasing the relationship with customers and understanding the valuable points across the whole experience.*

That's what your subscription model forces you to do.

Oh and since we've just used a checklist, let's just focus for a moment on the value of them (in fact, a potential problem with them).

Our friend, fellow author, and consultant Gary Boomer reminded us recently in an *Accounting Today* article of Atul Gawande's book, *The Checklist Manifesto.*

Gawande is a surgeon, writer, and public health leader who practices general and endocrine surgery at Brigham and Women's Hospital in Boston. The book includes several lessons from both the airline industry and (interestingly) the medical profession that apply to the need for professional firms to transform.

Gary makes the profoundly important point that checklists have a problem. He puts it like this:

> The problem comes when checklists attempt to become all-encompassing, long, and often resisted. The checklist can be a valuable tool [when it's] simplified and applied to the basic principles of value and best business practices.
>
> For me, this was the "Aha!" moment. Now, over 10 years later . . . a talent shortage, a pandemic, and enabling technology have provided a sense of urgency to exponentially transform.
>
> [Business transformation is] an umbrella term for making fundamental changes in how a business or organization operates. This includes personnel, processes, and technology. These transformations help organizations compete more effectively, become more efficient, or make a wholesale strategic pivot. Today we are seeing this as firms focus on the right clients, right services and the right business model. (Boomer 2022)

He leaves us with this observation: "Exponential growth is focused on culture and adding value to team members and customers."

Nice to have friends on the same page, isn't it?

Hilda Carrillo, Joseph F. Castellano, and Timothy M. Keune write: "Millennials have a deep desire to do work that benefits society and may gain enthusiasm for their work if they appreciate the firm's larger purpose. (They) don't want to sit still and have zero interest in employers that are afraid of change and still operate the same way they did 10 years ago" (Carrillo et al. 2017).

Successful firms need to be bold and willing to evolve—to the point that innovation becomes ingrained in everything that the firm does. This is the really big picture, culture-creating stuff.

So, let's get moving from big picture, culture-creating stuff to a BIG question on our ladder now.

ARE YOUR CUSTOMERS BETTER OFF AS SUBSCRIBERS TO YOUR BUSINESS?

That's clearly a question best answered by your customers.

But let's give you some insights so that your customers will answer the question with a resounding "Yes!"

The question is so important because again it underscores the point that this is not just about moving to a subscription pricing model; it is about changing up your entire story. That story starts with the way you draw your organization chart (Figure 5.8).

One hopefully obvious point—we're absolutely not suggesting your organization must have all these layers. But, just for the moment, let's imagine some companies that do!

Traditionally, organization charts begin with the CEO or the board on top and then everyone else beneath them, as in Figure 5.8.

The customer-driven organization charts start with the customer at the top and everyone else "supporting" them (Figure 5.9). It flips your mindset and the mindset of the team.

FIGURE 5.8 The traditional organization chart.

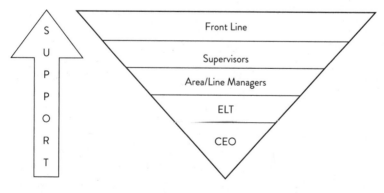

FIGURE 5.9 A better way of drawing the organization chart.

It makes a huge difference—one of the companies I own is so fixed on the idea they show the organization chart as a tree—the strong trunk supporting growth in the branches and the leaves doing the job of providing energy to the structure.

A key metric for a professional knowledge firm now is not their revenue or profits—it is the revenue and profits that they're helping produce for others. One of the companies I work with proudly talks openly about the improvement in profitability of the clients they serve (it's currently 247%, by the way).

You see that in the office environment (and websites, too) with photos and videos proudly showcasing the outcomes of the firms' work (as opposed to the normal photos of the board and CEO in "About Us"—surely there should be a tab called "About Our Outcomes" before the "About Us").

And guess what impact-driven companies have on their websites— yes, a tab called Our Impact. And when you really "get" this, you'll make sure that impact is updated automatically daily (it's easily possible to do that, by the way).

We give you much, much more on that in Chapter 6. For now, let's go up to the next rung on our ladder.

IS YOUR COMMUNITY BETTER OFF BECAUSE YOUR BUSINESS IS IN IT?

This question gets back to the very essence of belonging.

It's not just about *customers* feeling that they belong, it's clearly team members who need to feel they belong, too. Let's put it simply and directly: You cannot have a successful subscription business with low churn rates and significant MRR unless your team members (and, of course, your customers) are great ambassadors for you. And that's true irrespective of the role those team members might play in your business.

So . . . when you're doing great things getting everyone rowing (faster in unison toward that North Star that's bigger than you) in the same direction and everyone is truly on purpose and measuring your impact, those self-same people are more likely to be connected into their communities and doing great things in them (wearing their company T-shirts, of course). Re-read the story about the food parcels just a few pages ago to get the essence of what we're talking about here.

Encourage it—you'll be amazed at the difference it makes.

But it's more than just Team Members—it's your customers, too. For example, just imagine you building your firm by implementing all the ideas here to the extent that your customers do it as well—and they do it because you become the guiding light in a very real sense. And when we say "you" here, we don't mean "you, the person." Remember, you're leading, not necessarily doing. So the "you" in this context means "you the firm."

Think about what that means for a moment.

Just take a minute to get your mind around that concept—you're not an isolated firm living in its own bubble.

You are deeply connected—yes deeply—to your customers. And you're transforming their businesses with them by applying key insights from your model—imagine you actively helping them do that. (More on that later.)

And doing that impacts the top rung of the ladder, as you'll see right now . . .

TOP RUNG: IS THE WORLD BETTER OFF BECAUSE YOUR BUSINESS IS IN IT?

Straight to the point: You can only answer a resounding yes to that if, and only if, you're building your new subscription model on this story arc that I introduced you to in Chapter 2 (Figure 5.10).

FIGURE 5.10   The key story arc.

Let's go a little deeper now. And to do that, it's time to introduce you to Tim Duggan.

He expressed what we're talking about here really well in his first book *Cult Status: How to Build a Business People Adore.* The book won the prize for the 2021 Australian Business Book of the Year—pretty good for a first book!

Tim gives us a new word early on—the *untrepreneur*—an entrepreneur who is undoing the old ways of doing business.

In the opening chapter, Tim lays out what he labels as "7 Steps to Creating a Business with Cult Status."

I nearly flipped when I read the first item on the list. It's simply this:

Define Your Impact.

He writes: "The old way of thinking about business was making as much money as possible. The new way of thinking is to balance profit with the impact you want to have. Instead of starting with a dollar figure, start with the number of people you want to affect."

Think about that . . . it's "human" right from the get-go.

Straightaway, it's bigger than yourself.

And as a professional knowledge firm helping your customers achieve better results, every time you do that, you're multiplying your impact too.

Just imagine now if you could measure that impact (and more).

The great news is, you can. And you can do it simply by integrating impact right at the heart of every business process. You've already done that (just in case you didn't know) by investing in this book. When you did that, five children in need got daily access to game-changing education. And like so many businesses around the world now, we made that happen through B1G1.com.

And in case you're not familiar with how that works, take as just one example this legal firm in Perth, Western Australia, Lynn and Brown:

Internal Triggers

We have set a series of "triggers" or company goals across various business functions and departments here at Lynn & Brown Lawyers. Each month, as we achieve our goals we give to causes close to our hearts such as providing an e-Learning hub for Aboriginal communities in Australia, feeding children in crisis in Vietnam, or giving clean water to a school in Zambia.

At the beginning of each month we review the previous month's goals and when our firm achieves set targets we issue a "giving" through B1G1.

Some of the triggers that result in us giving are:

- Each time we receive a positive Google review or testimonial we give 20 cups of rice to children in crisis.
- When a lawyer gives an external presentation, we provide 20 days of computer education to children in need.
- When a client returns to Lynn & Brown Lawyers, we give 10 days of clean water to students in Zambia.
- When an initial appointment is attended, we give 20 days of clean water to students in Zambia.
- When the Lynn & Brown Lawyers website receives 4 visits, we give 1 day of clean water to a student in Zambia.
- When a guest attends one of our seminars or networking events, we give 10 cups of rice to children in crisis.
- When a client purchases a complete Wills package, we give 5 cups of rice to children in crisis.
- When a staff member has a birthday, we provide 10 days of computer education to children in need.
- When a client engages for the L&B Exclusive package, we give 30 cups of rice to children in crisis.
- Plus many other internal triggers!

Source: Lynn & Brown, https://www.lynnandbrown.com.au:/resources/b1g1/, accessed April 4, 2022.

And there really are many other internal triggers. What's really great is that the triggers are set by the team. The firm owners refer to it as "democratizing our impact globally."

Notice too it's not your normal CSR initiative as in "ABC firm proudly supports XYZ charity." This is very, very different. B1G1 Founder and CEO, Masami Sato explains:

> We're privileged to work with 1000s of businesses from around the world in more than 40 countries. We have projects right now in 47 countries.
>
> Those projects are run by great organizations that we assess and vet very carefully—it's quite tough to become a B1G1 Project. And so you may wonder how it's done.
>
> It's not like normal giving where you can donate $1,000 to an organization. What we do is carefully break everything down into tiny micro-units. For example, for just 61 cents you can provide business training to a woman in need so that they can actually start and run their sustainable business.
>
> Or it could be game-changing education for just 20 cents. There are hundreds of examples.
>
> And then your company can (like thousands of others now) link literally any type of activity directly to those projects with B1G1 passing on fully 100% of the giving you choose to do.
>
> So a company might say, "every time we have a great team meeting, we provide one day's support to a woman in business."
>
> What happens then is that everything in the business becomes something to celebrate and be grateful for. It means that the team members in the company can come together and unite under the shared mission to do good for somebody else, not for themselves, but for others.
>
> And so the power of B1G1 is actually the power of stories. The stories make it meaningful. It's like a secret mechanism. You become integral with those giving stories.
>
> And when you do this with genuine intent to make a difference, you transform, how you communicate with your team transforms, how the team feels transforms and that spreads out in ripples to your customers too.

In this model, giving is no longer a once-off event. We're about to pass 300 million giving impacts worldwide. Business owners and their teams are taking action every day. That's why we do this.

Now it might seem as though we've made a jump here—jumping from outcomes for customers (in the sense that their lives are enriched) to outcomes that impact people we may never even get to meet.

But what's really cool is that Lynn and Brown's customers ARE involved. When impacts are made that involve them, they (the customers) get beautifully done Gratitude Certificates sent to them that specifically refer to the impacts created. Figure 5.11 is a typical example.

Now, of course, you may well use different language. And you can easily customize the style directly to your own brand book guidelines.

CONGRATULATIONS.

Specifically we want to thank you and congratulate you for being a client.

One of the things that's really important to us is to make sure something great happens every time we connect.

So with that in mind, we thought you'd love to know that 26 children just got access to game-changing education as a direct result of the meeting we had together today.

Our simple goal here is to keep on making great things happen in our world ...... together with you.

FIGURE 5.11   Imagine receiving this after a meeting.

The important thing here is that you get the idea, not the specifics. The specifics are the way YOU choose to implement the ideas.

Central to that implementation are some key foundational ideas from Chapter 2:

Our world has changed big time.

And because you and your firm are part of that world, you need to change-up your story, your model, and your focus on being impact-driven and enriching lives.

There's much more where that comes from in Chapter 6—just turn the page.

inspire™
Core Values

Dream Big

- Shoot for the moon.
- Challenge yourself and others to greatness.
- Step outside of your comfort zone and take a risk.
- Be creative—do something that wasn't asked of you, put yourself out on a limb.
- Step up and get better.

Make An Impact

- We're here to GSD or "get sh*t done". Make an impact and get results.
- Do meaningful work—you're not here to look good and go nowhere.
- Fulfill business and personal potential—be productive in all you do.

Remember Your Roots

- Wake up every day and feel excited. BE the source of inspiration.
- Connect and communicate with everyone that touches the business.
- Inspire is a BS free zone. No politics. Zero bitching. Drama, gossip, and moaning have no place here.

WHY WE EXIST

We are numbers people and we believe that FAMILY is number one. We exist to help Young Families use their Small Business to get Cashed Up.

OUR MISSION | We're on a mission to become Australia's Most Impactful Accounting firm. Ultimately it's about helping our clients pull more money, time and happiness from their business—measured in Freedom Days or Net Wealth / Cost of Living per Day. The 10 year vision is to give the proactive advice that helps create 10,000,000 Freedom Days, across 10 cities.

ENVIRONMENT
DICTATES PERFORMANCE

Dream Big. Make an Impact. Remember Your Roots.

This is our version of "Code of Conduct." Unlike a traditional policy document, we wanted to be more human about things.

The following 14 Agreements point to the fact that in business (and in life), all we can do is manage our agreements.

Marathons & Sprints.

Like Dog Years, a single year at Inspire could be likened to seven years in a more traditional firm. We run at a serious pace. To avoid burnout, we run our business to a "3 x 4" rhythm or 3 x 4 month quarters in a year instead of the traditional "4 x 3". Each quarter will have a clear theme and focus, and every team member will know their role to play, climaxing with a month of Celebration.

Celebrate	Activate	Recalibrate	Accelerate	Celebrate	Activate	Recalibrate	Accelerate	Celebrate	Activate	Recalibrate	Accelerate
Nov	Dec	Jan	Feb	Mar	Apr	May	Jun	Jul	Aug	Sep	Oct

Sharpening the axe.

Celebration months are a great opportunity for "Service & Maintenance" as it's the only time that "the speed train"—that is inspire—slows down long enough to onboard new team members, allow team to take a well earned holiday or do some epic personal and professional development. In November, March and July each year for example, we celebrate our wins with a 2 day offsite team retreat called Thinking and Thanking Day.

The Game Plan.

Like a team in a locker room moments before running onto the field, our retreats help every person on the team know exactly the role they each play in winning the game. Client Service Coordinators, Account Managers, Business Development Managers and Quality Controllers, each have a different (but complementary) role to play for the quarter, summarised in one key Measure of Success. For example, "5 x Proactive Advice Meetings / week" or "5 x 2nd Opinions on Tax / week" when repeated 13 times over the 13 weeks in a quarter keeps us each "on track" to win as a team. Because we are all dependant on each other, it's fine to be ahead, or on track but **it is not ok to be behind.**

Own the day.

To help you create space for personal or family success, we do an "early start, early finish" with office hours between 7:20 and 3:50. Daily at 747 sharp we assemble in a circle for a Standing Team Huddle where we each share 3 things— What am I grateful for? What are my top 3 priorities for today? Am I ahead, on track or behind with my Measures of Success?

Think of "747" as everyone standing around a campfire and the goal is to get everyone warmed up. What you say and how you say it can be like either throwing cold water or fuel on the fire. Please be brief, inspirational and to the point.

Get sh*t done.

Ever noticed how productive you are when you've worked either on an airplane, from home or at a cafe with your headphones on? *Distractions are the enemy of productivity.* That's why "747" is followed by 2 hours of GSD time—no emails, no client meetings, no phone calls and best of all, no one tapping you on the shoulder to ask a question, until 10 am. Seriously, unless there's a comet about to hit our office, don't bug anyone.

Batch-sh*t crazy.

The relentless pursuit of GSD also sees us "batch" all our client meetings on Tuesday–Thursday, leaving Monday's & Friday's to prepare and follow up. It's also why we don't live in our inboxes. Emails are only "let in" to our inbox 3 x times a day—thanks to a software called Boomerang.

Inbox Zero.

Every day we achieve Inbox Zero. Every email in our inbox is either acknowledged or actioned on the day it's received. Most client emails are actually answered by our team of Client Service Coordinators and Junior Accountants. So it's just the curly ones that make it through to you. Inbox Zero helps us stay well within our promise to our clients of a "guaranteed 24 hour response to your questions, *or we'll send you a bunch of flowers".*

Gratitude is a gamechanger.

Every Friday morning we do Team Thankyou. A standing circle of gratitude where we THANK each other for the impact we've heard or seen each other make during the week. There's laughter, there's smiles and sometimes even tears. Definitely the highlight of the week.

Deadlines become Lifelines.

Preparing Tax Returns & Financial Statements is like driving in a car looking through the rear vision mirror. While being compliant with the ATO is important, we ultimately want to help our clients make the 7 Smart Financial Decisions of a Cashed Up business. That's why we turn ATO Deadlines into Business Lifelines through early lodgment and proactive advice—this is like looking through the front windscreen, helping clients take the shortest and fastest route to their destination. For example—

- Quarterly BAS are finalised *2 weeks before* they're due, so clients have time to plan cashflow.
- Tax Planning is done with every client by May 15, so clients *still have 6 weeks* to implement before 30 June.
- We run an "Annual General Meeting" with each of our clients when we finish their Tax Returns & Financial Statements in October, so they still have Nov–June to make this the best financial year yet.

Death before Timesheets.

You may know by now we don't do timesheets. So ... what do we measure then? *Impact*.

- Tax Savings
- Increases in Profit & Business Value & Wealth
- Reduction in Cashflow Days, Debt & Cost of Living.
- The ultimate impact is Freedom Days. which calculated by "Net Wealth / Cost of Living per Day" is really the sum of all these impacts combined.

At Inspire we believe that "Advice Precedes Impact." Instead of timesheets, everyday and every week we track the number of "Proactive Advice Meetings" we've delivered, then every quarter we measure the impact of our advice on our clients business and lives.

Communication over Calculation.

He who communicates best, wins. To date your career progression has been focused around upping your technical knowledge. From here on in it's about becoming a MASTER COMMUNICATOR. Knowing your sh*t is important, but that just gets you a foot in the door. "Making an impact", becoming a "Life Changing Accountant" and helping people get "Cashed Up" will require you to learn how to communicate in such a way that people listen, take action and leave feeling inspired.

Dress to Impress.

The dress code at Inspire is Super Smart Casual. We want to strike the fine balance between "I'm down to earth and approachable" and "I'm a qualified professional, ready to make an impact". You'll **never** see us in a suit or tie. Some cool jeans or a skirt with an Inspire T Shirt and a collared shirt over the top will do the trick. In short, we want people to judge us by the impact we make, not the clothes we wear. However we'd never want to dress in such a way that people find it hard to have *instant trust* in sharing with us their most intimate financial details.

Leave, leave, leave.

Annual Leave . . .

Celebration months are a great time to take leave, but you're free to take annual leave whenever you like with plenty of notice. Just put your initials on the dates you're thinking of taking in the Activities Calendar. At our Quarterly Retreats we help you to plan your holidays a year in advance so you always have something to look forward to.

Sick Leave ...

If you're sick, you're sick. Just take the day off and get better. We'll see you again tomorrow, when you're 100%. I'm sure your emails and client meetings will still be there for you when you get back. No need to work from home.

I'm-not-really-feeling-it-so-I'm-working-from-home-or-leaving-early-leave ...

We're definitely not a team of clock-watchers, but out of respect for the team we are part of, we show up on time and ready to make an impact. We don't duck off early and there's not really a culture of working from home. We recognise that we are part of an inspirational team of game changers, and value the opportunity we have to work side by side with people we actually respect (and even love).

High-five the status quo in the face—with a chair.

We are best selling authors. We've won multiple awards. We regularly get invited to feature in the media and speak on business and personal success around Australia and internationally. Although we've just begun, we're already worthy of the title "Australia's Most Impactful Accounting Firm." None of which is possible without a culture of *extreme* innovation, profound rejection of the status quo and a strong desire for everyone to embrace change. **You up for the challenge?**

6

THANK GOODNESS—A NEW DEFINITION FOR ESG THAT REALLY DOES MAKE A DIFFERENCE

We've talked a lot already about being purpose-led and moving beyond words to taking action to become impact-driven.

Here we're going deeper, much deeper, on that.

And we've stressed time and time again that becoming a subscription-led or subscription-based business is all about relationships and belonging as opposed to simply transacting.

Naturally you want those relationships to be long-term, to be sustainable, and sustained.

And here, we're going to go deeper, much deeper, on that too.

First, let's jump back to purpose and state the obvious: it's very, very hard to measure purpose. By contrast, it's quite easy to measure impacts!

But professionals—particularly accountants—want to measure everything that moves (and everything that stays still too, as well as some things we can't really get our hands on).

And that penchant for measuring things—every thing—sometimes makes life extraordinarily challenging.

That's the case with ESG. And just in case you're not up to date with that acronym, it currently stands for environmental, social, and governance. [Special note: Please do not read into this that we think this measurement process or the focus on it is necessarily cool. In fact, in a May 2022 *The Soul of Enterprise* podcast, Ron and our colleague Ed Kless focused on ESG and headed the episode (#389), "ESG—We Respectfully Dissent."]

Here's a key, I think there's a much better use of that acronym for your new subscription-led firm. It's this:

Embed

Social

Good

Put simply, do what Lynn and Brown and thousands of other businesses are doing, described in Chapter 5.

But since the regular ESG is getting lots of press now (in spite of Ron and Ed's disagreement), let's first go through a quick history lesson on the term.

It starts in 2004 with the late Kofi Annan, then the UN Secretary General, connecting with a large group of (apparently more than 50) CEOs drawn from the financial sector—presumably people we might call heavy-hitters.

Like many people even way back then, Annan was becoming concerned about the damage we business owners were doing to the environment and social structures. He wanted to find ways to integrate what we now refer to as sustainability into capital markets.

The first outcome of that group was a then groundbreaking study conducted by the Swiss government and the International Finance Corporation. And it was groundbreaking in its simple title, "Who Cares Wins." Do pause and note that—it's central to the subscription model—you need to really care to make it work. And when you do, you'll see the results it brings you—you'll see that who cares really does win.

That groundbreaking study is where the ESG acronym was first coined.

It looked at environmental issues across the three dimensions of environmental, social, and governance; specifically lower energy consumption, reliance on renewable resources, reducing carbon footprint, employee welfare, relationships with all stakeholders of companies (moving beyond shareholders for the first time), and looking at how those issues could be included in a company's accounting and financial practices.

There were four broad areas covered in the study; how companies:

1. Respond to climate change.
2. Treat their employees.
3. Build trust and foster innovation.
4. Manage the relationships with various stakeholders.

Perhaps not that surprisingly, it had limited impact given the financial climate of the time. That's a climate that's best characterized by events like those shown in *The Wolf of Wall Street* movie. It was very much (until the Global Financial Crisis of 2008 hit) the "greed is good" time.

Some companies got the lesson early on. And what's now known as ESG investing started to happen.

And that picked up pace when early studies around the 2013/14 period started to show links between an ESG focus and financial results. Businesses who "stood up" for good actually did good financially.

Then ESG or impact investing started to take off. From the initial cynicism we now have a position where ESG funds (impact investment funds) have seen much higher inflows from investors than "traditional" share market funds every year since 2013.

It's estimated that ESG funding now accounts for a total of 33% of the $51.4 trillion of funds under management in the United States. That 33% is projected to grow to 50% in the United States by 2025.

Even rating agencies now have their own ESG indices. And it's becoming increasingly (and rapidly) important.

For example, Reuters reports that shareholders have filed a record 529 resolutions related to ESG issues for the annual meetings of publicly traded US companies so far in 2022, up 22% from the same point in 2021 (Kerber 2022).

Jamere Jackson is the CFO of AutoZone and the audit committee chair at Eli Lilly and Company. In a *Wall Street Journal* article, reposted on Deloitte's website, he points out that change and ESG issues overall have become business imperatives:

> My board and CFO perspectives intersect at many points. As a CFO, I generally look at ESG through more of a shareholder value strategy lens because, done right, ESG goals and actions can help us grow the business and improve competitively—and those goals connect directly to my CFO role. Companies that spend time thinking about how to become more environmentally conscious in a cost-efficient way have an opportunity to mitigate business risks and improve their bottom lines while serving a broader group of stakeholders. Similarly, a deep commitment to taking care of employees and setting robust diversity, equity, and inclusion (DEI) goals can be a competitive advantage in terms of talent management and brand. (Marks 2022)

Clearly, "normal" financial metrics are inadequate for measuring ESG impact because they focus primarily on monetary aspects.

And as an important sidebar, it turns out that "normal" financial metrics really are inadequate when it comes to measuring growth in your subscription business model growth, too.

In his *Winning on Purpose* book, Frederick Reichheld and his co-authors propose a new accounting measure—it's called earned growth. It's the first measure to take proper account of the effect of loyalty and is, we'd suggest, going to be important in the comparison of subscription models.

Earned growth has two components: NRR—net recurring revenue measuring the percentage of revenue coming from customers who were with you last year, and ENG—earned new growth, new revenue coming (essentially) from people who were referred by those existing customers.

You can see more on that in the original Reichheld piece in *Harvard Business Review* (Reichheld et al. 2021) and in this follow-up piece by Maxie Schmidt-Subramanian, the principal analyst at Forrester Research (Subramanian 2021).

But let's get back to the rapidly becoming commonplace now—ESG. And here's an example of just how commonplace it is:

> At BDO, we view sustainability as an investment in the strength of our culture, the resilience of our business, and the future of our planet. We are committed to making ESG synonymous with BDO, ensuring that sustainable business practices are integrated into everything we do. We believe we have an obligation to make an impact and do our part to be a force of change—to strive for business that's better than usual—for our people, our clients, and our communities.

And Christopher Tower, BDO USA ESG Strategy and Services Leader and Executive Team Member puts it this way:

> We recognize the unique opportunity we have as advisors to the middle market—not only to do our part to advance ESG within BDO—but in our ability to help our clients integrate ESG into their own business models—resulting in not just better business, but in ensuring a sustainable future for us all.

You can see more at BDO's excellent ESG site at www.bdo.com/resources/esg.

In May 2022, Mastercard reported that ALL employees now have ESG targets linked to their bonus pay. The payments processor is extending a compensation model previously put in place for senior executives, which links incentive pay to targets related to carbon neutrality, financial inclusion, and gender pay parity. The new plan applies to all employees starting this in 2022.

And on Earth Day, April 22, 2022, Tien Tzuo (Founder of Zuora) and one of our favorite subscription model proponents and cheerleaders wrote an excellent piece on how we need to focus on the "E" of ESG and be really concerned with sustainability.

In the piece he points out that in 2011, only 20% of the S&P 500 published sustainability reports; today almost all of them do.

He references (as we have elsewhere) Larry Fink and Blackrock (managing over $10 trillion in assets) have dedicated the firm to sustainable investing.

He quotes Larry Fink as saying in an investor letter to CEOs, "As more and more investors choose to tilt their investments toward sustainability-focused companies, the tectonic shift we are seeing will accelerate further."

And because this will have such a dramatic impact on how capital is allocated, every management team and board will need to consider how this will impact their company's stock."

Tzuo continues, "ESG principles aren't just important for our investors, of course. They're also important for our employees, our customers, our kids, our fellow living animals, and ourselves. Clearly, sustainability is not a 'nice to have' anymore. It's a fundamental corporate priority" (Tzuo 2022).

I agree. But I want to suggest that ESG as it currently stands is making doing it overly complex. And because of that, things don't get done (you may remember a quote we mentioned earlier on: "Simple scales; complex fails.").

What we need, I suspect, is something new, something easy, AND, perhaps most importantly, something that makes IMPACT not just an integral part of what you do but also an integral part of what you could choose to do for your subscription model customers, too.

That "something" is a wonderful "tool" for your firm that directly integrates impact into the very core of your firm—it turns the potentially complex ESG we've just spoken of into the very simple definition we gave you at the start of this chapter (well, it's really more of a designated action):

Embed

Social

Good

In fact, you could link this back to the "Standard—Standout—Stand For" story arc we described in Chapter 3. It might look like this:

Standard	Standout	Stand for
. . . .	. . . .	
Do nothing	Be impact-led	Embed social
. . . .	. . . .	good

And you can do that very, very easily—almost effortlessly in fact. You've already seen it in action. It's officially called B1G1: Business for Good. And you can find more details on it right here: www.b1g1.com.

It's a unique and powerful way to "ESG"—embed social good. And it links right back to where we were in Chapter 2, when we talked about the need for a brand-new story.

When you go to that link, you'll see how it lets you embed social good by creating giving stories, just like you saw when we talked about Lynn and Brown a few pages back. Figure 6.1 is another example from one of the many thousands—this one from Pivot Wealth, advisors in the financial planning space:

Fantastic stories. Stories that really connect.

And with leverage in mind, we wonder what stories your customers will create too. With "belonging" in mind, you might even create what B1G1 calls a hive—a place where all your embedded social good impacts are automatically linked together, impacting and measuring your specific and broad impact on our world together. The potential here really is astonishing in scope.

And you'll see more of that potential in our next chapter, too. Just turn the page . . . .

FIGURE 6.1   How Pivot Wealth proudly display its impacts.

7

THE ONGOING UPWARD SPIRAL—PERHAPS A DIFFERENT KIND OF LEGACY

If ever you've been involved in helping your customers move forward in any way (some might call that consulting or advisory), you'll be aware that there's a classical five-step model to do it.

It looks like Figure 7.1 (there's one key difference here, which we'll come to in a moment).

It's simple and logical.

Step 1: You show your customer (or ask potential ones) where they're at right now. And you could do that by focusing on some key numbers like revenue, profit, and so on. But it's much more important (at least initially) to talk about the potential customer's feelings about their current situation. And as you do that, remember to ask a question based on Tamsin Wooley-Barker's great observation: "Nature doesn't look for problems, it looks for potential."

That is precisely the point of Step 2: Ask questions about where they could get to, where they want to go, etc. You reframe "problems" into "potentials" as in: "I understand that's an issue right now, Sally. If everything was running right in that area, what's the potential we could unlock here, and what do you feel would be the impact of that?"

Potential really is so powerful, isn't it?

As you note all of those details, you move gracefully to Step 3 by asking "What shifts do you think we need to make to make that possible?"

Step 4 is the transformation—creating a plan of action to make it all happen. This leads you to Step 5, measuring and monitoring per formance to plan.

Now we said a few moments ago that the diagram is quite different than the normal one. Here's why: Normally it is shown as a circle that you keep moving around.

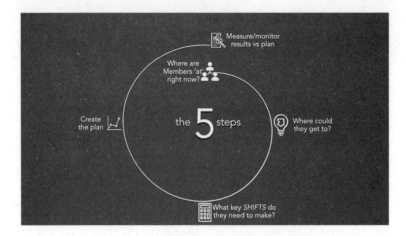

FIGURE 7.1 The usual consultancy questioning sequence.

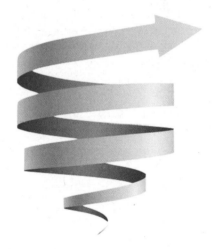

FIGURE 7.2 The upward spiral model.

But it's not a circle—it's an upward rotating and expanding spiral like Figure 7.2.

As you continue to move up the spiral with your customers, it's important to develop rituals, habits, and processes to keep it moving.

One very simple way of doing that is to always have a predefined agenda for each regular (let's say monthly) meeting you or (more importantly) your team have with your members/customers.

By the way, that "members/customers" phrase was not a slip of my fingers on the keyboard. Like every other phrase in this book, it has intent. Here's a personal example:

I well remember working with a dentist—Dr. Paddi Lund in Brisbane—who was the first dentist I'd ever met who did not call his "patients" patients.

Paddi and his team referred to the people every other dentist on the planet referred to as a "patient" as "a client."

When I asked him why, he said, "It's all about mindset, Paul, theirs and ours. When they're called 'a patient' it sets up something in their mind where they're the unwell patient and we're the well doctor. More importantly, though, when they see themselves as patients, they think it's up to us to 'fix' them. Our experience is that when we refer to them and think of them as 'clients,' we become so much more respectful to them. And they see themselves as partnering with us in the process of getting well."

Paddi continued, "We see it in the stats and outcomes. For example, in the past when we referred to everyone as a patient, we'd show them how to floss their teeth and give them a recommend schedule to do it. But we could tell from our notes that very, very few 'patients' followed the recommendation. That changed the very day we decided to refer to them as 'clients.' Increasingly, they saw themselves as partners with us in the process of healing as opposed to it all depending on us."

That's a great upward spiral, isn't it?

So now, let's get back to habits and rituals that lock it all in for you because of the process you have in your meetings with your members (let's just go with that phrasing/naming for now to see how it feels to you moving forward).

And we'd strongly suggest that this becomes part of your "This Is How We Do It Here" processes.

Labeling plays a huge part in this. So don't have agendas, have *moving forward plans*. My close friend Dr. David Dugan of

Abundance Global uses what he calls RAP Sheets, where RAP stands
for Review, Align, Plan. It's a really nice sequence.

Whatever you call them, here's a recommended sequence:

---

1. **Wins for the month:** Here you and your Member document their wins AND (most importantly) as they do that
   (after congratulating them, of course) you ask if they see
   any pattern. You ask why they think those wins occurred—
   specifically, what behavior or process brought them
   about. And of course, you'll want to relate them back to
   key numbers on their financials.

2. **Overall progress toward the goals we set last month.**

3. **Where we might need help** (of course, you've already got
   your items ready for this section based on your work
   before the meeting).

4. **Our three high-value activities (HVAs) for the month
   ahead:** Here you align on what the actions and goals must
   be going forward.

It's simple—deceptively simple, in fact. What it does is give you
and your Member a firm *structure* moving forward.

When people see structures, whether it's in meetings or in buildings, they see certainty. It's these structures and processes that create
your "This Is How We Do It Here" playbook.

In a very real sense, everything we've written here is not just about
getting a brand-new playbook, it's about getting a brand-new way of
thinking, a way of thinking that leads to a way of behavior that leads
to an upward spiral for you and your customers.

This upward expanding spiral is exactly what we'd like you to see
as the outcome of your investment in this book and the multiplicity of
ideas in it that you've worked your way through.

You applying those insights and ideas gets you started on a fascinating journey.

And what a journey it is—one where you really do enrich your life
and the lives of people whom you serve.

That's all about creating the new story we spoke about in Chapter 2—setting the vision, the values, and the agenda for an entire generation yet to come.

That simple realization gets you thinking on other dimensions too—for example, it may well get you thinking about what you leave behind—your legacy, if you will.

Interestingly, when most people think of legacy, they think of it as "leaving a legacy." So let's pause and make the point that you *are* going to leave one—we have no choice in that at all.

We are only able to choose what type of legacy it is. And much as I don't like binary choices, this one does come down to this: Is it a legacy of consumption or contribution? Simple as that.

But there's more to it than that, too. You'll know from previous examples in our book that I like alliteration—a string of (typically) three words that begin with the same letter or have the same sound.

So when I started thinking about legacy that way, I realized there was a perfect alliteration like this:

| Living Your Legacy | Leveraging Your Legacy | Leaving |
| .... | .... | Your Legacy |

Why not live it every day—for example, Embedding Social Good? Why not leverage our legacy by inspiring others with our story?

And when you think that way, your legacy becomes bigger than perhaps you've ever imagined.

With that in mind, you may remember right at the start we mentioned this quote from Barry Melancon:

> We won't recognize the profession in five years. The change is going to be phenomenal going forward.

Time's UP thinking about it. The time is now to do it. As the Chinese proverb reminds us: "The best time to plant a tree was 20 years ago. The second best time is now."

And doing it—actually getting that tree planted as it were, requires you to see what it might look like.

Remember the diagrams we introduced you to in Chapter 4. You first move clockwise, starting with vision (Figure 7.3). And it starts with you actually not just seeing it but seeing it with total clarity. Once you have that, you need to get your team fully involved.

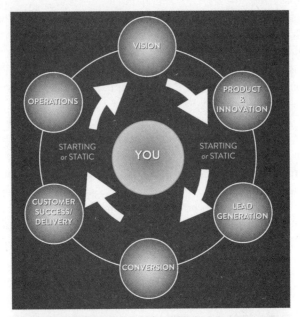

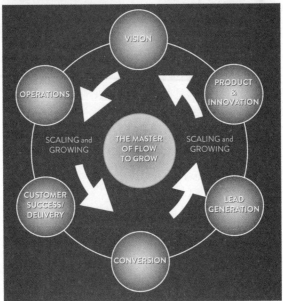

FIGURE 7.3   Driving the Six Engine Rooms.

We've already spoken about vision. Let's see how it translates into reality (a tough reality at that). Our colleague Ric Payne showed us an interesting exercise many years ago—it's still relevant today.

Imagine the following. Three groups of 10 individuals are in a park at lunchtime with a rainstorm threatening. In the first group, someone says:

"Get up and follow me." When he starts walking and only a few others join in, he yells to those still seated: "Up, I said, and NOW!"

In the second group, someone says:

"We're going to have to move. Here's the plan. Each of us stands up and marches in the direction of the apple tree. Please stay at least two feet away from other group members and do not run. Do not leave any personal belongings on the ground here, and be sure to stop at the base of tree. When we are all there . . ."

In the third group, someone tells the others:

"It's going to rain in a few minutes. Why don't we go over there and sit under that huge apple tree. We'll stay dry, and we can have fresh apples for lunch."

Which one would you choose, and why?

We wonder . . .

Here's what John Kotter had to say about the exercise:

I am sometimes amazed at how many people try to transform organizations using methods that look like the first two scenarios: authoritarian decree and micro-management. Both approaches have been applied widely in enterprises over the last century, but mostly for maintaining existing systems, not transforming those systems into something better.

When the goal is behavior change, unless the boss is extremely powerful, authoritarian decree often works poorly even in simple situations, like the apple tree case. Increasingly, in complex organizations, this approach doesn't work at all. Without the power of kings and queens behind it, authoritarianism is unlikely to break through all the forces of resistance. People will ignore you or pretend to cooperate while doing everything possible to undermine your efforts.

Micro-management tries to get around this problem by specifying what employees should do in detail and then monitoring compliance. This tactic can break through some of the barriers to change, but in an increasingly unacceptable amount of time. Because the creation and communication of detailed plans is deadly slow, the change produced this way tends to be highly incremental.

Only the approach used in the third scenario above has the potential to break through all the forces that support the status quo and to encourage the kind of dramatic shifts found in successful transformations. This approach is based on vision—a central component of all great leadership. (Kotter 2012, pp. 67–68)

With that in mind, here are nine key steps to make it happen.

NINE STEPS TO TRANSFORMATION

Step 1—Establish a Sense of Urgency

We believe that when you do that, when you examine the marketplace and competitive realities, when you look at the potentials and the risk of *not* moving, you'll decide that the only time is now.

Step 2—Form a Powerful Guiding Coalition

It's tough to do this stuff alone. You need to assemble a group with enough power and commitment to lead the change. And you need to encourage the group to work together as a team

Step 3—Get On Purpose

Define a North Star—something bigger than you. Remember the website we showed you in Chapter 3—"We're doing this SO THAT WE CAN . . ."

Again, when you're *really* clear on your purpose, when it's what you stand for, when it's front and center of everything, when everyone on your team lives and breathes it, then in that moment what you do becomes profoundly more attractive and compelling *and* you're on the path to *stand out*.

Step 4—Create a Compelling Vision

Wrap your purpose into a more detailed vision—a vision that inspires, a vision that then flows into very specific strategies moving forward now.

Step 5—Communicate the Vision . . . Constantly

Use every possible means to articulate the vision—Figure 7.4 shows some examples of posters I've seen in firms' offices (and as background images on Zoom calls).

Of course, you must teach the new behaviors by example.

Step 6—Empower Others to Act on It

It's critically important that you get rid of obstacles to change and that you change any system or structure that undermines the vision.

FIGURE 7.4   Great-looking wall posters.

It's crucial, too, to actively encourage risk-taking and nontraditional ideas, activities, and actions.

Step 7—Plan for and Create Short-Term Wins

You must define and engineer visible performance improvements. By *define* we mean you're going to set targets like "we're going to complete this by . . ." And make this timeline as short as you possibly can. And then, of course, you recognize and reward team members involved in the improvements.

Step 8—Consolidate and Produce More Change

It's important that you use the increased credibility you and your team get from early wins to keep on changing things that no longer fit the vision. That spills over, of course, into your hiring and promotion processes—you must hire, promote, and develop team members who can implement the vision. Be really clear too on the need to reinvigorate the change process with new projects, themes, and change agents.

Step 9—Institutionalize the New Approaches

All through the change process—the transformation process—make sure you're articulating the links between the new connections and your ongoing success. You need to put systems and processes in place to create and support leadership development and success consistent with the new behaviors.

Tick off these steps each week—they become a key to you committing to the process. Consider each step as a milestone along the way.

This really is the start of an inspiring adventure.

Thank you for starting this journey to a new business model with me. You know there's much, much more to come with Ron. He is going to take you passionately deeper.

Make sure you enjoy the journey ahead with Ron.

And then, of course, you'll be ready to continue your own journey.

From what you know already, that's one that's bursting with potential—potential for you, for your team, and, of course, your customers—every second, every day and in every way.

II

THE WORKSHOP

8

A RENAISSANCE: THE SUBSCRIPTION ECONOMY

Companies that sell products to strangers aren't going to last long in this new subscription economy.

—Tien Tzuo, founder, Zuora, author of *Subscribed: Why the Subscription Model Will Be Your Company's Future—and What to Do About It*

From the fourteenth to the seventeenth centuries, the Renaissance spawned some of the world's greatest authors, statesman, artists, and scientists. Global trade expanded, opening up new cultures and lands for European commerce. The Renaissance is credited with "bridging the gap between the Middle Ages and modern-day civilization" (History.com editors n.d.).

We are living through another Renaissance in business model evolution, crossing the bridge from the traditional model constructed upon volume product and service transactions to one focused on relationships; access rather than ownership; customization of transformations rather than deliverables; continuous innovation and value creation instead of planned obsolescence; a seamless, frictionless customer experience that not only offers convenience, but also provides peace of mind, and surfaces simplicity. Welcome to the subscription economy.

Ironically, the history of the subscription business model goes back to the Renaissance, in the 1500s, when European map makers had customers who subscribed to their offerings. Newspapers and magazines also were sold on a subscription basis in seventeenth-century Europe.

Yet the current model is radically different from older subscription models. The focus on the customer relationship is obsessive, recognizing its lifetime value rather than the math of the moment as with transactions.

The growth of the subscription economy empirically proves the point. UBS, one of the world's largest banks, issued a report detailing how the subscription economy is on track to become a $1.5 trillion market by 2025, up from $650 billion in 2020. The Subscription Trade Association reports that subscription revenues grew at an average annual rate of 17% between 2014 and 2019, attracting approximately $3 billion in venture capital between 2018 and 2020. During the COVID-19 pandemic, subscription businesses showed remarkable resilience, often growing above 10% while nonsubscription revenue was declining.

The subscription software platform company Zuora, founded by Tien Tzuo, publishes the Subscription Economy Index (SEI). Here are some statistics from its February 2022 report, for the 12 months ending December 31, 2021:

- The SEI has experienced 17.5% 10-year Compound Annual Growth Rate (CAGR) versus 3.8% for the S&P 500.

- Revenue growth in 2020 and 2021 (during COVID-19) was 13.3% and 16.2%, respectively. This compares with –3.7% and 12% for S&P 500 revenue.

- The churn rate (lost customers) was 6.3% in 2020 and 5.4% in 2021—subscription companies are keeping most of the gains made during COVID-19 (Tzuo 2022).

Customers have become acclimated to the ease of subscribing to products and services, while businesses have made it more convenient, including providing a more valuable offering to the customer. The number of goods and services now offered on subscription is staggering, and it is difficult to keep up with. You are already familiar with—indeed, may already subscribe to—many of them. No doubt, as with any economic boom, an indeterminable number of these ventures will fail, but many will thrive.

WHY NOW?

A lot of factors are cited for the growth of the subscription economy, such as technological advancement, digitization, big data, even the millennial generation being more enamored with experiences and access over ownership. I find these explanations necessary but not sufficient.

A better theory is offered by economist Michael C. Munger in his book, *Tomorrow 3.0: Transaction Costs and the Sharing Economy*. Munger defines transaction costs this way: "Transaction costs are the expenses, including time, inconvenience, and actual payments required to use the item, and the problems involved in trusting others to deliver on their promises and not to rob us." *To customers, all costs are transaction costs.* Take the Sears catalog, the older version of Amazon's platform model. It reduced transaction costs for customers by offering quality, reputable products that were backed by a company with an incentive to guard its reputation and goodwill.

From eBay, founded in 1997, portable technology has enabled entrepreneurs to shift from selling more things to selling reductions in transaction costs, providing customers with more access to underutilized assets or excess capacity—think Uber, Lyft, and Airbnb. Viewing ownership through the lens of transaction costs, you quickly realize that ownership can be an albatross: time spent shopping for and deciding which product to buy, assessing the purchase price against upkeep, repairs and maintenance, storage, and disposal, all add significantly to the original price. Munger defines three types of transaction costs and how new business models reduce each one:

1. **Triangulation**: Matching a willing buyer with a seller, agreeing upon terms, etc.
2. **Transfer**: Of the product or service, and the payment thereof
3. **Trust**: Honesty, performance (buyer and seller ratings, brand, and reputation all fulfill this role)

Combine lower transaction costs with the psychology of subscribing to a business rather than merely purchasing from it, and you have a completely different relationship. Former Amazon employee Vijay Ravindran said of Amazon Prime: "It was never about the $79. It was really about changing people's mentality so they wouldn't shop anywhere else." There is an enormous difference between *purchasing* from Amazon and *subscribing* to it; hence the power of the subscription model at generating customer loyalty.

Loyalty is not dead in the business world, though a reason to be loyal may not always be present. If we want customers to invest in us, we have to invest in them. This mentality transcends transactions, scope of work, and deliverables—it is all about delivering recurring value, where, when, and as needed. When we accomplish this, we are living our professional purpose, the reason we chose to enter our profession in the first place.

Given the myriad subscription offerings available, Tzuo predicts: "In five years, you won't buy anything, but subscribe to everything." I am not sure I would go that far—ownership of things will always be important. Anne Janzer, author of *Subscription Marketing: Strategies for Nurturing Customers in a World of Churn*, perhaps predicts a more probable future: "In five years, you'll have the *option* of subscribing to everything—and every business will have to accommodate that fact." This becomes more true with each passing day, requiring another evolution in the professional firm's business model.

HISTORY OF THE PROFESSIONAL FIRM BUSINESS MODEL

My prior book, *Implementing Value Pricing: A Radical Business Model for Professional Firms*, documents the history of the business model. A business model is herein defined as: **How your firm creates value for customers, and how you capture a portion of that value**. Within the business model is the "revenue question" that Marco Bertini and Oded Koenigsberg ask in *The Ends Game: How Smart Companies Stop Selling Products and Start Delivering Value*: "What are we asking our customers to pay for? This is separate from the pricing question (how much are we asking them to pay)" (Bertini and Koenigsberg 2020).

Historically, what have the professions asked their customers to pay for? Hourly billing, which began in 1919 in the legal profession, answers that the customer pays for hours, efforts, overhead, and a desired profit—in other words, *inputs*. The accounting profession began to adopt this model in the 1960–1970s; prior to that, it set a fixed price that was still built on time and overhead, usually in the form of daily rates. When I entered the CPA profession in 1984, we charged a fixed price for a defined scope of work (an audit, tax work, etc.), though that price was built on estimated hours and did not include out-of-scope work, which was billed separately, always hourly, and nearly always after the fact. In effect, we were charging for *outputs*.

The value pricing movement that began in earnest in the accounting profession in the mid-1990s taught firms that they should price the *customer*, not the services, by establishing a customized price for each one based on their wants and needs, which also included offering three or four options. This method requires conducting a value conversation with every customer, at least every year, to incorporate changing circumstances and services. It attempts to price customer *outcomes*, since that is where the value lies. It is more optimal than hourly billing and fixed prices because it takes into account the specific value being created for each customer. It is still a viable business model. However, with the market evolving toward subscriptions, it needs to be modified.

My colleague Ed Kless defines the subscription model this way: periodic recurring payments for frictionless, ever-increasing value, and serial transformations. Each word in that definition is doing a lot of work, and we will unpack each of them in the following chapters.

The subscription model prices the *relationship* and the *portfolio*. You are probably asking, "What is the difference between pricing the customer and the relationship—isn't that just semantics?" No. It's an enormous difference, as we see with the psychology of Amazon Prime subscribers. The subscription model puts the customer relationship at the heart of the business. There are no silos or profit centers; it is a true "one-firm" business model. It reframes the firm's value proposition because the focus is less on deliverables and scope of work. It is more of a membership attitude than a financial arrangement. Your customers aren't buying services, they are subscribing to your firm, allowing you to have a larger impact on them across more areas of their lives. We will explore this in depth in later chapters.

In Jeff Bezos's shareholder statement from 1997, he wrote:

> There are many ways to center a business. You can be competitor focused, you can be product focused, you can be technology focused, you can be business model focused, and there are more. But in my view, obsessive customer focus is by far the most protective of Day One vitality.

Professional firms have always claimed to be based on relationships, and by and large that is true. However, when you analyze what firms monetize, you clearly see outputs and deliverables, with few firms truly monetizing outcomes. This misalignment between customer desires and expectations becomes very evident when you operate in a subscription business model. In other words, I believe professional firms are, by and large, paying lip service to the importance of their relationships. I know that's harsh, but economists teach *revealed preference*: Look at what people *do*, not what they *say*. What are we asking customers to pay for? Unequivocally, it is still outputs. As professionals, we must do better.

WHAT SHOULD PROFESSIONALS BE PAID FOR?

What does it mean to be a professional? Certainly, the first two laws of medicine apply: (1) First, do no harm; and (2) Prescription without diagnosis is malpractice. Yet this deals more with the doctor than the patient. When you think about the question from the customer's perspective, the answer is more evident. My favorite definition of a professional comes from Michael Hammer: "A professional is someone who is responsible for achieving a result rather than performing a task."

This definition clearly illustrates the disconnect between what professionals charge for—a series of tasks, deliverables, scope of work, etc.—and what we should ultimately be accountable for—the outcome. This misalignment is possible under value pricing, but it is much harder for it to exist within a subscription business model where the focus should be on the ultimate outcome for the customer. Consider the following examples.

Fender is the largest manufacturer in the world of electric guitars. Founded in 1946, it flourished during the COVID-19 pandemic. What outcome are people looking for when they buy a guitar? To own a guitar? Or to be able to play, at the level to which they aspire? Fender knows that 90% of new guitar buyers quit within three to six months. If that happens, the guitar sits in the closet, and the customer never buys another. Worse, he may gift it to someone else, depriving Fender of a customer.

On July 6, 2017, Fender launched the Fender Play app, which offers over 3,000 video lessons, from beginner and beyond. Within three years, it had more than 200,000 subscribers and a 95% retention rate. Further, those subscribers spent 40% more on Fender products than nonsubscribers.

During the COVID-19 lockdowns, Fender offered a free trial subscription that increased its subscriber base to over 1 million, and sold more guitars in 2020 than it ever had in the past. Ultimately, Fender understood it wasn't selling guitars—it was selling the ability to play them—*musicianship*. The focus is more on lifetime value and customer engagement than unit sales and gross margins. It is an excellent illustration of how teasing out what the customer is really purchasing can enhance lifetime value, loyalty, and profits.

The optical industry is a perfect example of a mature industry that hasn't changed in decades. The transaction costs of getting an eye exam, a new prescription, and then the glasses or contacts being made is the bane of anyone who needs all of this for better eyesight. Along comes Synsam Group, Scandinavia's largest optical chain, consisting of over 500 clinics and 3,500 employees.

In 2016, it launched Synsam Lifestyle™. All the "experts" said it would never work, no one wants to subscribe to glasses. By 2021, it had over 280,000 subscribers and well over €100 million in revenue. It covers an annual eye exam, and if your prescription changes, it updates all your glasses. Synsam reframed the value of its offering from eye exams and glasses/contacts SKUs to selling *perfect eyesight*. All from removing customer friction and decision-making load at each step of the process, lowering transaction costs, while providing convenience and peace of mind.

What's more, it transcends the transaction. In Latin, the word *transaction* is derived from *trans*, across, beyond; through. It is the action after the exchange, which here is a lifelong relationship—subscribers are the gift that keeps on giving. Similar to stock valuations, subscriptions are forward-looking revenue models.

I'm sure by now you are asking yourself, "How can this apply to professional firms?" Fortunately, the trail has already been blazed by the medical profession. Let us meet these disrupters.

9

THE DIRECT PRIMARY CARE
DISRUPTERS

*I became a concierge physician for the same reason I became
a doctor—I want to help people. Patients deserve to be
involved in their care and receive the valuable service of
planning for optimal health with the guidance of a family
physician who is dedicated to the care of the patient.*

—Dr. Brian Nadolne, MD, Marietta, GA (quoted in *The Doctor's
Expanded Guide to Concierge Medicine*)

If you have ever interacted with the health care system in the United
States, you've experienced *battered patient syndrome,* a term I
learned from Dr. W. Ryan Neuhofel, founder of NeuCare, a direct
primary care physician in Lawrence, Kansas. Between the bureaucracy of the insurance system and the physician's back office to the
electronic health records that force doctors to spend more time focused on their screens than on the patient, this system is broken. One
doctor complained he was becoming a better typist than physician.

It is beyond the scope of this book to discuss why this is so. Suffice
to say, the similarities between the medical profession and the professions we focus on here are vast. Doctors are concerned with maintaining our physical health while accountants protect our financial
health. Yet just as there is no diagnosis code for caring in medicine,
there is no billing code on the timesheet for investing in relationships
with our customers in the professions. We are as much on a fee-for-
service treadmill as are doctors, facing the same incentives to continuously sell more services to more customers rather than taking the

time to truly transform the customers we have into a desired future state, one at a time.

Doctors complain about being de facto employees and bill collectors for third-party payers (insurance companies and governments), as opposed to working in their patients' best interests. One doctor complained that insurance companies are so involved in the clinical decisions of his patients that they are practicing medicine without a license.

This fee-for-service business model incentivizes doctors to do things *to* you—ordering tests, diagnostic procedures, office visits, etc.—rather than *for* you. Further, the average general physician in the United States has a panel of patients of 2,400, which is why they spend a sum-total of roughly 5 to 10 minutes with each of some 30 to 50 patients per day. This simply doesn't allow them time to fulfill their purpose of helping people maintain their health, but rather focuses them on curing the presenting problem. There is no time for preventative care. Unfortunately, dignity and quality of life don't show up on financial statements. Nor does physician burnout.

According to a 2016 study by Medscape, 51% of doctors experience burnout, characterized by three major symptoms:

1. Exhaustion and loss of enthusiasm for work
2. Depersonalization and cynicism, with a tendency to see patients less as people
3. Reduced sense of personal accomplishment and meaning

Part of the reason is the loss of autonomy and agency in the day-to-day practice of medicine. There is nothing more demoralizing than bearing the ultimate *responsibility* for patient outcomes while at the same time having no *control* over how those outcomes will be achieved. Responsibility without authority is unreliable and unpredictable. Combine that with the overwhelming number of patients needed to feed the revenue model and the system has crafted the perfect cocktail for burnout.

Are doctors destined to work in such a broken system? Are they suffering from some sort of Stockholm syndrome—a psychological phenomenon in which hostages have empathy toward their captors? As Doctor Paul Thomas said to me during our interview on our podcast, *The Soul of Enterprise: Business in the Knowledge Economy*

(The Soul of Enterprise 2019): "If half of your lightbulbs went out, you wouldn't blame the bulbs but the electrical system." The electrical system in this case is the business model, and we should call it what it is: physician abuse.

But just because the business model is broken doesn't mean the people inside the profession have to be. We have it within our power to *create* a better future, not just forecast one. Fortunately, there are pioneers who have ventured into the unknown, blazing a trail for the rest of us, while leaving behind some maps for the curious.

THE DISRUPTERS

Two such pioneers are Howard Moran and Scott Hall, who in 1996 founded MD²® (pronounced MD squared®) in Seattle, the largest high-end concierge medical practice in the country. Moran was the team physician for the Seattle Sonics NBA basketball team. He explains:

> I appreciated that I could get to know each team member intimately, and that I could provide exceptional care as a result of knowing them so well. I wondered why people who weren't elite athletes couldn't get the same kind of relationship from their physician. That's really where the idea was spawned.

In an interview in the July 2005 *Worth* magazine, Maron was asked to describe a typical patient experience at MD²®:

> We don't have a waiting room. Our office is locked. It's fully staffed. The door is closed, but it's available all the time by appointment. When a patient comes to the door, the door is locked behind him and he has the entire office to himself. We're not in a hurry. If a patient needs to do business in the meantime, needs to attend to a phone call, fine, we'll wait. Again, how can a doctor do that unless he has very few patients? (Moran 2005, p. 71)

Visit the website of MD² under "Our Story" and you will read this:

> Dr. Howard Maron founded MD²® in 1996 based on the belief that delivering exceptional medical care must fundamentally revolve around, honor and protect the most sacred of relationships—that

between a physician and a patient. This is only possible when you limit your patient threshold to so few; 50 select families, cared for by 1 exceptional physician who is committed to elevating their craft of medicine. This is a vow we are honored to uphold.

At its finest, we believe medicine has the power to transform the lives of both patients and physicians. With this in mind, every detail and decision that went into creating MD^2 was intentional, highly designed, and exceedingly personal.

Dr. Maron wasn't setting out to ignite a whole cottage industry or pioneer a new category of medicine—but he did.

The website explains the justification for why each doctor only handles 50 families. (see box below, "This is the power of personal medicine.")

Though its prices are not posted on the website, according to *The Doctor's Expanded Guide to Concierge Medicine*, the annual price is $13,200 for an individual and $20,000 per family, with an extra $2,000 per child. In addition to the above, other services that can be accessed include direct access to your doctor (text, email, etc.); expedited appointments with medical specialists at top hospitals; genetic testing; in-office radiology services with same

---

This is the power of personal medicine

When you're one of only 50 families seen by a masterful physician, everything changes. You receive a much higher caliber of care, day or night, from someone who knows you well. And you gain a medical champion who will protect your well-being, lifestyle, and privacy.

Only MD^2 physicians dedicate their practices to just 50 families.

This affords them the luxury of time to give every patient the very best: their full energy and focus, their absolute availability, and their true potential. It's an unparalleled standard of care built upon a powerful relationship—the one between you and a truly exceptional physician.

Source: https://www.md2.com/#why-50:1.

day readings; medical jet evacuation; and access to international doctors and hospitals.

I wrote about MD²® in my 2006 book, *Pricing on Purpose: Creating and Capturing Value*. Nothing better illustrates the inadequacy of our language to articulate the meaning of how revolutionary this model was at the time that I labeled it a "retainer-based model of health care." It is not retainer-based, it is subscription (or membership) based. I also wrote this:

> Critics claim that this form of elitist medical care is more style over substance, putting forth the argument that no studies have proven doctors who spend more time with a patient, or who have smaller patient loads, result in longer life spans or earlier diagnosis of life-threatening maladies for their patients. They also claim this is a form of "cherry-picking" healthy and wealthy patients, which creates shortages of doctors for middle- and lower-income patients.
>
> Yet medical care is a luxury good, an item people will purchase more of when their income rises. Patients are not concerned with medical studies that prove that this type of personalized attention has salutary effects across a range of patients; they are only concerned with how this type of care effects them. Value is subjective, and they are paying for peace of mind and instant access, since the opportunity cost of their time is so high (they have more money than time). It may be too early to judge the success (or failure) of this type of care, but there is no doubt that a certain group of customers are willing and able to pay for it, and hence providers are willing to supply this type of concierge medicine. (Baker 2006, p. 258)

It is no longer too early to judge the success of this model. The empirical evidence is in, and it is overwhelmingly positive, and not just for the high-end of the market to which MD²® caters. As you would expect in any dynamic marketplace, a wide range of value and price points will arise to serve as much of a market as possible, which is exactly what has happened with the rise of the direct primary care (DPC) physicians, who usually cater to a lower price point in the market, and have a panel of patients on average of between 600 and 800. According to DPC Frontier (DPC Frontier n.d.), there were 1,783 direct primary care physicians across 48 states and Washington, DC. The growth rate has been less than the demand for this revolutionary method of health care. Far from contributing to the shortage of primary care physicians, this business model might be the ultimate solution, as it restores why doctors chose their profession in the first place and prevents burnout.

According to *The Doctor's Expanded Guide to Concierge Medicine* the average prices for these DPC practices across the United States are as follows:

6.8% = less than $50/month/person
18.45% = $51–$100
10.68% = $101–$135
28.16% = $136–$180
13.59% = $181–$225
21.36% = $225+

As you can see, often at a lesser price point than the average smartphone or cable bill, this type of health care is hardly only available to the wealthy. In addition, many of these DPC practices have 10% charity cases.

WHAT ABOUT PATIENT OUTCOMES?

Most people conflate health care with health insurance. But there are many people who have adequate health insurance who rarely visit a doctor and are not getting healthier. It might be obvious but needs to be said: just having health insurance does not improve your health or reduce your risk of getting a chronic disease. When you subscribe to a business, you have "skin in the game" and are more likely to value and utilize the service. Because of the lower capacity of DPC doctors, the average office visit is one hour, oftentimes longer. This allows more time to learn about their medical history, habits, desires, and other issues that may have an impact on their health. This creates a deeper and richer experience for the patient, restoring the sacred doctor-patient relationship that is the hallmark of efficacious, not to mention humane, care.

It also leads to better health outcomes as patients are more likely to follow the advice of their physician, including regularly taking their medications, getting recommended screenings, and other preventative interventions. It also reduces the incentive for the doctor to order and perform unnecessary procedures—so-called *defensive medicine* to avoid lawsuits. Patients of DPCs have fewer emergency room and hospital visits, take fewer prescription drugs, enjoy the benefits of convenient access (via telemedicine, text, email, home and workplace visits, same day appointments, etc.), and easy access to their health records. Care coordination with specialists is another valuable component of this type of relationship, which is unmatched by most general physicians. The DPC doctor acts like a train conductor, ensuring the right health care is delivered to the place it needs to be, and keeps the patient on track and arriving safely.

The battered patient syndrome is over for DPC customers, with average retention rates between 85% and 97%, much higher than traditional fee-for-service practices. Since a general physician can handle between 60–90% of the average patient's medical needs, this is a far more cost-effective way to deliver health care.

Continuous innovation is baked into this model, as these practices constantly expand their offerings, such as dieticians, physiologists, blood tests, screenings, body scans, genetic testing, hearing tests, educational workshops, even their own pharmacies—none of which change the membership price when they are added. This reframing of value reinforces in the customer's mind how worthwhile the relationship is and makes future price increases much more palatable.

The patient receives convenient, frictionless, and peace-of-mind care. There is no *scope creep*, or visits to the Department of Paperwork to determine Change Requests, and other hurdles we frequently put in front of customers. There are no more annual pricing discussions, as the customer has already made the decision to subscribe once, not with every change in services delivered. All the non-value-added bureaucracy has been removed, and the relationship with the customer becomes the ultimate focus. What customer wouldn't want this type of relationship with their CPA, lawyer, or other professional? As a customer, wouldn't you want this level of care? As Zauro CEO Tzuo says, "Your company and customer experience is either *expendable* or *indispensable*." By improving the customer experience, you become indispensable. This business model does not entail less work, but it does provide a different pace and more fulfilling work.

THE DOCTOR OF THE FUTURE IS THE PATIENT

My only challenge thus far has been to convince people to call me before they go to the ER or urgent care. Many of them still imagine their phone calls or secure messages are "bothering me," despite my reassurance that this is exactly why I charge a monthly fee.

—Rob Lamberts, MD, DPC Physician from Augusta, GA

I can hear your questions and objections: "What if the customer abuses the relationship, constantly contacting us and is very demanding? What if they ask for more than is reasonable? What about one-off projects that fall outside my normal offerings? I have heard horror stories of 'all you can eat' offerings from colleagues, and so forth." These are all valid points, yet we do not believe they are insoluble.

Let us dispense with the first objection, deferring the others to future chapters: the fear of abuse. Doctors have become all too familiar with *cyberchondria*—"a clinical phenomenon in which repeated Internet searches regarding medical information result in excessive concerns about physical health." I heard the same types of objections when I advocated inserting "unlimited phone calls and meetings" into your fixed price agreements. The fact is, customers simply do not abuse this service. In fact, the onus is still on the firm to stay in constant contact with the customer. Even DPC doctors have experienced that over 80% of the calls they receive are during normal business hours. And if your customers need to call you over the weekend, wouldn't you want to hear from them? It is usually something serious. If a customer did serially abuse you or your team, you always have the option of terminating the relationship. Yet if anything, doctors describe how they have to reeducate their patients to visit them *more* so they can maintain and improve their health. This is part of the reframing of value that is so important in the subscription business model.

We've looked at the benefits of this model for the customer—recurring, convenient, and frictionless value coupled with peace of mind. What are the benefits to the professional? The model moves us closer to aligning the revenue model—what do we want our customers to pay for—to why we entered the profession in the first place—to

help people. It is the most outward-focused business model that's
been developed (so far) since it is built exclusively around the customer relationship and his or her needs. Here are some other
major benefits:

- Living your purpose and rekindle your passion for the profession
- Avoids excessive overhead and bureaucracy
- Reduction in malpractice insurance and chance of lawsuits
- Less burnout and cynicism
- More differentiation of value in the marketplace, commanding
  higher pricing power
- Increases customer loyalty, retention, and lifetime value
- Allows professionals to be more selective with whom they work
- An increase in the value of the firm because Annual Recurring
  Revenue is more valuable and predictable than reoccurring rev-
  enue that is based on transactional services. This model will
  command a valuation at a multiple far beyond the standard 1
  times gross revenue

Perhaps the above advantages explain a poll taken in 2018–2019 of
DPC doctors who, after 10 years of practicing under this model,
reported they are more satisfied while 0% answered less satisfied
(4.17% said neither).

Even better, we finally have a model that values the customer's
time more than the professional's. If we are going to track time, let us
track it under two dimensions:

1. The time customers spend interacting with our firm
2. The time we save the customer so they are freed up to pursue
   higher-valued activities

This is how value is created, reducing the friction and transaction
costs the customer encounters in dealing with us. Customer loyalty is
not enhanced because of the efficiency of our processes and workflow management systems, but how we make them feel. We can be
efficient with things, but we must be effective with people. No one
defines their marriage as "efficient," nor should we do the same with
the customers we are privileged to serve.

It has become a cliché to say "Time is our most precious resource." It is not true. Ultimately, time is a *constraint*. In the end, it is what we do with the time we are given that matters. Yet I do believe that *health* is one of our most precious assets, and as with financial health, it takes time, effort, and investment to sustain and grow. The reason I have taken the time to explain the DPC doctors is because they have introduced disruptive change in their profession. They help their patients develop a vision of a preferred future, and then guide the transformation to that destination, over and over, as the customer moves through their natural life cycle. It is not a one-time transaction built by piling up services brick-by-brick, but rather cultivated on recurring value creation and innovation, as explained by Michael Tetreault speaking at the Concierge Forum in Atlanta, October 2018:

> There is a mystique, a temperament and a curious fascination about doctors who spend an inordinate amount of time with their patients. It's so simple, it's weird. There is just nothing like that in healthcare today. And like it or not, a patient wants and deserves your time and attention. That's why they pay the subscription, keep calling you and keep texting you. They are entrusting you with their life. Today, we're hearing routinely that a patient will leave a private, direct style medical practice in a matter of weeks if they feel they are not a priority. (Tetreault and Sykes 2019)

Seth Godin says: "Perhaps the reason price is all your customers care about it because you haven't given them anything else to care about." A suboptimal pricing model focuses customer attention on what they have to pay; an optimal pricing model makes price nearly invisible, focusing the customer's attention on what they are receiving. That is precisely what will happen when you reframe your value around recurring, frictionless, convenient, and peace-of-mind offerings. *Only unconventional offerings will command premium prices.*

As Dr. Paul Thomas (2020) wrote in *Startup DPC: How to Start and Grow Your Direct Primary Care Practice*: "You should start a direct primary care practice because you can become the doctor you're meant to be." The Japanese [have a] concept called *Ikigai*: your reason for being.

If you are intrigued by this model, you are among the 2.5% of your peers, those innovators who, like the pioneers, take the arrows and all the adjacent skepticism that goes along with it. The dog always barks at what he doesn't understand. As Mark Twain apparently did not say, but should have: "History does not repeat itself, but it rhymes." When Paul and I published *The Firm of the Future* we received the same skepticism and criticisms for our views, and still do, actually. But ask yourself:

- What about your practice and profession today does not provide you with purpose?
- Are you making a meaningful impact on the lives of those you serve?
- Are you doing what you were born to do (or, at the least, doing what you originally joined the profession to do)?
- Is your current business model the most optimal you can imagine?
- Has our profession lost its soul?
- Do we have the vision and courage to build a better model for posterity?

Where there is no vision, the people perish (Proverbs 29:18), which is why the motto of Jeff Bezos's Blue Origin space startup is *Gradatim Ferociter*, which means "step by step, ferociously." We realize this business model is not for everyone, and that is fine. There is plenty of room in the marketplace for multiple business models. For those of you who are interested in evolving your firm and blazing the trail toward a more fulfilling future, let us next, together, explore this model in greater detail.

10

Business Model Evolution

If we want things to stay as they are, things will have to change.

—Giuseppe Tomasi di Lampedusa, *The Leopard*, 1958

Shawn Fanning was a 19-year-old college dropout in 1999 when he created Napster. In the first three months of 2001, 2.5 billion music files a month were being downloaded, validating the economist's theory of demand, which states that the lower the price, the larger quantity demanded, especially a zero price. The music industry collectively cried foul, accusing millions of young people of intellectual theft. Yet when you have millions of potential customers downloading billions of your product, you do not have a crime wave; you have a *marketing* problem—more specifically, you have a business model problem. It took Steve Jobs of Apple to capitalize on this opportunity with iTunes, and now, that model has evolved once more, and most of us stream our music on a subscription basis.

The Napster saga is just one in a long history of revolutions taking place outside the confines of an existing industry, in what the Austrian economist Joseph Schumpeter labeled the "perennial gale of creative destruction." The reason entire industries can be brought down is because new competitors offer more value to the customer than the status quo. Schumpeter understood this phenomenon at the macro level: "Creative destruction is the essential fact about capitalism. Stabilized capitalism is a contradiction in terms. [Responsible businesspeople] know they are standing on ground that is crumbling beneath their feet."

119

The late Harvard Business School professor Clayton Christensen recognized that it is very difficult for a business to disrupt itself. Despite how many times leadership insists we live in a VUCA world—volatility, uncertainty, complexity, and ambiguity—it is a rare leader who is willing to truly disrupt the status quo by creating, capturing, and measuring value in new and more meaningful ways. As Christensen wrote, "Generally, the leading practitioners of the old order become the victims of disruption, not the initiators of it." It is more *self-destruct* than self-disrupt. Paul expressed it well in Chapter 1: "What got you here won't get you there. . ."

In a meeting with Clayton Christensen, the late Intel CEO Andy Grove made the point that "disruptive threats came inherently not from new technology but from new business models." Perhaps this is why Grove titled his own book *Only the Paranoid Survive*. Fintech has a saying: "Banking is necessary, banks are not." Might this be true for some of the work presently done by the professions? Accounting is necessary, accounting firms are not. Before we discuss how the professional firm business model has evolved, it is worthwhile to explore why models are so useful.

THREE WAYS OF UNDERSTANDING THE WORLD

We need models to explain what we see and to predict what will occur. We use models for envisioning the future and influencing it.

—Emanuel Derman, *Models Behaving Badly: Why Confusing Illusion with Reality Can Lead to Disaster, on Wall Street and in Life*, 2011

Emanuel Derman is a physicist who went to work on Wall Street. His book *Models Behaving Badly: Why Confusing Illusion with Reality Can Lead to Disaster, on Wall Street and in Life* is an excellent exploration of the difference between theories and models:

> . . . I will argue that there are three distinct ways of understanding the world: theories, models, and intuition. Theories are attempts to discover the principles that drive the world; they need confirmation, but no justification for their existence. Theories. . .must stand on their own two feet.

Models stand on someone else's feet. They are metaphors that compare the object of their attention to something else that it resembles. Resemblance is always partial, and so models necessarily simplify things and reduce the dimensions of the world. In a nutshell, theories tell you what something is; models tell you merely what something is like. Intuition is more comprehensive. It unifies the subject with the object.

We need models and theories because of time. Unless you can live in the perpetual present, you need theories and models to exert some control. (Derman 2011)

We all walk around with mental models of how the world works. This is particularly true in business, where there are many sacred principles that we seem to isolate from challenge or debate—maximizing margin over cash flow, hourly billing, the necessity of timesheets, being just a few examples. Thinking is hard. Models provide a shortcut through complexity while saving mental energy.

Derman also coined the term *pragmamorphism,* which is the "naïve tendency to attribute the properties of things to human beings." Humans are more than mathematical equations, or materialistic properties. Enterprise has a *soul* precisely because humans are involved. No business model captures the full reality of any enterprise, any more than a model airplane depicts a real one. "This looks like a bird, but no bird looks like this."

Consider the construction of an airplane, boat, bridge, and building. With nearly 100% success, the plane will fly, the boat will float, and the bridge and building will stand, even against the perils of inclement weather. Now consider a marriage, or a business. Why is the success rate so much lower? Because, as my colleague, Ed Kless, likes to say: "Business ain't science."

Humans have a *physical* and *spiritual* dimension, illustrated by how we are able to weigh and measure a violin in a laboratory with absolute precision, but not being able to explain why it makes you weep—or march off to war, or dance like no one is watching—when it is played. No model is ever going to capture the full richness and wonder of human beings; it would be folly to attempt to construct such a device.

With that caveat in place, let us turn to how the subscription business model has been evolving, and then we will apply it to professional firms to see the next iteration, a sort of *Firm of the Future 2.0,* if we dare.

THE NINE SUBSCRIPTION BUSINESS MODELS

In *The Automatic Customer: Creating a Subscription Business in Any Industry*, John Warrillow (2015) compiles nine types of subscription business models. Obviously, there exists much overlap plus various hybrid models—such as Amazon Prime. Yet it is useful to see these listed to see how many elements fit your firm and spark creative thinking. Here are the nine models, with a few examples to illustrate each:

1. The Membership Website model: *Wall Street Journal, New York Times, The Economist*

2. The All-You-Can-Eat Library model: Netflix, Spotify, Apple Music.

3. The Private Club model: Country clubs, Disney's Club 33.

4. The Front-of-the-Line model: Priority access, such as Clear in airports, Peach Pass, and FasTrak for highways and bridge tolls.

5. The Consumables model: Based on replenishment, Harry's Razors, Diapers, Quip.

6. The Surprise Box model: Wine, beer, fruit of the month.

7. The Simplifier model: Porsche Drive and Hassle-Free Home Services (more below).

8. The Network model: Partial access to expensive infrastructure: NetJets, Zipcar, Airbnb.

9. The Peace-of-Mind model: A form of insurance, such as Tagg for pet tracking, direct primary care (see Chapter 9).

You may be asking yourself, "These are all direct-to-consumer (D2C) models; what do they have to do with my firm?" The answer is that our D2C experiences are driving our business-to-business (B2B) expectations. The fact is, *we compete against any organization that has the ability to raise customer expectations.* Amazon has raised the bar for digital interaction across the board, for all companies. My local grocery store's website experience is atrocious compared with Amazon's, to its peril. Combine a frictionless, convenient, and seamless experience with peace of mind and you demonstrate to the customer you value *their* time more than your own.

Consider Hassle Free Home Services, Inc., which provides home maintenance and allows you to "reclaim your weekends." When one-off projects are desired by the homeowner, such as a kitchen or bathroom remodel, the company will handle the project management and roll it up into your monthly payment, which accounts for approximately 50% of its revenue. This is what is meant by putting the relationship at the center of the business. By establishing trust with the customer every month while taking care of their routine maintenance, who will they hire to perform larger jobs? The subscription builds a moat around the competition.

Contemplate Porsche Drive, which allows you to subscribe to a single-vehicle plan or a multiple-vehicle plan, in an all-inclusive monthly subscription that covers everything—insurance, roadside assistance, maintenance, registration, and white-glove concierge service—except gas and tolls, with monthly pricing ranging from $1,700 to $3,600. People ask, "What's the difference between signing up for this and buying (or leasing) a Porsche?" It is not tied to a car (transaction); you are *subscribing to Porsche*, the company. It's a direct, one-to-one relationship that reframes its value proposition and is far more psychologically binding. When we subscribe to a company, we have entered into a covenant, and are more likely to be loyal. Approximately 80% of the customers who signed up are new to the brand. What will they most likely drive for the rest of their lives?

Both offerings confer recurring, frictionless, and convenient value, combined with peace of mind and an exceptional customer experience, providing the companies with a source of differentiated value that can command premium pricing. If you have read this far, you are beginning to see the link between these two subscription models (The Simplifier and The Peace-of-Mind models) and the direct primary care model, which is most applicable to professional firms.

THE FIRM OF THE FUTURE 2.0

I'm willing to be occasionally wrong. But what I hate most in life is to stay wrong.

—Paul A. Samuelson, Nobel laureate economist

When Paul and I published *The Firm of the Future*, the intent was to posit a better business model for professional firms, overturning the "predominant" model, which unfortunately still has substantial—albeit diminished—sway among professionals. For our purposes, a business model is defined as: *How your firm creates value for customers, and how you capture a portion of that value.*

In 2003, the predominant model was as follows; think of it as the Firm of the Past:

$$\textbf{Revenue} = \textbf{People Power} \times \textbf{Efficiency} \times \textbf{Hourly Rate}$$

This model built the archetypal pyramid firm by leveraging people hours and hourly rate realizations. Want to make more money? Add more people, or work the people you have more hours. David Maister called it "the donkey strategy;" by carrying a bigger load, we will prosper. Nor do you want much spare capacity in this model since you are selling time and not really building relationships.

Nor do you want to become more efficient, since that will lower your revenue. Perhaps this is one of the reasons firms have been slow to invest in technology—it eats hours. Yet nearly all firm leaders say the firm has to become more efficient without understanding *there is no such thing as generic efficiency*. It all depends on what your purpose is, and how much you are willing to pay. The Golden Gate Bridge is, by definition, not efficient. So what? It is very effective in being an iconic symbol of a city that draws tourists from around the world. Innovation, dynamism, customer service, and investments in human capital are all the antithesis of efficiency. We can be efficient with *things*, but we must be *effective* with people—defined as doing the right thing.

Hourly rates are a form of cost-plus pricing, the real antecedent of which is the labor theory of value, posited by economists of the eighteenth century and by Karl Marx in the middle nineteenth, and falsified by the 1871 Marginalist Revolution, which proved that all value is subjective (see Chapter 14).

Last, consider revenue. It is one thing to get *more* business; it is quite another to get *better* business. The "bigger is better" mentality is an empty promise for most firms. Acquiring more customers is not necessarily better. Growth for the sake of growth is the ideology of the cancer cell, not a strategy for a viable, profitable firm. Eventually, the cancer kills its host.

What is worse, this model limits the profit you can earn, by design. Want to make a million more dollars, bill a million more hours. More pernicious, it is a limit professionals themselves have created, not their customers. Plainly, this is a suboptimal business model. It is a valuable accomplishment in and of itself to point out defects in a model—or falsify it entirely. Another way to advance knowledge is to posit a better model, which is what we did in *The Firm of the Future*:

Profitability = Intellectual Capital × Effectiveness × Price

We started with profit because revenue is vanity, profit is sanity. Growth without profit is perilous. Think of how many companies have grown their way into bankruptcy. We laid out the three types of intellectual capital: human capital; structural capital; and social capital (more on these below). A fascinating study by the World Bank documents that 80% of the developed world's wealth resides in human capital, not physical resources, such as oil, real estate, earth minerals, etc. Human capital is vital to any knowledge firm.

We explained the profound difference between efficiency and effectiveness, the former being a mindless ratio (outputs divided by inputs), whereas effectiveness concentrates on doing the right thing, which requires a judgment, not merely a measurement.

Last, we explained why value pricing was superior to hourly billing for capturing value created. Businesses have prices, not hourly rates, set in advance of doing the work. We advocated pricing the customer, not the services, or outputs (deliverables) since value varies by customer. At the time, this was considered a radical model, but recall that *radical* comes from the Latin for "getting back to the root." I expanded on this model in my book, *Implementing Value Pricing: A Radical Business Model for Professional Firms*. Therein, I wrote: ". . . if the model posited here is someday replaced with a better one, I will have contributed to the advancement of the professions—and nothing would please me more."

The perennial gales of creative destruction—manifested in new business models do not stop blowing simply because a book has been published. We always knew this model could be replaced based on the ever-changing conditions in the marketplace. This is the dynamism of free markets that continuously enhance the standard of living for all of us.

Given the Renaissance in subscriptions (Chapter 9), it is past time to posit a more optimal business model. Ed Kless, Paul, and I have been working on this for several years, attempting to synthesize the various subscriptions models into one that is optimal for professional firms. We are fully aware that what we are positing here is *inchoate*— derived from a Latin word, *incohäre,* meaning "to begin" or to make a first effort at. As physicist Niels Bohr said, "If an idea does not appear bizarre, there is no hope for it." Keep that in mind as you contemplate this new model:

Customer Lifetime Value = Intellectual Capital
× Transformations × Learning and Innovation
× Ensurance × Portfolio Pricing

I admit this model could use a good shave from Occam's Razor to get it to $E=MC^2$ level of simplicity (not simplistic). But we wanted to build on the model presented in *The Firm of the Future*—where Intellectual Capital, Effectiveness, and Value Pricing were introduced. Recall my colleague Ed Kless's definition of the subscription model: Periodic recurring payments for frictionless, ever-increasing value, and serial transformations. In that spirit, we will unpack the meaning of each the components in the above equation in more detail in subsequent chapters. For now, let us describe how we define each of these terms.

Customer Lifetime Value

The present value of the future net profit earned from the entire duration of the relationship. There are many nuances to this calculation (do you use revenue, gross margin, or net profit?), but the important point for now is CLV must be *modeled*, it is not computed by generally accepted accounting principles (GAAP), which is why it does not appear on the income statement. We will discuss the income statement, metrics, and KPIs in Chapters 18–20.

Intellectual Capital

The Intellectual Capital Management Gathering Best Practices conference in 1995 defined intellectual capital as "knowledge that can be converted into profits," which is an adequate definition for our purposes since it equates knowledge with a verb (Lev 2001, p. 155). Intellectual capital should not be confused with knowledge management, which is merely a process, whereas IC is an entity that is far broader than mere intellectual property (IP).

However, our understanding of the role IC plays in generating wealth is not well recognized by accountants, or accurately measured by them for that matter. GAAP do an abysmal job of valuing IC, as most of the cost of creating IC is treated as a period expense for GAAP. This explains how Microsoft's GAAP assets, as reported on its balance sheet, account for less than 10% of its market capitalization. Contrary to what every accounting student is taught, in the real world, debits do not equal credits.

Today, intellectual capital is sometimes thought of as nothing more than another buzzword. IC has *always* been the chief driver of wealth, as economists have argued since the term human capital was first coined in 1961, and as far back as the late eighteenth century when Adam Smith discredited the idea of mercantilism. Wealth does not reside in tangible assets or money; it resides in the IC that exists in the human spirit, which is then used to create valuable goods and services. Yet since this is hard to measure (How does one measure the ambition of Steve Jobs to "put a dent in the universe"?), we tend to ignore it until it becomes so obvious, as in the case of Apple, Google, and Tesla, that we have to acknowledge our old theories of wealth creation are no longer relevant.

For our purposes, we are going to separate a company's IC into three categories, as originally proposed by Karl-Erik Sveiby, a leading thinker in knowledge theory, in 1989:

- **Human capital (HC).** This comprises your team members and associates who work either for you or with you. As one industry leader said, this is the capital that leaves in the elevator at night. The important thing to remember about HC is that is cannot be *owned*, only contracted, since it is completely volitional. In fact, more and more, knowledge workers own the means of your firm's production, and knowledge workers will invest their personal HC in those firms that pay a decent return on investment, both economic and psychological. In the final analysis, your people are not assets (they deserve more respect than a desk and a computer); they are not resources to be harvested from the land like coal when you run out. Ultimately, they are *volunteers,* and it is totally up to them whether they get back into the elevator the following morning.

- **Structural capital.** This is everything that remains in your firm once the HC has stepped into the elevator, such as databases, customer lists, systems, processes, procedures, intranets, manuals, technology, business models, and all of the explicit knowledge tools you utilize to produce results for your customers.

- **Social capital.** This includes your customers, the main reason a business exists; but it also includes your suppliers, vendors, networks, referral sources, alumni, joint ventures and alliance partners, professional associations, reputation, and so on. Of the three types of IC, this is perhaps the least leveraged, and yet it is highly valued by customers.

The crucial point to understand here is that it is the *interplay* among the three types of IC above that generates wealth-creating opportunities for your firm. Human capital, for example, can grow in two ways: when the business utilizes more of what each person knows, and when people know more things that are useful to the firm and its customers. And since knowledge is a *nonrival* good—meaning we can both possess it at the same time without diminishing it—knowledge shared is knowledge that is effectively *doubled* throughout the organization. That is why former Hewlett-Packard CEO Lew Platt said: "If HP knew what HP knows, we would be three times as profitable."

It also explains why IC is the real leverage in any professional firm. Because IC can be in more than one place at a time, not to mention used by more than one customer at a time, it is the main leverage in a firm. The Firm of the Past model puts the leverage into hours; but an hour is a *rival* asset, as we can only do one thing at a time. You simply cannot leverage time, which is why hours are the wrong measuring device for knowledge worker wealth creation. As Archimedes said, "If you give me a lever and a place to stand, I can move the world."

Another useful way to think about IC is by ownership. Human capital is owned by the knowledge worker; structural capital is the only component of IC that is owned by the firm; and social capital is owned by no one, though it can be leveraged, monetizing benefits to the owners of the firm. Utilizing this framework, even world-class brands are not really owned by the company's stockholders. Yes, technically in a legal sense they are, but not from an economic point of view. One of the best illustrations of who really owns a brand is Coca-Cola's decision to remove Old Coke and begin offering New Coke. There was literally a customer revolt, proving beyond a shadow of a doubt that it is customers who ultimately decide the value of a brand. When Robert Goizueta, then CEO of Coca-Cola, was asked what the lesson was from the New Coke debacle, he replied that he learned that Coca-Cola did not own its brand—the consumer did (Tedlow 2001, p. 105). Ask yourself what the world's most valuable brands would be worth tomorrow if everyone in the world suddenly developed amnesia?

Knowledge firms are the ultimate "asset-less" organizations, since 80% of their value-creating capacity is owned by the volunteers who work there. Before we leave this brief discussion of IC, it is necessary to explain something that may, at first impression, not seem obvious.

NEGATIVE INTELLECTUAL CAPITAL

When IC is discussed, it is normally done in a very positive context, as most of the examples used are from successes in leveraging IC, such as Tesla or Apple. But it is important to understand there is such a thing as *negative* human capital, *negative* structural capital, and *negative* social capital. Not everything we know is beneficial. Think of the IC a thief possesses; it is knowledge in the sense he knows how to perform his craft, just as much as United Airlines knows how to fly planes and transport people around the world. But that does not make the knowledge valuable; and with respect to thieves, the social loss they impose is a societal negative.

Think of countries that dogmatically adhere to the principles of socialism or Marxism, even though both of these theories of social organization have been repudiated by empirical evidence. There has been enormous negative social capital built up over the past six-plus decades in Cuba, just as there was in the former Soviet Union. Fidel Castro *thought* he expropriated the most crucial capital from the capitalists, all their land, stores and buildings, and so on, to create a great

Cuban city. He did—in Miami, since the crucial human capital left Cuba.

Examples of negative intellectual capital in a professional firm would include a rigid adherence to old methods that are hindering your people from achieving their potential, and subtracting from value creation. High on this list would include cost-plus pricing; Industrial Age efficiency metrics and time tracking, focusing on activities and costs rather than outcomes and value; and other forms of negative IC that have embedded themselves into the culture. These negative ideas have permeated each type of knowledge discussed herein—human, structural, and certainly social—and have become part of our tacit and explicit knowledge systems.

Transformations

This idea comes from Joseph B. Pine II and James H. Gilmore, in their book *The Experience Economy: Work Is Theatre and Every Business a Stage*, wherein they put forth a hierarchy of value. The heuristic—mental short cutout—they used at the end of each level was, "How do you de-commoditize (the previous level)?" which led them up to the next offering (based on our interview with Joseph Pine on the radio show, *The Soul of Enterprise: Business in the Knowledge Economy* (The Soul of Enterprise 2015). Here is their echelon of customer value:

- If you charge for *stuff*, then you are in the *commodity* business.
- If you charge for *tangible things*, then you are in the *goods* business.
- If you charge for *the activities you execute*, then you are in the *service* business.
- If you charge for *the time customers spend with you*, then you are in the *experience* business.
- If you charge for the *demonstrated outcome the customer achieves*, then and only then are you in the *transformation* business (Pine and Gilmore 1999, p. 194).

We will discuss transformations more in Chapter 13. For now, ask yourself: How does our firm provide transformations to our customers?

What are the outcomes we take responsibility for creating? Transformations move your firm from effectiveness—doing the right thing—to efficaciousness—having the power to produce the maximum desired effect. The good news is that professional firms perform transformations every day, but as with fish in water, they are not aware of it, nor do they use the precise language to articulate, exactly, what it is they are creating.

Learning and Innovation

A business does not exist to earn a profit, despite the conventional wisdom. Of course, any business needs to earn a profit to survive; indeed, profit is the measurement of how much value an organization adds to the lives of others—an index of its *altruism*, as my mentor, George Gilder, eloquently explains. It is also a premium earned for risk and uncertainty.

That said, to think that a business exists solely to make a profit is to confuse cause and effect—we must distinguish between the *purpose* of a business with its *goal*. As Peter Drucker indefatigably pointed out in his writings, not only is the notion that businesses exist to make a profit false, it is irrelevant. Profit is a *result* of customer behavior. More accurately, profit is a *lagging indicator* of customer behavior. The real results of any organization take place in the hearts and minds of its customers.

We have already seen how wealth is equal to knowledge. As economist Thomas Sowell wrote in *Knowledge and Decisions*:

> After all, the caveman had the same natural resources at their disposal as we have today, and the difference between their standard of living and ours is a difference between the knowledge they could bring to bear on those resources and the knowledge used today. (Sowell 1980, p. 47)

The caveman had oil and other natural resources we use today to make drugs and other useful items he just lacked the knowledge that we have today about combustion engines, energy, and medical science.

If knowledge equals wealth, where does economic growth come from? The answer is learning (accumulated tested knowledge) and

innovation. Not just book learning, or continuing professional education, but real entrepreneurial experiments subject to the test and
whims of the marketplace. Knowledge is about the past, while entre-
preneurialism is about the future. Even when a new product, service,
or venture fails, we gain knowledge, an epistemic yield—learning.
Consider Silicon Valley. We can easily see the successes, but those
businesses stand on top of a mass graveyard of failures, sometimes
from the very founders of the present successful firms.

If we do not allow our human capital investors to spend a portion
of time investing in innovation and learning—such as Google's 20%
time to work on a project that interests you—we will continue to fall
below our potential of serving customers as professionals. This
requires spare capacity and not putting growth for the sake of growth
above all other goals. Busyness and efficiency do not equate to profitability, and indeed are the antithesis of learning and innovation,
which are, by definition, inefficient.

Ensurance

This aspect of the subscription model is truly uncommon, a form of
coverage that spreads the firm's risk across the entire portfolio of its
customers. As with DPC physicians, whatever the customer needs
that the doctor can perform with competence, it is covered. This
allows flexible capacity to be built into the system to be able to handle emergencies, or short-term deadlines, while providing customers
peace of mind that, no matter what they may need in the future, they
will be adequately cared for. There are still strategies you can use to
segment customers, offer various levels of "covered and noncovered"
services, which we will discuss in Chapters 15–17.

That said, this is not *insurance*, whereby the customer secures a
payment in the event of a loss. Nor is it *assurance*, such as CPAs
auditing a financial statement creating a sense of confidence in the
numbers presented. As Pine and Gilmore explain: "Services insure;
Experiences Assure; and Transformations Ensure: Secure an event,
situation, or outcome" (Pine and Gilmore 2019). Focusing on transformations will provide your firm with the ability to command premium pricing; merely providing services—even at a value price—is
not nearly as optimal.

Portfolio Pricing

This is a *suitcase term*—there is a lot packed into it. Some of the items are your firm's purpose, strategy, positioning, brand, lowering of transaction costs to your customers, and actuarial principles of pricing risk. Many principles of value pricing still apply, such as assessing customer value; price-justifying costs, not costs determining price, offering options, etc. There is no room, however, for any hourly billing mentality or measures in this model; you are *pricing the relationship*, not the services, or even the customer. By ignoring the math of the moment and instead focusing on customer lifetime value, you will increase your pricing power. We will discuss pricing the portfolio more in Chapters 15–16.

One more point needs to be made about business model changes. At least two things change when you observe a new business model: The pricing strategy is adjusted to reflect the new offering's value proposition. We go from purchasing $20 compact disks, to iPods and 99¢ per song, and now most of us are streaming our music on subscription. Uber introduced surge pricing to account for both demand and supply of the ride market.

The other change is what is measured inside of the organization. The key performance—and I say, predictive—indicators (KPIs) change. This one is usually ignored by most firms and consultants as they transition to new business models. We witnessed this when firms moved from hourly billing to value pricing because many clung on to their timesheets for dear life. But this measures the wrong thing, which is why timesheets are so pernicious. If your customers are not buying time—and we are not pricing upon it—why are we measuring it? The subscription business model ushers in an entirely new dashboard of metrics, none of which are focused on time. *Time's Up* indeed. We will explore KPIs in Chapters 18–20.

NOT FINAL THOUGHTS

Life is traveling to the edge of knowledge, then a leap taken.

—D.H. Lawrence, poet

Look before you leap. Sometimes it is good advice. Other times, especially in a dynamic, changing marketplace, it is precarious. It is the *leap*, not the look, that provides the crucial knowledge. Always remember that knowledge is about the past, while entrepreneurship is about the future, and often creating a future that we did not even know was possible. Creativity and innovation always take us by surprise; otherwise we could run the economy with artificial intelligence. What we think is possible is only determined by venturing into the impossible.

When my VeraSage Institute colleague Ed Kless and I began discussing the subscription business model on our radio show, *The Soul of Enterprise*, in November 2018, we started to receive fervent pushback from our colleagues: This is not possible, it's not scalable, it's not an optimal pricing model, etc. It very much reminded me of introducing value pricing back in 1994. I received intense pushback from the very colleagues I was trying to help. It was the same when Paul and I introduced the new business model outlined above in *The Firm of the Future*.

One thing I've learned is that if your ideas are irritating people, they are probably worth pursuing. It certainly does not mean the ideas are right, or that they will work, but it does demonstrate that you are asking the right questions. The late Clayton Christensen used to say, "Without a good question, a good answer has no place to go."

We all walk around with our theories and models of how the world works, and we rarely challenge our most deeply held beliefs. Richard Feynman, the Nobel Prize physicist, had this wonderful advice: "The first principle is that you must not fool yourself—and you are the easiest person to fool." With subscription-based businesses growing nearly five times faster than the S&P 500 over the last 10 years, according to Zuora (see Chapter 8), how can we ignore the impact this will have on professional firms? Peter Drucker used to say that he didn't predict the future, but he did look out the window and observe what was happening.

There is an obvious disconnect between what professionals say and what their business model does. We say the relationship comes first, but we monetize the services. We have too many customers, and too many who are "one and done," which keeps us on a treadmill to continuously feed the lead-generation funnel. We do not measure the lifetime value of customer relationships—nor do we consider the lifetime value of the firm to its customers—but rather, focus on the math of the moment. We struggle to attract the best talent because stars do not work for firms that force them to track every minute of their day as if they didn't trust them to do the right things, nor does it allow them the freedom to be creative and innovative, traits to which we pay enormous lip service, not willing to put our money where our mouths are.

These contradictions are simply not worthy of a proud profession. It is past time for us to align our rhetoric with our calling, and restore the relationship to the center of the firm. The ground beneath the feet of the professions is beginning to shift, again. New and more effective business models are being developed and refined every day that recognize the realities of the subscription economy and more robust revenue models that continuously ask, "What do we want the customer to pay for?"

Skeptics will call for an incremental approach, which is how they maintain the status quo. I am, frankly, discouraged that in the year 2022—103 years after the first law firm introduced hourly billing and the timesheet—we are still having this debate among some of our fellow professionals. Alfred Sauvy, the French thinker, used to worry about "a society of old people, living in old houses, ruminating about old ideas."

There is no limit to what we can achieve, as long as we do not lose faith in ourselves. The professions are built on relationships; indeed, life is all about relationships, the rest is details. A stark reality is that relationships do not scale—they are developed and nurtured over time, one at a time. If we truly want to provide transformations to those we are privileged to serve, our business model's economics must reflect that fact. This is the subscription economy mandate.

11

PURPOSE, STRATEGY, AND POSITIONING

*To know what a business is we have to start with its purpose.
There is only one valid definition of business purpose:* to
create a customer. *Because its purpose is to create a customer,
the business enterprise has two—and only these two—basic
functions: marketing and innovation. Marketing and innovation produce results; all the rest are costs.*

—Peter Drucker, *People and Performance*, 2007

Imagine you or a loved one has made the painful and difficult
decision to obtain a divorce, a high-stress, high-anxiety situation.
Searching for a local family law attorney, you will discover *what* and
how they do what they do, their credentials, areas of practice, etc.
What very few will inform you is *why* they do what they do. Then
you run across the website of Chinn & Associates PC, in Jackson,
Mississippi (full disclosure: Mark Chinn is our VeraSage Institute
colleague):

> At Chinn & Associates, we believe that divorce may end a marriage,
> but it doesn't have to end a family or ruin your future. We are here to
> protect your interests.

What is meaningful about this is he is letting potential customers
know *why* he does what he does, what he stands for, what he believes.
As Simon Sinek says, people buy *why* you do what you do, not just
what you do. This conveys something deeply personal about Mark's
philosophy, his worldview, which is vital, as we humans are defined
by what we *believe*, not what we *know*.

137

Defining your purpose is crucial because we believe everything else derives from a clearly articulated purpose—your firm's strategy, marketing, positioning, selling, and pricing. In fact, purpose is so important it was the first question Peter Drucker listed in his 2008 book, *The Five Most Important Questions You Will Ever Ask About Your Organization*:

1. What is our mission? (we are using "purpose")
2. Who is our customer?
3. What does the customer value? (Most important and least asked)
4. What are our results?
5. What is our plan?

These questions are timeless. Let us think about each of them in the context of Purpose, Strategy, and Positioning. Innovation and Risk-taking will be explored in Chapter 12, while pricing will be covered in Chapters 14–17.

PURPOSE

As Paul discussed in Chapter 3, excellent organizations all have one thing in common: a clear purpose. Think of Apple, Google, Disney, the Mayo Clinic, or any other firm you admire. You will notice they stand for something. They have a particular culture. Certainly, great companies are cultlike. The word *cult* shares an origin with *culture* and *cultivate*, and comes from the Latin *cultus*, a noun with meanings ranging from "tilling, cultivation," to "training" or "education" to "adoration" (Merriam-Webster). The Disney Institute defines a corporate culture as "the system of values and beliefs an organization holds that drives actions and behaviors and influences relationships." Cultivation, in this context, would imply an active soil to nourish customer relationships.

In his book *Purpose: The Starting Point of Great Companies*, Nikos Mourkogiannis sums it up masterfully:

> Purpose is bigger than tactics. Purpose is bigger than strategy. It is a choice to pursue your destiny—the ultimate destination for yourself

and the organization you lead. Purpose is your moral DNA. It's what you believe without having to think. (Mourkogiannis 2006, p. 6)

Your purpose should start with "We believe," such as the Mayo Clinic's: "We believe the needs of the patient come first."

Our VeraSage Institute colleague Tim Williams provides the following criteria to determine if you've reached deep enough to find your purpose in his book, *Positioning for Professionals*:

- It's inspiring and motivating.
- It's about meaning, not money.
- It comes from the inside, what you really believe (not what others think you should believe, or focus groups, or customer comments).
- It's difficult—maybe impossible—to fully achieve (Williams 2010, pp. 53–54).

As Tim writes, a purpose is discovered, not created—it already exists in the DNA of your firm. He offers the following useful questions to unearth the purpose of your firm that you can use with your management team:

- Why does this organization exist?
- What inspires us to come to work each day?
- Besides making money, why are we in business?
- What is the meaning in what we do?
- What significant contribution do we want to make to the industry, the profession, or the world?
- What are some of our "unrealistic" expectations?
- What important problem would we like to solve?
- What would we like to create that may have never existed before?
- What would happen if our company or brand ceased to exist?
- What kind of lasting difference do we want to make?
- What do we preach?
- What are we crusading against?

- What would our enterprise be like if we were leading a movement instead of running a business?

- If our people were volunteers instead of employees, what would they be volunteering for?

- What would we want to achieve if we knew we could not fail? (Williams 2010, pp. 52–53).

Think audaciously when you answer these questions. When we launched VeraSage Institute, our purpose was: "We believe the only place time spent should matter is in prison," even going so far as drafting a Declaration of Independence that anyone could sign (https://www.verasage.com/dofi), setting forth our quest to bury both hourly billing and trashing the timesheet (not one or the other, *both*). Is this realistic? No, and I still don't think it will be fully achieved in my lifetime, though tremendous progress has been made—the death of these plagues on the profession may not be within *reach*, but they are within *sight*. Your purpose should be debatable—it should cause dissent, ruffle feathers, and take a stand. If it is not debatable, it is too bland.

Your purpose also needs to be broadly communicated both internally and externally. Disney University founder Van Arsdale France explains in his book, *Window on Main Street*, Disney's theme park operation philosophy, embedded in four elements, listed in their order of importance:

1. **Safety.** When guests come to Disneyland, they put their safety in Disney's hands.

2. **Courtesy.** We represent the entire Disney organization in the guests' person-to-person contact with us.

3. **Show.** Disneyland is a spectacular show, and we are show people. We may work "on stage" or "backstage," but all our efforts combine to create the world's greatest show.

4. **Capacity.** We have a limited capacity. Every seat must be utilized. (We later changed this key to *efficiency*) (France 2015).

Notice how efficiency is last, and how high courtesy is ranked. This is why Cast members in Disney parks are allowed to go "off-task" to be "on-purpose," creating happy guest experiences—what it calls "moments of magic." Can your firm's team members do the same? Or are they penalized for reducing "efficiency and billable hours" to go above and beyond in the care of customers? As Ralph Waldo Emerson wrote in his journals, "It is not enough to be busy; so are the ants. The question is: What are we busy about?" Do not confuse being busy—or efficient—with purpose, making an impact, or even being profitable. This leads us to another popular misconception: The *purpose* of a business is to make profits.

Purpose and/or Profits?

Profit is as necessary as the air we breathe. But it would be terrible if we were only in business to make money, just as it would be terrible if the only reason we lived was to breathe.

—Hermann Josef Abs, CEO of Deutsche Bank after World War II

Is there an inherent conflict between purpose and profits? It is fashionable today to believe there is, manifested in the stakeholder theory versus the shareholder theory of a company. The *stakeholder theory* insists that a firm be run not only for its owners—the shareholders— but also for its stakeholders: customers, employees, suppliers, the community, the environment. The *shareholder theory* insists a firm should be run in the best fiduciary interests of its owners in the form of profit maximization (not shareholder value, but profits). It is beyond our scope to dive into the nuances of these two theories; suffice to say I do not believe there is a conflict between living your purpose, earning profits, and serving your shareholders and stakeholders. It needs to be said we are speaking about profits ethically earned, otherwise companies could run meth labs and earn profits. Robert Bosch, founder of Bosch in Germany, said: "I don't pay good wages because I have a lot of money. Rather, I have a lot of money because I pay good wages." When a company is earning profits, its stakeholders, by definition, will also prosper. This is how free markets have lifted billions out of poverty in the short time span of approximately 250 years. Businesses that fail to earn a profit are, in effect, wasting societies' resources that could be utilized in more valuable ways.

Any business needs to earn a profit to survive. Peter Drucker repeatedly made the point that "profit is a condition of survival. It is the cost of the future, the cost of staying in business." Profit also simply means not suffering a loss. Beyond that, profit is a measurement of how much value an organization adds to the lives of others. This is why George Gilder labels profits "an index of a firm's altruism"—that is, how well it is serving the needs of others.

This is why I have always turned to economics and its definition of profit, rather than that of accountants, because economists use a different definition of profit from that of the typical financial statement. They consider both parties to the transaction because both parties must receive more value than each is giving up; otherwise no transaction would be consummated in the first place (assuming no fraud or coercion). US Representative Samuel Barrett Pettengill (1886–1974) gave an excellent definition of *profit* from an economist's perspective:

> The successful producer of an article sells it for more than it costs him to make, and that's his profit. But the customer buys it only because it's worth more to her than she pays for it, and that's her profit. No one can long make a profit producing anything unless the customer makes a profit using it.

A most articulate expression of the above definition came from Stanley Marcus (1905–2002), chairman emeritus of Neiman-Marcus, one of the ultimate authorities on excellence in customer service:

> You're not really in business to make a profit, but you're in business to render a service that is so good people are willing to pay a profit in recognition of what you're doing for them.

Figure 11.1 illustrates for every voluntary transaction that occurs, both the seller and the buyer earn a profit. The total value the seller creates over and above its costs is the economic value added to society. The price the seller charges is the portion of the total value created it captures, while the excess value over price accrues to the buyer. To the extent the seller can create more total value the price can more easily be increased to capture a fair share of that marginal value. In reality, there is no way for a seller to capture all of the economic value created—the buyer must also earn a profit.

How do economists know that the customer profits from a transaction? After all, we do not measure the customer's profit, either in our home or business accounting, nor our national accounting statistics

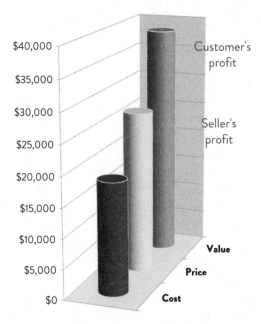

FIGURE 11.1   Value creation and capture.

(gross domestic product, national income, etc.). They know it nonetheless because transactions can only take place when the buyer and
seller *disagree* about value. I realize that sounds counterintuitive.

For example, if I am attempting to sell you my house, I will no doubt
think it has higher *value* than you do, but that won't prevent us from
reaching mutual agreement on an acceptable *price*. Prices are how people divide up value. Yet our accounting—both national and business—
ignores the customer's profit. Economists have tried to estimate the
customer profit—what they call the *consumer surplus*—across the
entire economy. Nobel Prize–winning economist William Nordhaus
famously found that entrepreneurs on the scale of Henry Ford, Steve
Jobs, Bill Gates, Jeff Bezos, and so on, capture approximately 2% of
the total value they create for customers and society (Boudreaux 2018).
Like dark matter in the universe, we can't measure this customer profit
precisely, but we know it is there and adds immeasurably to the world's
standard of living and eradication of poverty.

This is also why, in the real world, debits do not equal credits.
Exchanges don't take place on an equal basis but rather because

people have different perceptions of value. Generally accepted accounting principles (GAAP) were designed only to record historical transactions based on prices paid, not value received. This is why GAAP cannot account for value, and the book value of stock market companies only explains approximately 10% to 20% of their market capitalization. The difference is what accountants call goodwill—a word they use to label their ignorance with respect to value.

One other way economists know that trade is mutually beneficial: the double thank-you moment at the cash register. You hand over your money, the representative hands over the merchandise and you both say, "Thank you." Why is that? Because you are both benefiting—you are both made better off from the exchange. If this was not the case, would not one of you reply, "You're welcome"?

For a business to maximize profits, leaders should focus on the wealth-creating capacity of their organization. The more customers profit, the more the firm will prosper. Perhaps our time horizons are too short in how we measure the impact we are having on the lives of others. Maybe Edwind Land, co-founder of Polaroid, had it exactly right when he said, "The only thing that matters is the bottom line? What a presumptuous thing to say. The bottom line's in heaven."

STRATEGY: YOUR FIRM IS DEFINED BY WHAT YOU DON'T DO

Strategy is the rare and precious skill of staying one step ahead of the need to be efficient.

—Jules Goddard and Tony Eccles, *Uncommon Sense, Common Nonsense: Why Some Organizations Consistently Outperform Others*, 2012

One way to think about your firm's strategy is that it is the road less traveled. Harvard Business School professor Michael Porter, one of the leading thinkers on strategy, says, "The essence of strategy is choosing what not to do." Strategies develop from insights and learning, not planning. You are searching for an ethical, unfair advantage that leverages your firm's strengths in an unexpected way. The reason

I prefer the definition from Goddard is that it recognizes that effectiveness—doing the right thing—is often achieved by being inefficient. If you want to innovate, you need slack time. Innovation keeps you ahead of the curve, gives you pricing power, and increases the wealth-creating capacity you are able to offer your customers.

Strategy involves tradeoffs. You cannot be all things to all people. Imagine fast-food, steak, and vegan dishes all being sold in the same restaurant. Diversification, in a business model context, is what we do when we don't know what to do. The most profitable professional firms all share one characteristic: They are narrowly niched. Over time, firms tend to lose their focus. By chasing growth, or market share, they take on a variety of different customers requiring different services. This imposes a "complexity tax." It is based on a flawed business model that places growth above profit. In the Firm of the Past business model from Chapter 10, the bias is to grow the top line, especially once the break-even point has been reached, allowing marginal dollars to drift to the bottom line. Hence, the attitude of taking on all customers, never meeting a billable hour you didn't desire, and other deleterious effects.

To reiterate, growth for the sake of the growth is the ideology of the cancer cell, not a sustainable, flourishing firm. If your firm generates an acceptable profit, then growth can be a choice rather than an imperative. The focus should be on becoming better, not just bigger. Firms that are driven by market share growth tend to be competitor-focused (think Android), whereas firms focused on wealth creation and innovation tend to be customer-focused (think Apple). Peter Schutz, who led Porsche in the 1980s, liked to say that "The second Porsche on the same street is a catastrophe" (Simon 2015). (Our CPA colleague Dan Morris replies, "the fourth Porsche in your garage is a blessing.")

Consider the difference between a general physician and a specialist. Patients from around the world will flock to the Mayo Clinic in Rochester, Minnesota, to consult an oncologist who specializes in their type of cancer. We are going to search our Zip Code for a general physician (ideally, a DPC—see Chapter 9). Specialists work on more interesting customers, attract a much wider geographical customer base, have an easier time marketing, attracting the right talent, and commanding premium prices.

Peter Drucker proposed two questions to Jack Welch, who had just taken over as CEO of General Electric:

1. If you weren't already in a particular business, would you enter it today?
2. If the answer is no, what are you going to do about it?

These are useful questions to examine every few years to make sure your services and markets are not past their sell date. Pursuing tomorrow means casting off yesterday's winners at some point. Tim Williams, our VeraSage Institute colleague, taught me that a brand can only stand for one thing. Here's how he explains it in a blog post from his firm's newsletter, *Propulsion,* titled "Is Your Firm Competing with Itself?":

> As the iconic David Ogilvy observed decades ago, a brand is meant to stand for one thing. The strongest brands don't have a "multi-pronged strategy"—they have a laser-like focus that features a well-defined product or service targeted to a well-defined market. This applies not only to consumer-facing brands, but to professional service brands like yours.
>
> Contrast this fundamental aspect of brand strategy with the way most [professional firms] define themselves: "Full-service, serving a wide variety of clients." The problem is, a firm that works in many different businesses not only lacks deep expertise in any one of them, it is also obliged to devote talent and money in many dissimilar directions.

As G.K. Chesterton observed: "Why be something to everybody when you can be everything to somebody?" Your firm is defined by the customers you *don't* have and the services you *don't* offer. Hewlett-Packard has over 10,000 stock keeping units (SKUs) and Apple has less than 100, illustrating the power of intense focus. And if you are thinking narrow equates to small, think Starbucks.

One last point. Please do not fall into the trap of believing that technology is a strategy, or a differentiator, for your firm. It is clearly not, since it is widely available to all of your competitors. Too many firms have inserted technology between themselves and the customer, removing the human contact that is so crucial in professional firms. We are all for being efficient with things, just not people. We must be effective with all of our relationships. People crave the human touch. Technology cannot be sympathetic, compassionate, nor build lasting, meaningful relationships. It also cannot think. As Edsger Dijkstra, a pioneer in artificial intelligence, once remarked, asking whether a computer can think is a bit like asking "whether submarines can swim" (*The Economist* 2015, p. 21). You want your customers to have a deep emotional connection with your firm's brand, which is what the subscription economy is all about.

POSITIONING

In its simplest form, a compelling positioning strategy
lives at the intersection of these two crosshairs:
Be something. . .for someone

—Tim Williams, Ignition Consulting Group

The late Anthony Bourdain, along with a colleague, planned a garden party for his employer that was a smashing success. Afterward, the two printed up business cards for their new catering venture, Moonlight Menus. Bourdain tells the story in his book, *Kitchen Confidential*:

> We proceeded to hand these things out to local businessman, telling them blithely that not only did we not need, or even want their business, but they couldn't possibly afford us, as we were easily the most expensive and exclusive caterers on the entire Cape! Two highly trained specimens like us had more than enough business, thank you very much.
> . . .We knew well how much these people were paying for cocaine— and that the more coke cost, the more people wanted it. We applied the same marketing plan to our budding catering operation, along with a similar pricing structure, and business was suddenly very, very good. In no time, we were able to leave our regular jobs at the Dreadnaught and Mario's (Bourdain 2008).

He further discusses the differences between line cooking in a restaurant and running a catering operation:

> Line cooking—the real business of preparing the food you eat—is more about consistency, about mindless, unvarying repetition, the same series of tasks performed over and over and over again in exactly the same way. The last thing a chef wants in a line cook is an innovator,

> somebody with ideas of his own who is going to mess around with
> the chef's recipes and presentations. Chefs require blind, near-fanatical
> loyalty, a strong back and an automaton-like consistency of execution
> under battlefield conditions (Bourdain 2008).

Does this distinction sound familiar inside a professional firm? Are
your knowledge workers line cooks or caterers? We're not arguing
that you don't need both, but if you want innovation and creativity you
have to have some caterers. The line cook is a craftsmen, the caterer
more an artist. This story is also an excellent lesson in positioning
your value. The *framing effect* is the idea that people draw different
conclusions from equivalent information depending on how it is presented. For instance, saying 90% lean meat is better than saying 10%
fat. By framing their value as caterers, as opposed to chefs, Bourdain
and his colleague were able to command premium pricing for essentially the same offering. They were no longer being compared to restaurants, but to others who could create a memorable experience.

Positioning is the battle for the customer's mind. What do the following brands immediately make you think about: Volvo (safety);
FedEx (reliability); Apple (innovation); Disney (happiness);
Nordstrom (excellent service). Anthropologists agree that one of our
deepest habits is to copy others and fear of being too focused. This
might have served us well on the plains while hunting when we
needed situational awareness of the threats surrounding us, but it is a
suboptimal business strategy.

Examine the websites of professional firms and you will see the
same vocabulary used: Excellence, quality, partnership, professionalism, tailored solutions, leading provider, proven results, full service,
etc. But none of these communicate a positioning strategy. They are
more focused on how and what the firm does rather than the results
customers will receive. Customers do not purchase a wide range of
expertise but rather a specific kind of expertise.

Tim Williams posits a litmus test for your firm's language: Consider
what it would be like to claim the opposite:

Full service	Partial service
Excellence	Mediocrity
Professionalism	Unprofessional
Leading provider	Lagging provider
Proven results	Unproven results

You do not have to be better than your competition, just different. Better yet, be *remarkable*—that is, worth noticing or commenting on. One effective way is to communicate how your firm *thinks* differently, including the language you use. Tim also provides the following set of questions to answer to validate your positioning strategy:

1. Does it allow for clear identification of prospective customers?
2. Does it help us say no to the wrong prospects?
3. Does it help expand our geographical footprint?
4. Does it result in fewer competitors?
5. Does it allow us to charge higher prices?
6. Does it make our business development cycle shorter and less expensive?
7. Does it make it easier to attract the right talent?

Recall that a brand can only stand for one thing. You cannot sell Rolls Royces and Chevys out of the same dealership, which many firms attempt to do by serving all types of different customers at a wide-range of price points. Positioning strategy teaches that you should separate these two ventures into two different brands, with separate locations, marketing, etc. This is exactly what our VeraSage Institute colleague Dan Morris did when he created Express Tax.

As Dan was starting out, like many firms, he took on all customers. But as he began to mature, became more niched, more selective of whom he worked with, he realized they were devoting too much capacity to low-value customers, mostly relatively simple individual tax return customers. It's hard to sell a $50,000 engagement to a high-net-worth individual when he asks you, "Don't you do my brother-in-law's taxes for $500?" Rather than terminating these relationships, Dan set up a separate firm across the street, branding it Express Tax. It had a cheaper price point than the mother ship CPA firm, and was managed entirely by an enrolled agent. If any of its customers reached the point of needing a CPA, they would transition to the CPA firm.

Strategy and positioning are all about tradeoffs. Leadership is essential, and leadership demands tough decisions (the word *decision* comes from Latin *decidere*, meaning "to cut off"), and sometimes individual opinions have to be sacrificed for the good of the firm. Too many firms operating under the partnership model find it hard to introduce innovations because it requires consensus. If any one or two partners object, the entire initiative can be killed. This is another reason why professional firms have not abandoned the billable hour—the partnership model is simply not conducive to innovation. Margaret Thatcher, former prime minister of the United Kingdom, was fond of pointing out: "Consensus is the negation of leadership."

SUMMARY AND CONCLUSIONS

At the beginning of this chapter, we quoted Peter Drucker, who believed that the purpose of a business was to create a customer. We then discussed his Five Most Important Questions, which led us to purpose, strategy, and positioning. These three topics lay the foundation for your firm. Collectively, they will drive your marketing, branding, pricing, even the language you use to communicate and articulate your value.

Recall also that Drucker said, "Because its purpose is to create a customer, the business enterprise has two—and only these two— basic functions: Marketing and Innovation. Marketing and innovation produce results; all the rest are costs." These two functions represent his idea of the marketing concept, which, along with risk, we will turn to next.

12

MARKETING, INNOVATION, AND RISK

The very nature of creativity is that it always comes as a surprise to us. In a free economy, a high degree of apparent randomness does not mean actual randomness. An apparently random pattern is evidence not of purposelessness but of an entrepreneurial economy full of creative surprises.

—George Gilder, *Knowledge and Power*, 2013

Harrison "Buzz" Price was a consultant with Stanford Research Institute between 1951 and 1955. In 1953, he received an interesting assignment: Do a location and feasibility study for Disneyland, a new theme—not amusement—park idea from the legendary Walt Disney. He recounted how the highlight of that study was the amusement park annual convention and trade show in November 1953 at the Sherman Hotel in Chicago. Buzz and a group of Disney executives did a two-hour presentation of the idea of Disneyland to four of the nation's leading amusement park owners, while liberally pouring Chivas Regal and feeding them caviar. These were the leaders in the industry: William Schmitt, owner of River View Park in Chicago, Harry Batt of Pontchartrain Park in New Orleans, Ed Schott of Coney Island (in Cincinnati), and George Whitney, of Playland at the Beach in San Francisco. "The reaction was unanimous. **It would not work**" (Price 2004, p. 29, emphasis in original).

Keep in mind the adage that knowledge is about the past and entrepreneurship is about the future. The "experts" explained a litany of reasons why Walt's fantasy would not work, which is delightful to read with hindsight, since we know the ending:

- All the proven moneymakers are conspicuously missing, no roller coasters, no Ferris Wheel, no shoot-the-chute, no tunnel of love, no hot dog carts, no beer, and worst of all, no carny games like the baseball throw. Without barkers along the midway to sell the sideshows, the marks won't pay to go in. Customers are likely to leave with money left in their pockets.
- Overall, there isn't enough ride capacity to make a profit.
- Custom rides will never work. They will cost too much to buy and they will be constantly breaking down, resulting in reduced ride capacity and angry customers. Only stock, off-the-shelf rides are cheap enough and reliable enough to do the job. And besides, the public doesn't know the difference or care.
- Most of Mr. Disney's proposed park produces no revenue but it will be expensive to build and maintain. Things like the Castle and Pirate Ship are cute but they aren't rides, so there is no economic reason to build them.
- There is too much wasteful landscaping.
- Town Square is loaded with things that don't produce revenue, like the Town Hall, the Fire Department, and the Square itself.
- The horse cars, the horseless carriages, and western wagon rides will cost so much to run; they will lose money. They don't have enough capacity to make a profit.
- You can't operate an amusement park year around; 120 days is the only way to go.
- Walt's design has only one entrance. This will create a terrible bottleneck. Entrances should be on all sides for closer parking and easier access.
- The jungle cruise idea will never work because the animals will be sleeping and not visible most of the time.
- Walt's screwy ideas about cleanliness and great landscape maintenance are economic suicide. He will lose his shirt by over-spending on things the customers never really notice.

- Bottom line, Mr. Disney's park idea is too expensive to build and too expensive to operate. "Tell your boss to save his money," they said. "Tell him to stick to what he knows and leave the amusement business to people who know it" (Price 2004, pp. 30–31).

Thankfully, Walt ignored their advice while at the same time employing two of the doubters as consultants (George Whitney and Ed Schott). Physicist Richard Feynman use to say that "Science is the belief in the ignorance of experts." Entrepreneurs are people who constantly prove the experts wrong because imagination precedes knowledge. This is one of the limitations of logic—it kills off magic. People who worked for Walt recount how it was a career-limiting move to tell him one of his ideas wouldn't work, usually by saying, "No, because. . ." You were better off replying to Walt, "Yes, if. . ." This is an excellent framework for creativity and innovation.

Ward Kimball, one of Walt's "Nine Old Men" (animators), once said, "If you want to know the secret of Walt Disney's success, it's that he never tried to make money." He was more inspired by ideas, money was just the means to bring his ideas to fruition, as Walt himself explains:

> You reach a point where you don't work for money. . .. When I make a profit, I don't squander it or hide it away; I immediately plow it back into a fresh project. I have little respect for money as such; I regard it merely as a medium for financing new ideas. I neither wish nor intend to amass a personal fortune. Money—or, rather the lack of it to carry out my ideas—may worry me, but it does not excite me. Ideas excite me.
>
> I could never convince the financiers that Disneyland was feasible, because dreams offer too little collateral.

Another remarkable lesson from the story above was the contemptable attitude of the existing amusement park owners toward their customers, labeling them "marks," and suggesting they wouldn't notice the finer things such as landscaping, architecture, cleanliness, and all of the other innovations Walt designed into Disneyland. Advertising maven David Ogilvy's famous quip is very relevant here: "The consumer is not a moron, she is your wife." The right customers will recognize value and gladly pay for it.

Innovation and creativity always take us by surprise. When we think of innovation we tend to think of new products, such as the Apple iPhone or iPad. Yet innovation is not a single event, but a continuing process, and it can be far more expansive than merely a new product or service offering, or a new technology. Think holistically. Work back from the customer to the firm. Peter Drucker coined the term *marketing concept* in the early 1960s to teach that the purpose of any organization—from a governmental agency or nonprofit foundation, to a church or a corporation—exists to create results *outside* of itself. The result of a school is an educated student, as is a cured patient for a hospital, or a saved soul for a church. A business exists to create wealth for its customers.

The only thing that exists inside of a business are costs, activities, efforts, problems, mediocrity, friction, politics, crises, and a grapevine. In fact, Peter Drucker wrote, "One of the biggest mistakes I have made during my career was coining the term *profit center*, around 1945. I am thoroughly ashamed of it now, because inside a business there are no profit centers, just cost centers" (Drucker 2002, pp. 49, 84). The only profit center is a customer's check that does not bounce. Customers are indifferent to the internal workings of your firm in terms of costs, desired profit levels, efficiency of your systems, efforts, and hours. Nobody wants to hear about the labor pains—they want to see the baby.

What makes the marketing concept so breathtakingly brilliant is that the focus is always on the outside of the organization. It does not look inside and ask, "What do we want and need?" but rather it looks outside to the customer and asks, "What do you desire and value?" While the marketing concept has existed for decades, it is regularly ignored because professional firms lose sight of the fact that the sole reason they exist is to serve customers outside of their four walls. In the final analysis, a firm does not exist to be efficient, control costs, perform cost accounting, implement efficient processes, or give people fancy titles and power over the lives of others. It exists to create results and value *outside* of itself. This is why, like Walt Disney, your firm should be governed by ideas, not hierarchy.

Unfortunately, one often reads that professional firms—especially law and CPA firms—are *not* a business but rather a *profession*. This is no doubt true, but this makes the marketing concept even more salient. The term profession comes from the Latin noun *professio*, which is derived from the past participle *professus*. Professionals are said to "profess" something; they stand for something. They are responsible for creating a result.

For now, let us just point out that as a professional, it is much easier to focus on the technical aspects of what we do rather than the humans beings we serve. The best professionals, in any of the professions, are those who care deeply about their customers as fellow humans. David Maister makes this very point in his splendid book *True Professionalism*, which should be *required* reading for all professionals: "The opposite of the word *professional* is not *unprofessional*, but rather *technician*. Professionalism is predominantly an attitude, not a set of competencies. A real professional is a technician who cares" (Maister 1997, p. 16).

In any event, innovation can be manifested in new business models—such as Concierge and direct primary care (DPC) physicians; pricing strategies, meaning not just *how much* but *how* you present your pricing—offering options, anchoring, the psychology of price, and more; reframing your value; enhancing the customer experience by building in frictionless touchpoints, convenience, and peace-of-mind; and the language you use with customers to articulate your value. These are part of the two basic functions of any business, marketing and innovation.

PLUSSING AND REFRAMING YOUR VALUE

Walt was famous for constantly *plussing* the park, adding touches that would enhance the guest experience. This is a vital component of the subscription business model—you cannot simply go-to-market with your existing offering. You have to *plus* it, offer a higher value experience.

This can be done by reframing your firm's value, much like Walt did by replacing the "amusement park" with a "theme park," which moved it significantly up the value curve, allowing Disney to command much higher prices. We are seeing this across industries. Ponder certified pre-owned (CPO) cars, which easily sell for between $500 to a few thousand dollars extra, all due to the *framing effect*, pre-inspection, and a limited warranty. Evian Natural Spring Water (11.2 ounces) retails for about $1.25 per bottle (11¢ per ounce). Evian

Facial Spray sells for $10.00 per 10-ounce bottle, or $1.00 per ounce. Different purpose—skin hydration—higher value, increased price.

In February 2005, Amazon launched Amazon Prime, offering unlimited two-day delivery, plus other benefits, for $79 per year. This was a new way to frame the value of doing business with Amazon, illustrated by this simple, unequal formula: $7 \times 1 \neq 1 \times 7$. Before Prime, customers had to bundle, say, seven items, to exceed a certain order threshold to receive free shipping. After Prime, a subscriber could simply order one item seven times, or seven different items one time, and not have to worry about shipping costs on any of them. Which one is more likely to serve customers better, and to compound and grow? This is why the simple formula is actually not equal—one is psychologically different. As Jeff Bezos explained about Prime: "I want to draw a moat around our best customers. . . and change the psychology of people not looking at the pennies differences between buying on Amazon versus buying somewhere else." Amazon Prime is now in roughly 51% of US households, where members spend an average of $2,486 per year compared to $544 for non-Prime members.

Rory Sutherland, vice chairman, Ogilvy in the UK, told an amusing story during his Google Zeitgeist talk. Speaking of the train between London and Paris, Eurostar, the value proposition was framed by engineers solely in terms of duration. If you could reduce the time for the trip, people would pay a premium. The problem is, it was quite expensive to build. As Rory points out in his book *Alchemy*, "Making a train journey 20% faster might cost hundreds of millions, but making it 20% more enjoyable may cost almost nothing." He satirically suggested that you could take 10% of the Eurostar budget, invest in male and female supermodels to serve Chateau Pétrus during the journey, and customers would ask for the trains to *slow down*. An excellent example of reframing value.

One of the most advantageous aspects of the subscription business model, combined with the DPC physician framework, is how it reframes your value as a firm. How is a prospective customer going to compare your value proposition with that of a fee-for-service competitor when you are offering significantly more value in the form of transformations, ensurance, peace-of-mind, convenience, even services they do not yet know they will need? This separates you from the competition, which can only be achieved by being willing to innovate and take the risks necessary to gain competitive advantage.

There is no such thing as a free competitive advantage, which leads us to another perilous philosophy.

THERE IS NO SUCH THING AS A COMMODITY

There is no such thing as a commodity. All goods and services are differentiable.

—Theodore Levitt, *Harvard Business Review,*
January-February 1980

During the days of Prohibition, 25 of Chicago's top bootleggers were rounded up in a surprise raid. During their arraignment, the judge asked the usual questions, including the occupation of each suspect. The first 24 were all engaged in the same activity. Each claimed he was an accountant. "And who are you?" the judge asked the last prisoner. "Your honor, I'm a bootlegger," he said. Surprised, the judge laughed and asked, "How's business?" "It would be a lot better," he answered, "if there weren't so many accountants around."

G.K. Chesterton once wrote, "Competition is a furious plagiarism." One of the most discouraging questions asked of those who preach innovation and differentiation is, "Who else is doing this?" Only the truly excellent companies get to answer, "No one." Name the grocer that stocks no brand merchandise, has no sales, accepts no coupons, does no advertising, and has no loyalty program? No one—except for Trader Joe's, which has the highest sales per square foot of any grocer. Which car brand has no dealers, never discounts its cars, and accepts only online orders? Not one—except for Tesla, which continues to creatively destruct the major automotive companies. Its remarkable Model S "slapped Detroit sober," as Elon Musk's biographer Ashlee Vance wrote.

Transforming your firm should not depend on other firms transforming theirs. The goal of being on the bleeding edge is to *differentiate*, not *duplicate*. To be *distinctive*. If firm leaders had to wait for someone else to be first, we would still be in caves rubbing rocks together. With respect to your firm, customers should be able to say, "When you've seen one professional firm, you've seen one professional firm." Study top performing firms and you will notice these characteristics: continuous innovation, risk-taking, experimentation, putting the customer and her experience first, and high prices.

Many leaders push back on the idea that they can charge higher prices, since a lot of services are "commodities." For instance, the tax return, or accounting and other compliance services, are *grudge purchases* because customers only buy them to stay out of jail. But this is empirically false. Economists refer to *negative goods* to describe products or services we really do not enjoy buying but do so because we have to. The list would include gasoline, insurance, aspirin, prescription drugs, and so on. Do you buy the cheapest of these categories because it is a "grudge" purchase? My guess is you don't, as most people even have branded aspirin, not generic, even though aspirin is aspirin according to the Food and Drug Administration.

The fact of the matter is there is *no such thing as a commodity. Anything* can be differentiated, which is precisely the marketer's job. Believing your firm—and the services it offers—is a commodity is a self-fulfilling prophecy. If *you* think you are a commodity, so will your customers. How could they believe otherwise? This notion of selling a commodity is one of the most pernicious beliefs, which leads to price wars; incessant copying of competitor's offerings; and lack of innovation, creativity, and dynamism, not to mention suboptimal pricing strategies.

Consider candles, an industry literally in decline for the past 300 years. Yet Blyth Industries custom tailors its candles for the specific location, companion, and occasion. Blyth commands premium prices as a result.

Jim Stengal, former global marketing officer of Procter & Gamble, is even more vigorous about the commodity trap, which he calls a cop-out:

> I hate it when someone says they're in a commodity category. We don't accept that there are any commodity categories. We are growing Charmin and Bounty very well and if there is any category that people could say is a commodity, it's paper towels and tissues. We have developed tremendous equities, tremendous loyalties from our consumers. So, no, I think that is a cop-out. That is bad marketing and an excuse. We are not in any commodity categories (Colvin 2007).

If toilet paper and paper towels can be differentiated and command premium prices, what is the professions' excuse? If only professional firm leaders had more imagination and vision, then maybe they would not suffer from the commodity trap thinking that drives down their prices. Instead of innovating, most firms seem content with gazing at each other's navels and copying each other, such as with benchmarking.

THE PERILS OF BENCHMARKING

The best swordsman in the world doesn't need to fear the second-best swordsman in the world. No, the person for him to be afraid of is some ignorant antagonist who has never had a sword in his hand before; he doesn't do the thing he ought to do, and so the expert isn't prepared for him; he does the thing he ought not to do, and often it catches the expert out and ends him on the spot.

—Mark Twain (1835–1910), *A Connecticut Yankee in King Arthur's Court*, 1899

Another cause of the commodity trap is ruthless imitation on the part of companies, cloaked in the names of benchmarking and best practices. Rather than investing in research and development and experimenting with innovation, a lot of firms are spending precious executive attention trying to figure out where they are relative to the competition by studying financial indicators and other forms of competitive intelligence.

While no doubt useful for some applications, benchmarking is not a way to build a strategic advantage. By definition, best practices are *past* practices. You are simply copying others, not leading. It is as if entire industries are bathing in the same bathwater, rather than looking for ways to change the rules of the game. Pouring over lagging indicators such as financial ratios—revenue per person, net income percentages, labor as a percentage of revenue, etc.—rarely spurs innovation and dynamism within an industry.

The major problem with benchmarking studies and best practice reports is that one is studying the *results* of a process, but not the process itself. They tend to confuse cause and effect. Financial averages can be devastatingly misleading without understanding the underlying causes of the results one is observing. Furthermore, there is a *selection bias* in the data being analyzed; rarely is it a truly random sample or a statistically significant sample size.

Avoid benchmarking your competitors—why benchmark mediocrity? Truly effective benchmarking usually takes place outside of one's industry, such as when Henry Ford was inspired to create the assembly line from a visit to a slaughterhouse where he observed the overhead trolley system. What was standard in one industry became a revolution in another—old ideas in new places.

Purging the Commodity Word

Unless your firm decides to compete based on price—such as Walmart, Costco, H&R Block, and Southwest Airlines—you cannot create a loyal customer based solely on being the low-cost provider. If customers are attracted by your low price, they will easily leave for another firm that offers an even lower one. Cutting your price to attract a customer rewards customers to constantly ask for future price concessions, thereby subsidizing your worst customers at the expense of your best ones.

Entrepreneur Richard Branson challenges his people to answer the following question before entering a new industry: "Tell me 10 things you never hear about this industry." They then go about thinking about the industry in a different way, creating a better customer experience.

In any event, there is absolutely no excuse—none—for firms to think of themselves as commodities. Any company can compete on price; it is truly a fool's game. On the other hand, competing based on excellent customer experience and transformations requires more thought, creativity, and investment. The commodity trap is a self-fulfilling prophecy, breeding cynicism and stifling creativity, dynamism, and innovation.

If your firm finds itself continually competing on price, it is taking the easy way out—since lowering price is always the easiest way to make marginal sales. It is also the apparent factor to place blame on for an organization's lack of remarkable service and providing a memorable experience. Constant price discounts signal you are targeting the wrong customer segments, or not developing a viable value proposition and positioning strategy that separates you from the competition. Do not allow your firm to acquire a core competency in cutting prices by falling into the commodity trap. Another concept that can help avoid the commodity trap is to understand the indispensable importance of risk.

WHERE DO PROFITS COME FROM?

Twenty years from now you will be more disappointed by the
things you didn't do than by the ones you did. So throw off the
bowlines. Sail away from the safe harbor. Catch the trade
winds in your sails. Explore. Dream. Discover.

—Apocryphally attributed to Mark Twain [author unknown]

In seminars around the world, we have presented to participants the following factors of production in any economy, and the type of income derived therefrom:

Land = Rents

Labor = Salaries and wages

Capital = Interest, dividends, and capital gains

We then ask a deceptively simple question: Where do profits come from? The answers range from entrepreneurs and value, to revenue minus expenses, and customers. Nevertheless, the real answer is that profits come from *risk*. The word *entrepreneur* comes from the French word *entreprendre*, meaning "to undertake." It is the basis for the English word *enterprise*. But not just entrepreneurs (or feminine, entrepreneuses) make profits; so do established enterprises.

When a business engages in innovation, it is taking a risk. In Italian, the word *risk* derives from *risicare*, which means "to dare," which implies a choice, not a fate, as Peter L. Bernstein points out in his outstanding study of risk, *Against the Odds*. In other words, risk is an economic positive. There are five responses when confronted with risk: avoid it, reduce it, transfer it, accept it, or increase it. In the final analysis, a business cannot eliminate risk, as that would eliminate profits. The goal is to take calculated risks and choose them wisely. The dilemma in many firms is that they are allocating a disproportionate share of their resources in perpetuating yesterday and today rather than creating tomorrow. By setting a nice comfortable floor on their earnings (via the cost-plus, hourly billing pricing mechanism), they have placed an artificial ceiling over their heads as well. This is self-imposed, and it comes from the attempt to avoid risk and uncertainty (which is very costly in terms of lost opportunities). It is playing not to lose, rather than to win.

Consider labor unions, the epitome of an institution attempting to avoid risk. Talk with union members and you quickly discover they credit the union for their standard of living. Certainly, they are paid an above-market wage (Milton Friedman has proved this point), and receive good benefits, a healthy pension, and generous time off. But have you ever met a wealthy rank-and-file union member? The trade-off made for the union compensation package is an artificial ceiling that blue-collar workers can never rise above, at least not based on their union job, since seniority and other stultifying restrictions limit their potential. Risk avoidance is the antithesis to a successful enterprise, condemning it to mediocrity, perhaps even extinction. The goal should be to maximize wealth-creating opportunities rather than to minimize risk.

Businesses have very sophisticated means of measuring the costs and benefits of risks, *once they have been taken*. But the risk occurs only *before* the event, and cannot be accurately measured until *after* it has occurred. There is no theory—in economics or finance—that measures the cost of *not* taking a risk. Yet, it is precisely these losses that cost the business the most.

For customers, risk and uncertainty are the twin banes of existence. Consider what people will sacrifice to avoid them. Risk avoidance has created a multi-trillion-dollar worldwide insurance industry. It is why rental car companies make more from the collision damage waiver insurance they sell then they do renting cars. It is why buyers of appliances (e.g., microwaves, computers, and other electronic goods) will spend large sums on extended warranties for products that could be replaced more cheaply.

Peter Drucker classified risk into three categories: the affordable, the nonaffordable, and the compulsory:

> First, there was the risk a business could afford to take. If it succeeded at the innovation, it would not achieve major results, and if it failed, it would not do great corporate damage. Second, there was the risk a business could not afford to take. This risk usually involved an innovation that the company lacked the knowledge to implement, and usually would end up building the competition's business. Third, there was the risk a business could not afford not to take. Failure to undertake this innovation meant there might not be a business several years hence. (quoted in Flaherty 1999, p. 172)

Naturally, in this book, the third type of risk taking is being advocated, that is, taking those risks that will spur the firm to higher levels of effectiveness and profitability. Too often in firms, risk taking is seen as a negative, a reckless use of resources better spent on other functions. Nothing could be further from the truth. Firm leaders should not prevent risks from being undertaken. In fact, they need to make sure their colleagues feel safe in taking them, even if it results in failure, which is an inevitable consequence of trying something new. Profits are derived from risk; complacency is not an option.

INNOVATING THE LANGUAGE

The structure of language determines not only thought but reality itself.

—Noam Chomsky

In *The Kingdom of Speech,* Tom Wolfe wrote, "Speech is not one of man's several unique attributes—speech is the attribute of all attributes. Speech is 95% plus of what lifts man above animal!" Words mean things—language matters, especially in shaping a culture. Werner Erhard said, "All transformation is linguistic. If we want to change our culture, we need to change our conversation." Throughout this book, we use the words *customer, price, invoice, and team member* (or *colleague*) in lieu of, respectively, *client, fee, bill, and staff* (except when quoting from other sources). We do this because we believe these words convey better images and evoke more positive emotions of what they are attempting to describe.

For example, according to my dictionary, "among the ancient Romans a *client* was a citizen who placed himself under the protection of a patrician, who was called his patron; a master who had freed his slave, and retained some rights over him after his emancipation; a dependent; one under the protection or patronage of another." Are these the type of images we want to invoke? The welfare state has *clients*, while businesses have *customers*. A *fee* is negatively associated with a tax or some other charge, while *price* is a benign term most customers easily comprehend, eliciting no positive or negative emotions. *Value billing* is not used because billing takes place in arrears, after the work has been done, whereas pricing takes place up front, before the work is begun.

One major problem with our current lexicon of business is how it is drawn largely from war and sports analogies. In sports, a competition is usually zero-sum, meaning one competitor wins and the other loses. This is not at all relevant in a business setting. Just because your competitors flourish does not mean you lose. There is room for both Airbus and Boeing, Pepsi and Coke, and while their sparring might be mistaken as some war, as John Kay points out "not in Pepsi's wildest fantasies does it imagine that the conflict will end in the second burning of Atlanta [the location of Coca-Cola's head office]" (Kay 1995, p. 73). When Coca-Cola changed its recipe to New Coke, company spokesman Carlton Curtis stated, "You're talking about having some guts—and doing something that few managements would have the guts to do." If you find it amusing that grown men talk about *guts* and *recipes* in the same sentence, then it should be obvious business has nothing to do with war.

Business is not about annihilating your competition; it is about adding more value to your customers. Indeed, the competition is really about who gets to serve the customer, not battling each other. War destroys, commerce builds. Marketplaces are conversations, derived from the word for the Greek marketplace, the *agora*. It is where buyers and sellers meet to discuss their wares, share visions of the future, where supply and demand intersect with an invisible handshake. It is as far removed from war as capitalism is from communism, and perhaps these war analogies, too, need to be tossed onto the ash heap of history.

Contemplate the careful choice of language Walt Disney used for Disneyland, essentially creating a new patois for theme parks. It does not have "rides," it has "adventures, experiences, attractions, or stories." Customers are called "Guests," while team members are called "Cast Members"; jobs are referred to as "roles"; crowds were replaced with "audience"; the entire park is "the show," and so on.

In the spirit of impacting your firm's culture, Table 12.1 illustrates the vocabulary changes that we believe assist in the transition from hourly billing to subscription, or from value pricing to subscription. It is not meant to be an exhaustive list, but to spur further discussion and ideas around the importance of language.

TABLE 12.1   Innovating the Language

Hourly Billing	Value Pricing	Subscription
Training	Education	Customer success
Fee/billing/ hourly rate	Price the customer	Price the relationship and the portfolio
Discount/ write-offs	Preferred price	Special trial period
Client	Customer	Member
Revenue/Billings	Reoccuring revenue (not as predictable, or valuable, as annual recurring revenue) (see Chapter 21)/Profit	Lifetime customer value and annual recurring revenue
Change order	Change request	Covered/Not covered
Services	Results/Outcomes	Access/Transformations as a Service (TaaS)
Inputs	Outputs—Fixed price agreements	Outcomes, transformations
Staff	Team members	Colleagues
Efficiency	Effectiveness	Efficaciousness/Ensurance
Time capacity	Adaptive capacity	Emotional capacity
Needs/Wants	Value conversation	Transformation conversation
Utilization/ Realization	Profit	Accountability/Customer lifetime value

We believe this vocabulary list is more effective in communicating your value while also convincing your customers of that value. Let us now move to the top of the hierarchy of value and discuss customer transformations—one of the foundational attributes of the subscription economy in professional firms.

13

CUSTOMER TRANSFORMATIONS

With transformations, the customer IS the product!

—B. Joseph Pine II and James H. Gilmore,
*The Experience Economy: Competing for
Customer Time, Attention, and Money*, 2019

Imagine you are in the market for a landscaper for your relatively small front and back yards. Being prudent, you research online, find some highly recommended companies, and contact three of them for bids.

The first arrives and walks around your front and back yard with a clipboard. We all know what he is doing—scoping the work. How big is the lawn, how many trees, bushes, etc. He concludes by telling you he will handle the yard's maintenance at $80 per hour. Of course, that raises more questions than it answers: How long will it take? Will it vary every week, depending on who you have do the work? and so on. He is pricing based on *inputs*.

The second landscaper arrives and performs the same ritual. He informs you that he will do the work for a fixed price of $120 per month. This is better than the first company because it provides certainty in price and does not raise any of those useless questions such as how long it will take. He is pricing based on *outputs*—a specific scope of work. If something happens outside of that scope—a tree dies, a sprinkler head needs replacing, etc.—you will most likely go through a change request process and be charged an additional amount, agreed to in advance of the work.

Then the third landscaper arrives. He begins by asking you questions:

- Tell me a little about what you do.
- I got the impression from our phone conversation that you're not exactly Martha Stewart. Do you enjoy yard work?
- May I ask why you want to terminate your existing landscaper?
- Have you received notifications from your Home Owners Association for various violations with respect to landscaping?
- Do you have plans to sell the house? If yes, what's your timeline?

He concludes by offering you three options: The "basic maintenance" package at $150 per month. The "bring your yard up to neighborhood standards" package at $225 per month. The highest level, "The best curb side appeal in the neighborhood," is $350 per month. Since your timeline to sell the house is two to three years, he will gradually upgrade your landscaping. You always have the flexibility to slide down to a lower priced package. He is pricing based on *outcomes*—a specific transformation, *for each of the three packages.*

Assume you were currently paying $120 per month for a landscaper that was meeting your basic expectations, which landscaper would you select? Most people answer the third, since the expectation is to sell the house. Selecting the top package will drive a higher sales price.

Which landscaper communicated a higher value? Which one reframed their value from yard work to a specific return on investment? Which one provided three transformative options, at a fixed price, with all-inclusive packages providing frictionless service? Which one is nearly *three times higher* than you are paying now? Which one has you focused on the transformation rather than the price? The moral of the story: Which one will you be happier with? After you sell, I would venture to guess that you will maintain this landscaper and possibly slide down to a cheaper option. This illustrates the power of combining transformations with the frictionless subscription model. Landscapers provide recurring value; so do professionals, with a major distinction: Professionals can provide serial transformations across the life cycle of our customers—businesses or individuals— that will have an enduring, lasting impact on their lives and legacy.

THE HIGHEST LEVEL OF VALUE

Recall from Chapter 10 we introduced the hierarchy of value, posited by B. Joseph Pine II and James H. Gilmore, in their book *The Experience Economy: Work Is Theatre and Every Business a Stage*. The heuristic—mental short cutout—they used at the end of each level was, "How do you de-commoditize [the previous level]?," which led them up to the next offering:

- If you charge for *stuff*, then you are in the *commodity* business.
- If you charge for *tangible things*, then you are in the *goods* business.
- If you charge for *the activities you execute*, then you are in the *service* business.
- If you charge for *the time customers spend with you*, then you are in the *experience* business.
- If you charge for the *demonstrated outcome the customer achieves*, then and only then are you in the *transformation* business (Pine and Gilmore 1999, p. 194).

What is interesting about this proposed hierarchy is not only where professional firms are on it, but where their greatest potential is on the curve. Most firms would think of themselves as service providers, offering intangibles to their customers, and no doubt this is true. Certainly, we are mired in a "fee-for-service" mentality, monetizing transactions over relationships. Very few professional firms view themselves as being in the experience business, let alone the transformation business. Visiting a professional firm is not often thought of as an enjoyable experience, and is certainly not equated with visiting Las Vegas or a Disney theme park.

It is interesting to speculate how firms could be in the experience business. This does not mean to charge for the time—as in billable hours—the customer spends with you, but rather charge for the experience you create for the customer. As crazy as it may seem, how about this idea: Charge an admission price to enter your firm.

This is not as uncommon as you might think. Wineries in the Napa Valley charge for tasting. You can apply this thinking to a *minimum* price for all new customers. What is going to be included in your firm's standard offering to entice a customer to pay a minimum price to do business with you, one that is two to three times what your strongest competitor charges? It is an interesting thought experiment and one worth thinking about seriously. Only uncommon offerings command uncommon prices.

In any case, the main point to make is professional firms are already poised at the top of the value curve, since they are already offering their customers transformations, even though they may not think of themselves as doing so, nor does the language they use articulate this compelling idea. To prove this, let us see how Pine and Gilmore define *transformation*:

> While commodities are fungible, goods tangible, services intangible, and experiences memorable, transformations are *effectual*. All other economic offerings have no lasting consequence beyond their consumption. Even the memories of an experience fade over time. But buyers of transformations seek to be guided toward some specific aim or purpose, and transformations must elicit that intended effect. That's why we call such buyers *aspirants*—they aspire to be some one or some *thing* different. With transformations, *the customer is the product!* The individual buyer of the transformation essentially says, "Change me." So transformations cannot be *extracted*, *made*, *delivered*, or even *staged*; they can only be *guided*. Being in the transformation business means charging for the demonstrated outcome the aspirant achieves— the transformation itself—not for the particular activities the company performs. (Pine and Gilmore 1999, pp. 171–172, 177, 192)

Think of the difference between a fitness center, one that charges for membership, versus personal trainers. The latter earn more because they take personal responsibility for the *outcome* of their customer's fitness regimen. And because they take responsibility for the demonstrated outcome the customer achieves, they are more selective about whom they accept as customers, as well as more diligent in performing an up-front analysis of each customer's expectations and willingness to change. This is a critical analysis, because if the customer is not willing to follow the trainer's advice, his or her attempt at transforming the customer is bound to fail. The same is true for direct primary care (DPC) physicians versus fee-for-service doctors—the former focus on maintaining health and the latter focus on curing illnesses after the fact.

Today's sophisticated customers are demanding more from their professionals than merely providing services and a good experience;

they want transformations, and they will hold the professional accountable for guiding the journey.

Professionals, such as accountants, financial planners, attorneys, and advertising agencies, already effectuate many transformations for their customers. For example, they can help their customers become millionaires, retire at a specific age, finance a child's education, grow and enhance the value of a business and brand, and carry out a customer's last wishes through estate and gift planning. These are inherently personal transformations, guiding individuals into their preferred vision of the future—guiding them from where they are to where they want to be, helping them flourish from womb to tomb and beyond, rendering your customers healthy, wealthy, and wise.

There is no similarity between this offering and a commodity or even a bundle of intangible services. You are literally touching your customer's soul, forging a unique relationship with them virtually impervious to outside competition and commanding prices commensurate with the value of the results you are creating. Consider the emblems people possess to commemorate the transformations they have achieved: Rings, crosses, diplomas, medals, and so forth. As Pine and Gilmore point out: "No one can force someone to change. All transformations occur within the very being of the customer." And these transformations have to be sustained through time. So many firms engage in "one-and-done" services that seldom effectuate a transformation—they are delivering services, not serving. This is why DPC physicians have a larger impact on their patients; they are practicing integrative medicine, not just treating diseases but looking after their patient's emotional and spiritual needs as well.

What is so compelling about transformations is how they activate people's potential. You are longer confined to thinking that you are solving problems, though professionals will continue to do that quite diligently. This is at a higher level than mere problem solving. As Peter Drucker states in his book, *The Effective Executive*: "It is more productive to convert an opportunity into results than to solve a problem, which only restores the equilibrium of yesterday." Solving problems ends up fueling your failures, starving your strengths, and achieving a costly mediocrity—you end up propping up the past at the expense of investing in tomorrow. Focusing on capacities is far more valuable than curing deficiencies. The traditional *inadequacy marketing* that businesses have used delivers the message that the customer lacks something that can only be fixed with a product or service. With transformations, *the customer is the hero.*

As the Greek philosopher Heraclitus wrote, "No man ever steps in the same river twice, for it's not the same river and he's not the same man." Because professionals have the ability to provide serial transformations throughout the life of the customer—assuming they want to change— there is no other comparable offering that communicates higher value.

This explains why *services insure*, meaning to secure payment in the event of a loss; *experiences assure*, securing confidence, encouragement, trust, or feeling of satisfaction; while *transformations ensure*, to secure an event, situation, or outcome. This ensurance creates substantial value on behalf of your customers, which can be priced into your offerings—think of it as a luxury good. How you go about guiding these serial transformations?

THE ATTENTION ECONOMY

All companies have customers. Lucky companies have fans.
But the most fortunate companies have audiences.

—Jason Fried and David Hansson, *Rework*, 2010

The *attention economy* was identified by Nobel Laureate economist Herbert A. Simon. He hypothesized that attention was the "bottleneck of human thought," and also that "a wealth of information creates a poverty of attention." Information is not scarce; attention is, and money follows attention. This is why it is better to have audiences than customers. With customers you have to pay to get their attention whereas audiences happily give you their time and attention.

While professional firms track the time their professionals spend working on behalf of customers, what they should be tracking instead is the time their customers willingly spend with them, along with how much time the firm is saving the customer. Are your customers increasing or decreasing the amount of time they spend interacting with your firm? Perhaps audience member is too aspirational of a goal to seek, though we are not sure why not. Think of the people you willingly give your attention to on a regular basis, be they radio, television, podcast hosts, or comedians, actors, etc. How is that relationship psychologically different than others that you have?

Guiding customer transformations requires thorough diagnosis, implementation, adjustment, and follow-through, preferably utilizing an after-action review (AAR) (discussed in Chapter 20). It requires the posing of questions, and a significant investment of time from both sides. Relationships require constant nourishment, as they are either getting stronger or weaker over time. Yet our present business model rewards volume over value and depth of lifetime relationships.

The present model also rewards providing answers to technical questions, but rarely motivates posing better questions. Former long-shoreman and self-educated philosopher Eric Hoffer wrote in *Reflections on the Human Condition*, "Language was invented to ask questions. Answers may be given by grunts and gestures, but questions must be spoken. Humanness came of age when man asked the first question. Social stagnation results not from a lack of answers but from the absence of the impulse to ask questions." We would say that "value" stagnation results from the absence of asking questions, taking the time to thoroughly understand the answers, and following up with a plan to guide the customer to their preferred future. Merely providing services is no longer enough.

Conducting quarterly (or monthly, or more frequently if required) business reviews can point out new transformational opportunities. You have to pick a cadence that makes sense for your type of practice, be it individuals, businesses, and not-for-profits. The importance of these review meetings cannot be overemphasized. This is what separates traditional firms, focused more on compliance volume, from subscription-based firms dedicated to guiding transformations.

Today we hear how data about customers is the new oil. But insight, and wisdom, is what refines that oil to turn it into something valuable. That requires a substantial investment in the relationship with each customer to truly understand their business, which is what a lot of firms say that they do—"we want to be our customer's trusted advisor," and so on. But what does that mean, and is it enough?

TRUSTED ADVISOR IS A TABLE STAKE

Phrases such as *trusted advisor* have become common in firms' mission and value statements. In fact, many believe that trust is a *core competency* and a *competitive differentiator* of the profession. I disagree.

There is no doubting the importance of trust in business relationships. Accounting itself owes it origins to this very issue, since, from
the late fifteenth century on, firms that were originally based on kin-
ship and family ties grew to a size that made it imperative to hire
outsiders. In addition, as personal finances became further separated
from business finances, double-entry bookkeeping was a necessity
for the principals of an enterprise to watch over the agents they hire.

In any economy, a high level of trust acts as a lubricant to commerce,
reducing the need for lengthy negotiations, protracted contracts, and
costly litigation, or what economists refer to as *transaction costs*. Nobel
Prize–winning economist Kenneth Arrow explains the function of trust:

> Now trust has a very important pragmatic value, if nothing else. It is ex-
> tremely efficient; it saves a lot of trouble to have a fair degree of reliance
> on other people's word. Unfortunately this is not a commodity that can be
> bought very easily. If you have to buy it, you already have some doubts
> about what you've bought. Trust and similar values, loyalty or truth-
> telling, are examples of what the economist would call "externalities."
> They are goods, they are commodities; they have real, practical, economic
> value; they increase the efficiency of the system, enable you to produce
> more goods or more of whatever values you hold in high esteem. But they
> are not commodities for which trade on the open market is technically
> possible or even meaningful. (quoted in Fukuyama 1995, pp. 151–52)

With high levels of trust, commerce is more fluid and transaction
costs can practically be lowered to zero. You can't purchase trust; it is
a table stake in a free market economy, and not just for professionals,
but for *all* businesses. All transactions require trust; it is a basic expectation when conducting business. It certainly *is not* a core competency
or competitive differentiator because it is not an attribute you can do
better—or at lower cost—than your competitor. Trust is complex and,
obviously, there are different levels of trust, as it is a contextual concept. It is one thing to purchase prescription medication from a phar-
macist without having to count the number of pills, and quite another
to trust a babysitter with your child. But it is a mistake for any firm to
advertise or market its trustworthiness; it is frankly something that
must be demonstrated and earned. Merely having trusting relationships with your customers does not ensure they will remain loyal.

I fly quite extensively on United Airlines; I trust them with my *life*,
which certainly requires a higher degree of certainty and confidence in
a complete group of strangers than in selecting my accountant or

lawyer. In the airlines, safety is simply a *table stake*—it is necessary, since it is hard to sell anything to a corpse—but it doesn't ensure customer loyalty, or even profitability. If United's service ever begins to decline, I will defect. We witness the same response among customers of professional service providers. Moreover, no airline would advertise: "Fly with us, we won't kill you." The majority of transactions that take place in the worldwide economy are done under an umbrella of trust. Professionals are among the most trusted advisors. So what? This is a subtle point, but an important one. The profession—or any firm therein—does itself no favors by continuously trumpeting its level of trust. Like your technical quality, it is merely a *table stake*, absolutely necessary but not sufficient to develop customer loyalty. Those who talk about it, injure it, and are perceived less believable. *Trusted advisor* is a term your customers use to describe you.

Joey Havens is the managing partner at Horne LLP, a top 100 accounting firm. He wrote a thought-provoking and blunt 2016 LinkedIn post titled "What If I Really Am a Trusted Advisor?" He discusses the common gap between how firms define themselves and what customers actually experience. If we are truly "trusted advisors," he provides a litmus test that I am paraphrasing:

> List your top five customers, and write down their strategic goals. What do the customers see as their biggest challenge or risk? Write down the date when you proactively had a meeting to discuss these issues. (Havens 2016)

Not many firms would be able to thoroughly answer these questions. Mark Gandy, host of the podcast *CFO Bookshelf*, and author of *Becoming a Part-Time CFO: 30 Questions in 30 Days Before Making a Decision*, has an even more severe litmus test of whether you are a trusted, strategic advisor. Here is how he defines a part-time CFO:

> A CFO is a professional who can step into the role of the CEO for one entire year without sales, profits or the value of the business dropping. More than likely, one or all three of those measures will increase under your watch.

That is a high bar to set with your customers, but is there any doubt that meeting this aspirational goal would make you invaluable to your customers? How many customers is it possible for you to act in this capacity? I am not arguing that you would need to fulfill this role, but

I do believe that you need to know what the strategic issues are for each of your business customers beyond the accounting.

O'Byrne & Kennedy (OBK) is a chartered accounting firm outside of London, and our VeraSage colleagues. Tragically, Paul O'Byrne passed away far too soon in November 2008, but his legacy lives on through the work of his partner, Paul Kennedy, and the firm they founded. On April 20, 2017, our colleague Ric Payne published a blog post, "A Day in the Office with Paul Kennedy: How One Firm Transitioned from Compliance to Advisory," wherein he describes Paul Kennedy's philosophy of working with customers. As Ric writes:

> The Perceived Value Curve diagram below explains the rationale that underlies Paul's strategy.
>
> Compliance services will take a defined period of time (up to point A on the graph) which will vary in length for different clients but for any given client the length of time does not increase the perceived value to the client and may even reduce it. The relatively low and flat perceived value characteristic associated with compliance is the reason Paul is very happy NOT to do this work at all. In fact he mentioned in passing "we like to start where other firms finish."

THE PERCEIVED VALUE CURVE

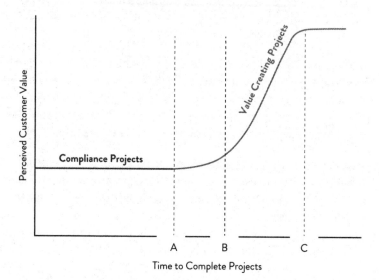

Source: Payne 2017.

Think of those "value creating projects" as transformations, then you will begin to see how powerful this framework is for providing recurring, frictionless value. We are not suggesting that compliance has no value, or that it will disappear anytime soon (I have heard that since I entered the CPA profession in 1984). What we are saying is that guiding transformations is the most valuable work you can do, and you cannot devote adequate time, emotional capacity, and the energy it requires if your volume of compliance work is too high. Think of compliance work as adding a complexity tax to your firm, costs that are better invested higher up the value curve.

SUMMARY AND CONCLUSIONS

B. Joseph Pine and James Gilmore originally proposed their hierarchy of value in 1999. Nearly a quarter century later, it is as relevant today as it was then. It is the embodiment of the landscaper's "best curbside appeal" as told at the beginning of this chapter. Every customer has a desired future state, usually for both their business and personal life. Professionals can guide them to that destination, and that is the apotheosis of value that you can create as a professional.

Think about how much harder it would be for a typical product or service company to move up the hierarchy of value. Take Starbucks. It moved coffee up to the experience level by providing a "third place"—between home and work—where one could relax, enjoy fine coffee, read a book, chat with friends. Today, it has created a new chain, Starbucks Reserve, which founder Howard Schultz envisioned would be the "Willy Wonka of Coffee." It has allowed Starbucks to increase the price, but it is still an experience, subject to the same "been there done that" competitive pressure as other experiences.

Why are Google and Amazon opening brick and mortar stores? It is to get back to those customer relationships. Yet, they are tied to tangible offerings, which make it far harder to move up to the top of the value curve. Tire companies, such as Bridgestone and Michelin, are beginning to offer tires as a subscription. Combined with the Internet of Things, IOT-enabled sensors in the tires can alert users when they need air, repair, or changing, all done with the convenience of the customer at the center. It removes the albatross of ownership, optimizes tire life, improves safety, fuel efficiency, and so on. This is moving up the curve from selling products to wrapping services around them, and even, to some extent, providing a better experience.

The point is, a lot of companies simply don't have the flexibility, or the capability, of moving up to transformations. Professionals firms do, providing myriad opportunities to provide innovative value.

You may be wondering, as I did after studying the hierarchy of value: What is beyond transformations? I asked Joseph Pine this very question when we interviewed him on *The Soul of Enterprise* (The Soul of Enterprise 2015), and he also answered it in the most recent edition of *The Experience Economy*:

> "What's next after transformations?" There can be no greater differentiation than a transformed person or company; no one can commoditize the most important aspect of a transformation: the unique relationship formed between the guided and the guide. It is the tie that binds.
>
> The only offering that can displace a transformation is yet another transformation—one aimed at another dimension of self, or at the same dimension but from a different worldview.
>
> Like every other economic offering, transformations will be scrutinized, lionized, and criticized—but not commoditized. Still, they must be customized to remain differentiated.
>
> What would the ultimate customer-as-product be? The utmost would be perfection, the perfect human being. According to our own worldview, there can be no sixth economic offering because perfecting people falls not in the domain of human business but under the province of God, only as an atoning act of God. And so, we contend, transformations are the fifth and final offering. (Pine and Gilmore 2019)

Elevating transformations into your language and marketing communications will position your firm as providing unique value, focused on outcomes, not merely transactions. Combined with the subscription characteristics of ensurance, peace of mind, frictionless touchpoints, and convenience, you will be able to create higher subjective value and hence command premium pricing. But first, let us discuss the practicalities of value and price, the subject of our next chapter.

14

TWO TIMELESS TRUTHS AND TWO THEORIES

*In the final analysis, I find nothing as intellectually satisfying
as the history of ideas. . . . (W)ithout the history of economics,
economic theories just drop from the sky; you have to take
them on faith. The moment you wish to judge a theory, you
have to ask how they came to be produced in the first place
and that is a question that can only be answered by the
history of ideas.*

—Mark Blaug, *Not Only an Economist*, 1997

Before he died, a father said to his son, "Here is a watch that your
grandfather gave me. It is almost 200 years old. Before I give it to
you, go to the jewelry store downtown. Tell them that I want to sell it,
and see how much they offer you."

The son went to the jewelry story, came back to his father, and
said, "They offered $150 because it's so old."

The father said, "Go to the pawn shop."

The son went to the pawn shop, came back to his father, and said,
"The pawn shop offered $10 because it looks so worn."

The father asked his son to go to the museum and show them
the watch.

He went to the museum, came back, and said to his father, "The
curator offered $500,000 for this very rare piece to be included in
their precious antique collections."

The father said, "I wanted to let you know that the right place values you in the right way. Don't find yourself in the wrong place and get angry if you are not valued. Those that know your value are those who appreciate you; don't stay in a place where nobody sees your value" (Author unknown).

There are two timeless truths embedded in the above story. The challenge is, to learn them, you have to be guided by the proper theory. "No theory, no learning," as W. Edwards Deming used to say. Let me explain the two truths, and then provide a tale of two theories.

FIRST, ALL VALUE IS SUBJECTIVE. SECOND, ALL PRICES ARE CONTEXTUAL.

You can think of these as *the first and second law of marketing*. They are universal, with enormous ramifications for how companies establish and present pricing. These truths exist no matter what your firm's business model. They are true under hourly billing, value pricing, as much as the subscription model, and whatever comes next. They are timeless because they are rooted in human nature and long, empirical evidence.

THE TALE OF TWO THEORIES

Why are diamonds more expensive than water? None of us would be able to live beyond a couple of weeks without water, yet its price is relatively cheap compared to the frivolous diamond, which certainly no one needs to stay alive. This conundrum led to some incredible discoveries, advancing our understanding of value.

Most people confronted with this paradox would resolve it by replying the supply of diamonds is sparse compared to water, and hence they command a higher price. This is an intuitive and very reasonable solution, since diamonds are found in only a limited number of places in the world, and the supply is even further restricted by diamond cartels.

Yet the scarcity theory lacks explanatory power. If it was true, we could sign your copy of this book in pink crayon, then create a non-fungible token (NFT) to authenticate this is the only one signed in this way. It is a Picasso, one of a kind—scarce. How much is it worth?

Just because something is scarce does not make it valuable. There must be a better theory that solves this puzzle.

The Labor Theory of Value

Throughout history, man has always correlated labor with value, inputs with outputs. In medieval English, the word *acre* meant the amount of land a team of eight oxen could plow in a morning. Along comes Karl Marx and his labor theory of value, which still wields enormous influence over our present-day concept of value and price. Here is how Marx explained his theory in *Value, Price and Profit*, originally published in 1865: "A commodity has *a value*, because it is a *crystallisation of social labour*. The *greatness* of its value, or its *relative* value, depends on the greater or less amount of that social substance contained in it; that is to say, on the relative mass of labour necessary for its production" (Marx 1995, p. 31).

This, too, sounds quite reasonable, until you put this theory to the test of explaining how people spend their money in the marketplace.

Marx's theory cannot explain how land and natural resources have value, since there is no labor contained in them. Taken to its extreme, the labor theory of value would predict those countries with the most labor hours—such as China or India—would have the highest standards of living. But this is demonstrably false, and what we witness instead in countries with *less* labor inputs and more entrepreneurship—as well as secure private property and other institutions conducive to economic growth—are vastly higher standards of living, including shorter hours for workers.

If Marx's theory was correct, a rock found next to a diamond in a mine would be of equal value, since each took the same amount of labor hours to locate and extract. Yet how many rocks do you see in the local mall's jewelry store? If you were to have pizza for lunch today, under Marx's theory, your tenth slice would be just as valuable as your first, since each took the same amount of labor hours to produce. One glaring flaw in Marx's theory was that it did not take into account the law of diminishing marginal utility, which states the value to the customer declines with additional consumption of the good in question.

The Marginalist Revolution of 1871

There are particular epochs that occur throughout history, when an assembly of people construct the events that cause a substantial advancement for human society. One such era was 1871–1874, when three economists ushered in the "neoclassical" marginalist revolution and solved the diamond-water paradox that so beleaguered the classical economists, and was the undoing of Marxian economics.

Three economists, from three different countries, developed the theory of marginalism and created a revolution, which took approximately 20 years to become generally accepted theory: William Stanley Jevons (1835–1882), from Great Britain; Leon Walras (1834–1910) from France; and Carl Menger (1840–1921) from Austria. "Swedish economist Knut Wicksell, who lived through the marginalist revolution, described it as a "bolt from the blue" (Skousen 2001, p. 169).

Value is like beauty—it is in the eye of the beholder. This was a refutation of the Marxian labor theory of value. This subjective theory of value has enormous explanatory and predictive capabilities, because it explains, for instance, why people dive for pearls. Marx would say pearls have value because people dive for them (thus supplying labor). The Marginalist economists would retort that people dive for pearls *because* other people value them.

Philip Wicksteed, a British clergyman, wrote the first scientific critique of the Marxian labor theory of value in 1884, where he explained:

> A coat is not worth eight times as much as a hat to the community because it takes eight times as long to make it . . . . The community is willing to devote eight times as long to the making of a coat because it will be worth eight times as much to it. (quoted in Howey 1989, p. 157)

Yet there are endless examples of this confusion, especially in professional firms that indoctrinate their professionals to believe that value resides in billable hours. But there is no guarantee of consumer acceptance just because costs were incurred; the high rate of product and business failures is a testament to this fact. In the long run, a product or service will *continue* to be produced only if people value it enough to pay a price that can *justify* its full costs of production.

Why Are Diamonds More Expensive Than Water?

Besides being abundant, water tends to be priced based on the marginal satisfaction of the last gallon consumed. The German economist Hermann Heinrich Gossen (1810–1858) developed what is known as *Gossen's law*: The market price is always determined by what the last unit of a product is worth to people.

While the first several gallons of water may be vital for your survival, the water used to shower, flush the toilet, and wash the dishes is less valuable. Less valuable still is the water used to wash your dog, your car, and hose down your driveway. The market price of water reflects the last uses of the good for the aggregate of all consumers of water. On the other hand, the marginal satisfaction of one more diamond tends to be very high.

If water companies knew you were dehydrated in the desert, they would be able to charge a higher price for those first vital gallons consumed, and then gradually adjust the price downward to reflect the less valuable marginal gallons. Since they do not possess this information—the cost of doing so would be prohibitive—the aggregate market price for water tends to be based on its *marginal* value.

As a consumer, if I'm dehydrated in the desert, near death, a bottle of Evian water is *priceless* (nearly *infinite value*), compared to the same quantity of water used to wash my dishes or dog. If my basement is flooded with water, now it has a *negative* value to me, since I will have to pay someone to remove it. Like prices, value is not only subjective, it is contextual.

To argue that you can measure value in hours is to claim the value of Jonas Salk's polio vaccine is based on how long it took him to develop it. The same logic applies to timesheets; it is a futile and superfluous measure in professional firms.

Now that we are equipped with the correct, subjective theory of value, we can lay out some axioms of value:

- Value is subjective.
- Value is indivisible.
- A transaction can only take place when the buyer and seller *disagree* about value.
- Value is a *feeling*, not a number.

- "Price is a story. It is not an absolute number."—Seth Godin
- Prices are contextual—there is no such thing as absolute value.
- Time ≠ Value; Time ≠ Cost; Time = Constraint.
- There is no such thing as "value billing." Billing is done in arrears; pricing is always done upfront (with one exception, which we will discuss in Chapter 17, the TIP Clause).

We have already discussed many of the above axioms, but others need further explanation. What does it mean to say value is indivisible? Think of a four-star Michelin restaurant. The chefs command a higher wage than the janitor. But what about seen through the eyes of the customer? There is no way to divide the value between the chefs and the janitor, since eating delicious food in a environment that smells like a sewer is not a valuable experience. Notice, we are focusing on value from the customer's perspective, not cost or price, which are determined by the restaurant.

Value and price are separate items in a subtractive relationship, that is, value equals benefits – price. Value is not proportional, which is the flaw in thinking that value equals benefits divided by price. An eight-cylinder engine is not 33% more valuable than a six-cylinder engine (8 – 6/6 = 33%). An eight-cylinder engine might provide much more value, if you are towing another vehicle, live in a mountainous region, etc.

If value is a feeling, there is no way to quantify it. This is why customer profit is not included in national income accounts, but makes up a large part of our wealth as a society. Value is emotional; your body physically reacts when you experience superior value, such as the feeling of a perfect meal matched with the perfect wine. It is the difference between eating and dining. When superior value is created between a seller and buyer, they are in sync, with opportunity to grow.

Unlike value, price is a number, but it is much more than that as well. It is a story about your firm. Think of the price of a Porsche, or an Apple product—much of the value is told through that price. You wouldn't trust either of those products sold at a steep discount.

There is no such thing as absolute value, which means that context is critical for comparing pricing. If I asked you, "Would you like to buy my unicorn," you would have no idea how much to pay, since you have never purchased one. This is why offering pricing choices is so important. Restauranters know the same menu items can command drastically different prices depending on how it is named and described. As advertising legend Rory Sutherland says: "A flower is simply a weed with an advertising budget."

We also need to stop thinking about time as somehow equated to value, or even cost. It's not. Time is a constraint. You cannot sell it, store it, hoard it, trade it, or buy more of it. All businesses—indeed, all living things—are constrained by time. Your business model should not be.

If one were to lay the two theories of value—labor and subjective—side by side, it would look like this (adapted from Nagle and Holden 2002, p. 4):

Cost-Plus Pricing—Labor Theory of Value

Services » Cost » Price » Value » Customer

Value Pricing—Subjective Theory of Value

Customer » Value » Price » Cost » Services

Notice how value pricing turns the order of cost-plus pricing inside-out, by starting with the ultimate and sole arbiter of value—the customer. Services do not magically become more valuable as they move through the firm and have hours allocated to them. The *costs do not determine the price*, let alone the value. It is precisely the opposite, as the marginalist economists pointed out; that is, the *price determines the costs* that can be profitably invested in to deliver a service desirable for the customer, at an acceptable profit for the seller. This subtle reordering of the value/service chain has a dramatic impact on value, price, and profit.

Being restricted by the final price at the outset focuses the firm like a laser beam on incurring only those costs that will add value to the customer. What separates this method from cost-led pricing is *when* costs are considered. As Henry Ford said, "No one knows what a cost ought to be." It is *planned* costs, not *past* costs, that are critical since all pricing decisions deal with the future. As Nagle and Holden point out: "The job of financial management is not to insist that prices recover costs. It is to insist that costs are incurred only to make products that can be priced profitably given their value to customers" (Nagle and Holden 2002, p. 4).

There is a long history of firms that became obsessively focused on minimizing costs at the expense of providing a service of value to the customer. The fact of the matter is you can make a pizza so cheap no one is willing to eat it. The obsession with cost-cutting can be counterproductive to fulfilling the real mission of any business: to create wealth for the customer.

Firms that use price-led costing will soon realize that perceptions of value can often be raised in the minds of customers. Cost is not the starting point for price; it is the final stage in the process. The importance of this can be seen in company's expanding into developing and poorer countries. For example, when Procter & Gamble expands into a poor country, it begins with the question, "How much can a consumer reasonably be expected to pay?" It then works backward through its supply-chain, keeping its overall costs below that price. It does no good to know your costs to the penny if the customer does not agree with, or cannot afford, your offering.

Wisdom Is Timeless

If you follow the price-led costing strategy, what would your firm have to do differently in terms of creating value, setting prices, and planning costs than it does now? History is a good teacher. Even Henry Ford understood price-led costing—long before it was diagrammed, as in the above illustration—recognizing no cost is truly fixed and that value drives price. While price may be taught in business schools as the last of the four Ps of marketing (Product, Place, Promotion, and Price), Ford knew value had to be understood first. Oscar Wilde's famous quip about "a man who knows the price of everything and the value of nothing," was his definition of a cynic, not a businessman—and certainly not Henry Ford.

With respect to the pricing revolution taking place in businesses around the world, Ford's understanding of this topic was truly prescient, as demonstrated in his autobiography, *My Life and Work*, published in 1922. It is worth quoting at length for the historical lessons it teaches since putting the customer first is just as relevant to the professional firm of today as it was in Ford's day. The idea that cost determines price was not foreign to Ford, but here is how he refutes this thinking:

> If the prices of goods are above the incomes of the people, then get the prices down to the incomes. Ordinarily, business is conceived as

starting with a manufacturing process and ending with a consumer. If that consumer does not want to buy what the manufacturer has to sell him and has not the money to buy it, then the manufacturer blames the consumer and says that business is bad, and thus, hitching the cart before the horse, he goes on his way lamenting. Isn't that nonsense? But what business ever started with the manufacturer and ended with the consumer? Where does the money to make the wheels go round come from? From the consumer, of course. And success in manufacturer is based solely upon an ability to serve that consumer to his liking. (Ford 1922, pp. 135–36)

Keep in mind that Ford's primary objective was the mass consumption of the automobile, so he focused more on driving the price down to increase volume. In a growing industry, this is a viable strategy. In mature markets in which professional firms are more likely to be operating, it is more strategic to increase value, thus allowing higher prices.

Another aspect to notice is that, in the final analysis, all costs are actually prices, subject to the same subjective value considerations as all other goods and services. Businesses do not always buy the cheapest inputs, especially human capital, but rather, those that provide the most value to achieve their objectives.

Ben & Jerry Learn the Subjective Theory of Value

The history of business is the history of epiphanies, and sometimes the fog clears up and the right path is seen. This certainly happened—with respect to pricing—for Ben Cohen and Jerry Greenfield, founders of Ben & Jerry's ice cream. In an essay written in 1997—before they sold the business on August 3, 2000, to Unilever, the British-Dutch food company—"Bagels, Ice Cream, or . . . Pizza?," they explain what they term was their "famous pricing epiphany":

> We were working our hearts out for the first two or three years, and every year we just barely broke even. The first year we were thrilled to break even. We'd made our overhead; we could see the light at the end of the tunnel.
>
> Then the next year came and we'd just broken even again, even though our sales had grown by $50,000. This went on for three years . . . . One day we were talking to Ben's dad, who was an accountant. He

said, "Since you're gonna make such a high-quality product, instead of pumping it full of air, why don't you raise your prices?"

At the time we were charging fifty-two cents a cone. Coming out of the sixties, our reason for going into business was that ours was going to be "ice cream for the people." It was going to be great quality products for everybody—not some elitist treat.

Ben said, "But, Dad, the reason we're not making money is because we're not doing the job right. We're overscooping. We're wasting ice cream. Our labor costs are too high—we're not doing a good job of scheduling our employees. We're not running our business efficiently. Why should the customer have to pay for our mistakes? That's why everything costs twice as much as it should."

And Mr. Cohen said, "You guys have to understand—that's human. That's as good as people do. You can't price for doing everything exactly right. Raise your prices."

Eventually we said, either we're going to raise our prices or we're going to go out of business. And then where will the people's ice cream be? They'll have to get their ice cream from somebody else. So we raised the prices. And we stayed in business. (Krass 1999, pp. 462–63)

Excellent advice from an accountant. Physician, heal thyself.

SUMMARY AND CONCLUSIONS

Why does cost-plus pricing remain so endemic in the professions today? One explanation is that professionals perpetuate this pricing method because it is *safe* and *simplistic*. Sometimes a theory is accepted because it serves a purpose, not because it is right or wrong. It *satisfices*, to use a term coined by Herbert A. Simon—the combination of satisfy and sufficient. It is not optimal, but it is good enough, so do not let the best be the enemy of the good. There's a funny meme circulating that reads: "Ehh, good enough," with a bust of a Greek-looking philosopher, signed "Mediocrates." Yet business practices do not progress in this fashion; seniority and sufficiency do not define how markets work.

Now that we have examined the timeless truths with respect to value, price, and cost, it is time to turn our attention to the aspects of pricing that *do change* in the subscription economy.

15

PRICING THE RELATIONSHIP

A man had better overvalue than undervalue himself. Mankind
in general will take his own word for his own merit. . . .
[K]now your own value, whatever it may be, and act upon that
principle; but take great care to let nobody discover that you
do know your own value. Whatever real merit you have, other
people will discover, and people always magnify their own
discoveries, as they lessen those of others.

—Lord Chesterfield

Nelson Mandela said, "There is nothing like returning to a place that remains unchanged to find the ways in which you yourself have altered." Ever since we began discussing the subscription economy the number one question we received was, "How does this differ from value pricing's rule that you price the customer, not the product or service?" As we further researched this area we began playfully referring to Value Pricing 1.0—as taught in our book, *The Firm of the Future*, and my later work, *Implementing Value Pricing*—and Value Pricing 2.0, the subscription model.

There are many foundational theories and principles that are still the same, as we explored in Chapter 14. The subjective theory of value is still true, as well the fact that price *justifies* costs incurred, not that costs *determine* price. Pivoting to a subscription business model entails the same changes as any other business model change: Different pricing, and a different dashboard, that is, the key performance indicators that we monitor (the latter will be discussed in Chapters 18–20). Also, the profit formula is different, moving from transactional and gross margin calculations to relational customer lifetime value.

We continue to receive a lot of pushback to the idea that in a subscription business you are pricing the *relationship*, not the *customer*. People thought we were just playing with semantics, but the difference is significant. We have heard these criticisms:

- There is no more optimal pricing strategy than pricing the customer.
- It is difficult to implement with existing customers.
- Small firms do not have the resources to scale with this model.
- Attracting new customers is a sales and marketing challenge.

These are all understandable objections, and I had them myself. The dog barks at what he doesn't understand. Yet all of these challenges continue to exist, no matter which business model you deploy.

We have not given up on our quest to help professional firms create and capture more value for the customers they are privileged to serve. Everything we have written and taught is an attempt to help firms increase the value they create while concomitantly increasing their pricing power. It is why we work with sellers, not buyers. It is why we recommend the skim pricing strategy (see below), deploying enlightened strategy and positioning approaches, niching, providing transformations, changing your language, and so on. These were all ways of creating and reframing value in the minds of customers.

But business models change, and we cannot be oblivious to the market signals and empirical evidence that exists. The subscription model reframes the value once again, and we believe in a more customer-centric direction. The market values annual recurring revenue more than transactional revenue—what is known as reoccurring revenue—because it is more predictable, while being based on higher customer loyalty. The advantages of the subscription model over transactional models are:

- Predictable revenue and cash flow—you start on the 50-yard line every day, not the end zone.
- Focus is more on marketing and innovation than selling mere services.
- Get paid automatically, with less financing and collection costs.
- Customer switching costs are higher.

- You are not selling services but creating annuities with a life-time value that far exceeds whatever you paid to acquire them.

- Collective knowledge of your customers is a competitive advantage that cannot be duplicated by your competition.

- Allows for one-to-one marketing, creating bespoke transformations for customers.

- You are pricing the relationship (lifetime value), transformations, peace of mind, frictionless access, and ensurance (see Chapter 13).

- By focusing on outcomes, you are living and working in alignment with what it means to be a professional (taking responsibility for a *result*, not performing a series of tasks).

- It aligns the revenue model with what professionals say they care about: the relationship (not the transactions).

- You can plan cash flow and capacity more effectively.

- Moving beyond merely solving problems for your customers and into helping them achieve possibilities and potential.

- The subscription model breaks down silos in firms because it molds the firm around the needs of the customer—the customer is at the center, creating a true "one-firm" model.

- It takes an actuarial approach to pricing, recognizing the objective is to maximize profit across the portfolio of customers, not each hour, job, or customer.

- Subscription businesses are more resilient to recessions (and pandemics, as we learned during COVID-19).

Let us now examine the other elements that go into crafting your firm's pricing strategy and revenue model.

SEARCH, EXPERIENCE, AND CREDENCE ATTRIBUTES

From a marketing perspective, products and services can be separated into three classes: search products, experience products, and credence products. Search products or services have attributes customers can readily evaluate before they purchase. A hotel room price, an airline schedule, television reception, and the quality of a home entertainment system can all be evaluated before a purchase is made. Well-informed buyers are aware of the substitutes that exist for these types of products and thus are likely to be more price sensitive than other buyers, unless there exists some brand reputation or customer loyalty.

Experience products or services can be evaluated only after purchase, such as dinner in a new restaurant, a concert or theater performance, a new movie, or a hairstyle. The customer cannot pass judgment on value until after he or she has experienced the service. These types of products tend to be more differentiated than search products, and buyers tend to be less price sensitive, especially if it is their first purchase of said product. However, since they will form an opinion after the experience, if it is not favorable, no amount of differentiation will bring them back. Brand and reputation play an important role in experience products, due to consistency of quality and loyalty. For instance, when customers travel, so does reputation, as with airlines, hotels, rental cars, and so on.

Credence products or services have attributes buyers cannot confidently evaluate, even after one or more purchases. Thus, buyers tend to rely on the reputation of the brand name, testimonials from someone they know or respect, service quality, customer experience, and price. Cheaper credence products do not inspire trust in potential customers. Credence products and services would include health care; legal, accounting, and other professional services; baldness cures; and pension, financial, and funeral services. Credence services are more likely than other types to be customized, making them difficult to compare to other offerings. Because there are fewer substitutes to a customized service, and there is more risk in purchasing these types of services, price sensitivity tends to be relatively low—the majority of customers purchasing credence services are relatively price insensitive compared to search or credence goods. Keep this category in mind as you review the following macro pricing strategies. Professional firms almost always are credence services, unless you are just performing the most routine, repeatable, and predictable tasks at volume.

UNDERSTANDING CUSTOMER RISK

Any purchase entails risk. Services are relatively more risky than products, especially credence services discussed above. This is one reason why there is greater loyalty to service providers than product manufacturers, though the subscription model is changing this dynamic since the relationship is now at the center of the business. The six types of customer risk follow:

Performance risk is the chance the service provided will not perform or provide the benefit for which it was purchased.

Financial risk is the amount of monetary loss incurred by the customer if the service fails. Purchasing services involves a higher degree of financial risk than the purchasing of goods because fewer service firms have money-back-guarantees.

Time loss risk refers to the amount of time lost by the customer due to the failure of the service.

Opportunity risk refers to the risk involved when customers must choose one service over another.

Psychological and social risk is the chance that the purchase of a service will not fit the individual's self-concept. Closely related to psychological risk is social risk, which refers to the probability a service will not meet with approval from others who are significant to the customer making the purchase. Services with high visibility will tend to be high in social risk. Restaurants and hair stylists are examples of service industries that are perceived to have a high level of social risk. Even for business-to-business marketing, social risk is a factor. Corporate buyers are concerned that a service they purchase will meet with approval of their superiors. Thus, IBM's famous slogan: "No one ever got fired for choosing IBM."

Physical risk is the chance a service will actually cause physical harm to the consumer (Kurtz and Clow 1998, pp. 41–42).

It must be emphasized that the above risks are *perceived*, not necessarily *actual*, risks, and the perception is in the mind of the customer. The actual probability of service failure is immaterial. Usually, all things being equal, the service provider that offers the lowest perceived risk will be chosen. FedEx's guarantee of "Absolutely. Positively. Overnight." was a strong factor that led to—and maintains—its dominant share of the overnight delivery market at a premium price. This guarantee was especially important when FedEx began since no one knew whether it could actually deliver on its promise.

Customer Risk in the Subscription Model

Deciding whether to subscribe to a professional firm is a consequential decision for customers. Yes, it is reversible, but you would prefer to get it right and be able to have a loyal relationship over the long term. It reduces transaction costs for the buyer and makes life easier.

Subscribing requires an explicit act to enter into, and to exit. To stop paying for the service, you must "cancel." Psychologically, this is a different relationship. Consultant Robbie Kellman Baxter calls it a "forever transaction," and it "happens when a customer starts behaving like a *member*, is committed to your organization, and stops looking at alternatives."

The sooner you establish trust, the easier it will be to get customers to subscribe. In the value pricing model, you would offer price certainty, a value guarantee, a change request policy for any work that was not initially agreed upon, unlimited phone calls and meetings, payment terms structured around the customer's cash flow cycle, not the firm's work flow, and so forth.

In the Subscription Model, the Customer Can Cancel at Any Time

You must make it as easy as possible to do so, as counterintuitive as that sounds. This is not about locking the customer into a long-term contract. It is more about having faith in the value you are providing that will keep the customer a loyal member. There is enough empirical evidence to show that when customers know it is easy to cancel their subscription, they are less likely to do so. It builds trust. You might still utilize a value guarantee for one-off engagements, discussed below. Essentially, the subscription model is a built-in guarantee to the customer, who is provided the option to cancel at any time.

Customers should also be given the choice to select a different option or pause, whenever they want. During the COVID-19 pandemic, having subscribers allowed firms to get out in front of the crisis. They provided their customers the option to pause payments for a period of time, or to make other changes that more fit their financial circumstances. This created even more loyalty to the firm.

Cancellation is another scary topic, one that creates a lot of push-back to this model. But losing customers is going to happen no matter which business model you operate under. The evidence so far is that professional firms that use subscriptions have approximately the same amount of loyalty, if not more, than transactional-based firms. Professional firms already have higher rates of loyalty than the average business, due to the credence nature discussed above of their offerings. Value pricing further strengthens customer loyalty. The subscription model raises the bar even higher because it forces you to place the customer's needs and relationship at the center of the firm, while monetizing the relationship and transformations, not transactions.

One way to prove this assertion is with the audit function. There was a debate for many years whether the value guarantee impaired the independence of CPA firms who perform audits. The AICPA finally ruled that it does not. However, the subscription model remains untested in terms of impairing independence, and the people at the AICPA who I have spoken with tell me that it *would* impair the independence of an audit firm.

I do not agree with this conclusion, but it is as of yet unsettled. I believe what really impairs auditor independence is that they are paid by the very companies they are auditing. But no one wants to discuss that issue, or they retort, "No, the audit committee selects the auditors, and therefore they are independent." This is simply not true, unless the audit committee is spending its own money on the auditors. You simply cannot be paid to be independent.

Fixing this issue has long been discussed by economists and think tanks, but the profession is not very interested in debating the topic or looking for alternatives to the status quo. The idea that the stock market exchanges should be the ones to select and pay the auditors for its listed companies makes the most sense to me, as well as insurance companies offering financial statement insurance. Neither is a perfect solution, but either would be an improvement over what we have today.

In any event, if the subscription model does impair independence, then ask yourself, why? Because it creates a more loyal relationship with the customer, exactly what all firms say they want. To us, this is not a bug, it is a feature of the superiority of this business model. The revenue model is finally aligned with what we say is the most important, which is the relationship with the customer.

MACRO PRICING STRATEGIES

It is easy to overcomplicate pricing. At the macro level, there are only three pricing strategies. There are only two rules you need to follow. The first is, you must decide on a strategy. It may seem obvious, but many firms do not have a specific pricing strategy, which is a mistake. The second rule is you must be prepared to change your strategy if your market dynamics change. Pricing is not fixed in stone; it is an iterative process.

Think of Wal-Mart, Southwest Airlines, Costco, H&R Block, or Timex watches. All of these companies have used price as an effective competitive differentiation and have relentlessly driven out needless costs from their operations, passing the savings on to its customers. On the opposite side of the spectrum there is Apple, BMW, Bose, Disney, FedEx, and Nordstrom, all of which command premium prices because they offer premium quality and exceptional customer experiences. In the middle are companies such as Seiko and Casio watches, UPS, Sony, and Toyota, where price plays a more neutral role.

Selecting one of these three positions is a major strategic marketing decision, not to be taken lightly, and must be adopted by the leaders of the organization because it will create an acoustic message in the marketplace regarding the firm. The price a firm puts on its offering is a distinct story you tell to potential customers of what the value of the relationship is, and this narrative usually dwarfs any advertising, marketing, and promotion the firm executes.

Many companies make the serious mistake of underpricing a new product or service under the assumption it is necessary to induce customers to try the new offering. *Underpricing is far more prevalent than pricing too high.* Far too many firms assume they need to offer a lower price than the competition to establish themselves. This results in attracting low-value customers, which the firms usually regret in the long run.

The different prices reflected in these three strategies are not defined by the firm's price relative to that of competitor's similar offerings, but rather a strategy to drive revenue, or in the case of subscriptions, to drive customer lifetime value. The price in each of these strategies is actually defined relative to the value of the service *being offered by the firm itself*. Here are the three strategies to choose from.

SKIM PRICING

In any market, there is a certain segment of buyers who are relatively price insensitive because they value the offering so highly. Think of early adopters in the technology industry who rush to purchase the latest and greatest gadgets.

Skim pricing is a conscious decision to sell to this segment at premium prices more commensurate with value, thereby earning more profit than could be made selling at a lower price to an albeit wider market. The firm is not so much interested in market share as it is in extracting more of the perceived value from this smaller segment of the market. *A profit-maximizing price is almost always higher than a revenue-maximizing price.* A price that optimizes customer lifetime value most likely falls in between, though it needs to be constantly tested.

When Howard Moran launched MD^2®, the concierge medical practice discussed in Chapter 9, it used a skim pricing strategy. Some of the direct primary care physicians that emerged afterward used a more neutral—and some even a penetration—pricing strategy to expand medical care to lower-income populations. In a healthy, dynamic marketplace, there is always a wide range of value/price points. For example, hotels, restaurants, and automobiles all cater to particular types of customers, from frugal to frivolous.

None of the above is meant to imply there are not disadvantages with a skim price strategy. As with all pricing decisions, there are no absolute solutions, only tradeoffs, and these must be considered strategically, depending on the objectives the firm is trying to achieve in the long run. Some disadvantages of a skim price follow:

- It will not induce customers to try the service as much as a neutral or penetration price.

- It will take longer for a product to diffuse and become generally accepted in the market.
- If a skim price generates supernormal or windfall profits, it will attract competitors.

PENETRATION PRICING

Penetration pricing is when the firm decides to set the price significantly below the service's value to the customer, thereby ensuring a larger customer base, hopefully in a shorter period of time. It is the tradeoff of higher revenue versus higher profits, and can be a very effective strategy, especially for new entrants into particular markets.

Penetration prices are not necessarily lower than similar competitor offerings. They are lower *relative to value being provided by the firm itself.* Consider Southwest Airlines. Its pricing is relative to you driving or taking the bus, not other airlines' pricing. Penetration pricing is appropriate when:

- Demand for the service is sensitive to price changes.
- Search or experience services are involved that can be easily judged by customers before or after use, such as air travel, hotels, and televisions.
- Economies of scale or scope can be achieved in producing massive quantities.
- The threat of competitor imitation is very strong.
- Not a large enough segment is willing and able to pay a higher price.
- Network effects are an integral part of the business model—that is, the more people who use the service, the more the platform is worth, such as Facebook, Twitter, and LinkedIn.
- The firm has available capacity and financial wherewithal to produce in large volume.
- A low introductory price may prevent competitors from entering the market.

Penetration pricing is a strategy that is usually successful only for a few sellers in any industry. Not everyone can be, or wants to be, Wal-Mart and H&R Block.

NEUTRAL PRICING

The neutral pricing strategy is generally the default strategy for most companies. In effect, this strategy minimizes the role of pricing in the marketing mix, not utilizing price to gain or restrict market share. A firm may select this strategy when it knows its service, promotion, or distribution offers other more powerful advantages to the customer. The neutral price does not mean a price in between that of competitors, but in relationship to the firm's value.

Many new boutique accounting, law, and advertising firms have been launched in recent years specifically to take advantage of the discontent over hourly billing. These firms are offering a broad array of pricing strategies, from fixed prices and risk-sharing plans based on creating results to subscription plans. The problem is many of them are positioning themselves as "cheaper alternatives" to their larger competitors, since they have smaller overheads—in effect, justifying price based on costs, not value. Some have selected a penetration pricing strategy to gain acceptance among customers.

This is a strategic mistake. If these firms are truly offering new and innovative pricing policies, then at the least they should be utilizing a *neutral* pricing strategy. An enormous component of their value proposition lies in the fact that they are aligning the incentives of the firm with that of its customers, which is an enormously valuable offering in and of itself. It is folly to provide a cheaper price simply because your firm has less fixed overhead. What matters is the value you can create, and if you have remarkable intellectual capital—especially human capital—then offering it for a lesser price sacrifices an enormous amount of profits. A case could also be made that these firms should be using a skim strategy to send the message to those customers frustrated with the billable hour and willing to pay a premium for certainty in pricing.

These three strategies are the same in the subscription business model. Your firm must choose one of them. But because the subscription offering is being *plussed*—Walt Disney's term for adding more value—even if you select a neutral strategy, your price should still be able to increase due to the perceived value of your offering being enhanced tremendously—with transformations, frictionless access, peace of mind, and ensurance.

ONLY UNCOMMON OFFERINGS COMMAND UNCOMMON PRICING: YOU ARE WHAT YOU CHARGE FOR

Ultimately, a business is defined by that for which it collects revenue, and it collects revenue only for that which it decides to charge.

—B. Joseph Pine II and James H. Gilmore,
The Experience Economy, 1999

It is a deceptively simple question, but one for which the answer is taken for granted: **"What are we asking customers to pay for?"** (Bertini 2020). Marco Bertini believes the answer is the definition of your *revenue model*. Like one of Peter Drucker's five most important questions—what is value to the customer?—it is assumed that leaders know the answer. But they rarely do, since the customer is really purchasing the satisfaction of a want, not merely a product or service. They are buying the hole, not the drill—that is, the result, not the means to achieving the result.

As we have been suggesting, we believe it is beyond time for professionals to move off of charging for services performed and pivot to customer transformations. We have to get beyond thinking of the math of the moment—profit margins for each type of service, number of services utilized, and so forth—and focus on doing whatever is necessary to effectuate higher value transformations. This is another mind shift change that we recognize is not going to be easy; it is undoubtedly as challenging as moving away from hourly billing to value pricing.

Yet we enthusiastically believe it is time to align our rhetoric with our revenue model. As mentioned, professionals are said to "profess" something, they stand for something. What do you want your firm to stand for? Are you selling services, or are you transforming your customers into a preferrable future? Are not the services merely a *means* to this *end*? I know we say "pricing the relationship," but perhaps we are really discovering and capturing the *potential* of the relationship. Either way, we should hold ourselves to a higher standard than merely performing and pricing services.

The topics discussed in this chapter are the foundational principles to keep in mind as you contemplate your pricing. There are a lot of debates around pricing, and a lot of unsettled issues, especially in the subscription business model. Once you understand what your customers truly value, and your revenue model is aligned with that value, it gives you a framework to choose pricing strategies that work for you, irrespective of what other subscription businesses are doing. There is no one optimal policy when it comes to pricing. There are only tradeoffs. It demands continuous experimentation and testing. Your pricing strategies are not set in stone; they can be adjusted based on customer feedback and changing market conditions.

One of those tradeoffs is between complexity and trust. One of the biggest complaints we continue to receive about implementing value pricing is the amount of time it takes to execute, usually each year. You have to conduct a value conversation, customize three options for each customer, and so on. It creates bureaucracy, especially if you empowered a value council to have final authority over pricing decisions. You had to deal with scope creep and change requests, which added to the bureaucracy, and the unpredictability the customer felt (What is in-scope or out-of-scope? What is the final price?). The biggest disadvantage with value pricing is forcing the customer to confront the entire value/price decision each year, or at each service (with change requests). These are the right tools for the value pricing business model, but they are no longer relevant in the subscription model if you align your revenue model with what customers are really paying for—transformations.

Any unnecessary complexity and cognitive load (frequent pricing decisions) undermines customer trust. The subscription model *surfaces simplicity*, as Zuora CEO Tien Tzuo likes to say. Being transparent about your pricing, while offering certainty and predictability on how it is to be paid, goes a long way to fostering trust. Transparency enhances trust. *Price transparency* is achieved when a customer knows what they will pay before they enter into the transaction.

Pricing transparency is achieved when a customer understands how your firm *arrives* at a price. For instance, Amazon and airlines have *price* transparency, but not *pricing* transparency, since both use dynamic pricing that can change frequently based on demand. The US health care market—outside of concierge and direct primary care doctors—has neither price nor pricing transparency, which is why it is not truly a free market. In any case, the level of transparency is a means to the end of creating delighted customers.

Complicated pricing confuses customers, which can erode trust. Your customers should not have to become experts in your pricing, like some people do with the airlines, trying to second-guess their algorithms with respect to movements in airfares. Keep your pricing simple for the customer. That does not mean it will be simple for you to create, far from it, but it is important to remember that pricing is the servant to the master of your purpose, strategy, and positioning.

Southwest Airlines (n.d.) has branded its transparent approach to pricing to differentiate itself from the competition:

Transfarency® [Trans-fair-uhn-see] n.

1. Philosophy in which Customers are treated honestly and fairly, and low fares actually stay low—no unexpected bag fees, change fees, or hidden fees.

Low fares. No hidden fees.

Of course, Southwest Airlines uses a penetration and neutral pricing strategy, hence the emphasis on low fares. But the point remains: this is exemplary communication to customers and inspires trust and peace of mind that they will not be nickeled-and-dimed to death. We will discuss branding your pricing approach more in Chapter 17.

Another tradeoff—and fierce debate within the subscription pricing community—is between a fixed-priced subscription versus usage-based pricing. This debate reminds me of the debates in the early years of value pricing, whereby firms would simply estimate the amount of hours it was going to take to do a job and fix the price in advance. I labeled this practice the billable hour in drag, since it was based on the falsified labor theory of value.

TechCrunch ran an article on January 29, 2021 with this headline: "Subscription-based pricing is dead: Smart SaaS companies are shifting to usage-based models." Tzuo responded in his November 6,

2021, newsletter, "Sorry, I'm not falling for this one. . . . The best outcomes are often achieved when the two pricing models are combined."

I agree with Tzuo, especially for professional firms. Unfortunately, predictability and certainty in price still command premium prices in the professions because so many firms use the labor theory of value to establish their prices. None of us as customers want to pay for what we do not use, but we also do not want to be on the clock, or worry about running over our data plans on our internet connections, which makes binging Netflix far less enjoyable. Could you imagine Netflix charging for each show? It is why we will pay a premium for unlimited data plans, we just don't want the hassle of worrying about it. I wonder if anyone has ever considered the customer's feelings toward the unpredictability of usage-based pricing? After all, hourly billing was justified for the same reason—we spend more time, the customer pays more. I understand the goal is to *land and expand* the customer, and usage pricing appears to do that, though I believe far less than people think.

In fact, Tzuo points out that the Subscribed Institute has found that "companies with usage-based pricing making up between 1% and 25% of their overall revenue mix grow faster than companies with no usage, but also faster than companies with more than 25% of their revenue coming from usage." We will have more to say on this topic in the next chapter.

SUMMARY AND CONCLUSIONS

In summary, we have covered a lot of foundational pricing principles in this chapter:

- Pricing the relationship by ignoring the math of the moment and focusing on the lifetime value of the customer
- The many advantages of the subscription model over a transactional model
- The difference between search, experience, and credence goods and services, and why price is such an important indicator of quality for credence services
- The seven types of customer risk and how the subscription model deals with them

- The three macro pricing strategies—penetration, neutral, and skim—and how your choice depends on your firm's purpose, strategy, and positioning

- You are what you charge for, i.e., your revenue model—what are you asking your customers to pay for?—and why the alignment between our rhetoric and revenue model is so important

We are not done with pricing yet. We have discussed the first law of marketing: *All value is subjective*. Now it is time to turn our attention to the second law: *All prices are contextual*, where we will discuss how to construct and offer choices in your pricing that will enable you to segment your customers based on value, willingness to pay, and commensurate with the value you are creating for them, the subjects of Chapter 16.

16

CUSTOMER SEGMENTATION AND PRICING TIERS

*Like money, price talks. It changes perceptions. Price changes
the actual experience of using the service: A high price
actually improves the experience. Watch what your price says.
Push price higher. Higher prices don't just talk, they tempt.*

—Harry Beckwith, *The Invisible Touch*

One of the most customer-centric strategies your firm can deploy
is to offer an array of choices to your customers. It is very "outer-
directed," rather than just offering a one-size-fits-all, take-it-or-leave-
it option. Humans prefer options, especially in today's world where
they face a plethora of choices regarding who, when, what, and how
to patronize a business.

From the iconic American Express Green, Gold, and Platinum
charge cards, to Starbucks' tall, grande, and venti options, businesses
have nearly always offered choices. Almost always three, sometimes
four, rarely more. Why? Because smart pricing is about price segmentation and searching, not just offering one price. There is a range
of acceptable prices we are willing to pay, and the smart pricers are
constantly searching the boundaries of this range. I would bet where
you get your car washed you are being offered at least three options.
In fact, there has been an enormous private-equity play in this space,
converting car washes into subscription businesses.

There is strong empirical evidence—from both the rational and
behavioral schools of economics—that offering customers different
options can often result in them purchasing more, at a higher price,

than merely offering one take-it-or-leave-it option. This simply recognizes that different customers have different value perceptions, and
firms that engage in price searching are deploying a more optimal
pricing model.

Offering pricing tiers creates the *anchoring effect*, whereby the
customer is now comparing prices to your highest offering. The
first lesson is, if you do not offer a high-end premium package,
how could your customers ever select one? Second, list your most
expensive option first. The third lesson is that by offering three
options, you almost always sell more of the middle option and less
of the cheapest offering. Once again, this confirms what most pricing experts know: People are not just price sensitive; they are value
conscious.

Having the customer make the selection of which option they prefer allows them to decide on that all-important value/price tradeoff.
It also ensures they have buy-in to the decision, and will convince
themselves they made a good decision. There is a hilarious scene in
The Simpsons where Homer and Marge are on a date at an expensive
French restaurant. Homer bellows to the waiter, "Garcon! Another
bottle of your second-least-expensive champagne." You have probably experienced a similar wine list in an upscale restaurant, with
prices starting as high as $10,000, then ratcheting down to perhaps
$100. Most likely, you will not select the cheapest, but somewhere
above, and you will be delighted with your choice. The psychology
is very powerful.

This is why the rapid increase in pod coffee machines was so
successful. Even though the pods were expensive relative to buying
coffee by the pound, they were being compared with a Starbucks
purchase and hence were an attractive substitute.

Recall the *framing effect*—the idea that people draw different conclusions from equivalent information, depending on how it is presented. With choices, the customer is comparing your offering against
your other offerings. You have the ability, somewhat, to control what
they are comparing you to. This reframes the question in the buyer's
mind from, "Should I work with XYZ firm?" to "How should I work
with XYZ firm?" This is a completely different question that usually
leads to a more favorable decision for the firm, especially if the competition is *not offering* choices.

SEVEN GENERIC CUSTOMER SEGMENTATION STRATEGIES

According to Tom Nagle and Reed Holden in their 2001 book *The Strategy and Tactics of Pricing*, there are seven effective segmentation strategies to specifically identify different types of customers in order to capture a higher price:

1. **Buyer identification.** Senior discounts, children's prices, college students, nonprofits, and coupons are all examples of ways to identify different buyers with different price sensitivities.

2. **Purchase location.** Dentists, opticians, and other professionals sometimes maintain separate offices, in different parts of the same city, or in different cities, which charge different prices based on the economic and demographic makeup of each.

3. **Time of purchase.** Theaters offering midday matinees, restaurants charging cheaper prices for lunch than dinner, and cellular and utility companies offering pricing based on peak and off-peak times are all examples of segmenting by time of purchase.

4. **Purchase quantity.** Quantity discounts are usually based on volume, order size, step discounts, or two-part prices. Customers who buy in large volumes tend to be more price sensitive, and they have more incentive to shop for a cheaper price. Thus, they are offered volume discounts. Two-part pricing involves two separate charges to consume a single product. Night clubs charge a cover at the door as well as for drinks and food.

5. **Product design.** Offering different versions of a product or service is a very effective way to segment customers, either by adding more features or taking some away.

6. **Product bundling.** Restaurants bundle food on the dinner menu as opposed to à la carte, usually at cheaper prices. Symphonies, theaters, and sports teams bundle a package of events into season tickets. IBM and Hewlett-Packard bundle hardware, software, and consulting services to increase the value of their respective offerings.

7. **Tie-ins and metering.** Razor blade manufacturers design unique razors requiring customers to purchase its blades for refill, and a certain toner must be used on specific printers.

In addition to these seven generic strategies, other characteristics that can be used to offer different options to the customer include:

- Guaranteed response time; start time; and turnaround time
- Access to specific talent within the firm
- Bundling educational events your firm may conduct
- A systems review, risk audit, or other needs and diagnostics your firm offers
- Attendance at the customer's board meetings, and how often (monthly, quarterly, etc.)
- Intellectual property ownership belongs to the firm rather than the customer (mostly for advertising agencies)

Once again, this is not an exhaustive list of criteria that a firm could use to offer different levels of choices to its customers. The process of creating these pricing tiers is one of creativity, innovation, and constant experimentation. This is one major advantage that professional firms have over product manufacturers; the latter are tied to a tangible product, usually having to wrap a service around it, whereas professionals are not tied to any tangible offering and can adapt to what the customer needs.

LinkedIn segments its users based on buyer identification. It has four categories of users, each offering a different selection of prices depending on the value derived, with recruiters being priced the highest since they derive the most value from the platform:

1. Job seekers
2. Professionals
3. Salespeople
4. Recruiters

Direct primary care doctors will usually price by the age of the patient, another type of buyer identification. Pediatricians actually charge higher prices at younger ages, with the price declining as the child gets older. One could think up other ways to segment, such as lifestyle—are you a leisure or business traveler, for instance?

AIMS360 is an enterprise resource planning (ERP) software company for fashion brands. At first, it priced each customer, using a tailored approach whereby the customer could mix and match various services. What it learned is that this approach confused the customers, presenting them with more than 40 different choices. If there are too many choices, the "paradox of choice" can set in, paralyzing the customer from making a decision. And even if they are able to make a choice, they will end up being less satisfied, either because they were not sure of the choice they made when they subscribed and/or continue to doubt whether or not they selected the correct option as they use the software. This is part of the tradeoff between complexity, transparency, and trust.

AIMS360 revised its approach and began to segment customers based on the size and stage of the growth of their businesses. It now offers three options: Emerging, Designer, and Luxury, each specifying different levels of service based on need. This change not only reduced customer anxiety and increased satisfaction, it reduced the churn rate AIMS360 was experiencing. I encourage you to have a look at these tiers, because there are similarities to how professionals could segment based on what stage a customer is at in the business life cycle (AIMS360 n.d.).

Segmentation by stage of growth, at least for business customers, might make sense for professional firms. The startup, growth, mature, and declining phases all have different needs that are a good fit for bundling into a pricing tier. Of course, your firm might specialize in just one of the phases, which is another viable option.

The larger point is to illustrate the tradeoff between pricing complexity and building trust. Also, looking at it from a portfolio perspective, because you know not every customer is going to be using every service all the time. The fact they have access to it should they need it is a large part of the value proposition. In addition to the seven segmentation strategies above, there is another framework that we have found useful in assisting firms develop their pricing choices: The Smile Curve.

THE SMILE CURVE

The Stan Shih Smile Curve in Figure 16.1 helps you think about the relative value of your various offerings, from the customer's perspective.

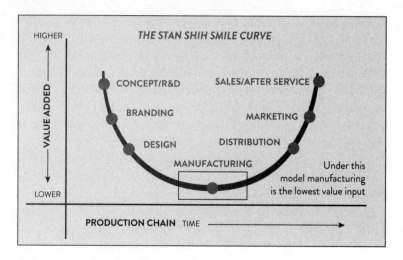

FIGURE 16.1   The Stan Shih Smile Curve.

The idea is that the lowest-value item in the production chain is the manufacturing, or assembling, of the product. Even though the Apple iPhone is assembled overseas, customers do not really care. The real value of these products is in the R&D, branding, design, distribution, and after-sale support (Apple stores, Genius Bar, AppleCare warranty, etc.). It is estimated that the value added by China in the assembly of the iPhone is around $30, which is why every iPhone states on the back: "Designed by Apple in California. Assembled in China."

There is a technical problem with the Smile Curve. Recall from Chapter 14 that all value is subjective, and that value is indivisible. We cannot distinguish between the value, to the customer, of the chef and the janitor in a high-end restaurant. Yet that is what the Smile Curve is doing, which is a technical error. That said, it is still a useful framework in helping you think through all the services your firm offers.

Of course, the Smile Curve can be adapted to the various professional sectors—legal, accounting, IT, advertising agencies. VeraSage Senior Fellow Ed Kless has adapted the Smile Curve to IT firms, as shown in Figure 16.2.

For advertising agencies, the Smile Curve would contain the following five elements instead of those shown in Figure 16.2:

1. Diagnose
2. Prescribe

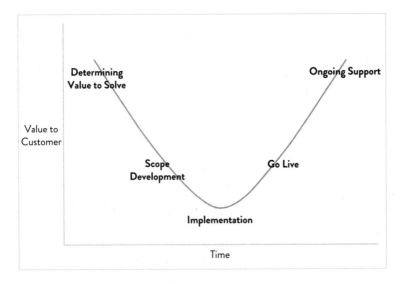

FIGURE 16.2   The Smile Curve for IT firms.

3. Create

4. Execute

5. Measure

It is the sides of the smile that contain the most relative value in the eyes of the customer. Yet, when you think about how most professional firms attempt to monetize their value, what are they trying to monetize? The equivalent of the manufacturing work. Even worse, they tend to either ignore, or not even charge for, the sides of the curve, inverting the Smile Curve to a Frown Curve, as shown in Figure 16.3.

Consider what a filled-in Smile Curve might look like for a typical customer accounting service (CAS) practice, as shown in Figure 16.4. The services listed, of course, are going to vary tremendously by firm, depending on niche, expertise, industry, and customer size, but it will give you a good idea of how the curve is filled in after a brainstorming session with your team.

Perform the same brainstorming for each practice area and you will then have a global Smile Curve for the entire firm. Avoid getting bogged down in thinking about monetizing specific services. Remember, the goal of the subscription business model is to provide transformations, and the services are merely a means to that end.

Smile Curve for implementations

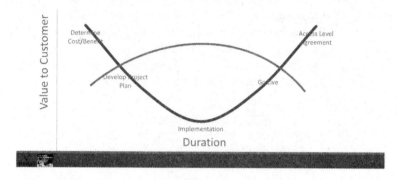

FIGURE 16.3   From Smile to Frown Curve.

CAS Smile Curve

Business Start-up consulting	Financial systems consulting & training	Initiating financial transactions	Basic Bookkeeping	Financial statements and income tax returns	Performance monitoring (exception reporting)	Business Consulting (performance improvement)
Business licencing and registration	Needs analysis	Customer payments	Source document management	Review bookkeeping	P&L budgets	Strategic planning
Incorporation	Requirements definition	Vendor payments	Data entry	Adjusting journal entries	Cash flow budgets	"What if" analysis
CRA/Min of fin/ WCB instalments and reporting	Process improvement recommendations and systems selection	CRA remittances and instalments	Account reconciliation	NTR financial statements	Actual compared to budget analysis and reporting	Industry benchmarking
Employee vs. independent contactor	Owner/ bookkeeper education and training		Review & approval	Owner/ manager remuneration		Value pricing
	Vendor selection		Sales tax & payroll	Other family tax planning		KPIs
	implementation		Basic Management reporting	Income tax returns		Advertising and marketing

FIGURE 16.4   CAS Smile Curve.

If you provide CAS services, for instance, then your services should include everything up to the middle of the curve. You don't need to break out services within that practice area—you should cover whatever it is the customer may need, similar to how a concierge doctor covers everything they are capable of handling. This would be the same for tax services—you would provide audit representation (assuming you have the expertise), handling tax agencies notices, Power of Attorney, tax forecasts and projections, etc. In the subscription model, we are not differentiating based on services, but instead on access level and other conveniences.

The objective is to have the customer's selected tier cover everything they might need in that specific area. If they decide at a future date they need advisory services, they can easily upgrade to a higher tier. Once done, they can also easily slide back down. This is part of the frictionless customer experience. Of course, you have to decide what is the minimal level of service you are going to offer. If you are willing to do CAS services with or without doing the tax work, that will complicate your tiers.

I am not a fan of offering a la carte menu options, because I think that complicates the pricing model and violates the tenets of subscribing to your firm. Even worse, it illustrates you have not thought through your strategy and positioning closely enough. You are still trying to be all things to all people. If tax services are not part of your strategy, then you might just offer a CAS pricing tier and a CAS plus business advisory tier. You can always add a third tier later for new innovative offerings.

This is another difference in the subscription model—innovation is baked in. As you roll out new innovations, you should include them in your highest tier, and then over time, make them available to lower tiers. For example, if you offer technology, cybersecurity, human resource compliance, or other types of advisory services, consider offering a mini-assessment in these areas in your lower tiers. Then, if you uncover opportunities to solve problems or pursue possibilities, the customer can upgrade to the higher tier that includes those services. But remember to make it easy for them to also slide back down to a lower tier once they are done utilizing the higher tier's services. Over time, some of these services will be included in the lower-priced tiers as they are replaced with new, innovative offerings.

Other innovative offerings that are not directly tied to offering services can first be included in a higher-priced tier. Examples include (I am indebted to my friend and colleague Mark Wickersham for some of these examples):

- Access outside of normal business hours
- Exclusive point of contact to partner
- Audio or video record all meetings

- Leveraging your social capital: Have other professional firms in your network—law, insurance, banks, and so on—offer free consultations, preferred pricing, seminars, etc., to your customers
- Online groups to help your customers and for them to help each other, such as a CEO or CFO roundtable (especially effective if you are in a niche)
- Mentoring group: Leverage your knowledge and that of your network's to offer content to your customers
- Access to a video or audio library of business advice on topics relating to purpose, strategy, positioning, pricing, KPIs, etc.
- Make available any research reports the firm may undertake, similar to how the McKinsey Institute makes its research available broadly, thereby enhancing the reputation of the McKinsey consulting firm
- Start a book-of-the-month club, which you can do by implementing it inside your firm and then simply invite your customers

These are examples of leveraging your firm's brains rather than selling its hands. There is a lot there, and it illustrates our limited imaginations that we must perform more services to add more value. No, you must leverage your knowledge—a *nonrival asset*, unlike the billable hour—which creates significantly more value than merely providing services.

Keep your pricing tiers simple. Remember, the goal is customer *transformations*, not piling up services brick by brick. The services are *merely a means to the ends*. Also, because you are pricing the portfolio, you can charge a premium for the added convenience and peace of mind provided to the customer. They are secure in the feeling that whatever they might need in that particular area—that you are *capable and competent* to do—they will be covered. This is the magic that is the concierge and DPC subscription model.

Another critical component of constructing your pricing tiers is to stay in your lane. Only include those services that you have expertise in, and can do with competence. It is all right to say no to a customer's request. In fact, it is a professional requirement to do so if you do not have the expertise to create the desired result the customer is looking for. A primary care physician is not going to perform heart surgery, nor would you want them to as a patient.

Saying no to a customer's request is better than giving a reluctant yes that leads to resentment and unprofessional behavior. "No" is a complete sentence. You do not have to justify it or explain it—get comfortable declining work that is outside of your expertise.

Professionals worry that this model is akin to "all-you-can-eat" and it scares them to death. But that is absurd. It is only all-you-can eat for the type of food that you decide to provide, and within the pricing tiers that you offer. For the things you don't supply, leverage your firm's social capital to find experts whom you trust, and refer to them.

THE ADAPTIVE CAPACITY MODEL

Your firm has a theoretical *maximum* capacity and a theoretical *optimal* capacity, and it is essential to see how that capacity is being allocated to each customer segment. Your maximum capacity is the total number of customers your firm can adequately serve (not how many hours you and your people have), while the optimal capacity is the point where customers can be served remarkably. For example, being told by your dentist when you have a bad toothache that it will be a couple of days before she can see you is not a frictionless, remarkable experience. We want our professionals to always have capacity to serve us, and will pay a premium for that luxury.

Usually, for most professional firms, optimal capacity is between 60% and 70% of maximum capacity. In the traditional transaction model, too many firms will add capacity—or reallocate capacity from higher-valued customers—to serve low-valued customers. Furthermore, firms will turn away high-value, last-minute work for its best customers because it is operating near maximum capacity and usually at the low-end of the value curve for price-sensitive customers. This is especially common during peak seasons and is one of the reasons I coined Baker's law: **Bad customers drive out good customers**.

The subscription model is an excellent antidote to Baker's law. It ensures that you always have adequate capacity because you are better able to plan in advance the predicable, recurring work, and build in plenty of spare capacity for contingencies and urgent situations. It also prevents you from cutting your price during slow periods since now you are viewing the entire portfolio of your customer base, increasing customer lifetime value, and not worrying about profit per hour, job, or customer. The goal is not to fill the capacity to 100%; it is to maximize profit and customer lifetime value, and if that can be done while operating at 60% capacity, so much the better. The excess capacity can be invested in innovation, CPE, and better serving your existing customers. This also prevents professional burnout and retains and develops top talent. Do not confuse being busy with being profitable. Innovation is the residue of wasted time.

SUMMARY AND CONCLUSIONS

We have covered a lot of value and pricing principles in the last several chapters, yet we are still not done. We have learned how important the distinctions are between pricing services, pricing the customer, and pricing the relationship; how the Smile Curve can help us think about our offerings and how to segment customers; how the adaptive capacity model can plan our capacity for optimal customer experience, profitability, loyalty, and talent development and retention.

There are a few more topics to discuss. Specifically, what do we mean by pricing the portfolio? What should firms do about one-off projects, which can be quite large and don't fit neatly into any pricing tier? How do you raise your prices in the subscription model? What should the cadence of the payment terms be—weekly, monthly, quarterly, or something else? All these topics are the subject of the next chapter.

17

PRICING THE PORTFOLIO

There is no such thing as a bad risk, only bad premiums.

—Actuarial Axiom

Coming off many successful years of windfall profits, an accounting firm decides to invest in a Hollywood studio. The partners are listening to a presentation from a senior studio executive about its plans for the upcoming year. "We will produce 10 movies. Five of them will bomb, and we'll lose money. Three will do okay, either break even or make a nominal profit. Two will be blockbusters, generating either supernormal or windfall profits."

One of the accountants raises his hand and asks, "Why don't we just make the two blockbusters?"

I am not comparing professional firms to movie studios. For one reason, professional firms could not handle the risk it entails, being bred in an hourly billing mentality where every hour must turn a profit. In the subscription business model, you are forced to nurture and grow lifetime customer value.

The strategies for pricing the portfolio revolve around robust customer selection and minimum pricing. Here is where your Purpose, Strategy, and Positioning (Chapter 11) play the senior role. Pricing strategy is the servant to these broader themes. Recall how your firm is defined by the customers it does not have and the services it does not perform. You already have a built-in constraint to what you are able and willing to do for customers. When you have a clear and concise offering it is much easier to stay in your lane and to know when a customer is not a good fit. No firm can meet every need for every customer. What they can do is meet very specific needs in the most transformative manner.

We have received a lot of objections to this idea of pricing the portfolio as part of the subscription model (italicized below). I am indebted to Matthew Burgess and Mark Wickersham for raising some of these questions. One of which is: *Customers should only pay for what they use, a defined scope of services.* Perhaps. Perhaps not. Maybe we only think that way because of our 70+ year-old business model of "We sell time." If we thought more about the customer's peace of mind, convenience, and most importantly, guiding transformations, some customers would gladly pay for that level of service. The concierge and direct primary care (DPC) doctors prove this, as do many other subscription companies.

This model is hard to scale, because professional firms only scale by adding human capital. Frankly, any business model is a challenge to scale. Is hourly billing easier to scale, or value pricing? Subscription generates annual recurring revenue, which is predictable and can be used as collateral to obtain financing. It is far more reliable than hourly billing's work in progress (WIP) reports, and even value pricing's signed fixed-price agreements. You can certainly tweak the payment terms, and use weekly instead of monthly, as Summit CPA does (Summit CPAs n.d.), or provide incentives to the customer if they pre-pay an entire year, which is useful if you are in the transition to subscription phase (see Chapter 22).

The trade-off between, say, monthly and annual payment terms is the cognitive load you are putting on the customer at renewal time. With annual payments, it is a much heavier load that could lead to higher customer churn. There is something optimal about a monthly payment cadence, turning it into a habit customers will become acclimated to relatively quickly.

In any event, scaling comes down to risk-taking while offering a value proposition that is desirable to customers, which is what being in business is all about.

Every, or most, successful subscription businesses scales primarily via tech, not humans. Not true. DPC doctors are scaling every day. Dr. Paul Thomas has gone from being a solo practice to employing two more doctors, and has plans to scale more. Consider Netflix. Yes, it's a digital company, but the content it produces is even more costly than professional knowledge workers—it is based on the creative talent of actors, actresses, directors, etc., some of the most expensive human capital in the world.

*Small firms don't have the resources to scale, and attracting sub-
scription customers is a sales and marketing challenge.* Again, what
business model automatically provides the resources to scale? As for
marketing and sales challenges, customers are craving predictability, convenience, and peace of mind, especially from the professional
firms they engage. I would rather offer subscriptions—that are based
on relationships and transformations—than sell services one at a
time. Even Porsche's Drive program has expanded, with nearly 80%
of the customers being new to the brand. This result is for a company
whose target customer is aging and dying off. These new customers have breathed new life into the brand, and a lot of them will be
driving Porsches for the rest of their lives. Focus on creating lifetime
annuities, not pricing every transaction.

*But pricing the portfolio creates a cross-subsidization situation,
similar to the U.S. Postal Service charging the same prices in remote
areas because those areas are subsidized by higher volume areas.*
The problem with this logic is in the subscription model; we do not
know, *ex ante*, who will use more or less services over any given
period of time. We are reserving capacity and pricing accordingly,
to account for our lack of knowledge and the risk about which, and
when, customers are going to demand our attention.

*There's too much risk with this model because customers could
demand a lot from us and we'd lose big on those.* Again, would you
be willing to offer this at the right price? Recall the Actuary's Axiom:
There are no bad risks, only bad premiums. At a high enough price,
you would be willing to offer any transformation your customer
desired, assuming you were capable of creating the result. Further,
what customers are able to demand from you is constrained by what
it is you offer. You aren't going to provide flying and cooking lessons.
This is where staying in your lane, and niching, become important. If
you only work with dentists, then you are well aware of the services
they may need from womb to tomb. This objection reminds me of the
joke about an actuary:

> An actuary's wife had a cat that continually annoyed him. In the
> middle of the night, the actuary got up and took the cat to a
> nearby lake. There he took a boat to the deepest part of the lake
> and put the cat in a bag filled with rocks. He securely closed the

bag and threw it overboard. The next day his wife was quite dis-
traught at the cat's disappearance. To show his concern, the actuary called the local newspaper to place a lost cat ad. For return of
the cat a $10,000 reward was offered. When questioned about the
size of the reward, the actuary stated, "When you are confident of
your contingencies, you can be liberal with your benefits."

Source: Actuarial Jokes n.d.

This may be why a computer is defined as an actuary with a heart.
Nevertheless, actuaries have a lot to teach professional firms about
pricing risk.

To borrow from the late Donald Rumsfeld, former secretary of
defense under U.S. Presidents Gerald Ford and George W. Bush: You
have *known knowns*—these are the services you know your customers will need on a recurring basis. They are even highly predictable.
There are *known unknowns*—these are the services you are aware of
that customers are likely to need, or might need, but you are not sure
which customers or which services, such as an IRS audit defense.
Then there are the *unknown unknowns*—these entail uncertainty, not
just probable risk. How many of these you can handle is primarily
dependent on your firm's expertise. You have a professional duty not
to take on one-off jobs that you have never performed before, or don't
have a track record of competency to perform.

At the right price, you can absorb all three of these types of risks,
and even the uncertainty, which is what actuaries do for a living. Not
focusing on the specific services, but rather on the customer lifetime
value, changes the profit formula entirely, which is why this business
model is different than one that value prices only services.

This is not necessarily an objection, but an excellent question:
What principles from value pricing remain relevant in the subscription model? Many, actually. Certainly the falsification of the labor
theory of value, along with the first and second laws of marketing:
All value is subjective, and all prices are contextual, as discussed in
Chapter 14. Price segmentation and offering choices are still relevant,
though two choices may work for some firms better than always striv-
ing to offer three. Also, the timeless truth that price *justifies* the costs

that firms can profitably invest in; not that costs (plus desired profit) determine price.

With value pricing, you priced the individual customer. With subscription, you are pricing across the entire customer portfolio. An analogy is to study the change in Disneyland's pricing from when it first opened in 1955. It used a classic price discrimination strategy of charging different customers different prices, depending on the attractions desired, rather than the entire park experience. Disneyland utilized an A–E ticket system (E stood for *exciting*) to price its attractions, developed by economists at Stanford Research Institute. On July 17, 1955 when Disneyland opened, A, B, and C tickets cost from 10 cents to 50 cents each, depending on the attraction. D tickets were added in 1956 and E tickets in 1959, priced at 50 cents each. From a pricing perspective, the A–E ticket system was a pure price discrimination strategy, whereby the park charged the highest prices to those guests who simply had to ride the most exciting attractions, and some rode multiple times. However, over time the problems with the A–E system began to outweigh the benefits, a clear example of the tradeoff between optimal pricing and customer experience. Disney had to print the tickets, its guests had to wait in long lines to purchase them (thus diminishing the fun and experience of the park visit), and the cast members at each ride had to handle and police the tickets, sometimes turning away guests carrying the wrong ticket—a moment of misery. The total costs of engaging in this type of customer segmentation began to exceed the marginal profits derived from it, and in 1982 Disneyland changed to the Disneyland Passport, a fixed-price, unlimited use of attractions, all-day pass.

You may be thinking, "That's fine for Disneyland, where the marginal cost of allowing one more guest into the park is practically zero, but it won't work in a professional firm, where the marginal cost of taking on an additional customer is much greater." Not quite. The theme park business is incredibly capital intensive, with competition demanding any park constantly add new, multimillion-dollar attractions, not to mention building new parks. It is much less risk to hire a few more professional knowledge workers than spend the capital needed to build a new roller coaster.

The objection with the most validity has been about the complex, high-priced, one-off engagements in which firms occasionally get involved with, which we turn to next.

PRICING COMPLEX, ONE-OFF ENGAGEMENTS

This is the same objection we received when we were advocating value pricing over hourly billing. But what about those engagements that are just so complex you have no idea how to scope them? I offered a few models in Chapter 30 of my book *Implementing Value Pricing*, such as Chris Marston's Concentric Circles, and the FORD Consulting Model. We hear this across the professions, those black-hole engagements where you just don't know what is going to be involved and therefore there is no way you could provide a fixed price. In fact, even in firms that claim they value price, some say on complex projects they revert back to the billable hour because of the level of *unknown unknowns*.

Whenever I hear this, the professional in me cringes. The last thing I want to hear from my surgeon as I am being wheeled into the operating room is, "Wow, look at that, I've never seen that before." We engage professionals precisely because they have seen this before, and we have confidence in their ability to handle the situation, even if unexpected events turn up. Certainly the surgeon has superior knowledge of the possible contingencies and complications; that's why I hired him. And if he doesn't have that knowledge, I certainly cannot be expected to as the patient, putting me in a high-anxiety situation. It is simply not good enough to consider the situation from the firm's convenience, we have to consider how we would feel if we were the customer. Do I want to hire a surgeon who merely "dabbles" in heart surgery, or engage a specialist who has done thousands of operations? How would you feel if the decision was for a parent, spouse, or child?

The pricer in me also cringes. It is hard for customers to believe you are competent in your field if you cannot quote a price upfront. They will lose faith in you, and it will take longer to build trust. More to the point, professionals usually know more about an engagement than they think. Breaking it down into phases is one way to price it based on value rather than hours. Either way, it is when projects are complex that you need to run away from the billable hour the fastest. These projects are usually high value, and the billable hour simply captures costs and a normal profit, leaving the opportunity for super-normal or windfall profits on the table.

Broadly speaking, there are two issues when it comes to one-off engagements. The first is professional due care, and the other is how to price these engagements. But if you cannot perform the engagement with professional due care, the second issue is moot—you should not be performing the service in the first place, at any price. It is the first rule of professional conduct: *First, do no harm.* I can only speak as a recovering (and inactive) certified public accountant, but the AICPA's Code of Professional Conduct is very clear with respect to the principle of due care:

.01 *Due care principle.* A *member* should observe the profession's technical and ethical standards, strive continually to improve competence and the quality of services, and discharge professional responsibility to the best of the *member's* ability.

.02 The quest for excellence is the essence of due care. Due care requires a *member* to discharge professional responsibilities with competence and diligence. It imposes the obligation to perform *professional services* to the best of a *member's* ability, with concern for the best interest of those for whom the services are performed, and consistent with the profession's responsibility to the public.

.03 Competence is derived from a synthesis of education and experience. It begins with a mastery of the common body of knowledge required for designation as a certified public accountant. The maintenance of competence requires a commitment to learning and professional improvement that must continue throughout a *member's* professional life. It is a *member's* individual responsibility. In all engagements and in all responsibilities, each *member* should undertake to achieve a level of competence that will ensure that the quality of the *member's* services meets the highest level of professionalism required by these Principles.

.04 Competence represents the attainment and maintenance of a level of understanding and knowledge that enables a *member* to render services with facility and acumen. **It also establishes the limitations of a *member's* capabilities by dictating that consultation or referral may be required when a professional**

engagement exceeds the personal competence of a *member* or a *member's firm*. Each *member* is responsible for assessing his or her own competence of evaluating whether education, experience, and judgment are adequate for the responsibility to be assumed. [Bold added]

.05 *Members* should be diligent in discharging responsibilities to *clients*, employers, and the public. Diligence imposes the responsibility to render services promptly and carefully, to be thorough, and to observe applicable technical and ethical standards.

.06 Due care requires a *member* to plan and supervise adequately any professional activity for which he or she is responsible. (AICPA 2016)

Under the value pricing business model, for one-off engagements you would simply issue a change order, scope the job, price it, and determine payment terms. What about with a subscription business model? There are several strategies you can deploy:

- **Upfront price.** Require a payment upfront to cover a portion, or the full amount, of the job.

- **Longer commitment.** Require a longer-term commitment from the customer, amortizing the project price over the term.

- **Declining price.** Increase the monthly price—or whatever cadence of payment term you utilize—then have it gradually decline over time until it is level with the normal subscription price.

- **Enterprise choice.** Offer a customized subscription plan for this one customer. This adds complexity to your pricing, which is a negative tradeoff. Over time, you should be able to "bake in" the most frequent one-offs into your tiers.

- **Trust your value.** Be confident that the investment in the customer will pay off over their lifetime and perform the work. If it is the right customer the risk is likely to pay off.

- **Use a TIP clause.** This is covered in a separate section later in the chapter.

There are pros and cons to each of these approaches. As we discuss each below, keep these questions in mind for your firm and its customers:

- Which pricing model produces the better customer experience?
- Which builds trust faster and actually enhances the customer experience?
- Which conveys and builds more confidence in your expertise?
- Which reduces internal bureaucracy in the firm, lowering its costs?
- Which lessens the cognitive decision burden on the customer of having to decide on paying an additional price?

There is much more to price than simply profit maximization. It can influence the behavior of your customer and enhance how they perceive your firm's value.

Upfront Price

Requiring an upfront price, separate from the subscription, is one strategy some subscription businesses have deployed, such as by Hassle Free Home Services, discussed in Chapter 10. When it undertakes a major project, such as building a deck or remodeling a kitchen, it is billed separately from its subscription plan. These projects account for approximately 50% of its revenue. Other firms simply charge an upfront price that will recover the cost of performing the work. The profit will be earned through the subscription. Charging an upfront amount lowers the risk to the firm, but it also burdens the customer with another decision point about price. One of the big advantages of subscription is the value/price tradeoff to the customer is made only once; it is decoupled from the workflow. This is what gives the firm the opportunity to add recurring value, build tremendous trust, all the while ensuring long-term loyalty.

Longer commitment

Require some minimum contract length with the customer so your monthly payments cover the marginal price of the one-off project. This might be easier on the customer's cash flow than an upfront

payment. Of course, you are adding risk to the customer while providing them another reason not to engage with your firm. We also
believe this violates the spirit—not to mention the psychological
advantages—of the subscription model. Subscriptions need to be
cancellable at any time; it is your value guarantee, and should not be
violated carelessly. Cellular and cable companies are notorious for
locking customers into service plans, with penalty clauses to get out,
which is not a remarkable customer experience nor a best practice
to emulate.

Declining Price

Up the subscription price to cover a portion of the project, then structure the monthly payment to decline gradually until it equals the normal subscription price. This is easier on the customer's cash flow
relative to the upfront price, with the added psychology of the monthly
price declining, a signpost of progress. This psychology is better
framing than requiring the customer to commit to a longer-
term contract.

Enterprise Choice

It is always an option to customize a subscription plan for an unusual
customer who does not fit within your normal parameters. Again,
remember the due care duty—is this a customer the firm should even
be serving? What is the malpractice risk if we take on a customer
outside our normal routine? Usually, these types of one-off engagements entail the highest risk of litigation. If it is an acceptable customer, then a customized plan might be the solution. However, keep
in mind, if you are doing this for a lot of your customers, it is a leading indicator that your purpose, strategy, and positioning are not
clearly defined. It could be that you are trying to be all things to all
people. Remember that you are defined by the customers and services you do not have.

   If you are niched in dentists, for example, it is going to be very rare
to come across a one-off project that you have never seen before, and
that cannot be built into your pricing tiers—this is what pricing the
portfolio is all about. The mindset that we have to earn our profit on
the math of the moment is simply obsolete in the subscription model.
Furthermore, burdening the customer with too many decisions can
cause analysis paralysis, leaving them less likely to make a choice.

The AIMS360 experience related in Chapter 16 is a cautionary example of what can happen when you try to price the customer rather than the portfolio in the subscription model.

If you are experiencing a lot of the same type of complex projects, bake them into your top tier. Allow customers to upgrade until the job is complete and then move back down to the tier they were in. You can also limit the number of projects you will perform at any one time. It is usually not a problem because most customer organizations do not have the bandwidth to handle more than two or three projects at one time.

The ultimate goal is to create a remarkable customer experience that is frictionless, hassle-free, and does not require you to add a Department of Paperwork to your firm's processes. Firms love to produce long, detailed scope of work documents that show the deliverables, timelines, and other processes in granular detail. Certainly some of this may be necessary, but customers are not buying your processes, or even outputs. They are buying outcomes—that is, transformations. Bureaucracy is a hidden tax that all organizations pay, and we should eliminate it everywhere we can.

Of course, none of this is to imply that engagement letters for various services—tax, audit, consulting, etc.—are no longer required. They are, in alignment with your professional liability insurance carrier. Be sure to run any standard agreements you use by them.

Trust Your Value
Simply perform the work with the confidence that the lifetime value is going to more than make up for this initial investment. After all, how much are you willing to spend to acquire a new customer? How many requests for proposals (RFPs), pitches, free meetings, free reviews, and sales calls do you perform in the hope of landing a customer? Shift these costs to performing some work, and chances are the long-term return on investment (ROI), customer trust, and loyalty earned will be higher. We are not suggesting that you do work for free, only that the profit formula under the subscription model is completely different than the transactional model.

In fact, we have heard from some firms that they get pushback from customers if they claim they will perform a large project upfront without changing the price or payment terms. Rightfully so, the customer questions the legitimacy of this—"if it's too good to be true, it usually is" logic—or the firm will not prioritize the project or give it adequate resources, and it will drag out. We do not believe these are insoluble issues. You have to earn and build trust through your performance. Emphasize the fact they can terminate at any time; that you are assuming all of the risk of the project. If it is the right customer, this will be much easier than you fear.

Use a TIP Clause

Tim was the managing partner of a top 200 accounting firm, and his best, long-term customer (of 20 years) had come to him wanting to sell his $250 million closely held business. He told Tim (and I am paraphrasing here), You've been my CPA for 20 years and I trust you with my life. It is time for me to sell my business and enjoy my golden years. Here is what I want you to do:

- Update our business valuation to maximize the sales price.
- Fly with me anywhere we have to go to meet with potential buyers.
- Be actively involved at every stage of the sales negotiation.
- Perform the due diligence, along with the attorneys, of the qualified buyers.
- Work with the attorneys on the sales contract to make sure my interests are protected.
- Perform tax planning and structure the deal in such a manner as to maximize my wealth retention.

Obviously, this was a very sophisticated customer, and it is true that Tim had no idea, at the outset of this engagement, how long it would take to close the deal, and how much firm capacity (his and his team members) it would require. But he did know more than an average salesperson would know, which is one of the enormous advantages professionals possess when it comes to pricing engagements such as this. He knew the customer's business was well niched, profitable, and growing. This would indicate a very high probability of a successful sale. He also knew this was an audit customer of the firm's and therefore he would not be able to charge a contingency price based on a financial outcome (such as a percentage of the sales price, or of any tax savings, etc.), since that would impair independence, which is illegal for an auditor.

When I asked Tim how he priced this engagement, he proudly proclaimed that every hour charged to this project was at the firm's highest "consulting rate" of $400 per hour—no matter who in the firm worked on the engagement—indicating, right from the start, Tim knew there was more value on this project than he would ever be able to embellish on a timesheet. He further explained how he had updated the business valuation, negotiated with two buyers, and did all of the other tasks requested by the customer. As a result of Tim's work, the customer received (and saved in taxes) an additional $15,000,000, and acknowledged that Tim was directly responsible for this outcome. In Tim's own words, the customer was "elated."

Tim then told how he priced the engagement. He reviewed all of the hours from the work-in-progress time and billing system, believed it did not adequately reflect the value provided, and marked it up an additional 25% over the $400 hourly rate. He then sent out an invoice for $38,000, which the customer promptly—and happily—paid. He believed he was value pricing. He was not—he was *value guessing*, since the customer had absolutely no input into the price paid, and only a customer can determine value.

I asked Tim what he thought the customer would have paid if he had utilized a TIP clause (also referred to as a *retrospective price,* or *success price*), such as the following:

> In the event that we are able to satisfy your needs in a timely and professional manner, you have agreed to review the situation and decide whether, in the sole discretion of XYZ [company], some additional payment to ABC [CPAs] is appropriate in view of your overall satisfaction with the services rendered by ABC.

The TIP is being based on the "overall satisfaction with the services rendered," and not any financial contingency, which is the origin of the acronym TIP—to improve performance. This TIP clause would be discussed with the customer *before* any work began. If needed, you could put a minimum price on the engagement (such as $40,000) to cover immediate firm capacity. But in this case, given the 20-year relationship with the customer, even a price *solely* determined by a TIP would have been acceptable, since the customer was not likely to take advantage of Tim after the outcome he achieved and the long-term relationship they had.

In answer to my question, Tim said his customer would most likely have paid him $500,000, a sum I believe to this day is below the real number—but at least better than the $38,000 he finally charged. Nevertheless, since Tim knows the customer better than I do, let us take his number as correct.

I informed Tim he had made the ultimate accounting entry:

Entry	Debit	Credit
Experience	$462,000	
Cash		$462,000

Tim was providing extraordinary value to this customer, yet the cost-plus pricing mentality prevented him from capturing a fair portion of it. Are we not ruled by our theories? This is why it is imperative to extinguish the cost-plus mentality from your firm, not to mention run away from the billable hour for complex engagements. No one in any seminar I have shared this story with believed Tim would have received less than $38,000 for his services on this engagement utilizing the TIP clause. In effect, Tim paid a *reverse risk premium*—he was assured he would not go below his hourly rate, but in return he gave up the added value the customer already believed he had created. This is not a risk worth taking if you want to maximize your firm's profitability. It is playing not to lose rather than playing to win.

The deleterious effects of this are deeper than just being deprived of a fair portion of the value you created on any one engagement. The problem lies at the very core of a firm's measurement system and points out how it does not offer the opportunity to learn from lost pricing opportunities, or pricing mistakes.

In his inimitable way, Yogi Berra explains this problem eloquently in his book *When You Come to a Fork in the Road, Take It!*:

> When we played the Pittsburg Pirates in the 1960 World Series, it was hard to believe we lost. It was real strange. We crushed their pitching. We won three of the games, 16–3, 10–0, and 12–0. We were the more experienced and stronger team. But we lost in a wild and weird

Game 7 when Bill Mazeroski hit that homer in the ninth inning over my head in left field. To this day, I thought the ball was going to hit the fence. Anyway, when a reporter asked me later how we could lose to the Pirates, I said, "We made too many wrong mistakes." (Berra 2001, p. 75)

In baseball, like everything, mistakes are physical or mental. In tennis, they say "forced and unforced errors." I like to say there's mistakes—and there's wrong mistakes. What I mean is that wrong mistakes are more serious, more avoidable, more costly. They're usually more mental than physical. There's nothing to be learned from a second kick of a mule. (Berra 2001, p. 74)

When it comes to pricing, the wisdom from Yogi is profound. Tim made the *wrong mistake*, and here is why: He will not learn anything from it because the firm's primary assessment is billable hours—once again the billable hour is the incorrect measuring device for value. When the partners review the realization report on this engagement, they will see 125%, which is excellent when you consider most firms realize between 50% and 95% overall on each hour. Most likely, Tim will get nothing but accolades and praise from his fellow partners. No one will ask where the $462,000 is because the billable hour metrics do not have a way to capture that type of information, which is precisely why pricing is more of an *art* than a science.

This is an excellent example of a wrong mistake for another reason: Tim (or the firm) will not learn anything from this lost pricing opportunity. The $462,000 simply vanishes into thin air (or, more precisely, more of the customer profit remains in the customer's bank account). No knowledge was gained by the firm on how to price the next similar engagement in accordance with value—it will simply perpetuate the same mistake, over and over. Being a more accurate activity-based cost-accountant, or even excellent project manager, would also not have helped Tim to capture the value. Pricing is an art, but it is also a skill similar to tennis or golf: the more you do it, the better you get.

Most feedback that firms receive on pricing is negative: "Your price was too high." Or it is ambivalent: "Your price was just right." No customer ever discloses how much money your firm left on the table. Since humans emerged from the cave and began to barter, it is the customer's job to do everything in his or her power to push down prices. There is nothing new about this, and it should not surprise any executive. Your firm's job, however, is to push back. The only effective way to accomplish this is by emphasizing value.

The cost-plus metrics, GAAP for financial statement reporting, cost accounting, even activity-based costing prevent firms from pricing commensurate with value since pricing mistakes (or missed opportunities) do not show up in any of these reports. As such, the company is denied the chance to acquire and develop intellectual capital on pricing so it can become a core competency within the firm. All of the traditional metrics of a firm focus on *internal* measurements, yet value is always an *external* issue—in the hearts and minds of the customers. Innovative pricing strategies, such as the TIP clause, that are outward focused and attempt to measure value have allowed more and more firms around the world to capture more of the value they provide, as the following case study illustrates.

THE MILLION-DOLLAR TIP

This story comes from Gus Stearns, a partner in an accounting firm, whom I met on September 25, 2000, at a conference in Las Vegas. Gus tracked me down at the dinner party, walked me over to the bar, and over a glass of wine told me his amazing TIP story. Here are the two emails I received from Gus explaining his success, the first one prior to our meeting in Las Vegas and the second one after:

Hello Ron,

I hope the tax season finds you well. I was fortunate enough to be at the Atlanta conference when you spoke and picked up an autographed copy of your book, which I devoured on the plane trip back.

The engagement which I refer to had already started a month or two before and I had used the old standard rate-time-hours routine and billed about $2,000 at a standard rate of $180/hour. After listening to you and reading the book, I was determined to reevaluate the price structure and simply went back to my customer and said, "Guys, this is what I am bringing to the table. It brings a lot of value which is etc., etc. I don't believe hourly rates based upon time is appropriate. I am unable to place a value on this. I need your help. You tell me what the value of all this is to you. You are the customer and only you can truly establish the value. I know I'll be happy with whatever you come up with." This is almost an exact quote.

I left it at that two months ago. I was handed a check for the first installment of $50,000 on the way out at the end of the engagement. I guess this is what you call "outside-in pricing." I like it.

Gus Stearns, CPA

It gets better, since this engagement was in two phases. Here is the follow-up email from Gus explaining the final result after the job was done:

Hello Ron,

Basically the large engagement was for a previous client that I had hired a controller for. He took over the tax work, at my suggestion, as he was a CPA. The engagement was an exit and management succession strategy, which involved some fairly hefty income tax savings as well. The total time expended was about 100 hours, although a lot of the time was on unrelated things that I did not want to charge for due to the magnitude of the price (we quit using timesheets some time ago).

I used a flip chart in the presentation, pointing out the value of what they were getting. At the end of the presentation, I asked how much they thought it was worth, and suggested $300,000, $500,000, a million? I wanted them to think in big numbers. The CEO was rather excited and said a million. Knowing that this would be difficult to obtain in one fell swoop I suggested $400,000 down and a retainer of $4,000 per month. They agreed but asked that I serve on the board of directors and attend quarterly meetings for the next eight years, when the note to the previous owners would be paid off. They were also kind enough to put me on salary so I could participate in their pension plan, which is a 25 percent direct contribution from the company. This all adds up to a little bit over $1 million.

Never once was the word "time" used or referred to by myself, or my client. They could have cared less about time. In all of our engagements, I never use the word. By concentrating on value and encouraging the client to participate in the valuation of the engagement our prices have skyrocketed. You were absolutely on-target when you said that accountants are terrible at valuing our services (myself included).

Keep up the wonderful work,

Gus

These types of engagements are certainly not the *rule* in any firm; they are the *exception*. Nonetheless, they do arise, and when they do it is critical to recognize the value you are creating and to utilize innovative pricing strategies to capture it. If you provide services similar to Tim and Gus, consider pricing those with a TIP clause. Just be sure to make this clear in your price messaging, that extraordinary services will be priced with a TIP clause. Conduct a thorough conversation with the customer in advance of doing the work explaining how the TIP works, and be prepared with whatever they decide to pay you. The turtle only makes progress when he sticks his neck out.

I include these stories not because I believe you will earn millions of dollars in TIPs but, rather, to illustrate how the cost-plus pricing mentality has placed a self-imposed artificial ceiling over the heads of firms. Never in their wildest dreams would Tim and Gus have placed such a high value on their work; but the customers did. Do they not deserve it?

RAISING YOUR PRICES

From time to time, you will need to raise your prices. Price increases are a sign of a healthy business because it is a leading indicator that you are adding even more value than the price you are charging. As this is being written in early 2022, and inflation is a major topic, we have seen many firms raise prices. One way to explain it to customers is to say, "Our costs are increasing." But as discussed in Chapter 14, prices are not determined by costs, but rather by value. It is much better to emphasize how your firm's value has increased in the interval between price changes. For example, as a Prime member, I received a notice from Amazon explaining its price increase:

Dear Prime Member,

Thank you for being a valued member of Amazon Prime: We are writing to you about an upcoming change to your membership.

As of February 18, 2022, the price of the monthly Prime membership has increased from $12.99 to $14.99, and the price of the annual Prime membership has increased from $119 to $139. The new prices, plus applicable taxes, will apply after March 25, 2022, on the date of your next renewal.

We continue to invest in making Prime even more valuable for members. Since the last price change in 2018, we have added more product selection available with fast, free, unlimited Prime shipping, and we expanded Free Same-Day Delivery from 48 to more than 90 U.S. metropolitan areas. In addition, Prime Video has tripled the number of Amazon Original series and movies; and this September, Prime Video will release the highly anticipated *The Lord of the Rings: The Rings of Power* and become the exclusive home of NFL's *Thursday Night Football*. This is all on top of billions of dollars in Prime Day savings over the years; the addition of new program benefits like prescription savings and fast, free delivery from Amazon Pharmacy; and the continued expansion of Amazon Music for Prime members, Prime Reading, and Prime Gaming.

> No further action is required. You may manage your Prime membership anytime by visiting Your Account.
>
> Sincerely,
>
> Your Amazon Prime Team

Notice how it emphasizes the continuous value Amazon is adding to the Prime membership. It's not blaming increases in inflation, inventory costs, supply chain disruptions, cost of labor rising, etc. It's informing you of the additional offerings to your membership. Customers do not care about your costs, nor are they buying them; that is the exact wrong revenue model to have. Nor do customers want to have to think about your costs. They do, however, enjoy comprehending and learning about the value you are providing.

Amazon didn't use euphemisms like "price adjustment" or "price change." It states plainly and clearly "price increase," informing you when it is to take effect, giving you plenty of notice. This is exemplary pricing communication because it doesn't rely on the old cliché of cost increases.

This is why it is so important to innovate your offerings. Over time, new offerings that you initially placed in the top tier should slide down, until eventually, they become part of your standard offering. When a subscription business adds value, it doesn't necessarily change your price. The two incidents are decoupled. My Amazon Prime membership didn't increase when a new season of *The Man in the High Castle* dropped, which I was addicted to, and binging on every season.

As you start off with your subscription pricing, you will probably need to make adjustments to your tiers and pricing levels. You can do so at any time by simply grandfathering existing members at the old price, and then tracking them in different cohorts. Provide plenty of advance notice, at least three months, if not six, and you can even offer existing members to pay a full year at the old price. Always try to add new offerings before you raise prices so you have something to emphasize other than cost of living increases. This will also differentiate you in the marketplace.

There is a lot of flexibility in your pricing. The most important thing is: Test, test, test. This applies to your tiered offerings, your prices, your payment terms (weekly, monthly, etc.), and feedback you receive from your customers on how well you are serving them. With the subscription model metrics and KPIs we will discuss in Chapters 18–20, you will be able to understand how price changes impact your churn rate—the amount of customers, and revenue, you lose per month, year, etc.

BRANDING YOUR PRICING

Consider branding your pricing approach. For example, the law firm Moores in Australia has branded its pricing approach with the acronym MAP (Moores Agreed Pricing), communicating certainty and predictability in price. Even though value pricing is becoming more common in the legal profession, Moores was an early adopter that benefited from having a unique, uncommon offering. Even though Moores is not subscription-based, here is how its website explains MAP:

Moores Agreed Pricing [MAP]

Where most firms charge by time, we are different. With Moores Agreed Pricing (MAP) you know exactly what you're getting and what it will cost. No estimates. No ranges. No hourly rates.

Before we talk to you about price, we take the time to understand your needs. Once we understand your situation, we prepare a proposal and provide a fixed fee cost. This gives you price certainty, with no annoying billing surprises.

SERVICE GUARANTEE

We can't guarantee outcomes, but like price, the quality of our service is another thing we can guarantee up front. If you think the quality of our service didn't match what was agreed, let us know and tell us how you think that should be reflected in the price you pay (Moores n.d.).

SUMMARY AND CONCLUSIONS

We are at the conclusion of our four chapters on pricing (Chapters 14–17). This chapter explained how "pricing the portfolio" differs from "pricing the customer," as is done under value pricing. We discussed the most common objections you are likely to hear about adopting the subscription business model in your professional firm, the biggest one being how to handle complex, one-off projects. We discussed the critical importance of the due care principle, then provided six different strategies for handling these types of projects—charging an upfront price; blending it in to the customer's subscription term length; structure a higher beginning price that tapers down to normal over time; offer an enterprise choice; trusting your value and just doing the work; and utilizing a TIP clause for truly extraordinary engagements when you are creating tremendous value. The important point is that the profit formula in the subscription model is different than one focused merely on value pricing transactions or selling time.

We also discussed best practices for raising your prices; why continuous innovation is so important in the subscription model; why you need to test, test, test, your prices, tiers, and make adjustments due to feedback from your customers; and finally, why you should consider branding your unique pricing approach to further enhance your firm's competitive differentiation. Only uncommon offerings command premium pricing.

When it comes to pricing, what you want is continuous progress, not perfection. Progress is made through constantly testing and iterating your pricing approach.

We have discussed how at least two things change when you change a business model: One is the pricing strategies that are deployed. The second are the metrics and KPIs that are used internally to assess the financial health of the firm. Before we get to specific KPIs for the subscription business model, it is worth discussing the consequences—both intended and unintended—of measuring, along with some warnings of why excessive measurement may create moral hazards.

18

MEASUREMENTS AND MORAL HAZARDS

*Grown-ups love figures. When you tell them that you have
made a new friend, they never ask you any questions about
essential matters. They never say to you "What does his voice
sound like? What games does he love best? Does he collect
butterflies?" Instead they demand "How old is he? How many
brothers has he? How much does he weigh? How much money
does his father make?" Only from these figures do they think
they have learned anything about him.*

—Antoine de Saint-Exupéry, *The Little Prince*, 1943

In the sixteenth century, a new word appeared in English
dictionaries—*pantometry*, which means universal measurement.
Ever since, man has been obsessed with counting things, from people and sheep to the amount of cars imported and the number of
McDonald's hamburgers served. Being able to count and measure is
one of the traits separating man from animals.

The problem for the pantometrists is the same one facing businesspeople today: What should be measured? Facts and figures do not
provide a context or reveal truth; we still need our observations, imaginations, and creativity. If we only focus on what we can measure,
we will become prisoners of our past, because it would be impossible
to create a future that would be different from an extrapolated and
precisely measured past. If everything important has to be quantified
to be comprehended, how are we to understand art, music, poetry,
literature—indeed, our own human feelings? Or new innovations,

since no quantified data yet exist? One could persuasively argue that the more valuable something is, the more likely it *cannot* be quantified. How do you measure and quantify the love you have for your child?

Measurements can certainly pronounce a fact, but they cannot explain it without an underlying context or theory. Numbers have an unfortunate tendency to supersede other types of knowing. Numbers give the illusion of presenting more truth and precision than they are capable of providing. Human genetic code is 98% identical with chimpanzees. We share even more DNA with whales. So what? Should we marry whales and chimps? That 2% is an enormous difference, so obviously the accuracy of the measurement misses the reality. These examples are all illustrations of *The Sagan Fallacy*: "To say a human being is nothing but molecules is like saying a Shakespearean play is nothing but words." Much of what is measured in today's firms suffers from the same fatal fallacy. Oliver Wendell Holmes once wrote: "We are mere operatives, empirics, and egotists, until we learn to think in letters instead of figures."

THE MCKINSEY MAXIM

We have all heard the famous saying, often referred to as the McKinsey maxim, named after the famed consulting firm: "What you can measure you can manage." This bromide has become such a cliché in the business world that it is either specious or meaningless. Specious since companies have been counting and measuring things ever since accounting was invented, and meaningless because it does not tell us what ought to be measured. Besides, has the effectiveness of management itself ever been measured? How about the performance of measurement? Measurement for measurement's sake is senseless, as quality pioneer Philip Crosby understood when he uttered, "Building a better scale doesn't change your weight."

This is not to imply we need to eliminate "hard data," but rather that we do not allow measurement mania to crowd out "soft" judgment. Since management itself cannot be measured, we have to rely on judgment. We can certainly use hard data to vouch for soft intuition, but we can also do the opposite—use soft judgments to check hard facts.

A lot of information is soft—gossip, hearsay, and intuition. The partner who learns his largest customer was golfing with a major competitor is not going to be served well by the time the lost revenue shows up on his profit and loss statement. As one manager quipped, "I would be in trouble if the accounting reports held information I did not already have" (Mintzberg 2009, p. 27). Accounting reports, timesheets, cost accounting, realization, and utilization rates—the matrix of measurements in most firms—are, by their nature, *lagging* indicators. Yet what is needed in firms today, similar to the canary in the coal mines of the last century, are *leading* indicators—early detection systems that allow firms to perform their ultimate function of creating wealth for the customers they serve. Running a firm based on financial reports and timesheets is similar to timing your cookies with your smoke alarm. The information is simply too late.

Another argument I constantly hear in defense of timesheets is they are a measure of opportunity cost: Is the firm investing its resources and receiving a high enough return? But opportunity cost has to be assessed *before* you do something, not afterward. If you decided to read this book for the next several hours instead of go to the beach, you made that tradeoff decision in advance of taking the preferred action, not afterward. Analyzing the action afterward is crying over a *sunk* cost, not an *opportunity* cost, and that is an enormous difference. Sunk costs are sunk; they are history that cannot be changed.

Traditional financial-based metrics are no longer as meaningful as they once were. They are a product of rationalists who are able to count the bottles rather than describe the wine. Though in an economy dominated by mind, not matter, intuition, discernment, wisdom, and judgment are far more important. Firms need better understanding before they can develop measurements that actually matter.

Blindly relying on this metric mania can obscure many oblique realities. The ultimate problem with numbers and measurements is what they *don't* tell us, and how they provide a false sense of security and the illusion of control—that we know everything that is going on.

Even the not-for-profit world is infected with this mentality. Consider the one measure that most people believe establishes the "efficiency" of a charity: What percentage of my donation goes to the cause? This metric explicitly assumes that a lower administrative and overhead structure leads to a more effective charity. Yet the empirical evidence does not warrant this false belief. This efficiency measurement, in and of itself, provides no information on the effectiveness of the outcomes—not merely the outputs—produced. If Jonas Salk had spent 50% on overhead and administration but developed the polio vaccine—saving countless millions of lives—should we conclude that his charity was "inefficient" because the ratio was only 50% spent on the cause? To ask the question is to answer it. Measurements can crowd out judgment and common sense.

Perhaps we need a corollary to the McKinsey maxim: *What is really important cannot be measured.* This will no doubt be met with tremendous resistance. It goes against the very grain of the MBA mindset, the modern-day pantometrists, who are taught that everything needs to be quantified and counted, and decisions should be based on the numbers: In God we trust, all others bring data, as is often said.

In other words, don't think, count. This is not to suggest that metrics are not relevant or useful. Rather, metrics, KPIs, and other quantifiable data are subservient to your firm's strategy, not the ruler of it.

Deep and meaningful transformations come from seeking answers to profound questions and engaging the imagination, not from more accurate measurements. If firms implement new strategies to adapt to the subscription economy, they will also need to usher in new measurements, otherwise they will get nothing but old behaviors. If it is true that we get what we measure, is it not about time we start to measure what we want to become? Let us stop measuring like mad and rather serve with soul.

To understand the limitations of quantifiable data, let us examine the vital difference between a measurement and a metric.

MEASURES VS. METRICS

Sometimes the numbers don't explain everything. The numbers are not the business—they are symbols of the business.

—Gerald Deitchle, Cheesecake Factory

Revenue, cost, profit, spending, income, and investment are all quantitative abstractions, a classic example of what philosopher Alfred North Whitehead categorized as the *fallacy of misplaced concreteness*—that is, when one mistakes an abstract belief, opinion, or concept about the way things are for a physical or concrete reality. Puppies are similar, believing that the fence defines physical reality. No one has ever actually seen or touched "a profit," a "profit center," or "a revenue." Firm leaders pour through financials and other metrics while ignoring the human relationships and concrete operations from which the numbers emerge. Rather than focusing on better ways to *organize and perform* work, they manipulate quantitative abstractions *about* the work (time tracking, hourly billing quotas, objectives and key results [OKRs], customer profitability, etc.).

To overcome this fallacy of misplaced concreteness, it helps to understand the enormous difference between a *measurement* and a *metric*. If you and I walk outside with two reliable thermometers, we will each get an accurate reading of the temperature. That is a measurement. Notice a measurement is not based on a choice or any assumptions.

But if we are valuing inventory to determine cost of goods sold, we will get a different number depending on whether we use the last-in, first-out (LIFO), or the first-in, first-out (FIFO) valuation method. If you are using cost accounting to determine cost allocations, you will get different results, depending on which cost accounting method you apply: standard, total absorption, average, lean, activity-based, or marginal costing. These calculations are all metrics, since they depend on the assumptions you are making.

Metrics are an excellent illustration of Lee Segall's law: "A man with one watch knows what time it is; a man with two watches is never quite sure." This explains the old joke about the accountant who is asked what 2 + 2 is, and replies, "What would you like it to be?" It is how Enron and Bernie Madoff can report windfall profits, while being cash poor.

Even though leaders understand cost accounting can be manipulated, we hear a lot of them say, "True, but it's better than nothing." Really? It is as if three friends are lost in New York City, and one happily reports, "Don't worry, I have a map." "Yes, but it's a map of Los Angeles," says the second friend, while the third says, "True, but it's better than nothing." It is better to be approximately right rather than precisely wrong.

Once you realize that costs are calculated, quite arbitrarily, it is easy to understand that they have nothing to do with cash, yet leaders spend an enormous amount of resources managing costs that have nothing to do with free cash flow.

Furthermore, even counting is not as straightforward as it seems. To count something, you first have to categorize it. Cash is easy and exact, yet costs are dependent on how they are allocated. If you are paying a team member $100,000 per year, you are spending that amount of cash regardless of how that person's capacity is utilized. Same with rent, technology, etc. Certainly you can allocate it out per hour to every job or customer, but that's not a cash transaction. If you didn't allocate those hours, or those hours simply went idle, would you save the equivalent of the hourly rate in cash? Of course not. This is the grand fallacy of cost accounting—not only is it *not* related to actual operations, it is not related to cash.

Enter Dr. Reginald Tomas Lee, author of *Lies, Damned Lies, and Cost Accounting: How Capacity Management Enables Improved Cost and Cash Flow Management*. He posits three reasons why cost accounting is a bad practice:

1. To get a cost, you have to create and force math and relationships that do not exist.
2. By doing this, you lose touch with your operations.
3. You create meaningless numbers that people consider as gospel (a single representation of an artificial reality).

Costs and profits are not absolute; they change based on the model you use to calculate them. The largest expenditure for most companies is capacity; space, labor, materials, equipment, and technology. Unless you model and manage capacity effectively, you will not achieve the cash flow results you seek (Lee 2016).

This debate between cost accounting and cash flow is not over. Much work is being done in this area. In 1987, accounting professor H. Thomas Johnson and Harvard Business professor Robert S. Kaplan published *Relevance Lost: The Rise and Fall of Management Accounting*, which was named in 1997 one of the 14 most influential management books to appear in the first 75 years of *Harvard Business Review* history. The book is credited with launching the activity-based costing (ABC) revolution. Yet, these two thinkers have gone down very different paths since then: Kaplan going on to pioneering work in the field of performance measurement, creating the balanced scorecard, and Johnson moving on to what he calls management by means.

I have drawn inspiration from both Kaplan and Johnson, along with Dr. Reginald Lee and Eliyahu Goldratt (author of *The Goal*), the latter three all being extremely critical of cost accounting, and I would encourage you to read each of these scholars because this field has evolved beyond what we were taught—and indeed, is *still* being taught—in our cost accounting courses in college.

H. Thomas Johnson's book, *Profit Beyond Measure*, is a seminal work. He profiles Toyota and Scania—the latter now owned by Volkswagen Group—as two manufacturers that *do not* have a standard cost accounting system. It is hard to argue with results. Toyota is one of the most respected companies in the world and has produced one of the highest-quality products at the lowest cost in the industry for years, dating back to 1926, when it started manufacturing and selling the automatic looms it had invented. It has an unbroken record of profits, is a fierce innovator, and ranks top in any measure of productivity you care to analyze.

As Glenn Uminger, a financial controller at Toyota Motor Manufacturing-Kentucky (TMM-K)—which Johnson studies in depth in his book—since 1988, says, "TMM-K has never had a standard cost system to track operating costs, and we probably never will." So how do they do it? How can a manufacturing company run without a standard cost accounting system? The answer lies in the subjective theory of value we explained in Chapter 14. Like Henry Ford, Toyota understands price justifies costs, not the economic fiction that costs determine price. Here is how Johnson explains it in his book, *Profit Beyond Measure*:

> None of these comments is meant to imply that Toyota does not have accounting and production planning information systems. Of course it does. Toyota has a comprehensive array of information systems, accounting and otherwise, with which to *plan*, in advance of operations, and to *report* results of operations after the fact. But information from such systems is *not allowed to influence operational decisions* (Johnson and Broms 2000, p. 106).

Johnson goes on to explain his theory that Toyota operates under "management by means" rather than "management by results." It is a thought-provoking viewpoint because it views the organization as a living system, based upon interdependent relationships, and those are nearly impossible to quantify. He notes Dr. W. Edwards Deming's observation that over 97% of the events that affect a company's results are not measurable, while less than 3% of what influences final results can be measured:

> Managers who adopt the new thinking offered here will accept as second nature the idea that what decides an organization's long-term profitability is the way it organizes its work, not how well its members achieve financial targets. It posits Toyota's principles as an example of new management thinking called "management by means." Management by means is the antithesis of "managing by results," practices identified . . . with Toyota's American competitors. Those who manage by results focus on bottom-line target and consider that achieving financial goals justifies inherently destructive practices. Those who manage by means consider that a desirable end will emerge naturally as a consequence of nurturing the activities of all employees and suppliers in a humane manner. (Johnson and Broms 2000, p. 12)
>
> Accounting measures are unable to penetrate the organic, multi-faceted union between customer and company that ultimately is the source of a company's financial results. This union is the reason any company exists. (Johnson and Broms 2000, p. 145)
>
> Because cost and profit are not objects, but are properties that emerge from relationships, quantitative measures can only describe them, they cannot explain them. Quantitative measures, unlike art, music, or the stories and myths that humans fashion with words, cannot convey understanding of the multidimensional patterns that shape the relationships from which results, such as cost and profit, emerge in a living system. (Johnson and Broms 2000, p. 188)

In other words, we can audit the drunk's bar bill, but we cannot explain why he is an alcoholic. Measuring outcomes without evaluating the processes that leads to those outcomes can be highly deceiving.

Andrew Carnegie use to say, "Watch the costs and the profits will take care of themselves." Johnson is saying: "Nurture the means. The results will take care of themselves." Robert Kaplan of balanced scorecard fame would say, "Measure the result and the means will take care of themselves" (this is dubious). We would say, along with Johnson's dictum, "Cultivate your value creation and customer relationships, and the profits will take care of themselves." Even the late Peter Drucker might agree:

I do not believe that one can manage a business by reports. I am a figures man, and a quantifier, and one of those people to whom figures talk. I also know that reports are abstractions, and that they can only tell us what we have determined to ask. They are high-level abstractions. That is all right if we have the understanding, the meaning, and the perception. One must spend a great deal of time outside, where the results are. Inside a business one only has costs. One looks at markets, at customers, at society, and at knowledge, all of which are outside the business, to see what is really happening. That reports will never tell you. (quoted in Flaherty 1999, p. 86)

As Eliyahu Goldratt says, "Products, services, and customers do not have costs; organizations do." It sounds heretical, but think about it: Would you save any cash on your rent even if you had no customers?

Cost accounting, and its more modern cousin activity-based costing—"a new way to be wrong" quipped Goldratt—does not deserve to be the apotheosis of value creation, or pricing, let along running your firm. No doubt, it has a role—for external financial and tax reporting—but that role is very specific and narrow, not one that should influence the managing of the internal operations of the firm.

To add insult to injury, tracking time and doing cost accounting does not help you price better; earn more profit; conduct project management more effectively; qualify your customers better; predict or improve the future performance of your team members; manage capacity more optimally; model cash flow; or measure what matters to your customers—and, it is a *lagging* indicator. Metrics and KPIs can also create moral hazards.

THE SEVEN MORAL HAZARDS OF MEASUREMENTS

As long as measurements are abused as a tool of control, measuring will remain the weakest area in a manager's performance.

—Peter Drucker

Exact measurements of the wrong things can drive out inexact, yet still useful, judgments of the right things. The illusion of certainty in our measurements creates—to borrow an important concept from the insurance industry—a *moral hazard*. Simply defined, people have an incentive to take more risks, or act carelessly, when they are insured. Fire insurance causes arson; life insurance causes suicide, or worse, murder; federal disaster insurance enables people to build on floodplains, or other places susceptible to natural disasters, since they do not suffer the costs of their choices. If people are insured, they may just act carelessly and cause the very thing they are insured against.

Our current cult of calculation, perpetuated by the infamous McKinsey maxim—what you can measure you can manage—creates the same type of risk, offering today's firm leaders the illusion of control and mastery of knowledge. Many times, numbers prove nothing, such as in start-ups, whose financial statements may look horrible but that may someday rise like the phoenix from the ashes and decimate the status quo infrastructure in a particular industry. The process of serendipity, trial and error, creativity, and discovery is just too impossible to measure, so the tendency is to ignore it as noise, subjective judgment, opinions, or just plain luck.

Peter Drucker is often cited as the source for, "What you can measure you can manage." But he never said it, wrote it, nor believed it. What he did say was that you will get what you measure, even to the detriment of your organization. This is because humans are scamps; they are experts at gaming any measurement system you deploy to control them.

Ed Catmull is one of the co-founders of Pixar Animation Studios and author of *Creativity, Inc.: Overcoming the Unseen Forces That Stand in the Way of True Inspiration*, all about how to run a truly creative enterprise. Here is what he has to say about the philosophy of what you can measure you can manage:

> "You can't manage what you can't measure" is a maxim that is taught and believed by many in both the business and education sectors. But in fact, the phrase is ridiculous—something said by people who are unaware of how much is hidden. A large portion of what we manage can't be measured, and not realizing this has unintended consequences. (Catmull 2014)

Some of those unintended consequences are the seven moral hazards of measures—be they metrics, KPIs, targets, or incentives. Analyzing them will assist firm leaders in avoiding these risks.

Moral Hazard #1: We Can Count Consumers, But Not Individuals

Josef Stalin's famous misattributed remark that "one death is a tragedy, whereas a million is a statistic" illustrates the danger of lumping individuals into aggregate, amorphous lumps as if they did not have a soul.

Stanley Marcus, the son of one of the founders of Neiman-Marcus, led the store through the difficult Great Depression, and one point he was especially fond of making was there was no such thing as a market, only customers:

> I am unaware of any store, or any business school, for that matter, that conducts a course or a series of lectures on "The Care and Treatment of Customers." I am referring to "customers" and not "consumers," for never in my retail experience have I ever seen a "consumer" enter a store. I've seen lots of "customers," for that's what they call themselves. (Marcus 1979, p. 211)

As economist Herbert Stein often said, "There is nobody here but us people." In the final analysis, *markets* and *consumers* are statistical abstractions, while *customers* are human beings who want to be treated specially and individually. Because benefits and costs are inherently personal and subjective, aggregation misses the individual. We can measure the objective temperature in a room at 70 degrees, but any one person can feel either warm or cold, and the differences cannot be used to cancel each other out. We simply cannot mathematically manipulate people. This is the tremendous advantage of the subscription business model—it puts the individual customer relationship at the center of the business, one human being at a time.

Moral Hazard #2: You Change What You Measure

Scientists call it the *Heisenberg's Uncertainty Principle*, which applies to all measures: That the observer in a scientific experiment affects the result. Central bankers call it *Goodhart's law*: Any target that is set quickly loses its meaning as it comes to be manipulated. People will always find ways to make their numerical targets, even if it leads them to ineffective or, sometimes, unethical or illegal behavior.

We witnessed this in the Wells Fargo Bank scandal where it used a cross-selling metric, which it mentioned in its third quarter 2016 earnings report, to "best align our cross-sell metric with our strategic focus of long-term retail banking relationships." The target was to cross-sell eight products to every customer, labeled internally "Going for Gr-eight." What did bank employees do? Opened 3.5 million deposit and credit card accounts without customers' consent. This ultimately led to $185 million fine from the Consumer Financial Protection Bureau, $6.1 million in customer reimbursements, and settling a class-action lawsuit for $142 million. It was also required to set aside a $3.25 billion accrual for future litigation expenses. In February 2018, it was hit with a joint $1 billion fine from the CFPB and the Office of the Comptroller of the Currency. That is a costly metric—there is no such thing as a free statistic, especially if you are using it to assess people's performance.

The lesson is, the bank never had a cross-selling *strategy*, it merely had a cross-selling *metric*. Its strategy was building long-term customer relationships. The strategy was hijacked by the metric. This is the process known as *surrogation*, which Wikipedia defines this way:

Surrogation

Surrogation is a psychological phenomenon found in business practices whereby a measure of a construct of interest evolves to replace that construct. Research on performance measurement in management accounting identifies surrogation with "the tendency for managers to lose sight of the strategic construct(s) the measures are intended to represent, and subsequently act as though the measures *are* the constructs." An everyday example of surrogation is a manager tasked with increasing customer satisfaction who begins to believe that the customer satisfaction survey score actually is customer satisfaction (Wikipedia n.d.).

This is an excellent illustration of why all measurements are subservient to your firm's strategy. If your metrics are not accurately reflecting your strategy, you probably need to change your metrics.

Moral Hazard #3: Measures Crowd Out Intuition and Insight

Once a measure becomes entrenched as part of the conventional wisdom, it is usually impenetrable to logic, intuition, critical thinking, or better ways to do something. Nowhere is this more true than the conventional metrics in a professional firm: billable hours, realization and utilization rates, job and customer profitability, and average hourly rate.

This is where H. Thomas Johnson's approach of "managing by means" versus "managing by results" is triumphant. We need deeper understanding and new processes to improve professional firm performance, not better measures, or even newer technology. After-action reviews are a superior process that all professional firms should use (to be discussed in Chapter 20).

If you have ever been bribed off an oversold airplane with a travel voucher, you have economist Julian Simon (1932–1998) to thank. Before airlines were deregulated in 1978, they frequently overbooked flights, causing enormous customer frustration. Even though the airlines measured load factors precisely, it provided little insight on how to solve this problem, which some airlines even denied existed. Simon came up with the solution one morning while shaving: Hold a reverse auction by finding those passengers who valued the seat the least, giving it to others who valued it more. It took years before the airlines, and the regulators, agreed to even test Simon's idea. Once they did, they discovered it solved the problem quite smoothly. Simon didn't have to pour over data; he used the economic way of thinking—logic combined with testable theories—and solved an issue those closest to it could not.

Daniel Boorstin, Librarian of Congress, wrote: "The greatest obstacle to discovery is not ignorance—it is the illusion of knowledge." To the extent our illusions of knowledge come from precise measurements that drive out critical thinking, we should constantly "hang our assumptions in front of us" to challenge our prevailing theories and look for better ways to do things.

Moral Hazard #4: Measures Are Unreliable

A company's balance sheet and income statement are subject to a margin of error that is never adequately disclosed to shareholders and other interested parties. Nor do financial statements make a distinction between revenue (or profits) increasing or decreasing due to inflation or deflation, or better pricing, for example. The former is external to the firm's control, while the latter can be influenced by executive decisions internally; yet the financials are mute as to the difference. We have already seen how GAAP do a pathetic job of measuring—or even acknowledging—intellectual capital. Why would we want to put so much faith in these numbers?

If the COVID-19 pandemic taught us anything, it is that leaders need to be far more sensitive to the errors in the data they use to make decisions. Many measures are not the oracle of Delphi, and we need to show more humility and less arrogance with respect to what we do not know.

Moral Hazard #5: The More We Measure, the Less We Can Compare

Engage in this thought experiment: You (or a loved one) needs heart surgery. You talk to doctors, nurses, friends, and other people you trust and respect, and two surgeons are consistently recommended to you. You go online to do some research on these two practitioners and discover their mortality rates (i.e., the risk of dying from surgery): surgeon A = 65%; surgeon B = 25%. Which surgeon would you choose?

I have conducted this thought experiment in seminars attended by various educated professionals—who certainly have taken a statistic class or two—and astonishingly, the overwhelming majority select Surgeon B. When I ask why, they say because of the lower probability of death. Perhaps they think they need to choose between the two without gathering more information. But that is not how I set up the thought experiment: I left it open as to whether they could ask further questions. Almost none do.

But wouldn't you want to know what type of patients the two doctors serve? What if surgeon A takes a disproportionate share of hard cases and thus has a higher failure rate? She just may be the better surgeon. We simply do not know without gathering additional information, both quantitative and qualitative, and making further judgments based on our own risk profile. Seeing the two numbers side by side seems, though, to give people a false sense of precision and, in this case, could lead to a deadly decision.

Moral Hazard #6: The More Intellectual the Capital, the Less You Can Measure It

Since 80% of the developed countries' wealth-creating capacity resides in its human capital—a lot of which is tacit knowledge, explained in Chapter 20—it is hard to capture in spreadsheets. We may be able to count the physical assets of a Google or Apple, but traditional accounting pays no attention to its human capital, what has been labeled the "invisible balance sheet." Traditional book value accounting—assets minus liabilities equals equity—can only explain about one-fifth of the value of the market capitalization on the nation's stock markets. Accountants call the difference between market value and book value goodwill; but that is just a label for our ignorance.

Retired accounting professor Baruch Lev wrote in *Accounting Today*:

> A study of mine showed that even if you could predict all the companies that will meet, or beat analyst's consensus earnings estimates—an impossible feat, of course—you wouldn't make real money. That's how useless earnings numbers are. (Lev 2021)

This remarkable finding speaks to the continuing irrelevance of historical financial statements. Knowledge work is difficult to measure, and the measures we do deploy—tracking time, realization, etc.—are totally inadequate for the job, similar to plunging a ruler into the oven to determine its temperature. Henry Mintzberg tells the story of someone he knew who once asked a British civil servant why his department did so much measuring. His reply: "What else can we do when we don't know what's going on?" (Mintzberg 2019). This is insightful and explains how measuring gives us a false sense of knowing and control.

Moral Hazard #7: Measures Are Lagging

Imagine driving your car with your dashboard gauges informing you of last month's speed, fuel level, temperature, oil pressure, RPMs, etc. This is precisely the status of accounting information; it is like walking into the future backward. It is a lagging indicator—or at best coincident, assuming real-time accounting takes place. This type of information can only tell us where we have been, never where we are going. Auditors come in after the battle and bayonet the wounded; they are historians with lousy memories (I know, I used to be one).

In a free market economy, innovation and dynamism are the life-blood of wealth creation. Profits come from risk. Yet from Prometheus—who democratized fire by taking it from the gods and making it accessible to mankind—onward, societies have feared the innovation and the innovator. The current whine seems to be: "They didn't tell me I could lose money!" We seem to want the trial without the error (or to privatize the gains, and socialize the losses). There are no sure bets. Data is only available about the past, never the future.

The Danish philosopher Søren Kierkegaard wrote: "Life is lived forward but understood backward." Certainly, measures help us reflect on past events, and aid us in improving our theories. But they can never take the place of dreams, imagination, passion, and the soul of enterprise where entrepreneurs toil and struggle to create our future. George Gilder articulates it well:

> Knowledge emerges not from chaos, or fixity, but from conditions of uncertainty. Under capitalism power flows to precisely the people who are willing to stake their money not on gambles or sure things but on testable hypotheses, thus generating knowledge and wealth for society.
>
> Entrepreneurs are trustworthy because they accept a moral code of testability and falsifiability rather than one based on sentiment, sanctimony, good intentions, good press, good luck, good looks or guarantees. (Gilder 2002)

No measure is capable of capturing the richness of free minds operating in free markets dreaming of better ways to improve our future, and it is folly to believe otherwise. It may even lead us into moral hazards, or a world where we are so preoccupied about measuring past performance we do not take the time to dream about a future that will make what we now measure obsolete.

SUMMARY AND CONCLUSIONS

We have attempted to slaughter some sacred cows in this chapter. First by refuting the infamous McKinsey maxim—the false idea that what you can measure you can manage. We discussed how metrics can obscure reality, crowd out judgment, wisdom, and common sense, all the while providing the illusion of control and false precision, leading us to being precisely wrong rather than approximately right.

We explored the crucial difference between a measurement and a metric, which helps to explain how cost accounting can lead to faulty decisions from an operations and cash flow perspective. The seven moral hazards of measurement were also analyzed to help avoid the worst excesses of too much measurement as a tool of control.

This was all done in preparation for discovering how the income statement is modified, along with the measures, metrics, and KPIs, in the subscription business model, the subject of our next chapter.

19

SUBSCRIPTION BUSINESS INCOME STATEMENT AND KPIs

Revamping a business model is not easy; it requires visible, consistent commitment from the top. It takes time. First, the more established an industry's norms, the more difficult it is to innovate business models. Everyone has a big stake in preserving the status quo, but it is critical to resist the temptation to do so.

—A.G. Lafley and Ram Charan, *The Game-Changer*, 2008

When Warner Brothers debuted the movie *The Suicide Squad* on August 6, 2021, the Hollywood press reported it was a failure due to its weak box office numbers. Yet the movie was watched on HBO Max's streaming service nearly 3 million times on just one weekend.

It is meaningless to impose old metrics on new models. The movie theater market is decelerating—especially since COVID-19—and whether it returns to its prior levels is yet to be seen. What we do know is that streaming services utilize a different business model, which requires new metrics. Movie theaters are essentially popcorn vendors facing increasing competition from alternative mediums of entertainment. Is it possible that streaming services will enter into this business, such as Netflix, or HBO? Also, think about how streaming services will change how actors and actresses are compensated. It certainly will no longer be based on gross box office receipts. New models demand new metrics.

Our old metrics and key performance indicators (KPIs) are still obsessed with counting the number of hamburgers, automobiles, and

SKUs sold. In the subscription business model, revenue and lifetime value per customer are far more important, but our metric mentality has yet to catch up to our new economic reality. As discussed in Chapter 12, since all transformations start with linguistics, this will also require learning a new language with respect to what is measured inside of firms. Even the traditional income statement looks different in subscription-based businesses. We will explore all of these issues, and more, in this chapter.

THE SUBSCRIPTION MODEL INCOME STATEMENT

A lot of rules have been added since the Venetian monk Luca Pacioli published the first accounting textbook, *Summa de arithmetica, geometrica, proportioni et proportionalita*, in 1494, introducing double-entry bookkeeping. It was a creation for future accountants that was as big as the invention of zero for mathematicians. Unfortunately, one could also make the argument that it was the last revolutionary idea to come from the accounting profession.

The balance sheet dates from 1868; the income statement from before World War I. Generally accepted accounting principles (GAAP) fits an *industrial* enterprise, not an *intellectual* one, or one based on **annual recurring revenue (ARR)**. The "three blind mice"—the balance sheet, income statement, and cash flow statement, and even their specific line items—have been frozen in time for the past 110 years, according to accounting professors Baruch Lev and Feng Gu in their groundbreaking 2016 book, *The End of Accounting and the Path Forward for Investors and Managers*. In it, they point out that "today's financial reports provide a trifling 5 percent of the information relevant to investors" (Lev and Gu 2016, p. xiii). They posit this is why privately held companies, whose investors are not making decisions based on this low-quality information, "invest considerably more and grow faster than publicly held companies" (Lev and Gu 2016, p. xvii).

To illustrate this point, in Chapter 1, Lev and Gu present the corporate financial statements for US Steel, from 1902 and 2012, side-by-side, and remark:

> Imagine if the report that people get today following a comprehensive physical checkup were identical to what patients received from their doctors 110 years ago. (Lev and Gu 2016, p. 2)
>
> Thus, the 1902 and 2012 investors, different folks to be sure—the latter, with vastly more powerful analyzing capabilities, access to alternative investments and investment tools (multiple hedging mechanisms, short sales, programmed trading)—received similar information from the two profit and loss statements. As for the balance sheets, the only items on the 2012 report absent in 1902 are goodwill and intangibles, the result of certain mergers and acquisitions conducted by the "modern" US Steel. . . . The sheer sizes of the two reports attest to this: The 1902 US Steel report is a slim 40-page document . . .whereas its 2012 counterpart is, in the best accounting tradition of mounting complexity and obfuscation, a hefty 174-page tome. (Lev and Gu 2016, p. 4)

Adding more arcane and picayune rules to GAAP, or converging existing GAAP with international accounting standards, will not solve this problem. The accounting model is suffering from what philosophers call a *deteriorating paradigm*—the theory gets more and more complex to account for its lack of explanatory power.

In all fairness to accounting, it never was meant to predict value prospectively, only to record transactions retroactively based on agreed prices. In effect, accounting can only count exchanges *after* they have taken place, at an agreed upon price. This is why accounting can only record the "goodwill" of a business until after is has been sold. Accounting has no way to place a value on that goodwill until a transaction takes place.

For these reasons and more, the subscription business model insists on a new income statement, one that is not focused on the cost of widgets sold, but rather on revenue per customer, and where costs are matched to future revenue streams, not period revenue. Here is a simplified example of a subscription income statement for two years:

	Year 1	Year 2
Annual recurring revenue	$1,000	1,200
Churn	(100)	(50)
Net ARR	900	1150
Recurring Costs:		
COGS (direct labor)	(200)	(300)
General & administrative	(100)	(125)
Research & development	(200)	(300)
	(500)	(725)
Recurring profit margin	**400**	**425**
Growth costs		
Sales & marketing	(300)	(400)
Net sales & costs		
Net operating income	100	25
New ARR	300	400
Ending ARR	1,200	1,550

This income statement is forward-directed, not just backward-looking, by showing how much in annual (or monthly) recurring revenue you are starting off with, and ending with, for the period.

Churn shows how much in lost revenue from customers who have defected. This critical indicator is now baked into your financials and you are more likely to pay much closer attention to customer churn in the subscription model than in a traditional transactional model. We will deal with strategies for curbing churn in Chapter 21.

Recurring costs in a professional firm consist of direct labor, research and development (continuing professional education and other learning expenses would be included here), and general and administrative expenses. These are the expenses that serve ARR. Since professional firms usually do not have inventory, these recurring costs are normally allocated in full to serving ARR.

Growth costs are primarily sales and marketing, and rather than reflecting how much is spent to generate past revenue, these expenses are matched to future revenue. These costs could include adding new customers, as well as growing existing customers.

The **recurring profit margin** shows how much is available to spend on future growth. Ending ARR is much more valuable than the traditional work-in-progress (WIP)—based on spent hours, or even a fixed price for a certain length—on traditional professional firm's financial statements, which can be more easily used as collateral to finance expansion. Tien Tzuo, founder and CEO of Zuora and author of *Subscribed*, explains how analyzing this income statement is different from a traditional P&L:

> When I was at Salesforce, we spent a lot of time and energy educating investors and analysts on the vast performance differences between subscription software companies and traditional software companies. Lots of them remained fixed on the P/E ratio, and could not fathom investing in a company trading—at that point—200x future earnings. We knew that operating profit was essentially meaningless to measuring our value. Honestly, as an investor, I would ding a subscription business that brought operating profit to the bottom line, seeing it as a signal from the company that it's cutting sales and marketing spending because it can't efficiently acquire new bookings!
>
> Here's the key takeaway — it is perfectly rational for subscription businesses to spend all their profits on growth, as long as their bucket doesn't leak. Remember, as long as you are growing your ARR faster than your recurring expenses, you can step on the gas. As Ben Thompson of Stratechery notes, "you're not so much selling a product as you are creating annuities with a lifetime value that far exceeds whatever you paid to acquire them." (Tzuo 2018, pp. 183–184)

The astute reader will notice that the subscription business model achieves something else—it blows up silos within the firm, transforming it into a truly one-firm model, all centered on customer relationships. For larger professional firms, this has been very hard to accomplish, especially in an hourly billing business model since separate P&Ls are run for each department—audit, tax, consulting, etc.—and even more absurd, analysis of P&L for individual customers, engagements, and even each hour. This is no way to run a business.

In the trial between Epic Games and Apple, there was an incredible revelation from Apple's CEO, Tim Cook. He was asked the profitability of the Apple App store. Cook responded by saying it was nearly impossible to figure that out because the company does not track expenses in that manner. He refuses to have his executives fight over cost allocations. He also pointed out that when Steve Jobs came back to Apple in 1997, the company was losing approximately $1 billion per year, yet every division (i.e., silo) was reporting a profit. How is that even possible? Because allocated costs have nothing to do with cash, or with making money. Jobs restored the entire company to one P&L (Aten 2021).

Firms should do the same, since it is an interdependent system, and you simply cannot expect to optimize each part, and in turn, expect that to optimize the whole. Some parts of a system need to be less efficient for the whole to be optimized, and this is certainly true in a relationship business. Thinking that if you focus on efficiency and do work faster you will be more profitable is ludicrously mistaken. It is not efficiency that is the goal; it is being effective in creating wealth for customers, while nurturing those relationships and offering a superior experience.

THE SUBSCRIPTION MODEL DASHBOARD: KPIS AND METRICS

Men have become the tools of their tools.

—Henry David Thoreau

When business models change, how you create, deliver, and price value changes as well. You simply cannot maintain the old measurements and expect to drive new behaviors. If we are what we measure, then we need to measure what we want to become. In the subscription model, there is simply no need to track time, compute customer profitability, or agonize over meaningless realization and utilization rates, along with all the other anachronistic metrics, because now the focus is on customer lifetime value and annual recurring revenue. There are no unit sales, just customers, and all of our costs are expended to create them. Recall customers and services do not have costs, only firms do. The unit of measure is the customer relationship, not the SKUs and services customers purchase.

Fortunately, a lot of work has been done on subscription KPIs and other metrics. I like the definition of a KPI provided by Bernie Smith (2021) in his book *Gamed: Why Targets and Incentives Fail and How to Fix Them*: "A KPI is measure of how we are doing at something that we care about." KPIs are only proxies for performance. You don't change your weight by weighing yourself more frequently, but rather through changing behaviors. This is why it is so important to work on the *means* if you want to change the *result*. Diet, exercise, adequate sleep, and so on are what is needed to effectively change your weight.

We will cover the fundamental KPIs below, based on two reports published by Andreessen Horowitz (Jordan et al. 2015; Casado 2020), the famed Silicon Valley venture capital firm, along with one published by Subscribed Institute (Subscribed Institute, n.d.), part of Tzuo's company, Zuora. You can find links to these reports in the Bibliography.

- **Bookings:** The total value of all the subscription agreements with the company. Of course, it is cancellable by the customer at any time. This would include one-off and one-time engagements, depending on how you price and invoice for them.

- **Revenue:** Revenue is recognized ratably over the life of the subscription agreement (usually monthly). How and when revenue is recognized should be done in accordance with GAAP, and is outside the scope of our discussion. The Accounting Standards Committee has promulgated ASC 606 that guides recognizing revenue for both public and private companies.

- **Active subscribers:** Number of subscribers with one or more subscription charges in a given period (typically a month, quarter, or year). Calculate: = Total number of customers who have subscription agreements.

- **New subscribers:** Calculate: = number of Active Subscribers (above) not active at the start of period, but became active during period.

- **ARR (annual recurring revenue):** A measure of your firm's recurring revenue, based on the annual sum of all your customers. It would exclude one-off or one-time (non-recurring) revenue.

- **ARR per customer:** This helps you analyze if your individual customer revenue is growing or declining, which will assist with offering new innovations, price increases, and pricing tier changes.

MRR (monthly recurring revenue): ARR converted to a monthly amount. Be sure not to include one-off or one-time engagements.

GRR (gross revenue retention): The percentage of recurring revenue retained in a given period of time. The highest GRR each customer can have is 100% since increases in revenue are ignored. If the customer spends less, say by selecting a lower-priced tier, the GRR percentage will decrease. This is an indicator of the long-term health of your customer base.

NRR (net retention rate): What existing customers spend, including upgrading, one-off projects, price increases, etc. It can be above 100%; in fact, the higher the better. A 140% NRR means the firm is growing at a 40% rate without adding any additional customers, which was Zoom's NRR when it went public, before the pandemic. Calculation: = Ending Cohort Gross MRR / Starting Cohort Gross MRR.

EARR (expansion annual recurring revenue): Percentage of new revenue generated from existing customers.

CRR (customer retention rate): ((CEP – NCDP) / CS) × 100. Where,

CEP = Number of customers at end of period

NCDP = Number of new customers acquired during period

CS = Number of customers at start of period

CAC (customer acquisition cost): Measures how much the firm is spending to gain customers against the number of customers it has acquired. Calculate: = Sales and Marketing costs for period / # of customers acquired over the period.

Average revenue per subscriber: Helps to understand your growth effectiveness. Calculate: = Gross ARR / Total number of active subscribers.

ASP (average selling price): To benchmark your CAC for new subscriptions and to assist in optimizing pricing. Calculate: = Total MRR (or ARR) in period for new subscribers / Number of active subscribers during that period.

Churn: Monitors health of customer relationships. Calculate: MRR at end of period (including customers who started in that period) / MRR at the beginning of the period. Also, calculate for number of subscribers: Monthly churn = Lost customers / Prior month's total.

Gross churn: Calculate: MRR lost in month / MRR at beginning of month.

Net churn: Calculate: (MRR lost *minus* MRR from upgrades) in month / MRR at the beginning of month.

CLV (customer lifetime value): Estimates the present value of the future *net profit* from the customer over the duration of the relationship. Helps to determine how much to spend on customer acquisition, and the value of the firm. First calculate average life span of customer (in months) = 1 / Churn rate. Then, CLV = Customer contribution margin* × average lifespan.

(* The customer contribution margin can be estimated in total across the entire portfolio of customers. There is no need to allocate costs to each customer as is done with timesheet cost accounting. Approximately right is good enough.)

The above are some of the more common KPIs and metrics associated with the subscription model. You have to test which ones are useful for your firm. Do not boil the ocean. Remember, just because you can measure it does not mean you should. Start with the fundamentals: Number of subscribers, MRR, ARR, CAC, and churn. Over time, you will discover which metrics work for you and which are superfluous. The goal of measuring is to improve performance. If that is not happening, look to your processes, not the result of your processes.

Another metric used by venture capitalists and other investors to appraise the health of subscription businesses is the heuristic of 3:1. That is, the ratio of customer lifetime value must be three times greater than the cost to acquire, as shown: CLV > 3 × CAC. Some of the most valuable subscription businesses achieve an 8:1 ratio.

As Wharton Marketing Professor Peter Fader has observed:

Decisions about customer acquisition, retention, and development shouldn't be driven by cost considerations—they should be based on future value.

If we could see Customer Lifetime Value as clearly as costs, all firms would get this. But because costs are so tangible and CLVs are a mere prediction, it's really hard to get firms to adopt this mindset. But it's the right one, and they should be working hard to become comfortable with CLV as the key driver to this kind of decision.

Another key issue to understand is the idea of win, retain, and grow, or as our friend Mark Stiving says, *Win, Keep, Grow*, the title of his book on subscription businesses. Of course you have to acquire the *right* customers that fit your firm's purpose, strategy, and positioning (see Chapter 11). Remember, your firm is defined by the *customers you do not have*. Once acquired, you have to minimize churn and hence grow your retention rates over time. This is accomplished by creating and constantly *plussing*—to borrow Walt Disney's phrase—your offering, while delivering to your customers a convenient, frictionless experience. Growing your customers is achieved by constant innovation that commands higher pricing and cultivating customer loyalty. Yet these levers are not equal in terms of their impact. You might assume that growing margins would increase CLV, but in reality, it does not move the needle much. Retention is the one that creates the largest impact on CLV. One study from Yale found that companies that improved retention from 60% to 90% had CLVs that quadrupled. By offering a model that is more focused on relationships than services, you will be more likely to create multiple transformations for your customers, increasing their loyalty to you as you are seen as reliable as Amazon, or a DPC physician.

Along with CLV, another important metric to monitor is free cash flow. In the old model, firms are fanatically focused on margins, but as Jeff Bezos used to quip when he was CEO of Amazon, "Percentages don't pay the light bill, cash does! He wrote in his 2004 Letter to Shareholders why he focuses on free cash flow:

> Why not focus first and foremost, as many do, on earnings, earnings per share or earnings growth? The simple answer is that earnings don't directly translate into cash flows, and shares are worth only the present value of their future cash flows, not the present value of their future earnings. Our ultimate financial measure, and the one we most want to drive over the long term, is free cash flow per share. (Rossman 2021, Appendix C, Free Cash Flow)

Of course, Amazon's strategy of hyper-growth is most likely different from yours, and the pricing power you acquire with this model will assist tremendously in growing your cash flow, but Bezos's quip that you can't spend margin is straightforward, which is why focusing on customer realization, based on an arbitrarily determined hourly rate, is so meaningless.

The above KPIs, especially CLV and free cash flow, are all examples of *lagging* indicators. They are also the most important of what John Warrillow calls *owner KPIs*, since they will ultimately determine the value of your firm when you are ready to exit. Your firm very well may be your largest single asset, and you want to be sure you are doing everything you can to maximize its sale value. Those with excellent CLV and free cash flow will command a premium multiple at sale.

Owner KPIs are differentiated in the mind of buyers from operational KPIs, such as net income, revenue, margins, and other lagging indicators that be can derived from the financial statements. At times, owner and operational KPIs will come into conflict, such as if you try to expand into different practice areas or diversify your customer base. When these conflicts arise, it is usually better to give more weight to the owner KPIs to maximize the value of the firm. Next, we explore *leading* indicators.

KEY PREDICTIVE INDICATORS

The only way to look into the future is use theories since conclusive data is only available about the past.

—Clayton Christensen et al., *Seeing What's Next*, 2004

When the late Milton Friedman taught his graduate courses in economics at the University of Chicago, he used to ask what his students came to call his two terrifying questions:

- How do you know?
- So what?

In terms of building a theory, these questions are profound: the first making us observe the world, the second forcing us to say what the effect is. To answer the latter, we need theory—a statement of cause and effect. Philosophers of science, such as Karl Popper and Thomas Kuhn, have explained how to build a theory, which is done in a cyclical pattern as follows:

- Observation
- Categorization

- Prediction
- Confirmation

This is why all scientific theories are formulated in a manner exposing them to being disproved. Scientists always ask, "What would it take to admit your theory is wrong?" If you answer nothing, you are arguing an assertion—a matter of faith—not reason. If you cannot be wrong, you cannot be right, either. This is why scientists are constantly looking for anomalies. Indeed, many scientific breakthroughs come from such anomalies, like the properties of helium seeming to defy gravity. Many papers in science are titled "An Anomalous Case of . . ." It is an iterative process, a never-ending quest of improvement, since only a better theory can replace an inferior theory. Nassim Taleb, author of *The Black Swan*, describes this as "Subtractive epistemology: the sucker thinks Truth is search for knowledge; the nonsucker knows Truth is search for ignorance." This is what the Scottish philosopher David Hume meant when he wrote "Knowledge is only ignorance postponed."

In his last book, *The Effective Executive in Action*, Peter Drucker explained the decision-making process:

> A decision is a judgment. It is a choice between alternatives. It is rarely a choice between right and wrong. It is at best a choice between "almost right" and "probably wrong." . . .
>
> But executives who make effective decisions know that one does not start with facts. One starts with opinions. These are, of course, nothing but untested hypotheses and, as such, worthless unless tested against reality. (Drucker and Marciariello 2006, p. 184)
>
> Then no one can fail to see that we start out with untested hypotheses—in decision-making as in science the only starting point. We know what to do with hypotheses—one does not argue them; one tests them. (Drucker and Marciariello 2006, p. 186)

Unlike management accountants and auditors, who tend to focus on lagging indicators—such as a business's financial statements—economists developed not only *lagging indicators* but also *leading* and *coincident indicators*.

- *Leading indicators* anticipate the direction in which the economy is headed.

- *Coincident indicators* provide information about the current status of the economy.
- *Lagging indicators* change months after a downturn or upturn in the economy.

This is not to claim economists can predict the future; far from it. There is a tremendous amount of history that supports the observation that no one can predict the future. That said, the indicators have no doubt expanded our knowledge of how an economy operates, and may even provide a clue as to where it is heading, but they are still a compendium of averages, and averages can be very misleading—you can drown in a lake that is, on average, four feet deep. Nonetheless, the indicators can be useful, for as Henry Hazlitt (1894–1993), wrote in his classic *Economics in One Lesson*: "The main purpose of economics is not to predict the future, but to learn what policies are likely to improve that future." The same could be said for businesses.

In a business context, *lagging* indicators are obvious—anything shown on the financial statements, or that can be computed from them. They provide *hindsight*. If you performed real-time accounting, where the financial statements and KPIs were literally updated for every transaction entered, that would rise to a *coincident* indicator—these provide *insight*. *Leading* indicators are different. They are nonfinancial, and they require us to posit a theory of cause and effect, then test it, then revise it, if necessary. The "canary in the coal mine" is a useful metaphor for thinking about leading indicators that help us see what is coming next. Usually, the cause and effect we are most interested in revolve around attempting to predict customer behavior, since we put such a premium on customer loyalty, reduced churn, and ultimately, CLV. Hence, leading indicators provide *foresight*, at least as best we can do in a complex, unpredictable universe.

This is a critical distinction being made between a key *performance* indicator and a key *predictive* indicator. A performance indicator is merely a mindless metric, such as the number of patents filed, or new revenue, but lacks a falsifiable theory. A predictive indicator, by contrast, is a measurement supported by a theory, which can be tested and refined, to explain, prescribe, or predict behavior.

The theory is the senior partner, as Einstein said: "It is theory which decides what we can observe."

Consider Dr. Paul Thomas, who you met in Chapter 9, founder of Plum Health, a DPC practice. He tracks some of the lagging KPIs shown above for a subscription business: MRR, churn, and so on, and obviously has up-to-date accounting reporting. But he also tracks these predictive indicators:

- How many hospitalizations prevented
- How many urgent care and emergency department visits we prevented
- Whether our patients with a weight loss goal are achieving those results
- Management of patient anxiety or depression
- How much money we have saved our patients (on drugs, diagnostic tests, and other procedures ordered, as well as unnecessary ones not being prescribed)
- Whether we have decreased morbidity and mortality in our communities (Thomas 2020).

Notice something about the above indicators? They measure the success of Plum Health the *same way the customer does*. And that is decisive because, ultimately, the success of any business is a result of loyal customers who return. None of those indicators would ever appear on a financial statement, but they have a predictive correlation with the success and profits of the practice.

Developing key predictive indicators is a metastrategy—that is, a strategy for defining strategies. They need to be intimately linked with the firm's value proposition, as well as quantitative measurements, or—and this is even more important in knowledge firms— qualitative judgments. They should have a common definition and be understood across the entire firm, with no ambiguity.

Having your entire team focused on KPIs not only gets the right job done daily, it also gives them a sense of commitment to the process of improving *how* that job gets done. Since they are at the coal face observing actual customer behavior, they know which processes work and which cause frustration, and can readily suggest improvements to make the customer experience more enjoyable. This process must be based on observed reality, and it must make sense in explaining *actual* customer behavior.

According to an article in the *Journal of Accountancy,* CPA firms lose customers for the following reasons (Aquila and Koltin 1992, pp. 67–70):

1. "My accountant just doesn't treat me right" (two-thirds of the responses).
2. CPAs ignore clients.
3. CPAs fail to cooperate.
4. CPAs let partner contact lapse.
5. CPAs do not keep clients informed.
6. CPAs assume clients are technicians.
7. CPAs use clients as a training ground (for new team members).

Turn the coin over, and this is why people select and stay with accountants (Winston 1995, p. 170):

- Interpersonal skills
- Aggressiveness
- Interest in the customer
- Ability to explain procedures in terms the customer can understand
- Willingness to give advice
- Perceived honesty

David Maister, Charles H. Green, and Robert M. Galford, in *The Trusted Advisor*, offer the most commonly expressed customer suggestions regarding what they want from their professional relationship (Maister et al. 2000, p. 180):

1. Make an impact on our business, don't just be visible.
2. Do more things "on spec" (i.e., invest your time on preliminary work in new areas).
3. Spend more time helping us think, and helping us develop strategies.
4. Lead our thinking. Tell us what our business is going to look like 5 or 10 years from now.

5. *Jump* on any new pieces of information we have, so you can stay up-to-date on what's going on in our business. Use our data to give us an extra level of analysis. Ask for it, don't wait for us to give it to you.

6. Schedule some offsite meetings together. Join us for brain-storming sessions about our business.

7. Make an extra effort to understand how our business works: sit in on our meetings.

8. Help us see how we compare to others, both within and out-side our industry.

9. Tell me why our competitors are doing what they're doing.

10. Discuss with us other things we should be doing; we welcome any and all ideas!

Despite all this evidence, many professional firms still track the hours its team members spend working on various assignments. There are many problems with this, the first being that no customer defines the success of their professionals by how many hours they spend on their work. It also focuses the team on efforts, activities, and inputs at the expense of transformations, and the customer experi-ence. Perhaps this explains why the surveys mentioned above on los-ing and gaining customers have not materially changed in the past half-century. The right measures, and judgments, are simply not on the dashboard of most professional firms. The canaries in the coal-mine are hacking and wheezing.

If a firm wanted to develop leading KPIs, it should study the pre-ceding factors to determine how it can create KPIs that would either discourage—or encourage—the behavior described. This requires positing a theory of factors important to measure and reward.

Here are some firm-wide KPIs selected by those firms that have quit using timesheets for a more customer-focused set of predictive indicators. It should be noted that not all of the following KPIs are leading, some are coincident, and some may even be lagging, depend-ing on how often they are disseminated throughout the organization.

Turnaround Time

Like FedEx, on-time delivery of services, as promised, is one way customers define the success of their firms. This can be tracked at the team member level and the firm-wide level. Peter Drucker's alliterative recipe to avoid the pitfalls of procrastination:

> Definition, delegation, and deadline. The executive needed to define the problem or the task, delegate accountability to a specific person along with responsibility for the specific thing to be accomplished, and establish a firm deadline for completion. The definition ensured a sense of purpose, the delegation identified who was going to do the actual work, and the deadline substituted action for inertia. (Flaherty 1999, p. 328)

If a particular team member is missing deadlines, it is a good indication the team member has been given too much work, does not have adequate education to do what has been assigned, is unclear on the assignment responsibilities, is simply not up to the job, or perhaps is having a personal problem. Whatever the reason, the turnaround time provides a leading indicator to firm leaders to intervene and correct any problems in real time. The timesheet does not provide this advantage, because once it has been discovered on the timesheet, the problems are history, and by definition, can no longer be managed. The bottlenecks are usually at the top of the bottle, and firms that don't have adequate workflow processes along with measuring turnaround time, not only don't deliver on time, they suffer from FISH: first-in, still-here.

Innovation Revenue

This is revenue generated from new offerings that didn't exist three to five years ago. Intel, for example, wants 100% of its revenue derived from products that didn't exist three years ago, a phenomenal innovation curve.

Innovation is essential to creating new wealth; as Gary Hamel asks, "What does it matter to an investor if a company is earning its cost of capital if its rivals are capturing the lion's share of new wealth in an industry?" (Hamel 2000, p. 285).

Customer Loyalty (or Net Promoter Score)

Frederick Reichheld, in his work with Bain & Company, estimated fewer than 20% of corporate leaders rigorously track customer retention. For professional firms, who derive anywhere from 80% to 95% of their revenue from existing customers, this is a major oversight. Also, when you consider it costs an average of 4 to 25 times more to *acquire* a customer than to *retain* one, not to mention that in the sub-scription model if you can retain a customer for one year, you have a 90% probability of maintaining them for life, these metrics must become part of the firm's value system.

Because word of mouth is the most effective way to acquire the right kind of customers, referrals from existing customers are a leading indicator that the firm is delighting its current customers. A firm has no business taking on new customers if its existing customers are not completely happy. Also, if the firm's leaders are interested in promoting rainmaking activities at all levels within the firm—and rewarding them commensurately—referrals can also demonstrate the firm is asking its current customers for friends or colleagues they believe could derive the same benefits as they do from doing business with the firm. A lot of firms do not get the referrals they could simply because they do not ask on a regular basis. I have always liked Chris Fredericksen's recommend response when you are asked by a customer, "How's business?" "Business is great, and we are looking for more."

One theory being tested in some companies to measure customer loyalty is Fred Reichheld's Net Promoter® Score (NPS®) from his book *The Ultimate Question*. The hypothesis is as follows: you only need to ask your customers one question.

How Likely Is It That You Would Recommend This Company to a Friend or Colleague?

The scores, on a 1-to-10 scale, are then divided into three categories:

1. *Promoters (P)*—loyal enthusiasts (score 9–10)
2. *Passives*—satisfied but unenthusiastic, easily wooed by the competition (score 7–8)
3. *Detractors (D)*—unhappy customers trapped in a bad relationship (score 0–6)

The NPS® calculation is then computed with the percentages from above, as follows (Reichheld 2006, p. 19):
NPS® = P – D

Reichheld concludes most companies have an NPS® score of only 5% to 10%, while those companies with the highest growth—due to higher customer loyalty—have NSP scores of 50% to 80%, such as Harley-Davidson, Costco, Amazon.com, eBay, Apple, and FedEx (Reichheld 2006, pp. 19–20). The accounting profession has an average NPS® score of 23.

Caveat: NPS® is merely a theory, which still needs to be tested. It has come under increasing criticism as of late, as companies learn how to game the metric—we humans are, indeed, scamps. For instance, Dell and Electronic Arts had high NPS® scores but encountered difficult times due to outdated business models. One reason is that the NPS® score is based on what people *say* in surveys, not what they *do*. That said, we have seen firms that use NPS® report higher levels of customer loyalty and profit, and it is one method to gauge customer loyalty. You have to test it to see if it is predictive for your firm. It may be better to test the next KPI first, before NPS®.

Customer Effort Score

Another popular indicator was proposed in the *Harvard Business Review* article, "Stop Trying to Delight Your Customers," by Matthew Dixon, Karen Freeman, and Nicholas Toman (Dixon et al. 2010). Their hypothesis was that merely delighting customers does not build loyalty, but reducing the customer's effort in dealing with your organization does. This is what is meant by a frictionless experience, and it is much easier to accomplish when you always have spare capacity available to deal with customer problems, challenges, and opportunities.

Like NPS®, this score is a theory, and needs to be tested to see if it predicts customer loyalty. It would certainly ensure the firm do everything it can to make the process of interacting with it as easy and painless as possible for the customer. It would be like doing a timesheet on your customers that tracks two items: Time you saved *them*, and time *they* spend with you. Since this is a function of the *attention* and interaction they have with your firm, it is one way tracking time might actually make sense. The major sin businesses create in our current economy is to waste the customer's time. It is unforgivable.

Value Gap

This measurement attempts to expose the gap between how much the firm *could* be doing for its customers compared to how much it actually is. We would recommend you measure this by how many transformations you could be guiding your customer through. What actions can your firm take to close the value gap? What would be the impact of creating more transformations for the customer?

Recency, Frequency, and Quality of Customer Contacts

Since two-thirds of customers defect from firms because of perceived indifference, why not encourage all of the firm's team members to meet regularly with the customers they serve? This keeps the firm visible and in front of the customer; aids in the development of communication and listening skills of team members; changes our mindset from Time equals Money to Time (*with the customer*) is *more valuable* than Money, since it is nurturing and growing CLV.

As a general rule, *all leading indicators are theories derived from information not found on financial statements*. It is important to note there is ample empirical evidence that between *three* to *five* leading indicators should be enough for *any* firm to have predictive value for customer behavior. Though we wanted to provide enough so you can at least begin to think in this direction—and perhaps develop even better leading indicators for your firm—it is important to keep in mind we are emphatically not suggesting you adopt *all* of the preceding KPIs. *Do not boil the ocean.* If you try to track too many KPIs, you end up knowing nothing, and would have simply replaced the old matrix of metrics with something even more burdensome.

Another caution: When choosing your firm's KPIs, do not over-intellectualize the process. Selecting KPIs is not merely a matter of left-brain analysis; your firm's right-brain is important, too. Recall the Julian Simon story of overbooked flights from Chapter 18. Simon did not need to know any KPIs from the airlines to imagine a new way of handling the problem. Ultimately, you are testing a theory, which will greatly influence what you are measuring and observing. You are looking for KPIs that will measure and reward results over activities, output over input, performance over methodology, responsibilities over procedures, and effectiveness over efficiency. Usually, when it comes to KPIs, less equals more.

KPIS = ACCOUNTABILITY

There ain't no rules around here! We're trying to accomplish something!

—Thomas Edison

There is little doubt that what you measure defines how people work, especially if those measurements determine pay, promotions, and other career advancements. Most firms, when they are guided at all by indicators, do not formulate a set of coherent KPIs focused on the real-time, day-to-day, customer experience. Most performance measures are simply abstracted from lagging accounting data, and while they may be able to report the score of the game, they provide no insight or guidance on how to improve performance.

Most people simply are not inspired to achieve the type of financial performance measurements dictated by the profit-and-loss statement. It is not inspiring to work somewhere simply to make "profits," or improve "realization by 5%." The firms who have gotten rid of their timesheets and replaced them with some (usually between two and three) of the firmwide KPIs above have also implemented this change in a very rational manner. That is, they involved the team members in the change. Although it is widely believed that people do not like change, we believe there is a difference between change *imposed* and change *adopted*. As Michael Basch reminds us: "People don't mind change. They mind being changed."

Let the team members decide for which KPIs they want to be held accountable. These are smart, bright, motivated and professional people who want to do an outstanding job not only for the customers and the firm, but also for themselves. They know what the key drivers of success are. Imposing controls such as billable hours, which do not have a palpable or predictive relationship with customer success, might cause obedience and a minimal level of exertion, but it will not drive discretionary effort on the part of team members, nor drive excellence.

The firms that have let the team decide on the KPIs discovered, usually to their pleasant surprise, the team chose KPIs that were tougher on themselves than the partners would have been. People who select their own goals are usually more demanding of themselves compared to when those goals are selected for them.

Social controls are also far more effective than financial controls for influencing your team member's behavior. This explains why most professional firms that have trashed timesheets tend to hold frequent meetings—both on marketing and work-in-process—in which everyone is held accountable for the selected KPIs. If you know your peers are holding you responsible and answerable for your activities, you are more likely to act in a manner consistent with the wishes of the group, not wanting to let your colleagues down.

Jim Casey, founder of UPS, said in 1947: "A man's worth to an organization can be measured by the amount of supervision he requires." *Time's Up!* for firms to remove the Sword of Damocles— the timesheet—hanging over the head of their professionals, and unleash them from a theory that is no longer applicable to the subscription economy of the modern firm.

We have discussed how the accounting statements and key performance indicators, along with key predictive indicators, for the subscription business model are different. Recall that with any business model change, not only the pricing strategy changes, but so, too, do the KPIs. To change the first, without changing the second, is the equivalent of looking for a gas tank on a Tesla. This is simply a different car that requires new conventions, practices, and dashboard.

Because professional firms are so dependent on human capital, it is time to cascade these key predictive indicators outlined above down deeper into the organization, at the individual knowledge worker level to align their day-to-day activities with the firm's overall purpose, strategy, and positioning. As W. Edwards Deming used to say, "No organization can survive with just good people. They need people that are improving." We will also present the most effective learning tool ever invented—next to the book—that every single professional firm should be utilizing to improve the future performance of its knowledge workers.

20

KNOWLEDGE WORKER KPIs AND THE AFTER-ACTION REVIEW (AAR)

What made the traditional workforce productive was the system—whether it was Frederick Winslow Taylor's "one best way," Henry Ford's assembly line, or Ed Deming's Total Quality Management. The system embodies the knowledge. The system is productive because it enables individual workers to perform without much knowledge or skill. . . . In a knowledge-based organization, however, it is the individual worker's productivity that makes the system productive. In a traditional workforce, the worker serves the system; in a knowledge workforce the system must serve the worker.

—Peter Drucker, *Managing in the Next Society*, 2002

Engage in this thought experiment: You want to build the world's finest automobile. You decide to use individual parts with a reputation for excellence from various cars around the world—the engine from a Ferrari, the brakes from a Porsche, the suspension from a BMW, and so on. What you would end up with is not the world's greatest automobile, but rather, a really expensive pile of junk.

This, in a nutshell, is the problem with the way we attempt to measure the "efficiency" of knowledge workers—we measure each task in six-minute increments in the false belief that maximizing the efficiency of each one will maximize the efficiency of the entire firm. Yet knowledge work is not repetitive, it is *iterative* and *reiterative*. That is, it is a process of the mind, a difficult place for metrics to have any meaning. Not many people would want a time-and-motion surgeon who equated efficiency with quality medical care.

The task at hand is formidable, since the relationship between inputs and outputs is not as well defined in the knowledge era as it was in the agricultural or industrial revolutions. In his Nobel Prize lecture, the economist Friedrich von Hayek urged policymakers to emulate gardeners, not engineers, by creating the environment for growth rather than trying to bring it about directly through command and control. This applies to knowledge workers as well. It does no good to admonish your team members to work *smarter*, not *harder*. It is not bad advice, it is just not very helpful—like telling people to be healthy, wealthy, and wise. We need to apply the same ingenuity and creativity management thinkers did with manual workers to increase the effectiveness of knowledge workers.

A MODEL FOR KNOWLEDGE WORKER EFFECTIVENESS

Knowledge work is not defined by *quantity* but by *quality*. It is also not defined by its *costs* but by its *results*. In knowledge work, the traditional tools of measurement need to be replaced by *judgment*, and there is a difference between a measurement and a judgment: a measurement requires only a stick; a judgment requires knowledge.

Knowledge work can only be designed *by* the knowledge worker, not *for* the worker. In a factory, the worker *serves* the system. The same is true in a *service* environment; but in a knowledge environment, the system should *serve* the worker. As technology continues its relentless drive to automate more and more tasks, the more complicated work requires judgment, experience, wisdom, and tacit knowledge, which is next to impossible to put into a standardized checklist, let alone believe there is "one best way" to achieve results.

We need new thinking and new models to *judge* the effectiveness of knowledge workers. Fortunately, Peter Drucker blazed the trail in this area, drawing an enormous distinction between *efficiency*—always a ratio of outputs to inputs—and *effectiveness*, which is the extent to which the desired result is realized:

> Effectiveness is the foundation of success—efficiency is a minimum condition for survival *after* success has been achieved.
>
> Efficiency concerns itself with the input of effort into all areas of activity. Effectiveness, however, starts out with the realization

that in business, as in any other social organism, 10 or 15 percent of the phenomena—such as products, orders, customers, markets, or people—produce 80 to 90 percent of the results. The other 85 to 90 percent of the phenomena, no matter how efficiently taken care of, produce nothing but costs (which are always proportionate to transactions, that is, to busyness). (Drucker 2007, pp. 34–35)

Wise firm leaders will build on this wisdom to usher in the new era of the knowledge worker. Drucker believed the main focus of the knowledge worker needs to be on the task to be done—with all other distractions eliminated as much as possible—and this is defined by the worker him- or herself. Asking knowledge workers the following questions (these are adapted from Peter Drucker and other sources) about their jobs is a rich source of learning a great deal about any firm:

What is your task?

What should it be?

What should you be expected to contribute?

How fair are those expectations?

What hampers you in doing your task and should be eliminated?

How could *you* make the greatest *contribution* with your strengths, your way of performing, your values, to what needs to be done?

What *results* have to be achieved to make a difference?

What hinders you in doing your task and should be eliminated?

What progress are you making in your career?

How is the firm helping you to achieve your professional goals and aspirations?

What does the firm do right, and what should it continue doing?

What are the firm's weaknesses, and what should it stop doing?

What critical things should the firm start doing?

It should be obvious at this juncture that leaders who are responsible for knowledge workers are going to have to become much more comfortable with intuition, judgment, and discernment over measurements, as well as verbal, visual, and visceral forms of information. You simply cannot manage people by numbers. Professor Henry

Mintzberg tells the story of one student who asked him: "How can you select for intuition when you can't even measure it?" (Mintzberg 1989, p. 83). This is a sad commentary on the state of current MBA education. We seem to be turning out greyhounds in counting but ignoramuses in dealing with human beings.

Emotions are essential to good decisions, since "most people reason dramatically, not quantitatively," as Oliver Wendell Holmes wrote. This is why people are inspired more by stories than spreadsheets. Martin Luther King did not proclaim, "I have quarterly objectives!" but inspired with a dream.

We need KPIs for knowledge workers that create an environment of responsible autonomy and accountable interdependence, where workers will decide for themselves—and in teams—what and how to perform their jobs, while taking full responsibility and accountability for the outcome.

KEY PREDICTIVE INDICATORS FOR KNOWLEDGE WORKERS

Many managers agree that the effectiveness of their organizations would be at least doubled if they could discover how to tap the unrealized potential present in their human [capital].

—Douglas McGregor, *The Human Side of Enterprise*, 1960

Many of the "hard" and "objective" measures we do use can be gotten around by the average worker with a modicum of intelligence. It is actually the "soft," "fuzzy," and "subjective" measures that are harder for leaders to deal with, because they require judgment and discernment. Measurements only require a scale, and it is much easier to be precisely irrelevant than it is to be approximately relevant. Measures also provide us with the illusion of control, as if you can manage people by managing numbers.

The following knowledge worker KPIs are offered in the spirit of flouting bureaucratic command-and-control rules and direct performance metrics from an externally guided standard, all the while maintaining a sense of pride in helping others, which is one of the most important intrinsic rewards people earn from their chosen profession. The following KPIs require judgment, and they have been found to be predictive of a successful professional.

Customer Feedback

What are the customers saying—good and bad—about the team member? Would you trade some efficiency for a team member who was absolutely loved by your customers? How does the firm solicit feedback from its customers on team member performance? Does the firm reward team members for delivering outstanding customer service or going above and beyond the call of duty for a customer? Are these stories shared with the rest of the firm so they can become part of its culture, as they are at Nordstrom, Southwest, FedEx, and Disney? Or is the firm simply rewarding billable hours while preaching customer service, creativity, and innovation—what leadership expert Steven Kerr described in his 1975 essay, "On the folly of Rewarding A, While Hoping for B."

Effective Listening and Communication Skills

If reading and writing go together, so too do speaking and listening. Yet is anyone really ever taught to listen? It is well known that speaking and listening are harder to teach than reading and writing; and if we lament the low level of reading and writing being taught in schools, just think how much less developed speaking and listening skills must be. Unlike reading and writing, which are solitary undertakings, listening and speaking always involve human interactions.

But how do you measure listening and communication skills? It is truly a soft measure, but is it not a critical skill for the development of a true knowledge worker, especially in an era where teamwork and wide collaboration with others are essential to perform their tasks? I observed a panel discussion at the American Institute of Certified Public Accountants' Group 100 meeting of executives in corporations and government agencies that hire CPAs, lawyers, and consultants. The number-one capability they look for—and it influences their decision to hire one firm over another, even before price or quality—is communication skills. These skills must be *judged and experienced*; they cannot be measured. Firms—and knowledge workers themselves—need to invest in the education necessary to make their team members exceptional in these abilities.

Risk Taking, Innovation, and Creativity

These are other soft measures (actually, judgments), but critical skills for any knowledge worker. How often do they take risks or innovate new ways of doing things for customers or the firm? Do they engage in creative thinking in approaching their work? Most leaders say they want their people to "think outside the box," but when you look at what they measure and reward, there is an enormous gap between what they say and what they do.

Innovation and creativity need not be thought of as separate from the rest of the firm, but rather an integral part of it. Shouldn't firms work to make innovation ordinary? This is why 3M implemented the "15% rule," which encourages technical people to spend up to 15% of their time on projects of their own choosing and initiative (Google provides 20%).

Yet I am met with *staring ovations* when I suggest professional firms adopt a similar policy, where at least the knowledge workers are given time to dream up better ways to innovate, improve systems, or add value to customers. As Ikujiro Nonaka says in *The Knowledge-Creating Company*, "Allow employees time to pursue harebrained schemes or just sit around chatting, and you may come up with a market-changing idea; force them to account for every minute of their day, and you will be stuck with routine products." Routine services will not suffice in the subscription model.

A survey conducted by the Net Future Institute found that most people do their best thinking not at the office but during their shower, commute, or while at home. Why? Because you are not distracted by other things in these environments—you actually have *time to think*. But in today's frenetic firms, contemplating, cogitating, daydreaming, and thinking lower efficiency, do not look good on your timesheet (there are no codes for these activities), and hence are underinvested in by most firms.

Knowledge Elicitation

Ross Dawson, in his book *Developing Knowledge-Based Client Relationships: The Future of Professional Services*, describes knowledge elicitation as "the process of assisting others to generate their own knowledge." Note that this encompasses more than simply learning new things; it involves educating others so they are able to generate their own knowledge. One of the most effective techniques for knowledge workers to learn any subject—especially at a very deep level—is to teach it. As they say, to teach is to learn twice. How often do the team members facilitate a lunch and learn on an article or book they have read or seminar they have attended? How good are they at educating their customers?

Effective Knowledge Producer and Consumer

This is designed to judge how well the team members draw from— and contribute to—the firm's intellectual capital (IC). Are they simply consumers of IC, or do they also produce IC? How many after-action reviews (AARs) have they performed? How many times were those AARs accessed by other members of the firm? (AARs will be discussed below.) How well do they convert their *tacit* knowledge into *explicit* knowledge the firm can reuse and make part of its structural capital? Do they look for the most effective way to leverage knowledge, or do they merely reinvent the wheel? This type of evaluation will help ensure the firm is leveraging what really counts—its IC—and developing more of it.

Ability to Deal with Change

How well do the team members adapt to discontinuity, ambiguity, and tumultuous change? How do they assist others—colleagues and customers alike—in dealing with change? Sure, this is another soft skill, but a critical one in developing the type of temperament required to become a successful professional.

Continuous Learning

What do team members know this year that they did not know last year that makes them more valuable to the firm and its customers? This is more than simply logging time in continuing educational courses; it would actually require an attempt to judge what they learned. Are they constantly enhancing their skills to become more effective workers? How many books have they read this year? More important, what did they learn from them? Does the firm adequately invest in its people's education to fulfill this mission? Firms are reluctant to invest in education because employees may leave. They can leave anyway, and the best ones will be more likely to do so if you are not investing in them. But what happens if you do not educate them and they *stay*?

Effective Delegator

Peter Drucker wrote: "I have yet to see a knowledge worker, regardless of rank or station, who could not consign something like a quarter of the demands on his time to the wastepaper basket without anybody's noticing their disappearance" (Drucker 2006, p. 17). If true, this is an astonishing statistic. Think of the additional capacity your firm would gain if its senior team members were to avoid up to 25% of their work, while delegating another 25% to 50% that could probably be more effectively done somewhere else in the firm. Not only would it provide needed skills for junior team members, it would make available greater capacity to service customers with more valuable transformations. Does your firm encourage its knowledge workers to become effective delegators, as opposed to hoarding work to meet irrelevant billable hour quotas?

Coaching Skills

How well does the firm develop team members who can coach and mentor those less experienced? Are adequate resources being invested in this area? I have seen my share of mentoring programs fail, or deliver lackluster results, and remain unconvinced of their worthiness. The reason is that a mentor cannot be thrust upon someone; rather, it is a voluntary relationship that develops over time. But this does not preclude it from happening within the firm. Knowledge workers cannot be managed—even Peter Drucker thought the word *manager* was becoming obsolete, and should be replaced by *executive*. They can, though, be coached, directed, focused, and inspired to perform based on their strengths.

Personal Development

What inspires knowledge workers? Why did they enter their chosen profession in the first place? What is their preferred vision of the future? How is the firm helping—or hindering—their professional development? Is it giving them the feedback they need to direct themselves? Ultimately, all development is self-development, and nowhere is this more true than with knowledge workers. These are all vital areas to address if you intend to develop your human capital investors, who are, ultimately, volunteers.

Pride

I agree with Jon Katzenbach, co-author of *The Wisdom of Teams*:

> Pride is a more effective motivator of professional's talent than money. And you can motivate that talent with pride in more than just belonging. There is pride in the specific work product that you deliver to clients, pride in the kinds of clients that you serve, pride in the expertise that you can apply, pride in the values of your firm. (quoted in McKenna and Maister 2002, pp. 147–148)

If you thought some of these other KPIs were hard to measure, how would you measure pride?

Passion, Attitude, and Commitment

These might be the three most subjective criteria, none of which is a substitute for actual talent, but can there be any doubt that passion, attitude, and commitment are important to the effectiveness of a true professional?

The glass can be either half empty or half full, depending on your disposition. Mathematically, these are the exact same positions, but in the arena of human decisions and actions, they lead to radically different temperaments—either a scarcity or an abundance mentality. As Homer Simpson explains to his daughter Lisa: "If adults don't like their jobs, they don't go on strike. They just go in every day and do it really half-assed." This is easier to do in a knowledge firm than a nuclear power plant.

HIGH SATISFACTION DAY™

I am indebted to John Heymann, CEO, and his Team at NewLevel Group, a consulting firm located in Napa, California, for this KPI, which is trademarked. When John's firm held a retreat for the purpose of developing their KPIs, the suggestion of High Satisfaction Day (HSD™) was made. An HSD is one of those days that convinces you, beyond doubt, why you do what you do. It could mean landing a new customer, achieving a breakthrough on an existing project, receiving a heartfelt thank-you from a customer, or any other emotion of exhilaration that makes you happy you got out of bed in the morning. Sound touchy-feely? John admits it is; but he also says the number of HSDs is a leading indicator—and a barometer—of his firm's morale, and its bottom line.

Reed Hastings is the founder of Netflix and author of *No Rules Rules: Netflix and the Culture of Reinvention*. The company is famous for its culture and how it treats its employees. It places people over process, innovation over efficiency, not to mention very few controls. Here is how Hastings explains Netflix's culture:

> If you give employees more freedom instead of developing processes to prevent them from exercising their own judgment, they will make better decisions and it's easier to hold them accountable.
>
> If you build an organization made up of high performers, you can eliminate most controls.
>
> Judgment is the solution for almost every ambiguous problem. Not process.
>
> Today, in the information age, what matters is what you achieve, not how many hours you clock, especially for the employees of creative companies like Netflix. I have never paid attention to how many hours people are working.
>
> We've been against performance reviews from the beginning. The first problem is that the feedback goes only one way—downward. The second difficulty is that with a performance review you get feedback from only one person—your boss. This is in direct opposition to our "don't seek to please your boss" vibe. . . .The third issue is that companies usually base performance reviews on annual goals. But employees and their managers don't set annual goals or KPIs at Netflix. (Hastings and Meyers 2020)

If you did not have any individual team member KPIs, how would you assess their performance? My guess is firm leaders already know who their A, B, and C employees are, without looking at any financial information. That is because you are *judging* them on some of the criteria laid out in the KPIs above.

Ed Catmull of Pixar explains his philosophy on talent in *Creativity, Inc.*:

> We start from the presumption that our people are talented and want to contribute. We accept that, without meaning to, our company is stifling that talent in myriad unseen ways. Finally, we try to identify those impediments and fix them.
>
> If you give a good idea to a mediocre team, they will screw it up. If you give a mediocre idea to a brilliant team, they will either fix it or throw it away and come up with something better.
>
> Getting the team right is the necessary precursor to getting the ideas right. It is easy to say you want talented people, and you do, but the way those people interact with one another is the real key. Even the smartest people can form an ineffective team if they are mismatched. That means it is better to focus on how a team is performing, not on the talents of the individuals within it. A good team is made up of people who complement each other.
>
> Unleashing creativity requires that we loosen the controls, accept risk, trust our colleagues, work to clear the path for them, and pay attention to anything that creates fear. Doing all these things won't necessarily make the job of managing a creative culture easier. But ease isn't the goal; excellence is. (Catmull 2014)

With the possible exception of Turnaround time, a firm with high caliber talent does not really need individual KPIs. You also do not need to do annual performance reviews, nor timesheets, especially if you implement AARs.

THE BEST LEARNING TOOL EVER INVENTED— AFTER-ACTION REVIEWS

We do not learn from experience. . .we learn from reflecting on experience.

—Philosopher John Dewey

A teacher tells one of his pupils to write a letter to his parents, but the student complained: "It is hard for me to write a letter." "Why? You are now a year older, and ought to be better able to do it." "Yes, but a year ago I could say everything I knew, but now I know more than I can say" (Gregory 1995, p. 59).

Albert Einstein's research assistant-turned-philosopher, Michael Polanyi, drew a distinction between *tacit* and *explicit* knowledge. To illustrate tacit knowledge, he said, try explaining how to ride a bike or swim. You know more than you can tell. Tacit knowledge is "sticky," in that it is not easily articulated and exists in people's minds. It is complex and rich, whereas explicit knowledge tends to be thin and low bandwidth, like the difference between looking at a map and taking a journey of a certain terrain. It is the difference between reading the employee manual and chatting with a coworker about the true nature of the job and culture of the firm. For tacit knowledge to become explicit knowledge—that is, stored somewhere where it can be viewed, reviewed, and used by others—it must first be converted from the mind to another medium (a database, white paper, report, manual, video, podcast, picture, etc.). Tacit knowledge tends to be dynamic, while explicit knowledge is static; both are required for innovation and leverage to take place.

Explicit is from the Latin meaning "to unfold"—to be open, to arrange, to explain. *Tacit* from the Latin means "silent or secret." Try describing, in words, Marilyn Monroe's face to someone, an almost impossible task; yet you would be able to pick her out among photographs of hundreds of faces in a moment. Germans say *Fingerspitzengefühl*, "a feeling in the fingertips," which is similar to tacit knowledge (Stewart 2001, p. 123). The French say *je ne sais quoi* ("I don't know what"), a pleasant way of describing tacit knowledge. The highest levels of knowledge and competence are inherently tacit, being difficult and expensive to transmit, which is why the concept of master and journeyman still exist, albeit in different forms in a knowledge economy. It also why the fad of "free" is nonsense, confusing data and information—which does move toward free, especially over the internet—with knowledge and wisdom, which is incredibly expensive to transmit.

This type of knowledge transfer is a "social" process between individuals, and is especially important in knowledge organizations where so much of the IC is "sticky" tacit knowledge. Studies have shown that managers receive two-thirds of their information through face-to-face meetings and phone calls, and during the physical meetings, body language can convey up to three times as much meaning as the words spoken for some types of interactions. Ikujiro Nonaka and Hirotaka Takeuchi postulate four different modes of knowledge conversion in their book *The Knowledge-Creating Company*:

1. From tacit knowledge to tacit knowledge, which we call socialization
2. From tacit knowledge to explicit knowledge, or externalization
3. From explicit knowledge to explicit knowledge, or combination
4. From explicit knowledge to tacit knowledge, or internalization (Nonaka and Takeuchi 1995, p. 62)

Managing explicit knowledge is certainly easier than managing tacit knowledge, since the latter exists in the heads of knowledge workers who are difficult to manage, to say the least. Nor is it possible to capture 100% of the tacit knowledge that exists in each team member's head, but that is not the goal. The goal is to capture as much of it as we can and place it somewhere (e.g., knowledge bank, Web portal, blog, social media site, etc.) where anyone else in the firm can get it when they need it. This way we are not constantly reinventing the wheel.

KNOWLEDGE LESSONS FROM THE US ARMY

The Army's After Action Review (AAR) is arguably one of the most successful organizational learning methods yet devised.

—Peter Senge

The Army never wants to build the same bridge twice is how one military expert describes the AAR. The Army's use of AARs began in 1973, not as a knowledge management tool but as a method to restore the morale, values, integrity, and accountability that had diminished during the Vietnam War. Thinking back on my own career in public accounting, I became convinced the AAR is a practice that would have many beneficial effects in a professional organization. I began to think about how well my firm learned from past mistakes, or how often we would reflect on what we did, rather than just moving on to the next project. Being generous, I can say there was plenty of room for improvement. We were not taught how the *evaluation* is ultimately more important than the *experience*. The average knowledge worker is so busy *doing* they do not have the time to *reflect* on what they have done, let alone discover major breakthroughs. But action without reflection is meaningless, as the T.S. Eliot poem expresses so well: "We had the experience but missed the meaning." In Latin, *reflect* comes from the verb meaning *refold*, implying the action of turning things inward to see them in a different way. Reflection without action is *passivity*, but action without reflection is *thoughtlessness*. Combine experience with reflection, and learning that lasts is the result.

Perhaps we ignore innovations in the military because its mission—to break things and kill people—is so divergent from that of a civilian organization. But this is far too parochial an attitude; and once again we discover a useful practice from another sector. In fact, because the AAR is such a useful method for turning tacit knowledge into explicit knowledge, not to mention to foster learning and sharing of knowledge throughout the organization, I highly recommend you read *Hope Is Not a Method: What Business Leaders Can Learn from America's Army*, by Gordon R. Sullivan and Michael V. Harper.

Here are the questions you need to ask in each AAR:

- What was supposed to happen?
- What actually happened (the "ground truth")?
- What were the positive and negative factors here?
- What have we learned, and how can we do better next time?

The Army suggests you divide your time in answering the AAR's questions into 25-25-50: That is, 25% reviewing what happened, 25% reviewing why it happened, and the remaining 50% on what to do about it and how can you learn from it to improve. The objective is not just to correct *things*, but rather to correct *thinking*, as the Army has learned that flawed assumptions are the largest factor in flawed execution—another way of saying there is no good way to execute a bad idea.

An AAR is more of a verb than a noun. It does not have to be a formal written report; it can be a conversation held among the team.

If the project is large and important enough, a facilitator is recommended to get the most from the process. The AAR could be videotaped, audio recorded, or summarized later in a transcript, any of which could be deposited into the organization's knowledge bank. The Army also recommends answering the following summary questions to wrap up the AAR:

- What should the organization learn from this experience of what worked and did not work?
- What should be done differently in the future?
- Who needs to know these lessons and conclusions?
- Who will enter these lessons in the knowledge management system, or write the case up for future use?
- Who will bring these lessons into the leadership process for decision-making and planning?

Imagine the benefits of having a library of AARs for almost any type of project, process, or method the firm may encounter. Imagine further creating a culture that rewards knowledge workers for taking the time to contribute to this stock of knowledge, and perhaps even determines its utility by tracking how many times particular AARs are accessed by others. Imagine further a culture that understands AARs are real work, where time is spent on not just *doing* the work, but also *improving* the way work is done. Perfectionist cultures, however, resist this type of candid reflection, as they tend to be intolerant of errors, and mistakes are associated with career risk, not continuous learning. Confucius said "Being ashamed of our mistakes turns them into crimes." The medical world has an appropriate axiom for mistakes made: *Forgive and remember.* Jim Collins calls this "autopsies without blame" (Collins 2001, p. 88). Fear is another reason for learning not taking place.

AARs mitigate fear, as long as they are not used as a method to place blame but rather as a learning tool that can identify best practices so they can be spread throughout the organization. AARs should not be used for promotions, salary increases, or performance appraisals. This is an enormous advantage of AARs compared to the annual performance appraisal. AARs provide instant feedback, where in their absence a supervisor may delay feedback—and hence learning—to a once-a-year review ritual.

In fact, the AAR can be done instead of the Kabuki theater that is the annual performance appraisal. For all the resources expended on this ritual, it does not improve future performance. AARs do. AARs can also be used in place of timesheets, since again, timesheets do not improve future performance.

I sat through an AAR in a hospital's Intensive Care Unit after a particular shift. I was utterly amazed that registered nurses, physician assistants, and other highly competent medical professionals were sitting in a circle in the middle of the ward discussing the events from that day's shift. Everyone spoke unencumbered, even admitting errors and mistakes—this is in front of the ER doctors, their bosses—in a psychologically safe environment that they knew would not threaten their jobs. This is all being done where the work is literally a matter of life and death. The lead doctor told me this practice, which they conduct at the end of every shift, has reduced the hospital's malpractice suits and increased the quality of patient care.

Pixar also conducts what it calls postmortems after every movie, dating back to 1998. Ed Catmull explains why:

> Ask yourself what happens when an error is discovered. Do people shut down and turn inward. . . .Is the question being asked: Whose fault was this? If so, your culture is one that vilifies failure.
>
> In a fear-based, failure-averse culture, people will consciously or unconsciously avoid risk. Their work will be derivative, not innovative.
>
> The goal, then, is to uncouple fear and failure—to create an environment in which making mistakes doesn't strike terror into your employees' hearts.
>
> Everyone was so engaged in rethinking the way we did things, so open to challenging long held ideas and learning from the errors we'd made. No one was defensive. Afterward, we decided we should do this kind of deep analysis after every movie. (Catmull 2014)

Once again, we can hear the objections from some partners on this note, who are myopically focused on efficiency rather than effectiveness and learning. Your firm's IC is the most important source of its long-term wealth-creating capacity. It must be constantly replenished and created to build the firm's invisible balance sheet. Constantly focusing on *doing* rather than learning, creativity, innovation, and knowledge sharing is the equivalent of eating the firm's seed corn. As Socrates said: "The unexamined life is not worth living."

Some firms even conduct AARs with customers, after significant projects, or at various intervals. It is far more effective than NPS® scores and customer surveys. You will generate candid feedback and if it is conducted in the same spirit as internal AARs—that is, used as a learning tool, not a blame game—customers will greatly value the process. You could even assist them in implementing AARs in their organizations.

Capturing the tacit knowledge that exists in the heads of your human capital and making it part of your organization's structural capital will ensure that your firm knows what it knows, and can deploy it more quickly and at a greater value than the competition. Sullivan and Harper summarize the importance and value of converting tacit to explicit knowledge succinctly:

> Earlier we argued that, as we face our external environment, "We don't know what we don't know." As we face our internal environment, it seems that the opposite is too often true: "We don't know what we *do* know." As an important organizational asset, knowledge is usable only if can be identified and disseminated so as to contribute value. The challenge is to discover what is known in any part of the organization and, if it is valuable, make it known to all. (Sullivan and Harper 1996, p. 206)

SUMMARY AND CONCLUSIONS

In this chapter, we discussed a new model for knowledge worker effectiveness, since most of our management theories were developed in the agricultural and industrial economies. This model will rely more on judgment and wisdom than on measurement and command-and-control. We also investigated some potential key predictive indicators for knowledge workers that actually correlate with the traits of a successful professional. Finally, learning from the military, we explored the most effective tool—after-action reviews—for capturing your firm's tacit human capital and creating explicit structural capital as a result, thereby building your firm's invisible balance sheet, which will stay with your firm even if your human capital should depart. This invisible balance sheet is also a large part of the value of your firm when you are ready to exit. The AAR can also replace timesheets and the annual performance appraisal ritual because it actually improves future performance while the others emphatically do not. They can also be used with customers to enhance the relationship and learn how to serve more effectively.

Is it not tragic that there are more knowledge workers today in the labor force than ever before, yet they are not really rewarded for thinking and reflecting because they are too busy tracking and billing time? In fact, I posit the following argument: most firms' legacy systems of measurements and reward systems—from productivity, efficiency, and other production-oriented metrics, up to our legacy accounting systems—have actually become embedded *negative structural capital*. As with negative human capital, these types of antiquated capital must be extricated from the organization to achieve its latent potential.

Now that we have looked at measuring the success of the firm the same way the customer does by utilizing key predictive indicators at the firm-wide level and the professional level, it is time to turn our attention to creating a positive customer experience that will reduce the incidence of customer churn, the topic of our next chapter.

ADDITIONAL RESOURCES

Listen to *The Soul of Enterprise: Business in the Knowledge Economy*, Episode #15, on after-action reviews. At the bottom of the show notes, you will find a link to a downloadable sample AAR agenda for knowledge firms, in Microsoft Word format (https://www.thesoulofenterprise.com/tsoe/aar).

Also, Episode #166 is an interview with Colonel Chris "Elroy" Stricklin (Ret.), a former US Air Force Thunderbird, who ejected from his F-16 during a live air show, just 40 feet off the ground. He tells the story of how the AAR—what the Air Force calls The Debrief and Lessons Learned—literally saved his life. It is an amazing story (https://www.thesoulofenterprise.com/166).

On Episode #262, Colonel Stricklin discusses his then new book, *Survivor's Obligation*, which details the flight that he ejected from, and the consequences of his surviving that crash, an amazing and inspiring story (https://www.thesoulofenterprise.com/262).

21

FROM ZERO DEFECTS TO ZERO DEFECTIONS

There is only one boss: the customer. And he can fire every-
body in the company, from the chairman on down, simply by
spending his money somewhere else.

—Sam Walton (1918–1992)

I recall obtaining a new customer—during my days practicing public accounting—who was the owner of a successful travel agency. Her husband had passed away the prior year and she never had to deal with the tax and accounting aspects of her business. Her husband had been using the same CPA for over 20 years, and when I asked (as I made a habit of doing) why she left her CPA, her answer was very laconic and poignant and one I will *always* remember: "He showed no compassion."

From what I could determine, the CPA's work was technically proficient. My customer had no complaints about his price or the quality of his work. She even trusted him. When I called him to ask for copies of certain documents, he was shocked he had been replaced. It wasn't the *technical quality*, but the *service quality*, that made all the difference to her, not *what* she got, but *how* she got it.

During the 1980s, total quality management (TQM) swept the business literature, and many companies rushed to institute a TQM program. TQM is a body of knowledge that dates back to the late 1800s, as part of the agricultural revolution. Yet applying TQM to a knowledge firm is no easy task, since it is a standards-based approach. The same is true for Six Sigma and Lean programs. From a customer value perspective, the breakdown is easy to diagnose: All of these programs tend to be an inside-out approach.

The organization can internally count, measure, and analyze against almost any standard. But weighing yourself 10 times a day will not reduce your weight. TQM and Lean Six Sigma may provide a scale but not the guiding light for what should be weighed. Some firms have embraced these programs largely because it utilizes mathematical and statistical methods we easily understand. But we need to shift our thinking from "everything begins and ends with management" to "everything begins and ends with customer value." Counting and measuring things for the sake of counting and measuring things will not be the *open sesame* to attracting and retaining customers.

The alternative to TQM is total quality service (TQS), which Karl Albrecht, the modern founder of customer service, defined as: "A state of affairs in which an organization delivers superior value to its stakeholders: its customers, its owners, and its employees" (Albrecht 1992, p. 72). Notice how this definition is a goal condition to be sought, not a particular method of operation. Methods are developed as a way to achieve the goal, not as ends in themselves. The reason TQS is a better beacon than the other methods for intellectual capital firms is that it recognizes the *subjective* value of what is delivered, not the *objective* quality. Customers expect their professional services to be technically accurate; TQS puts the focus and emphasis on the subjective value and the customer experience, the ultimate arbiters of whether the customer remains a customer. As Stanley Marcus used to admonish: "Service, or the lack of it, doesn't come through on the computer printouts; it has to be observed" (Marcus 1979, p. 42). There is a sign in a textile plant of Milliken & Company that reads: "Quality is not the absence of defects as defined by management, but the presence of value as defined by customers."

In the 1990s, along the line of reasoning that being customer-driven was the ultimate goal of a company, many organizations began to calculate the lifetime value of an average customer. Consultants began asking their customers, "How much are you willing to spend to acquire a new customer?" Once this amount was determined, they would respond: "Then you had better be willing to spend *at least* that much to retain one." It was the dawn of the customer-loyalty economics movement, given voice by Frederick Reichheld and his book *The Loyalty Effect*, among others.

The theory was businesses should look at the value of the relationship over the long term, rather than simply the math of the moment. You are more likely to handle a customer complaint differently, or resolve a dispute in favor of the customer, if you take into account their lifetime value.

This lifetime value paradigm also proved, empirically, that customer *retention* was more profitable than customer *acquisition*. Various studies showed that it cost between 4 and 25 times more (depending on the industry) to acquire a customer than it did to retain one. The American Institute of CPAs found it cost the average CPA firm 11 times more to acquire than retain a single customer. Reichheld also pointed out that increasing retention rates by just 5% can increase your profits by a staggering 25% to 95%. As a result, cross-selling became the mantra is most professional firms, with the focus shifting from market share to customer *wallet share*.

The loyalty movement created another positive effect, at least in terms of replacing the TQM paradigm: it focused the company away from zero *defects*, toward zero *defections*. This focus makes imminent sense, since a firm would never be able to achieve zero defects—to err is human, after all. And even if it did achieve this magical standard, customers would still defect over service quality, which is far more likely than a defection due to an error made on a tax return. Errors can be corrected—providing lousy customer experiences, not so much. Like trust, technical quality is a table stake, the basic expectation of the customer. You do not return to a hotel because it changes the linens and vacuums every day.

Even before Reichheld published *Loyalty Economics* in 1996, some businesses intuitively understood the importance and economic benefits of customer loyalty, such as the airlines with their frequent flyer programs, launched in their modern incarnation in 1981. Afterward, a string of loyalty programs emerged from grocery, drug, and office stores, to coffee and sandwich shops. These loyalty programs are essentially a bribe, a tactic to increase the customer's switching costs. The problem is, they are all still based on discrete transactions, a one-and-done and pray-the-customer-comes-back-at-some-point business model.

The subscription model, in contrast, formalizes customer loyalty into a relationship that is not based on individual transactions. Entering into a relationship by opting in to it gives the customer a vested interest in the business, and is psychologically much different than merely engaging in a transaction. If you study human behavior, people are loyal to their spouses, schools, neighborhoods, communities, not-for-profits where they donate money and services, and so on. It is not so much that loyalty is dead in the business world; it is a *reason* to be loyal that is rare. Firms have to continually earn the loyalty of their customers, which goes far beyond just being trusted and providing technically accurate services. It requires providing remarkable customer experiences, as well as personal transformations to guide them in achieving their dreams.

This is why the distinction is being made between *reoccurring* revenue and *recurring* revenue (I am indebted to John Warrillow, author of *The Automatic Customer*, for this distinction). For example, most accounting firms have *reoccurring* revenue because *some* of the same services happen repeatedly (year-end accounts, tax returns), but not all the services provided are of this nature. Some are sporadic, similar to a rash that comes and goes.

In contrast, *recurring* revenue happens over and over again, at regular intervals—it is far more predictable. In the subscription model, this is because the price being paid is based on the relationship, not just the services performed. Why is this distinction important? Because potential buyers of your business will value *recurring* revenue much higher than *reoccurring* revenue, which is why so many of today's unicorns—those businesses with valuations over $1 billion—utilize the subscription business model. Predictable, recurring revenue is also more likely, in the long run, to generate more free cash flow, which translates into a higher valuation when the business is sold.

Another advantage of the subscription model is that the customer makes one pricing decision, and then that barrier has been removed in their mind. It is not like discrete transactions, where the customer has to reassess each value/price tradeoff. This is why removing the friction of frequent pricing discussions—annual fixed price agreements, scope changes, change requests, and so forth—is so beneficial. Your pricing has already accounted for all of this, but now you are offering the customer the peace of mind and convenience that they are covered for whatever they may need that the firm can do. Professionals have known for a long time that they sell sleep, meaning the customer can rest peacefully, knowing their matters are in good hands. The subscription model actually monetizes this in a beneficial way because it focuses on the relationship, not the services that are merely the means, while that good night's rest validates your value, along with the higher price.

We explored why customers leave CPA firms in Chapter 19. These are *known unknowns*—that is, we know these reasons exist, we just can't predict which customers are going to leave when. Churn is going to be a fact of life, no matter which business model you choose. Humans are messy and idiosyncratic. They can leave because they get bored or a better price from a competitor. In a business-to-business environment there are many vagaries that expose professional firms to defections: they can lose their advocates inside the customer's organization; the customer's business could merge, be acquired, sell, or go under. Of course, there are also *unknown unknowns*, such as a pandemic, or war. All of these events are hard to predict, and preventing churn, arguably, is even harder. Some strategies to reduce churn, include:

- *Maximize onboarding.* Begin guiding a transformation for the customer within 90 days to score an early win and prove your value, or perform an upfront, one-off project to create value early.

- *Don't give your customer homework.* Stop making them visit the Department of Paperwork every year (especially true for CPAs and their dreaded tax organizers). Take on more of their burden to save them time, an essential component to commanding your premium price.

- *Provide something unexpected.* This could be an invitation to the firm's web events and seminars on a topic you know the customer is interested in, or a book you think they would enjoy that you could later have a meeting with them to discuss (the *E-Myth* by Michael Gerber seems to be a popular choice for small business owners, but there are many more).

- *Communicate often.* This is a major advantage of having fewer customers, you get to have more frequent conversations.

- *Get customer skin in the game quickly.* Some subscription consultants suggest charging upfront, to get the customer invested in beginning projects with you right away. As we discussed, you will have test the cadence of your payment terms, and whether or not you want to provide a preferred price (say 5–10% off) for a customer who pays an entire year in advance. This will vary significantly by firm.

- *Do not hide your cancel button.* Make it easy for your customer to cancel, suspend, or change the pricing tier on their subscription plan. Customers love knowing—along with being reminded—that they have freedom of exit, so they can reverse quickly any buyer's remorse or mistakes. Freedom breeds loyalty because freedom is a choice (liberty is the absence of coercion). Customers *choose* to be faithful to their spouses, religion, and your firm, and will be even more so if they know they have the freedom to leave at any time.

- *Explore what makes people stay.* For readers who are religious, I love the question that Robert Skrob asks in his book on the subscription model, *Retention Point*: Think of someone who goes to a church for the first time: What makes them decide to stay? Can these reasons be emulated in your firm?

- *Provide constant innovation and transformations to the customer.* When we say innovation, we are not just talking about new services, but perhaps helping your customers with new ventures, such as pivoting to a subscription model in their business. Or helping them with their KPIs, pricing, strategy, positioning, etc. By continuously learning, you will naturally find new areas that will help your customers achieve their potential.

This leads us to three other frameworks that are useful in combatting churn: firm lifetime value to the customer; moments of truth; and customer complaints.

FIRM LIFETIME VALUE TO THE CUSTOMER

As discussed in Chapter 19, customer lifetime value (CLV) is a critically important KPI, yet there is another way to think about this. Turn the telescope around and ask, What is the lifetime value of our *firm* to the customer? If you can grow this with continuous innovation and transformations, then you will have customers for life. Then when you are ready to sell your firm, it will be far more valuable as a result.

MOMENTS OF TRUTH

On an operational, day-to-day basis, another useful practice is being mindful of moments of truth. Karl Albrecht defines the moment of truth (MOT) as follows:

> Any episode in which the customer comes into contact with the organization and gets an impression of its service. (Albrecht 1992, p. 116)

Utilizing the MOT method is one of the most effective ways to enhance your firm's customer experience. The term has its roots in *the hour of truth* in bullfighting, to signal the third and final hour, the killing of the bull. In a business context, MOT certainly has a more prosaic meaning, but in terms of delivering excellent experiences to customers, and lengthening a firm's life, it is potentially just as fatal as to the bull.

Taken individually, each MOT is a minor event. Over time, however, each interaction is like a pebble placed on a scale, with one side being service excellence and the other being service mediocrity—the difference between being indispensable and expendable. Eventually, that scale will begin to tip in one direction or the other. Generally, there are three possible outcomes to each MOT:

1. Neutral experience (rarest)
2. Positive experience (moments of magic)
3. Negative experience (moments of misery)

Few customers come into contact with an organization and walk away with a neutral perception. When developing your firm's processes and interactions, it helps to map out each potential MOT with the customer and be as inclusive as possible. Even mundane things like how accessible your parking is affect a customer's overall experience of dealing with your firm. How easy is it for them to interact with you digitally, or reach a live person when they need to? According to former CEO of Disney, Michael Eisner, guests come into contact with Cast Members over 2.5 billion times per year at Disney theme parks, and each MOT is a chance to win over a customer or lose one (Disney Institute 2001, p. 74). Disney used the MOT mapping strategy and discovered many children visiting its EPCOT Park at Walt Disney World were disappointed there were no Disney characters wandering around as there are in the Magic Kingdom. Disney has since placed characters in all of its parks, creating literally millions of magic moments for its guests. Furthermore, many times a child waiting on line for an attraction is prohibited from boarding due to height restriction, a moment of misery to say the least. Thanks to the MOT strategy, cast members have a supply of special certificates entitling them to board the ride without waiting in line when they reach the required height, transforming a moment of misery into a moment of magic and almost guaranteeing a return visit (Disney Institute 2001, p. 161).

The key here is to understand how the MOT forces the company to focus on the *outcome*, not the *activity*, of each encounter. Each MOT in your company is an opportunity to deliver exceptional value to your customers and make them feel special, cared for, and appreciated. Every contact is an emotional connection and exchange with the customer; and if you thought intellectual capital was hard to measure, try sympathy and compassion. Albrecht articulates this core principle of service excellence: "When the moments of truth go unmanaged, the quality of service regresses to mediocrity." No MOT should ever be taken for granted, for no matter how small it may be, in the long run, collectively, they determine the destiny of your firm.

CUSTOMER COMPLAINTS

A customer complaint presents both a danger and an opportunity, depending on how it is handled. Since it is virtually impossible for a company to remove all defects from its work, and especially in its service delivery processes, handling complaints when they arise provides a competitive differentiation for your company and enhances customer loyalty and goodwill if they are handled properly. Furthermore, complaints handled quickly result in higher loyalty; and for that reason alone, one of the highest-value activities a firm can add to its repertoire of reducing churn is a proper complaint recovery system.

The empirical evidence proves the point. What is astonishing to realize is that customers who complain can become more loyal than if they had no problem at all—if the complaint is handled quickly and resolved to their satisfaction. Marriott found the following percentages of intent to return when customers had a problem during their stay:

- No problems during the stay = 89% return rate
- Had a problem during the stay and it *was not* corrected to customer's satisfaction = 69% return rate
- Had a problem during the stay and it *was* corrected to customer's satisfaction, *before they left the property* = 94% return rate

This is why it is so important to resolve all customer complaints quickly, or at least take action to resolve them immediately. Complaints are not like fine wines; they do not age well, especially in the age of social media and word-of-mouse. Customers complain because there is a gap between what they wanted to happen and what actually happened. Once they experience a problem, their expectation of having it resolved quickly is actually low (which is precisely why most customers do not complain—they think it will do no good), so a complaint is an excellent opportunity to improve their condition and turn the experience from a moment of misery into a moment of magic. You will redirect their focus on the *satisfying outcome*, rather than the original problem.

The golden rule when it comes to customer complaints: It is not *who is* right, it is *what is* right. Carl Sewell, author of *Customers for Life: How to Turn That One-Time Buyer into a Lifetime Customer*, has this advice: "Everything you need to know about handling mistakes you learned in nursery school: acknowledge your error, fix it immediately, and say you're sorry. Odds are, your customer, like your mom and dad, will forgive you" (Sewell 1990, p. 164).

When analyzing customer complaints and defects, ask *how* not *why*. Why questions tend to generate excuses and justifications, while how questions will lead to knowledge to correct the problem. "How can we prevent this from happening again?" is a much better question than "Why did this happen?" Also, follow this five-step recovery process to deal effectively with all customer complaints:

1. **Apologize.** Say *I am* sorry, not *we are* sorry.
2. **Urgent effort.** Fred Smith, founder of FedEx, follows the "Sunset Rule": "The sun will not set on an unresolved customer or employee problem that is not dealt with in some way."
3. **Empathy.** Show understanding and compassion; fix the customer before fixing the problem.

4. **Compensation.** Be generous, show remorse; better yet, ask the customer how they would like it to be fixed (usually, their request is less than you would have given up).

5. **Follow up.** Learn how the customer feels about the situation; provide closure.

Horst Schulze, the founder of Ritz-Carlton, empowered his team members with great latitude in resolving customer complaints, each one being authorized to spend up to $2,000 on solving customer problems. "When I announced this policy, my peers nearly fainted." "Look, the average business traveler will spend well over $100,000 on lodging during their lifetime. I am more than willing to risk $2,000 to keep them coming back to our brand of hotels" (Simon 2021). In the Ritz-Carlton Basics, a set of 20 guiding principles every team member is held accountable for, number 13 states: "Never lose a guest. Instant guest pacification is the responsibility of each employee. Whoever receives a complaint will own it, resolve it to the guest's satisfaction and record it." This "ownership" of customer complaints is quite effective, and every firm should have this attitude with respect to any customer problem.

The subscription model provides plenty of flexibility to deal with customer complaints, and easily provides compensation by pausing, say, their monthly amount, or granting to them a few free months. Forget the math of the moment and focus on the lifetime value, especially when recovering from a complaint. This is no time to be cheap.

Customer complaints can be more valuable than customer compliments because they provide the firm with information on aspects of its service delivery that need to be improved, a second chance to gain the customer's business, and an opportunity to actually increase the customer's goodwill and loyalty. Always let your customers know that you welcome any and all complaints, while realizing that when you do receive one, what separates excellent firms from mediocre ones is how they are dealt with.

A PUNCH IN THE GUT

I began this chapter with a success story from when I practiced accounting about acquiring a customer from another CPA firm. Let me share a failure story. In the early days of implementing value pricing in my firm, we had an "unlimited access" clause in all of our fixed-price agreements. This allowed the customer to call and/or meet with us anytime, anywhere, to discuss anything. One day, one of my customers called and complained that I had stopped contacting her to see how she was doing. I defensively replied, "But you have unlimited access, you can call me anytime." She replied, "It's not our job to reach out to you. You should be reaching out to us." I lost that customer, and it hurt. It is hard not to take it personally; it is a form of rejection, especially in such a demanding relationship business. I had developed some very valuable strategies for her that enhanced her business, but it wasn't enough. I had the attitude that she was paying for access, and if she didn't use it, even more profit for me. Terribly shortsighted.

That is an intolerable attitude in the subscription model. You want your customers to see you, have conversations with you, meetings, and even providing ancillary services that move them forward. Any firm can acquire new customers; it is keeping them that is crucial in making you successful. That is how you earn the annual recurring revenue as opposed to the more sporadic reoccurring revenue—you provide recurring value that subscriptions demand. Netflix understands this well, as this post from Eddy Wu, Product Innovation, illustrates:

> You know that sinking feeling when you realize you signed up for something but haven't used it in ages? At Netflix, the last thing we want is people paying for something they're not using.
>
> So we're asking everyone who has not watched anything on Netflix for a year since they joined to confirm they want to keep their membership. And we'll do the same for anyone who has stopped watching for more than two years. Members will start seeing these emails or in app notifications this week. If they don't confirm that they want to keep subscribing, we'll automatically cancel their subscription. If anyone changes their mind later, it's really easy to restart Netflix. These inactive accounts represent less than half of one percent of our overall member base, only a few hundred thousand, and are already factored into our financial guidance.
>
> We've always thought it should be easy to sign up and to cancel. So, as always, anyone who cancels their account and then rejoins within 10 months will still have their favorites, profiles, viewing preferences

and account details just as they left them. In the meantime, we hope this new approach saves people some hard earned cash. (Netflix 2020)

What would it have cost for me to make regular contact with that customer? Is that not a form of marketing? It is retention marketing, and it is essential to allocate a good portion of your marketing spend and your capacity to retaining your existing customers. This was not a case of having the wrong customer—I had a fantastic "A" customer who was paying a premium price. I took her for granted, another human trait we have to work hard to overcome.

You want to have regular customer interactions. If they aren't happening it could be a leading indicator the customer is not seeing value in your firm. This is precisely why so many subscription businesses have customer success departments that ensure proper onboarding and continuous use of the services. This is also part of your retention marketing. Do not fall into the cost accountant's trap of thinking the best customers are those who pay and do not fully utilize you. The onus is still on the firm to reach out and help the customer remain financially healthy by providing transformations. Stop worrying about how much time you are spending on a customer and start to worry if the customer decreases the time they spend with you.

Of course, there are some customers who you wish would leave. As my Dad taught me—like Charlie Brown, my father was a barber—"some customers you love to see come through door while others customers you love to see go out the door." This is why customer selection is so important. Do not pollute your river at the source. Your professionals have only so much emotional capacity, so you need to guard it like it was gold, or bitcoin. When it comes to hiring, the mantra is, "Hire slow, fire fast." I believe the same applies to customers. Ask yourself—and your team—periodically, "Knowing what we now know, would we have accepted this customer?" If the answer is no, graciously terminate the relationship. Churn is not always a one-way street. Do not simply raise their price three to four times, as chances are they will not leave. Grade "F" customers are like barnacles. They are not transformed into an A customer because they are paying you more. That is the ethic of the world's oldest profession, not the professional. What's more, there is nothing more liberating than terminating a customer who is either toxic or no longer a good fit.

Do not terminate a customer over email or a phone call. Do it face to face. You are a professional, and you want to make sure the customer understands why you made this decision, while providing them a safe place to land. Have some other firms lined up in which to refer them; inform them you will do everything you can to make the transition as smooth as possible. This is simply the right thing to do, and worthy of being a true professional who treats others with dignity. Our late colleague Paul O'Byrne used to say that firing a customer is like breaking up, akin to a Dear John letter: "It's not you, it's me. I've changed." Here is a script Paul Dunn wrote to help you ease into what we know is a difficult conversation:

Mary, we need to talk about how well we're working together. We need to be sure that the range of services we offer matches your needs.

Here in the firm we want to work with people where we can add significant value to their business, rather than just crunching some numbers and filling in some tax returns for them.

This means we are reducing the number of clients we work with and increasing the range of services we provide for them. We're working with them on growing their businesses by offering consultative services. Naturally, this means that our price levels are increasing too. Many of our customers are comfortable with that extra investment because of the value we are giving them in return.

Mary, my gut feeling is that unless I'm very mistaken, we simply can't provide you with that value. It seems to me that your needs would be better served by an accountant who just wants to stick to the numbers.

How do you feel about that?

Then there are those customers who will leave, perhaps writing nasty reviews, or for reasons you do not think were justified. Some folks simply cannot be pleased no matter how hard you try. An approach I learned from direct primary care physician Douglas Farrago is his phrase, "Be well." Here is how he explains it on his website:

> *Why get mad? It really isn't worth it. Let me tell you a story, and you can take from it any lesson you want. When I decided to do DPC, a physician who I thought was my friend and who had recruited me to his practice, responded to my long email about explaining my dream with two words: "Be Well." It threw me for a loop. It made me think for days. Two words? And then I realized what he was saying with "Be Well" was. . ."Go f%ck yourself." I got it. He said it without saying it. And I am sure he felt satisfaction inside. I really have no ill will towards him for that. It was brilliant. Where am I going with this? I am not sure. I think that saying "Be Well" to someone can be very authentic and very well meaning. For others, you may want your "Be Well" to mean what my doctor friend meant for me. It's up to you. Either way, it is a good mantra to LET THINGS GO! (Farrago n.d.)*

Now that we have discussed the dark side of the subscription model—losing customers—it is time to turn our attention to how you pivot from your existing business model to the subscription business model. We believe the economy is at an inflection point, which will affect your firm regardless of whether you change or not.

22

ADOPTION MODELS

*A strategic inflection point is a time in the life of a business
when its fundamentals are about to change. That change can
mean an opportunity to rise to new heights. But it may just as
likely signal the beginning of the end.*

—Andrew S. Grove, *Only the Paranoid Survive: How to Exploit the
Crisis Points That Challenge Every Company*, 1996

Economic revolutions don't care what you think about them.

—Michael C. Munger, *Tomorrow 3.0*, 2018

Remember department stores? Perhaps you grew up with one in your
town where you went to buy clothes, toys, and other goods. In 1960,
there were 316 department stores throughout the United Sates, some
small and others large, such as Macy's, Nordstrom, JCPenney, and
of course the Amazon of its day, Sears. At one point, Sears was 1%
of the USA's gross domestic product (GDP). Then an unknown little
startup in Bentonville, Arkansas, was founded in 1962. Walmart was
followed by other discount stores such as Kmart. As I write this, only
eight of the original large department stores still exist, with one of the
most successful being Dayton-Hudson.

The late Harvard professor Clayton Christensen's Harvard Business School course, Disruptive Strategy, detailed this history of the
department store industry. Our mutual Australian friend and colleague, Ric Payne, wrote up this case study on his blog, "The Six

Business Trajectories," explaining how Dayton's founder, John F. Geisse, responded to these low-end disrupters:

> In 1962, Dayton's John F. Geisse, could see an opportunity for an upscale discount store that was positioned between low-end discounters (Walmart hadn't really hit the straps at the time) and up-market department stores. He realised things were happening in the market that would present an opportunity even though Dayton was strong and growing at the time with no pressing need to change. Geisse, opened a new store called Target while still operating their existing business under the Dayton-Hudson brand.
>
> Target has continued to re-invent itself and today it now owns the retail space between the low-end discounters and Walmart. Its success took it to the point where, in 2000 Dayton-Hudson Corporation changed its name to Target, the business that had effectively disrupted its parent from outside its core over the past 38 years.
>
> The reason Target succeeded was that its management realized early that it needed a new business model with a different set of resources, processes, and profit model to support a new customer target (rising suburban middle class) with a new value proposition. Dayton operated two companies, one on the sustaining trajectory, one on the disruptive trajectory, and they managed that transfer from sustaining to disruptive by setting up a different business unit. But they were the only ones that have done that in the retail industry. There are a few in other industries. But in every case, they survived by setting up a different business unit to go after disruption.
>
> One of the most important lessons from the Target experience is the realization that the best time to invest in growth (and especially disruptive growth) is when the core is strong and growing and appears to be at the top of its game with a bright positive outlook.
>
> Source: Clayton Christensen, *HBX Course Material – Disruptive Strategy*, Harvard Business School, 2019, in Payne 2021.

THREE ADOPTION MODELS TO PIVOT TO SUBSCRIPTION

If you're going to be cannibalized it's best to dine with friends.

—Andy Grove, co-founder, Intel

The history of capitalism is one of dynamism and disruption. New ideas, inventions, technologies, and business models from the tinkers in the garage rise up and change the world, while rendering obsolete the existing modes of production, infrastructure, and business models. It is very difficult for a business to disrupt itself. What kills you usually does not look like you—it comes from outside your industry.

This makes selecting the right strategy to use to pivot to the subscription model imperative. Very few organizations can operate multiple business models inside of one firm, as we saw with the success of Dayton-Hudson creating a new entity, Target, which eventually cannibalized the old model.

Fortunately, there is some evidence from Tien Tzuo's company, Zuora, on the most successful methods to make the pivot. In his August 28, 2021, newsletter, Tzuo interviewed Robert Hildenbrand, Zuora's senior vice president of Global Services, regarding the evidence of the most successful pivots they have seen work. Essentially, there are three approaches to launch a subscription business model, as shown in Figure 22.1 (the diagram has been modified from the original article, but is inspired by it).

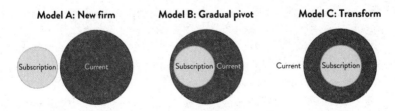

FIGURE 22.1   Three subscription adoption strategies.

A. **New firm.** Create a separate firm, the Dayton-Hudson approach with Target, eventually cannibalizing the old.

B. **Gradual pivot.** Gradually move customers over to subscription.

C. **Transform.** Wholesale transformation of the existing firm, converting the legacy systems, people, etc., to the new model. This is how Adobe made the change from selling software to software as a service (SaaS).

Tien asked Robert: "Now, given that Model C is your eventual goal, which approach should you start with?"

> Robert: "We've been working long enough together that I can confidently say my answer is the same as yours, Tien. It's door number one: Model A, build a separate system. . . .For the rest, it's Model C but you have to be really, really committed. And everyone should avoid Model B. That's a path to failure." (Tzuo 2021)

It is difficult to prescribe one of these models since every firm is different, but based on what we have experienced, Model B is the hardest to pull off. Because subscription requires new thinking, the *plussing* of your offering, different pricing, new KPIs and metrics, and even distinctive financial statements, all of these are destined to clash with the legacy systems of how you operate now—either hourly billing or value pricing. A relationship-based and a transaction-orientated model simply do not fit together. Subscription necessitates a new architecture and a new mindset, transitioning away from monetizing services to monetizing the relationship, cultivating customer lifetime value. If you simply try to slowly pivot to this model inside your legacy firm, that may be a lower-risk strategy, but it's also lower-profit strategy, and demonstrates a lack of commitment to deep, lasting change. It will take longer, it will confuse your team members, it will add complexity and costs to the operation of your firm, and worst of all, it will confuse the marketplace, both current and potential customers. It will also be easier for partners who are not onboard with this switch to sabotage the initiative. Better to keep them out at the outset, or transition them out of the firm completely. Disruption is not easy, which is precisely why most businesses cannot disrupt themselves. It requires tough decisions, tradeoffs, and personnel changes. Remember, profits come from *risk*—none of this is for the timid.

There has also been evidence from doctors attempting to pivot from a fee-for-service (FFS) model to either a concierge or direct primary care model. Needless to say, it is not easy. The FFS model requires insurance and Medicare billing, necessitating bureaucracy that adds no value to patients. Like hourly billing—and even value pricing to some extent—the FFS model monetizes services, procedures, lab work, office visits, etc., whereas DPC is all-inclusive. The focus shifts from providing services to keeping the patient healthy, the outcome they care most about. Most FFS practices are not able to utilize the gradual approach of Model B due to legal and regulatory reasons, so usually they employ Model C, whereby at some future date they transform to subscription. By informing their patients well ahead of time, they provide the option to stay under the new model or transition out. Obviously it is much easier if they start out of residency with a DPC practice, like Dr. Paul Thomas did when he founded Plum Health, discussed in Chapter 9.

Some businesses do attempt Model B, by treating subscription as merely another revenue model, and pricing strategy. HP's Instant Ink, launched in 2013, is an example. It had over 11 million subscribers by March 2022 (The Recycler 2022). Disney obviously has Disney+ and even has launched some subscription plans to its parks with Magic Key. Apple offers some service subscriptions, which account for approximately 16% of its total revenue. Needless to say, most firms don't have the resources, brand mystique, or managerial talent, of an Apple, HP, or Disney. Simultaneously operating two business models is like having two spouses—you can do it, but you might not like the consequences.

Interestingly, as I write this in March 2022, it was reported in Bloomberg that Apple is considering a subscription plan for its iPhone and other hardware products. We have been asking for years, when will it be possible to *subscribe to Apple*, rather than merely purchasing its SKUs? Understandably, transitioning from counting units sold to growing and nurturing annual recurring revenue is no easy feat, and time will tell whether Apple converts its entire revenue model to subscription. Paul and I, of course, hope it does.

The difficulty of the mind shift required cannot be overemphasized. History is littered with companies run by intelligent executives being disrupted by outsiders, as the late Clayton Christensen's life's work explores in detail. It is much rarer to see a company adapt, then cannibalize itself, as in the case of Intel and Dayton-Hudson. They do exist, but they are rare, such as with Charles Schwab, another case study Christensen told.

Prior to the internet, if you wanted to execute a stock trade, you called your broker. Merrill Lynch charged approximately $300 while Charles R. Schwab was determined to democratize investing for the little guy, launching a discount broker in 1975 and charging only $79 for a trade. Needless to say, he was quite successful. In 1995, Schwab launched an online brokerage, charging only $29 per trade. It knew the internet was going to be a major disruptive force, manifested in new business models. It also understood it would be too difficult to launch an online broker *within* the legacy firm—utilizing Model B above—because it would be viewed as less profitable, nor as lucrative for employees due to different incentive structures. Instead, Schwab established a new business unit. In 1996, there were 11,800 online trades per day, but by 1999 there were 200,000, one-third of which went through Schwab. By then, it had 2.5 million active accounts, and $219 billion in assets, recording just as much profit as the legacy brokerage firm.

Clayton concluded that if Schwab had tried to cultivate this new firm within its existing business, it would have gone nowhere. It was viewed as less profitable and people didn't want to give up their incentive structures at the old price. It was the mind shift that was critical: executives knew this new entity had a different profit formula, one where the price drops but volume increased dramatically. Yet that mind shift would have been much harder to nurture and grow within the legacy firm, hence our conclusion—and Clayton's—that it is very difficult to operate with two different business models under the same roof. Of course, we are recommending the opposite strategy: your volume of customers decreases while your price increases.

A business model is a theory of how the firm creates and captures value. When new business models or new technological innovations appear that challenge the status quo, it is human nature to reject any disruptive force. We have certainly seen this with the subscription model. Professionals have a very hard time moving beyond the idea of monetizing services and instead nurturing lifetime customer value. At the firm-wide level, it is even more of a challenge because a firm is usually far more conservative and resistant to change than are the professionals within it—people who leave, for example, obviously want a change.

Xerox fell into this mental trap when it failed to capitalize on the innovations that its Palo Alto Research Center (PARC) developed. This included the computer technology—the mouse and computer interface—that eventually led to the Apple computer and launched the personal computer revolution. Why couldn't Xerox see the opportunity? It was mired in the mentality that it was only paid by the page. In *Dealers of Lightning*, Michael Hiltzik hypothesizes:

> In the copier business Xerox got paid by the page; each page got counted by a clicker. In the electronic office of the future, there was no clicker—there was no annuity. How would one get paid? The hegemony of the pennies-per-page business model was so absolute that it blinded Xerox to an Aladdin's cave of other possibilities. (Hamel 2000, p. 112)

You are what you charge for, and new business models demand new pricing and revenue paradigms. Recall the subscription model definition: Periodic recurring payments for frictionless, ever-increasing value, and serial transformations. There is nothing about services, scope of work, or other attributes of prior models. This is not only a new revenue model, but also a completely different profit formula.

We realize this is not easy—I and our VeraSage colleagues have all struggled with it. But reality is changing, and we must adapt. As Clayton Christensen wrote: "Disruption is a process, not an event, and innovations can only be disruptive relative to something else." The kite rises against the wind, and the subscription model is no different.

Another question we have received: Can you go from hourly billing directly to subscription, without ever adopting value pricing? Time will tell on this, but here is our conjecture: Yes, you can. I say this because old models trap us into old thinking. The shift from hourly billing to value pricing is still taking place across the professions, and it is a massive mind shift change. But I still believe that you can leapfrog from hourly to subscription because it fundamentally changes the profit formula from either hourly or value pricing. We are already witnessing many value pricing firms struggling to get their heads around subscription, so I do not believe there is any great advantage to moving to value pricing from hourly billing before leaping to subscription. I vote you take the plunge directly to subscription.

You will not have as many legacy systems and mindsets to get in your way.

That said, there are many value pricing principles that still apply, as we detailed in the pricing chapters herein (Chapters 14–17). There are also many differences, and we have seen many pricers have difficulty understanding them. This is human nature—unlearning is hard. But economic revolutions do not care about your feelings, your revenue models, or your anxieties. You will be confronted with competitors offering subscriptions, so better for you if you climb down the learning curve earlier rather than later.

One more issue that you will confront adopting the subscription model is what Tzuo calls "swallowing the fish." In essence, it is all about cash flow, and you can Google the term Fish Model Subscription to see the graph that is in the shape of a fish, originally published in Tien Tzuo's book, *Subscribed*.

The fish's size is a function of the size of the firm. In a small firm, the fish is more like a minnow, whereas in larger firms it will be bigger. It took Adobe nearly two years to swallow and digest the fish, all the while its stock price took a beating. You can mitigate some of the cash flow issues by incentivizing customers to pay for a year upfront by offering a 3–5% preferred customer price, or one year for the price of 10 months, etc. Or you could use weekly payment terms rather than monthly.

Be aware of the trade-off between annual payment terms and a more frequent cadence. You are placing a high cognitive load on the customer at renewal time, which puts them at a higher risk for churning. As mentioned, there is something optimal about a monthly payment cadence. You will have test which is most optimal for your firm.

Whether your costs are going to increase depends on your capacity, since in most firms this is an issue of human capital. But remember, the number of customers is expected to decrease in the short term, which might very well mean less costs. We believe it is easier to scale in this model because cash flow is far more predictable than pounding the streets for new sales every day. Annual recurring revenue can also be used for financing far easier than trying to factor accounts receivable, either from hourly billing or even value pricing.

SIX QUESTIONS THAT KILL INNOVATION

*Cautious, careful people, always casting about to preserve
their reputation and social standing, never can bring
about a reform.*

—Susan B. Anthony, social reformer,
women's rights activist, suffragist

Soon after launching my own firm, I attended a four-day seminar titled "Increasing CPA Firm Profitability." In the tranquil setting of Lake Tahoe, Nevada, I learned three major strategies on how to increase my CPA firm's profitability:

1. Raise my hourly billing rate by at least $10.
2. Grade my customers "A," "B," and "C," and fire all the "Cs."
3. Offer my customers "fixed-fee agreements" on all services, with an appropriate "weasel clause" to cover any scope changes.

Inspired, I immediately shared all of these ideas, and more, with my new partner. We talked about become a "winning firm," the term the instructor used throughout the seminar, which meant, by today's vernacular, going from good to great. The course provided me with the tools I needed to put some of these ideas into practice immediately. In other words, it taught me *how* to do it.

What it did not teach me is *why* I should do it. It was all case studies and examples, but had absolutely no theory. So when I returned to my firm I had a hammer—the tool I needed to implement some of these new concepts—and I started furiously hitting things. I raised my hourly rate but did not simultaneously convince my customers that my value rose commensurately with that increase. I began grading my customers, and ridding the firm of the "Cs," but it wasn't until I began researching the ideas behind TQS that I learned that *our customers were not going to get better until we did.* We offered fixed pricing, but it was nothing more than estimated hourly billing in advance. Without a solid theoretical foundation of *why* I was doing these things, I failed miserably. Fortunately, we decided to stick with it because we felt—deep in our bones—it was the right thing to do for the customers.

This is one of the most glaring weaknesses in most business books and management ideas: *They are all practice with no theory*. Most do little else than propound platitudes and compose common sense into endless checklists and seven-step programs. Yet, all learning beings with theory.

When one reads a typical business book today, though, the author will usually begin by saying something to the effect that "this book is not based on some 'ivory tower,' theoretical model, but based on practical, real-world experience and examples that you can implement Monday morning."

Beware when you read such a qualifier, because as Dr. W. Edwards Deming used to say, "Without theory, experience has no meaning. No one has questions to ask. Hence without theory, there is no learning. Theory leads to prediction. Without prediction, experience and examples teach nothing" (Deming 1994, p. 103). It is worth repeating what the great mathematician David Hilbert wrote, "There is nothing more useful than a good mathematical theory," and the same is true with respect to economics and the study of human behavior. Theories build buildings and bridges that stand through time, fly airplanes that defy gravity, and put men on the moon. *There is nothing more practical than a good theory.*

William Cohen earned his PhD under Peter Drucker. Writing about his experience in *A Class with Drucker*, he frustratingly points out that Drucker understood the distinction made by Austrian economists—that is, *know-what* is far more important than *know-how*:

> Drucker taught what to do. He was very specific about this. However, he did not teach how to do it. That was left up to the student or to his consulting clients. It was sometimes frustrating. . .[but it] invariably led the recipients to whom these were given in order to apply and benefit from unimagined rewards in application, which would not have resulted had he simply told us how to implement his ideas. (Cohen 2008, pp. 61, 247)

Imagine if the Founders of the United States, after signing the Declaration of Independence, had sent it to King George in Britain, who then replied as perhaps a modern-day MBA, corporate strategist, or accountant would today:

Dear Mr. Jefferson:

We have read your Declaration of Independence with great interest.

Certainly it represents a considerable undertaking, and many of your statements do merit serious consideration. Unfortunately, the Declaration as a whole fails to meet recently adopted specifications for proposals to the Crown. So we must return the document to you for further refinement.

The questions that follow might assist you in your process of revision.

In your opening paragraph you use the phrase "the Laws of Nature" and "Nature's God." What are these laws? In what way are they the criteria on which you base your central arguments? Please document, with citations, from recent literature.

In the same paragraph you refer to "Opinions of Mankind." Whose polling data are you using? Without specific evidence it seems to us the "Opinions of Mankind" are a matter of—opinion.

You hold certain Truths to be "self-evident." Could you please elaborate? If they are as evident as you claim, they should not be difficult for you to locate the appropriate supporting statistics.

"Life, Liberty, and the Pursuit of Happiness" seems to be the goals of your proposal. These are not *measurable goals*. If you were to say that among these are the ability to sustain an average life expectancy in 6 of the 13 Colonies of at least 55 years; and to enable newspapers in the Colonies to print news without further interference; and to raise the average income of the colonists by 10 percent in the next 10 years—these would be *measurable* goals. Please clarify.

Your strategy for achieving your goals is not developed at all. You state the Colonies ". . .ought to be, Free and Independent States" and that you are ". . .absolved from all Allegiance to the British Crown..." Who or what must change to achieve this objective, and in what way must they change? What specific steps would you take to overcome the resistance? How long will it take? We have found that a little foresight in these areas might help to prevent careless errors later on.

How cost-effective are your strategies? Who among the list of signatories would be responsible for implementing your strategy? Who conceived it? Who will constitute the advisory committee? Please submit an organization chart and vitae of the principal investigators.

What impact will your problem have? Your failure to include any assessment of this inspires little confidence in the long-range prospects of your undertaking.

We hope that these comments prove useful in revising your Declaration of Independence.

We welcome submission of your revised proposal. Our due date for unsolicited proposals is July 31, 1776. Ten copies with original signatures will be required.

Sincerely,

Management Analyst to the British Crown*

* I am eternally indebted to Dr. Richard Ebeling, former president of the Foundation for Economic Education, for the idea, and the wording, of the above thought experiment, transcribed from an introduction Dr. Ebeling gave at an "Evenings at FEE event." See (Ebeling, 2004), in the References for more information.

Dr. Ebeling, former president of the Foundation for Economic Education, who conceived this thought experiment, concluded with a profound question: "I'd like to ask if the Founding Fathers had to have worked within such a framework would we be independent today?

The Framer's did not ask the following six questions that are always reasonable when individuals or organizations are confronted with a significant change, but when asked too soon and taken too literally may actually postpone the future and keep us encased in our present way of thinking. Peter Block describes these six questions in his eloquent and philosophical book, *The Answer to How Is Yes: Acting on What Matters*:

1. How do you do it?
2. How long will it take?
3. How much does it cost?
4. How do you get those [other] people to change?
5. How do we measure it?
6. How have other people done it successfully? (Block 2003, pp. 15–23).

How would Thomas Jefferson have answered these six questions?

1. I don't know.
2. I don't know.
3. Possibly your life.
4. I don't know.
5. I don't think you can measure Life, Liberty, and the Pursuit of Happiness.
6. No country has ever done it successfully the way we are proposing. Sign here.

Block suggests these better starting questions, and our colleague Ed Kless has modified number three:

1. "What refusal have I been postponing?
2. What commitment am I willing to make?
3. What is the value of it to me? [Block had "price" instead of value]
4. What is my contribution to the problem?
5. What is the crossroad at which I find myself at this point in my life/work?
6. What do we want to create together?" (Block 2003, pp. 28–32).

Peter Block explains why starting with "How to" questions are the wrong place to start. It is not that they are not important to answer, it's that they do not belong at the start of a change initiative:

> We often avoid the question of whether something is worth doing by going straight to the question, "How do we do it?" . . . Asking how is an escape from freedom and accountability. We wish to go to heaven and not die. Freedom asks us to invent our own steps. . . . Knowing how to do something may give us confidence, but it does not give us our freedom. Freedom comes from commitment, not accomplishment. (Block 2003, pp. 2, 47)

It is simply impossible to know how to do something until you attempt it. In a free market system, it is the leap, not the look, that generates the indispensable understanding and the necessary knowledge to generate wealth. There is no security, only a world of risk and uncertainty, where one must humbly serve the needs of others— supply before you can demand—against a constant tidal wave of rising customer expectations, with no guarantee of a predetermined return, or sustainable success. A world where companies "built to last" only exists in book titles, not in the "perennial gale of creative destruction" necessary to propel the economy forward.

Even though Paul I have done our best to provide you with some "how to" ideas, our approach in this book is more aligned with Peter Block's and Peter Drucker's about the importance of finding your own path. After working with literally thousands of professional firms worldwide, we have learned that no two paths to a business model transformation are ever the same. There is simply no one right way. There is no checklist with 10 things to do to change. I believe that has only worked once, involving Moses with a stone tablet. You need to discover your own path.

We are positive we have not answered every question that you will confront if you decide to transition to a subscription business model as described in this book. There are so many *known unknowns* that you will confront, along with the *unknown unknowns*. But we would ask you to begin with these questions as opposed to *how to* questions:

- Does the subscription model make sense?
- Does putting the customer relationship at the center of your firm comport with your purpose, your values, and why you entered the profession in the first place?

- Does it make sense that customers are really buying outcomes and transformations, not inputs, outputs, or services?
- Does it make sense that the services you provide are merely the *means* to the *ends* of creating those customer transformations?
- Is it worth doing? Is it the type of firm you want to build?

If you answered in the affirmative, congratulations. You will be one of the 2.5% of innovators that adopt a new idea. You can take comfort in Voltaire: "Our wretched species is so made that those who walk on the well-trodden path always throw stones at those who are showing a new road."

Embracing a new business model requires leadership and vision. It requires knowing you are doing the right things for the right reasons, not just doing things efficiently. It requires focusing the firm on the external value it creates for the customer and simultaneously building the type of firm people are proud to be a part of and contribute to—the sort of organization for which you would want your son or daughter to work. It requires a sense of dignity and self-respect that you are worth every penny you charge, and you will only work with customers who have integrity, whom you enjoy and respect. It requires an attitude of experimentation and abundance, not simply doing things because that is the way it has always been done. It requires less measurement, less fear, and more trust. It requires boldness and risk-taking, giving before you receive. There are no books in the library titled *Great Moderates in History*.

Skeptics will call for an incremental approach, which is how they maintain the status quo—long after the quo has lost it status. But how do you make incremental change to a business model that is already dying? There's no room for the polite protestors' chant: "What do we want? *Incremental change*. When do we want it? *In due course*." Due course is here and now, dear reader—*Time's Up,* to borrow a title. The freedom of choice is yours.

Science fiction writer William Gibson quipped, "The future is here. It's just not widely distributed yet." In that spirit, let us end by asking, "What's next?"

23

WHAT'S NEXT?

"What is the next thing?" The ineffability of that next thing
preoccupies me more than anything else.

—Carmen Gimenez Smith, poet, editor, publisher, educator

The logic of creativity is "leap before you look." You cannot
fully see anything new from an old place. . . . It is the leap, not
the look, that generates the crucial information; the leap
through time and space, beyond the swarm of observable fact,
that opens up the vistas of discovery.

—George Gilder, *Wealth and Poverty*, 1993

Friedrich A. Hayek, the 1974 Nobel Prize winner in economics, believed the human mind could not see its own advance; the future is unpredictable, and we simply cannot know now what still remains to be known. Knowledge is about the past while entrepreneurship is about the future. Knowledge is wealth, but all economic growth comes from learning, mostly entrepreneurial hypotheses and other innovations that get tested in the free market. This is why it is so important for businesses to run on ideas, not hierarchies. Knowing is just another way of saying, "I'm done thinking about it." But the economy is never done experimenting, creating, and leaping out of the liminal space, casting off the old and discovering the future for the rest of us.

This is why the future cannot be taught; if it could, there would be nothing for intrepid venture capitalists and angel investors to discover. Francis Bacon articulated the importance of imagination over knowledge: "The knowledge which we now possess will not teach a man even what to wish." Angel investors and venture capitalists place bets on contrarian thinkers who have a different vision of the future, and because the future is unknowable, the bets are worth placing even if only 1 out 5 (or 10) come to fruition. It is a reliable and relatively low-cost method for society to progress while at the same time creating wealth by serving others.

I, for one, would not want to live in a world where the future is knowable and rational, a population comprised of automatons calculating with logical precision exactly what needs to be done to optimize current performance, whether in a business or society. Dreams always die when they come true. "Without measureless and perpetual uncertainty," Winston Churchill said, "the drama of human life would be destroyed."

BUILT TO LAST VERSUS DYNAMISM

I would rather live in a world where my life is surrounded by mystery than live in a world so small that my mind could comprehend it.

—Harry Emerson Fosdick, American pastor

Since the macroeconomic environment of nearly any developed country is comprised of millions of businesses, the aggregate marketplace is a laboratory where multiple hypotheses get tested, where customers spending their own money ultimately falsify the business model of any one particular firm. All business ideas and theories are, ultimately, subjected to this perpetual authentication process, that of the sovereign customer.

For all of our advances in management thinking and the thousands of business books published each year claiming the path to success with some new fad, there is simply no economic theory that can predict which particular company will succeed and which will fail. If there were, competition itself would serve no purpose—knowing who is going to win the Super Bowl makes it pointless to play. And like the incalculable future, competition is incredibly risky, and full of uncertainty.

Think of the institutions in any society: Churches, the family, labor unions, professional organizations, government, bureaucracy, businesses. With the exception of businesses, nearly all institutions in society are conserving institutions, with the mission of preventing change, slowing it down, or preserving the status quo. Only the business enterprise is a destabilizing institution, organized for creative destruction. This is why economic dynamism and growth depend on innovation and the entrepreneur, because as organizations age they tend to regress to stability and homeostasis, not change. This is why most innovations take existing industries by surprise, as the late Harvard Professor Clayton Christensen has documented so well in his work.

Without entrepreneurs, economies are barren. Without the risk takers in society, growth would slow immeasurably, and we would be much poorer as a result. Discovery and innovation always take us by surprise; otherwise, we could run the economy with bureaucrats and our immense computational power—an idea falsified by the former Soviet Union, and other centrally planned economies.

A world where companies are "built to last" only exists in book titles, not in a dynamic, innovative economy. I would not want to live in a world where companies last forever. This is the ideology of communism and socialism, not a vibrant and dynamic free market economy. If a business is no longer creating wealth for its customers, I want the market—meaning sovereign customers—to ruthlessly drive it out of business for wasting society's resources. I do not want to inhabit a world built from the economist's perfect competition model, where businesses do nothing but provide job security, while cranking out commodities on a "level playing field," with no ability to effect prices, output, or customer preferences. How dreadfully boring. No innovation, no dynamism, no growth, no life.

I look forward to the *destruction* capitalism produces as much as I do the *dynamism*. Silicon Valley may be a font of creativity, but only because it rests atop a mass cemetery of bankrupted hypotheses—many more ventures fail than succeed—falsified by the sovereignty of the customer. The same applies to companies, which is why capitalism creates prosperity—it has a built-in falsification process whereby companies, like scientific experiments, can be proven wrong and removed from wasting society's oxygen. It is *not* survival of the fittest; it is survival of only those firms that continue to add more value to society than they consume.

This is precisely why entrepreneurs are so essential to growth and wealth creation. Existing organizations that have done something well millions and millions of times are usually not the best vehicles to perform something new for the first time. Niccolo Machiavelli said it well in *The Prince*: "Innovation makes enemies of all those who prospered under the old regime, and only lukewarm support is forthcoming from those who would prosper under the new." Let us turn now to what business model innovations we may see in the future.

GLIMPSING AHEAD

While subscriptions are all the rage at the moment, in our view they are a stepping stone toward other, more customer-focused revenue models rather than the final point.

—Marco Bertini and Oded Koeningsberg, *The Ends Game*, 2020

The Ends Game is a thought-provoking book, which we recommend you read to gain an understanding of experimentations that are already being piloted in the constantly evolving revenue and business models of companies. The authors' main argument is that companies are still selling the "means" to customers (products and services) and then promising that the desired "ends" will result. This is difficult to argue with, even in the subscription model. A lot of the ways it has been implemented are still far too dependent on discrete services, rather than continuous transformations.

The authors further argue that an exchange is inefficient if customers experience friction in any of these three touchpoints: access, consume, perform. Subscription has moved the needle in terms of access and consume, but not so much with perform. As professionals, we can't guarantee results. But why not? I know the ethical challenges with this: Professionals cannot guarantee results, outcomes, and so on. But put those aside for the moment. The following are some experiments that are already being done to move toward pricing the actual results, rather than just promises:

- Winterhalter, a German company, charges customers for clean dishes rather than selling dishwashers.
- Teatreneu, a comedy theater in Barcelona, Spain, installed facial recognition technology in front of every audience member

that could detect when they laughed, charging them 30 euro cents per laugh (to a maximum charge of 24 euros).

- "In 2007, Johnson & Johnson proposed a pay-by-outcome model for an oncology treatment in the United Kingdom, under which the company would refund any money spent on patients whose tumors did not remiss" (Bertini and Koeningsberg 2020).

- In 2017, Amgen would rebate buyers of its drug Repatha—that reduces the risk of heart attack or stroke—if the patient suffered a heart attack or stroke.

- Imagine if universities were to focus on student transformations, not just inputs such as tuition, class credits, etc. UATX, a nonprofit that is building a university in Austin (aka the University of Austin) is considering just that. A revolutionary new concept that is surely going to disrupt the higher-education market with its new business model, UATX is planning to welcome its first class of undergraduates and graduate students in 2024. It explains its new financial model: "We're completely rethinking how a university operates by developing a novel financial model. We will lower tuition by avoiding costly administrative excess and overreach. We will focus our resources intensively on academics, rather than amenities. We will align institutional incentives with student outcomes." To align these incentives, one idea it is considering is the following: "UATX is working on a proposal to guarantee the median salary in a student's major field for five years following graduation. If a graduate makes less than the median salary over the five-year period, UATX will pay the difference" (Nonpublic draft prospectus, UATX, personal communication, April 5, 2022).

- "Bugs" Burger Bug Killer Company (based in Miami, Florida, and run by Al Burger) is a pest control company specializing in the hospitality industry. Al knew most customers did not want to *control* pests, but to *wipe* them out, so he developed an *extraordinary* guarantee to ensure his customers he could do the job:

> You don't owe one penny until all pests on your premises have been totally eradicated. If a guest spots a pest on your

premises, BBBK will pay for the guest's meal or room, send a letter of apology, and pay for a future meal or stay.

If you are ever dissatisfied with BBBK's service, you will receive a full refund of the company's services *plus* fees for another exterminator of your choice for the next year.

If your facility is closed down due to the presence of roaches or rodents, BBBK will pay any fines, as well as any lost profits, plus $5,000.

Subscriptions demand that the firm focus more on the relationship, access, frictionless customer experience, and even transformations, as we advocate herein. Other than that, we do not have much skin in the game, certainly not as much as Al Burger. Of course, he charges quite a premium for this level of ensurance. Would you pay it?

One more example, this one again from Marco Bertini, from an article he wrote with Richard Reisman that originally appeared in the December 2018 issue of the *Journal of Revenue and Pricing Management* (Reisman and Bertini 2018) . It is called FairPay, which essentially gives pricing privileges to customers while allowing the company to rate the fairness of the price set by the customer, and retain the right to make the price revocable. It is not new, the band Radio Head allowed its fans to pay what they wanted, which worked out quite lucratively for them. The TIP clause we discussed in Chapter 17 is close to the FairPay idea, but it is not designed to be used across the entire firm, for all customers.

The question is, would a firm be able to run everything under this FairPay model? Time will tell, but there is no doubt in our minds that we will continue to witness further evolutions in the business models of professional firms. We simply have to raise the bar on the customer experience and focus on what they are buying—transformations.

Undoubtedly there will be ethical and independence issues in the attempt to price for outcomes, and for certain services—such as financial statement audits and other services that require CPAs to be independent—it will never materialize. However, given alternative models of ownership, private-equity, and other potential external investors into accounting firms, it might become possible. Top 100 accounting firm EisnerAmper spun out its audit function into a separate entity when it received private-equity funding in 2021, enabling it to have different revenue and business models in the other practice areas of the firm. External investors will not be so attached to old business models, so it will be interesting to see if this drives innovation.

Keep your eyes peeled on the edges, because that is where innovations in business models comes from. Continue to look outside at other industries and professions. Keep an open mind, and take Amelia Earhart's advice to heart: "Never interrupt someone doing something you said couldn't be done."

TRANSFORMATIONS REQUIRE LIMINAL THINKING

I remember when I first read about the first concierge medical practice, MD²®. Even though it was founded in 1996, it took me several years to discover this radical new business model. As I discussed in Chapter 9, I did not even have an adequate vocabulary, labeling it *retainer medicine,* like we labeled the first automobiles "horseless carriages," borrowing from the old to explain the new.

This model made me quite uncomfortable in trying to apply it to other professional firms. Even though I knew how revolutionary it was, I just could not escape the trap of thinking that our value was determined by the services we stack up for the customer, brick by brick. As these medical practices grew, along with its cousin, direct primary care, it was difficult to ignore. When you see something that challenges your worldview, you are experiencing *liminal thinking.* As Dave Gray explains in *Liminal Thinking: Create the Change You Want by Changing the Way You Think*:

> *Liminal* means boundary, doorway, portal. Not this or that, not the old way or the new way, but neither and both. A state of ambiguity or disorientation that precedes a breakthrough to a new kind of thinking. The space between. (Gray 2016)

Human beings are defined by their beliefs, not what they know. Therefore, it is natural that our beliefs are the biggest barriers to changing. It is scary for some people to be at the boundary of the known and the unknown, the past and the future. In a business context, we simply have to get comfortable in this liminal space, since, eventually, we will all get caught in the "gales of creative destruction." As T.S. Eliot wrote:

> Nothing pleases people more than to go on thinking what they have always thought, and at the same time imagine that they are thinking something new and daring: It combines the advantage of security with the delight of adventure.

The problem is, there is no security in the business world precisely because value is subjective, and consumers can change their minds tomorrow. As more and more customers are offered a better experience moving to subscription firms—even if this is just a way station to some other destination—the old model firms will become expendable, and rightfully so. We hope your firm becomes indispensable.

Keep yourself open to liminal thinking. It is a leading indicator that you are going to have some unlearning to do. The purpose of a business is to create wealth for its customers, a process of the inexhaustible human mind and spirit. John Perazzo, in his book *The Myths That Divide Us*, sums it up nicely:

> It requires courage to cast the accumulated myths of a lifetime to the wind. Our natural desire for simplicity, certitude, and the approval of others occasionally causes us to defend even our most flawed worldviews as if our very lives depended on them. Dead belief systems are difficult to bury, for in doing so we enter a world we do not recognize; we watch the carefully crafted towers of our understanding crash down in ruins; and we lose an integral piece of the only reality we have known, reinforced and imprinted on our minds by a thousand voices, internal and external. (Perazzo 1998, p. 17)

The author Gabriel Zaid wrote, "Wealth is above all an accumulation of possibilities." These possibilities lie hidden in the womb of the future, waiting to be discovered by human imagination, ingenuity, and creativity, manifested in free enterprise dedicated to the service of others. We would not want it any other way.

REFERENCES

Beware the man of only one book.

—Latin proverb

Actuarial Jokes (n.d.). Joke submitted by Michael Swiecicki, joke #130. https://actuarialjokes.com (accessed February 27, 2022).

AICPA (2016). "AICPA Code of Professional Conduct." USAICPA.org. https://us.aicpa.org/content/dam/aicpa/research/standards/codeofconduct/downloadabledocuments/2014december15contentasof2016august31codeofconduct.pdf (accessed February 27, 2022).

AIMS360 (n.d.). "Pricing plans." www.aims360.com/plans/ (accessed February 20, 2022).

Albrecht, Karl (1992). *The Only Thing That Matters: Bringing the Power of the Customer into the Center of Your Business*. New York: HarperBusiness.

Aquila, August J., and Allan D. Koltin (1992). "How to Lose Clients Without Really Trying." *Journal of Accountancy*, May 1992.

Aten, Jason (2021). "This Was Steve Job's Most Important Observation When He Returned to Apple. It Changed Everything." *Inc.*, May 26, 2021. https://www.inc.com/jason-aten/this-was-steve-jobs-most-important-observation-when-he-returned-to-apple-it-changed-everything.html (accessed March 12, 2022).

Baker, Ronald J. (2005). *Professional's Guide to Value Pricing, Sixth Edition*. Chicago, IL: CCH Incorporated. (Out of print).

Baker, Ronald J. and Paul Dunn (2003). *The Firm of the Future: A Guide for Accountants, Lawyers, and Other Professional Services*. Hoboken, NJ: John Wiley & Sons, Inc.

Baker, Ronald J. (2006). *Pricing on Purpose: Creating and Capturing Value.* Hoboken, NJ: John Wiley & Sons, Inc.

Baker, Ronald J. (2006). *Measure What Matters to Customers: Using Key Predictive Indicators.* Hoboken, NJ: John Wiley & Sons, Inc.

Baker, Ronald J. (2008). *Mind Over Matter: Why Intellectual Capital is the Chief Source of Wealth.* Hoboken, NJ: John Wiley & Sons, Inc.

Baker, Ronald J. (2011). *Implementing Value Pricing: A Radical Business Model for Professional Firms.* Hoboken, NJ: John Wiley & Sons, Inc.

Baker, Ronald J. and Ed Kless (2015). *The Soul of Enterprise: Dialogues on Business in the Knowledge Economy.* Petaluma, CA: VeraSage Press.

Wooley-Barker, Tamsin (2017). *Teeming: How Superorganisms Work Together to Build Infinite Wealth On a Finite Planet (and your company can too).* Ashland, OR: White Cloud Press.

Bariso, Justin (2022). "This CEO's Remote Work Policy Is Only 10 Words. It May Be the Best I've Ever Heard." *Inc.*, March 21, 2022. https://www.inc .com/justin-bariso/emotional-intelligence-gravity-ceo-dan-price-10-word-remote-work-policy.html (accessed April 20, 2022).

Basch, Michael D. (2002). *Customer Culture: How FedEx and Other Great Companies Put the Customer First Every Day.* Upper Saddle River, New Jersey: Prentice Hall.

Baxter, Robbie Kellman (2015). *The Membership Economy: Find Your Superusers, Master the Forever Transaction, and Build Recurring Revenue.* New York: McGraw Hill Education.

Baxter, Robbie Kellman (2020). *The Forever Transaction: How to Build a Subscription Model So Compelling, Your Customers Will Never Want to Leave.* New York: McGraw Hill Education.

Beatty, Jack (1998). *The World According to Peter Drucker.* New York: The Free Press.

Beckwith, Harry (2000). *The Invisible Touch: The Four Keys to Modern Marketing.* New York: Warner Books.

Berra, Yogi, with Dave Kaplan (2001). *When You Come to a Fork in the Road, Take It!: Inspiration and Wisdom from One of Baseball's Greatest Heroes.* New York: Hyperion.

Bernstein, Peter L. (2001). *Against the Gods: The Remarkable Story of Risk.* Hoboken, NJ: John Wiley & Sons, Inc.

Bertini, Marco, and Oded Koenigsberg (2020). *The Ends Game: How Smart Companies Stop Selling Products and Start Delivering Value.* Boston: The MIT Press.

Birla, Madan (2005). *FedEx Delivers: How the World's Leading Shipping Company Keeps Innovating and Outperforming the Competition.* Hoboken, NJ: John Wiley & Sons, Inc.

Blaug, Mark (1997). *Not Only an Economist: Recent Essays by Mark Blaug.* Cheltenham, United Kingdom: Edward Elgar Publishing Limited.

Block, Peter (2003). *The Answer to How Is Yes: Acting on What Matters.* San Francisco: Berrett-Koehler Publishers, Inc.

Boomer, Gary (2022). "Boomer's Blueprint: Checklists or questions—a key to increasing value." *Accounting Today*, January 7, 2022. https://www.accountingtoday.com/opinion/boomers-blueprint-checklists-or-questions-a-key-to-increasing-value (accessed April 10, 2022).

Boudreaux, Donald J. (2018). "Capitalists Get Rich but Consumers Capture the Benefits." American Institute for Economic Research. https://www.aier.org/article/capitalists-get-rich-but-consumers-capture-the-benefits/ (Accessed May 2, 2022).

Bourdain, Anthony (2008). *Kitchen Confidential: Adventures in the Culinary Underbelly.* New York: Bloomsbury Publishing.

Boyle, David (2001). *The Sum of Our Discontent: Why Numbers Make Us Irrational.* New York: Texere.

Carrillo, Hilda, Joseph F. Castellano, PhD, and Timothy M. Keune, PhD, CPA (2017). "Employee Engagement in Public Accounting Firms." *The CPA Journal*, December 2017. https://www.cpajournal.com/2017/12/25/employee-engagement-public-accounting-firms/ (accessed 09 April 2022).

Casado, Martin (2020). "11 Key GTM [go-to-market] Metrics for B2B Startups." Andreessen Horowitz, February 10, 2020. https://future.a16z.com/11-key-gtm-metrics-b2b-startups/ (accessed March 12, 2022).

Catmull, Ed, with Amy Wallace (2014). *Creativity, Inc.: Overcoming the Unseen Forces That Stand in the Way of True Inspiration.* New York: Random House.

Christensen, Clayton M. and Michael E. Raynor (2003). *The Innovator's Solution: Creating and Sustaining Successful Growth.* Boston: Harvard Business School Press.

Christensen, Clayton M., Scott D. Anthony and Erik A. Roth (2004). *Seeing What's Next: Using the Theories of Innovation to Predict Industry Change.* Boston: Harvard Business School Press.

Clear, James (2018). *Atomic Habits: An Easy & Proven Way to Build Good Habits & Break Bad Ones.* New York: Avery.

Cohen, PhD, William A. (2008). *A Class with Drucker: The Lost Lessons of the World's Greatest Management Teacher.* New York: AMACOM.

Collins, James C., and Jerry I. Porras (1997). *Built to Last: Successful Habits of Visionary Companies*. New York: HarperBusiness.

Collins, James C. (2001). *Good to Great: Why Some Companies Make the Leap. . . and Others Don't*. New York: HarperBusiness.

Colvin, Geoff (2007). "Selling P&G." *Fortune*. https://money.cnn.com/magazines/fortune/fortune_archive/2007/09/17/100258870/index.htm (accessed July 30, 2022).

Covey, Stephen R. (2004) *The 8th Habit: From Effectiveness to Greatness*. New York: Free Press.

Dawson, Ross (2000). *Developing Knowledge-Based Client Relationships: The Future of Professional Services*. Boston, Massachusetts: Butterworth Heinemann.

Deming, W. Edwards (1994). *The New Economics: For Industry, Government, Education*, 2nd ed. Cambridge, MA: MIT Press.

Derman , Emanuel (2011). *Models Behaving Badly: Why Confusing Illusion with Reality Can Lead to Disaster, on Wall Street and in Life*. New York: Free Press.

Disney Institute (2001). *Be Our Guest: Perfecting the Art of Customer Service*. New York: Disney Editions.

Dixon, Matthew, Karen Freeman, and Nicholas Toman (2010). "Stop Trying to Delight Your Customers." *Harvard Business Review*, July-August 2010. https://hbr.org/2010/07/stop-trying-to-delight-your-customers (accessed March 13, 2022).

DPC Frontier Mapper (n.d.). https://mapper.dpcfrontier.com (accessed August 4, 2022).

Drucker, Peter F. (1995). *Managing in a Time of Great Change*. New York: Truman Talley Books/Dutton.

Drucker, Peter F. (1999). *Management Challenges for the 21st Century*. New York: HarperCollins.

Drucker, Peter, F. (2002). *Managing in the Next Society*. New York: Truman Talley Books.

Drucker, Peter F. (2003). *Peter Drucker On the Profession of Management*. Boston: Harvard Business Review.

Drucker, Peter F. with Joseph A. Maciariello (2004). *The Daily Drucker: 366 Days of Insights and Motivation for Getting the Right Things Done*. New York: HarperBusiness.

Drucker, Peter F. with Joseph A. Maciariello (2006). *The Effective Executive in Action: A Journal for Getting the Right Things Done*. New York: Collins.

Drucker, Peter F. (2007). *People and Performance: The Best of Peter Drucker on Management.* Boston: Harvard Business School Press.

Drucker, Peter F., et al. (2008). *The Five Most Important Questions You Will Ever Ask About Your Organization.* San Francisco: Jossey-Bass.

Duggan, Tim (2020). *Cult Status: How to Build a Business People Adore.* Sydney, Australia: ReadHowYouWant.

Ebeling, Richard M. (2004). Introducing Dr. Richard Pipes, "Property and Freedom: The Inseparable Connection." Evenings at FEE, October 9, 2004.

Ebenstein, Alan (2003). *Hayek's Journey: The Mind of Friedrich Hayek.* New York: Palgrave Macmillan.

The Economist (2015). "Briefing: Artificial Intelligence." May 9, 2015, p. 21.

Edersheim, Elizabeth Haas (2007). *The Definitive Drucker.* New York: McGraw-Hill.

Farrago, Douglas (n.d.). "Be-Well" T-shirt." DPC Book website. http://dpcbook .com/be-well-t-shirt/ (accessed March 16, 2022).

Flaherty, John E. (1999). *Peter Drucker: Shaping the Managerial Mind.* San Francisco: Jossey-Bass Publishers.

Ford, Henry, and Samuel Crowther (1922). *My Life and Work.* Kessinger Publishing, www.kessigner.net.

France, Van Arsdale (2015). *Window On Main Street: 35 Years of Creating Happiness at Disneyland Park.* www.ThemeParkPress.com.

Fried, Jason, and David Hansson (2010). *Rework.* New York: Crown Publishing Group.

Fukuyama, Francis (1995). *Trust: The Social Virtues and the Creation of Prosperity.* New York: Free Press.

Gandy, Mark (2021). *Becoming a Part-Time CFO: 30 Questions in 30 Days Before Making a Decision.* Columbia, MI: G3CFO LLC.

Gawande, Atul (2010). *The Checklist Manifesto: How to Get Things Right.* London: Picador.

Gilder, George (1981). *Wealth and Poverty.* New York: Basic Books, Inc.

Gilder, George (1984). *The Spirit of Enterprise.* New York: Simon and Schuster.

Gilder, George (1992). *Recapturing the Spirit of Enterprise: Updated for the 1990s.* San Francisco: ICS Press.

Gilder, George (1993). *Wealth and Poverty: A New Edition of the Classic.* San Francisco: ICS Press.

Gilder, George (2002). "The Gilder Friday Letter." *Gilder Technology Report,* Friday, December 13, 2002.

Gilder, George (2013). *Knowledge and Power: The Information Theory of Capitalism and How it is Revolutionizing our World*. Washington, DC: Regnery Publishing, Inc.

Gilder, George (2018). *Life after Google: The Fall of Big Data and the Rise of the Blockchain Economy*. Washington, D.C.: Regnery Gateway.

Gilder, George (2023). *Life After Capitalism*. Washington, D.C.: Regnery Gateway.

Goddard, Jules, and Tony Eccles (2012). *Uncommon Sense, Common Nonsense: Why Some Organizations Consistently Outperform Others*. London: Profile Books.

Goldratt, Eliyahu M. (1992). *The Goal: A Process of Ongoing Improvement*, 2nd Edition. Great Barrington, MA: The North River Press.

Gray, Dave (2016). *Liminal Thinking: Create the Change You Want by Changing the Way You Think*. Brooklyn, New York: Two Waves Books.

Gregory, John Milton (1995). *The Seven Laws of Teaching*. Grand Rapids, MI: Baker Books.

Grove, Andrew S. (1996). *Only the Paranoid Survive: How to Exploit the Crisis Points That Challenge Every Company*. New York: Doubleday Business.

Hamel, Gary (2000). *Leading the Revolution*. Boston: Harvard Business School Press.

Harter, Jim (2022). "U.S. Employee Engagement Drops for First Year in a Decade." Gallup, January 7, 2022. https://www.gallup.com/workplace/388481/employee-engagement-drops-first-year-decade.aspx (accessed April 20,2022).

Hastings, Reed, and Erin Meyer (2020). *No Rules Rules: Netflix and the Culture of Reinvention*. New York: Penguin Press.

Havens, Joey (2016). "What If I Really Am a Trusted Advisor?" LinkedIn post, June 22, 2016. https://www.linkedin.com/pulse/what-i-really-am-trusted-advisor-joey-havens/ (accessed February 7, 2022).

Hazlitt, Henry (1979). *Economics In One Lesson*. New York: Crown Publishers, Inc.

History.com, editors (n.d.). "Renaissance." www.History.com. https://bit.ly/2FhCElH (Accessed November 28, 2021).

Hoffer, Eric (2006). *Reflections on the Human Condition*. Titusville, NJ: Hopewell Publications.

Howey, Richard S. (1989). *The Rise of the Marginal Utility School, 1870–1889*. New York: Columbia University Press (Morningside Edition).

Hunt, Vivian (2022). "Putting stakeholder capitalism into practice." McKinsey & Company, January 7, 2022. https://www.mckinsey.com/business-functions/strategy-and-corporate-finance/our-insights/putting-stakeholder-capitalism-into-practice (accessed April 20, 2022).

Janzer, Anne (2020). *Subscription Marketing: Strategies for Nurturing Customers in a World of Churn*, 3rd edition. San Luis Obispo, CA: Cuesta Park Consulting.

Johnson, H. Thomas and Robert S. Kaplan (1991). *Relevance Lost: The Rise and Fall of Management Accounting*. Boston: Harvard Business School Press.

Johnson, H. Thomas (1998). "Reflections of a Recovering Management Accountant." Society for Organizational Learning Initiative, First Research Forum, January 14–16, 1998.

Johnson, H. Thomas and Anders Bröms (2000). *Profit Beyond Measure: Extraordinary Results through Attention to Work and People*. New York: The Free Press.

Jordan, Jeff, Anu Hariharan, Frank Chen, and Preethi Kasireddy (2015). "16 Startup Metrics." Andreessen Horowitz, August 21, 2015. https://a16z.com/2015/08/21/16-metrics/ (accessed March 12, 2022).

Kay, John (1995). *Foundations of Corporate Success: How Business Strategies Add Value*. New York: Oxford University Press.

Kehrer, Daniel (1989). *Doing Business Boldly*. New York: Time Books.

Kerber, Ross (2022). "U.S. ESG shareholder resolutions up 22% to record level for 2022, study finds." Reuters, March 17, 2022. https://www.reuters.com/business/sustainable-business/us-esg-shareholder-resolutions-up-22-record-level-2022-study-finds-2022-03-17/ (accessed 20 April 2022).

Kotter, John P. (2012). *Leading Change*. Boston: Harvard Business Review Press.

Krass, Peter, Ed. (1999). *The Book of Entrepreneurs' Wisdom: Classic Writings by Legendary Entrepreneurs*. New York: John Wiley & Sons, Inc.

Kurtz, David L., and Kenneth E. Clow (1998). *Services Marketing*. New Jersey: John Wiley & Sons, Inc.

Lafley, A.G., and Ram Charan (2008). *The Game-Changer: How You Can Drive Revenue and Profit Growth with Innovation*. New York: Crown Business.

Lapin, Rabbi Daniel (2002). *Thou Shall Prosper: Ten Commandments for Making Money*. Hoboken, NJ: John Wiley & Sons, Inc.

Lee, Reginald Tomas Lee, Sr. (2016). *Lies, Damned Lies, and Cost Accounting: How Capacity Management Enables Improved Cost and Cash Flow Management*. New York: Business Expert Press, LLC.

Lee, Reginald Tomas Lee, Sr. (2018). *Strategic Cost Transformation: Using Business Domain Management to Improve Cost Data, Analysis, and Management*. New York: Business Expert Press, LLC.

Lev, Baruch (2001). *Intangibles: Management, Measurement, and Reporting.* Washington, D.C.: Brookings Institution Press.

Lev, Baruch, and Feng Gu (2016). *The End of Accounting and the Path Forward for Investors and Managers.* Hoboken, NJ: John Wiley & Sons, Inc.

Lev, Baruch (2021). "The sad state of accounting standards." *Accounting Today,* July 21, 2021. https://www.accountingtoday.com/opinion/the-sad-state-of-accounting-standards (accessed March 6, 2022).

Maister, David (1997). *True Professionalism: The Courage to Care about Your People, Your Clients, and Your Career.* New York: Free Press.

Maister, David, Charles H. Green and Robert M. Galford (2000). *The Trusted Advisor.* New York: The Free Press.

Marcus, Stanley (1979). *Quest for the Best.* New York: The Viking Press.

Marcus, Stanley (1995). *The Viewpoints of Stanley Marcus: A Ten-Year Perspective.* Denton, Texas: University of North Texas Press.

Marcus, Stanley (1997). *Minding the Store: A Memoir.* Denton, Texas: University of North Texas Press (facsimile edition; original publication 1974).

Marcus, Stanley (2000). *Stanley Marcus from A to Z: Viewpoints Volume II.* Denton, Texas: University of North Texas Press.

Marks, Andy (2022). "At the Intersection of ESG Oversight and Strategy." *Deloitte, January* 14, 2022. https://deloitte.wsj.com/articles/at-the-intersection-of-esg-oversight-and-strategy-01642088320 (accessed April 10, 2022).

Marx, Karl (1995). *Value, Price and Profit.* New York: International Publishers, (paperback edition, originally published 1865).

McKenna, Patrick J. and David H. Maister (2002). *First Among Equals: How to Manage a Group of Professionals.* New York: The Free Press.

MD²® (n.d.). "Our Story." https://www.md2.com/our-story (accessed January 13, 2022).

MD²® (n.d.). "Only MD²® physicians dedicate their practices to just 50 families." https://www.md2.com/#why-50:1 (accessed January 13, 2022).

Menger, Carl (1976). *Principles of Economics*, trans. James Dingwall and Bert F. Hoselitz. New York: New York University Press (originally published 1871).

Mintzberg, Henry (1989). *Mintzberg On Management: Inside Our Strange World of Organizations.* New York: The Free Press.

Mintzberg, Henry (2004). *Managers Not MBAs: A Hard Look at the Soft Practice of Managing and Management Development.* San Francisco: Berrett-Koehler Publishers, Inc.

Mintzberg, Henry (2009). *Managing*. San Francisco: Berrett-Koehler Publishers.

Mintzberg, Henry (2019). *Bedtime Stories for Managers: Farewell, Lofty Leadership. . .Welcome, Engaging Management*. Oakland, CA: Berrett-Koehler Publishers, Inc.

Moores (n.d.). "Moores Agreed Pricing." www.moores.com.au. (https://www .moores.com.au/here-for-good/#moores-agreed-pricing (accessed March 2, 2022).

Moran, Howard (2005). "Concierge Medicine: Weighing this Controversial Alternative to Traditional Health Care Providers. *Worth*, July 2005.

Mourkogiannis, Nikos (2006). *Purpose: The Starting Point of Great Companies*. New York: Palgrave Macmillan.

Munger, Michael C. (2018). *Tomorrow 3.0: Transaction Costs and the Sharing Economy*. Cambridge, England: Cambridge University Press.

Nagle, Thomas T., and Reed K. Holden (2002). *The Strategy and Tactics of Pricing: A Guide to Profitable Decision Making*, 3rd ed. Upper Saddle River, NJ: Prentice-Hall.

Netflix (2020). "Helping members who haven't been watching cancel." Netflix, May 21, 2020. https://about.netflix.com/en/news/helping-members-who-havent-been-watching-cancel (accessed March 16, 2022).

Nonaka, Ikujiro and Hirotaka Takeuchi (1995). *The Knowledge-Creating Company: How Japanese Companies Create the Dynamics of Innovation*. New York: Oxford University Press.

Novak, Michael (1996). *Business as a Calling: Work and the Examined Life*. New York: Free Press.

Payne, Ric (2017). "A Day in the Office with Paul Kennedy: How One Firm Transitioned from Compliance to Advisory." Ric Payne's Blog, April 20, 2017. http://theconsultingaccountant.com/a-day-in-the-office-with-paul-kennedy-how-one-firmtransitioned-from-compliance-to-advisory/ (accessed February 7, 2022).

Payne, Ric (2021). "The Six Business Trajectories." Ric Payne's Blog, October 5, 2021. http://theconsultingaccountant.com/the-six-business-trajectories/ (accessed March 16, 2022).

Perazzo, John (1998). *The Myths That Divide Us: How Lies Have Poisoned American Race Relations*. World Studies Books.

Pine, B. Joseph, II, and James H. Gilmore (1999). *The Experience Economy: Work Is Theatre and Every Business a Stage*. Boston: Harvard Business School Press.

Pine, B. Joseph, II, and James H. Gilmore (2019). *The Experience Economy: Competing for Customer Time, Attention, and Money*. Boston: Harvard Business Review Press.

Polman, Paul, and Andrew Winston (2021). *Net Positive: How Courageous Companies Thrive by Giving More Than They Take*. Boston: Harvard Business Review Press.

Price, Harrison "Buzz" (2004). *Walt's Revolution!: By the Numbers*. Orlando, FL: Ripley Entertainment Inc.

Rajamannar, Raja (2021). *Quantum Marketing: Mastering the New Marketing Mindset for Tomorrow's Consumers*. New York: HarperCollins Leadership.

The Recycler (2022). "HP Inc. grows instant ink to over 11 subscribers." *The Recycler*, March 1, 2022. (https://www.therecycler.com/posts/hp-inc-grows-instant-ink-to-over-11-million-subscribers/ (accessed March 17, 2022).

Reichheld, Frederick F. and Thomas Teal (1996). *The Loyalty Effect: The Hidden Force Behind Growth, Profits, and Lasting Value*. Boston: Harvard Business School Press.

Reichheld, Frederick F. (2001). *Loyalty Rules! How Today's Leaders Build Lasting Relationships*. Boston: Harvard Business School Press.

Reichheld, Fred (2006). *The Ultimate Question: Driving Good Profits and True Growth*. Boston: Harvard Business School Press.

Reichheld, Fred (2021). *Winning on Purpose: The Unbeatable Strategy of Loving Customers*. Boston: Harvard Business Review Press.

Reichheld, Fred, Darci Darnell, and Maureen Burns (2021). "Net Promoter 3.0." *Harvard Business Review*, November-December 2021. https://hbr.org/2021/11/net-promoter-3-0 (accessed April 16, 2022).

Reisman, Richard, and Marco Bertini (2018). "A novel architecture to monetize digital offerings." *Journal of Revenue and Pricing Management*, December 2018. https://www.researchgate.net/publication/323399666_A_Novel_Architecture_to_Monetize_Digital_Offerings; also see, https://www.subscribed.com/read/news-and-editorial/3-building-blocks-to-monetize-a-digital-business (accessed May 5, 2022).

Rossman, John (2021). *The Amazon Way: Amazon's 14 Leadership Principles*, 3rd edition. Clyde Hill Publishing.

Schoenwaelder, Tom, John Mennel, Amy E. Silverstein, and Shira Beery (2021). "The Purpose Premium: Why a purpose-driven strategy is good for business." Deloitte Monitor, 2021. https://www2.deloitte.com/content/dam/Deloitte/us/Documents/process-and-operations/purpose-premium-pov.pdf (accessed 10 April 2022).

Sewell, Carl (1990). *Customers for Life: How to Turn That One-Time Buyer into a Lifetime Customer*. New York: Pocket Books.

Shift (2022). "Connection: Driver of Company Culture." *Shift the Work*, January 4, 2022. https://www.shiftthework.com/blog/connection-company-culture (accessed April 4, 2022).

Simon, Hermann (2015). *Confessions of the Pricing Man: How Price Affects Everything*. Cham, Switzerland: Copernicus.

Simon, Hermann (2021). *True Profit!: No Company Ever Went Broke Turning a Profit*. Cham, Switzerland: Copernicus.

Skousen, Mark, and Kenna C. Taylor (1997). *Puzzles and Paradoxes in Economics*. Cheltenham, UK: Edward Elgar Publishing.

Skousen, Mark (2001). *The Making of Modern Economics: The Lives and Ideas of the Great Thinkers*. Armonk, New York: M.E. Sharpe.

Skrob, Robert (2018). *Retention Point: The Single Biggest Secret to Membership and Subscription Growth*. Membership Services, Inc.

Smith, Bernic (2021). *Gamed: Why targets and incentives fail and how to fix them*. Sheffield, UK: Metric Press.

Snow, Richard (2019). *Disney's Land: Walt Disney and the Invention of the Amusement Park That Changed the World*. New York: Scribner.

Southwest Airlines (n.d.). "Transfarency philosophy." www.southwestairlines.com. https://www.southwest.com/html/air/transfarency/ (accessed February 20, 2022).

Sowell, Thomas (1980). *Knowledge and Decisions*. New York: Basic Books, Inc.

Sowell, Thomas (1994). *Race and Culture: A World View*. New York: Basic Books, Inc.

Sowell, Thomas (2000). *Basic Economics: A Citizen's Guide to the Economy*. New York: Basic Books.

Sowell, Thomas (2004). *Basic Economics: A Citizen's Guide to the Economy*, Revised and Expanded Edition. New York: Basic Books.

Stewart, Thomas A. (1997). *Intellectual Capital: The New Wealth of Organizations*. New York: Currency.

Stewart, Thomas A. (2001). *The Wealth of Knowledge: Intellectual Capital and the Twenty-First Century Organization*. New York: Currency.

Stiving, Ph.D., Mark (2021). *Win, Keep, Grow: How to Price and Package to Accelerate Your Subscription Business*. New York: Morgan James.

Stricklin, Chris, and Joel Neeb (2019). *Survivor's Obligation: Navigating an Intentional Life*. St. Paul, MN: Elva Resa Publishing.

Subramanian-Schmidt, Maxie (2021). "Earned Growth: A Boon Even For Companies That Cannot Implement The Metric." Forrester Blog, November 18, 2021. (https://www.forrester.com/blogs/earned-growth-a-boon-even-for-companies-that-cannot-implement-the-metric/ (accessed April 16, 2022).

Subscribed Institute (n.d.). "Definitive Guide to Subscription Metrics: Core Metrics for Subscription Businesses." Subscribed Institute. https://www.subscribed.com/article/subscription-metrics-guide (accessed March 12, 2022). [Requires personal information to download report].

Sullivan, Gordon R., and Michael V. Harper (1996). *Hope Is Not a Method: What Business Leaders Can Learn from America's Army.* New York: Broadway Books.

Summit CPA (n.d.). "Virtual CFO Pricing." Summit CPA. https://www.summitcpa.net/vcfo-services/pricing (accessed May 8, 2022).

Sutherland, Rory (2019). *Alchemy: The Dark Art and Curious Science of Creating Magic in Brands, Business, and Life.* New York: HarperCollins (U.S. edition).

Taleb, Nassim Nicholas (2007). *The Black Swan: The Impact of the Highly Improbable.* New York: Random House.

Taylor, Frederick Winslow (1967). *The Principles of Scientific Management. New York: W.W. Norton & Company* (originally published 1911).

Tedlow, Richard S. (2001). *Giants of Enterprise: Seven Business Innovators and the Empires They Built.* New York: Harper Business.

Tesseras, Lucy (2022). "Starling Bank pulls Facebook advertising until it cracks down on financial fraudsters." *Marketing Week*, January 7, 2022. https://www.marketingweek.com/starling-bank-pulls-facebook-advertising (accessed April 20, 2022),

Tetreault, Michael, and J. Catherine Sykes (2019). *The Doctor's Expanded Guide to Concierge Medicine: Essential Education for Doctors & Healthcare Professionals Considering A Career In A Modern, Subscription-Based & Patient-Centered, Private-Direct Medicine Practice.* Alpharetta, GA: Concierge Medicine Today, LLC.

The Soul of Enterprise: Business in the Knowledge Economy (2015). "Interview with Joseph Pine," episode #34. https://www.thesoulofenterprise.com/34 (accessed February 22, 2022).

The Soul of Enterprise: Business in the Knowledge Economy (2019). "The Subscription Business Model in Medicine," episode #269. https://www.thesoulofenterprise.com/269 (accessed February 17, 2022).

The Soul of Enterprise: Business in the Knowledge Economy (2022). "ESG—We Respectfully Dissent," episode #389. https://www.thesoulofenterprise.com/389 (accessed May 17, 2022).

Thomas, M.D., Paul (2020). *Startup DPC: How To Start And Grow Your Direct Primary Care Practice*. Detroit, MI: Plum Health DPC.

Tzuo, Tien, and Gabe Weisert (2018). *Subscribed: Why the Subscription Model Will Be Your Company's Future—and What to Do About It*. New York: Portfolio/Penguin Random House.

Tzuo, Tien (2021). "Building for the Future, Not the Past: Talking Enterprise Architecture with Robert Hildenbrand." *Subscribed Weekly*. https://www.linkedin.com/pulse/building-future-past-talking-enterprise-architecture-robert-tien-tzuo/ (accessed March 17, 2022).

Tzuo, Tien (2022a). "The Lateen Sail: Sustainability & Cloud-Based Subscriptions." *Subscribed Weekly*. https://www.subscribed.com/read/news-and-editorial/the-lateen-sail (accessed April 22, 2022).

Tzuo, Tien (2022b). "The Subscription Economy in Five Charts." *Subscribed Weekly*. https://www.subscribed.com/read/news-and-editorial/the-subscription-economy-in-5-charts (accessed February 19, 2022).

Warrillow, John (2015). *The Automatic Customer: Creating a Subscription Business in Any Industry*. New York: Portfolio.

World Health Organization (2022). "14.9 million excess deaths associated with the COVID-19 pandemic in 2020 and 2021." World Health Organization, May 5, 2022. https://www.who.int/news/item/05-05-2022-14.9-million-excess-deaths-were-associated-with-the-covid-19-pandemic-in-2020-and-2021 (accessed May 7, 2022).

Wikipedia (n.d.). "Definition of Sustainable Development Goals." (https://en.wikipedia.org/wiki/Sustainable_Development_Goals (accessed April 20, 2022).

Wikipedia (n.d.). "Definition of Surrogation." https://en.wikipedia.org/wiki/Surrogation (accessed March 6, 2022).

Williams, Tim (2010). *Positioning for Professionals: How Professional Knowledge Firms Can Differentiate Their Way to Success*. Hoboken, NJ: John Wiley & Sons, Inc.

Winston, William J., Editor (1995). *Marketing for CPAs, Accountants, and Tax Professionals*. New York: The Haworth Press.

Wolfe, Tom (2016). *The Kingdom of Speech*. New York: Little, Brown and Company.

INDEX

80/20 rule, 42
80/225 rule, 42, 43f

A

Abraham, John, 10
Absolute value, impossibility,
    184–185
Accountants' Boot Camp, 18
Accounting firms
  mission statements, samples, 32
  necessities, 6
Accounting, problems, 244
Action plan, creation, 87
Active subscribers (fundamental
    KPI), 263
Activity-based costing (ABC),
    consideration, 244, 247
Adaptive capacity model, 215–216
Adoption models, 311, 313–319
A-E ticket system (Disney
    usage), 221

Affiliation, 17, 21
Affordable risk, 162
After Action Reviews (AARs), 60,
    173, 279, 285, 289–295
Against the Odds (Bernstein), 161
AIMS360 (ERP software company),
    209, 227
Albrecht, Karl, 298
"All-is-covered-for-you" subscription
    model, 21
Altruism, index, 131, 142
Amazon Prime, 156
  price euphemisms, avoidance, 236
  value, 235
American Institute of Certified Public
    Accountants (AICPA)
  Code of Professional Conduct,
    223
  Group 100 meeting, 283–284
Anchoring effect, 206
Annan, Kofi, 80

Annual recurring revenue (ARR), 258–260, 263

Answer to How Is Yes, The (Block), 323

Arrow, Kenneth, 174

Arsdale France, Van, 140

Aspirants (buyers), 170

Atomic Habits (Clear), 7–9

Attention
earning, 44–45
economy, 172–173
scarcity, 172

Attitude, impact, 287

Attractions, 20–21

Audit, Transfer, Fill (ATF), 54

Authoritarianism, 93–94

Automatic Customer, The (Warrillow), 122, 300

Autopsies without blame, 293

Average revenue per subscriber (fundamental KPI), 264

Average selling price (ASP), 264

B

Bacon, Francis, 327

Bad customers, impact, 215

Baker's law, 215

Balance sheet, origin, 258

Barrie, Corrie, 22–23

Basch, Michael, 277

Battered patient syndrome, 107, 113

Batt, Harry, 151

BCorp, 28, 29

Becoming a Part-Time CFO (Gandy), 175

Behaviors
change, 93–94
thoughts, relationship, 4

Belonging, 16, 21–22

Benchmarking, 159–160

Ben & Jerry's, value (subjective theory), 187–188

Berghoff, Jon, 47

Bernstein, Peter L., 161

Berra, Yogi, 230–231

Bertini, Marco, 102, 200, 332

Bezos, Jeff, 15–16, 104, 117, 143, 266

B Impact Assessment, scores, 29

Black Swan, The (Taleb), 268

Block, Peter, 323, 324

Blue Origin (Bezos), 117

Bookings (fundamental KPI), 263

Boomer, Gary, 63–64

Boorstin, Daniel, 251

Bosch, Robert, 141

Bourdain, Anthony, 147

Branson, Richard, 160

Brown, Sean, 25

"Built to last," 328–330

Bureaucracy, hidden tax, 227

Burgess, Matthew, 218

Burnout, 62, 108

Business, 47–48
cadence, 54
centering, 104
conception, 186–187
creation, dream, 3
engine rooms, 49f–53f
improvement, 48–56
leading, 55
lexicon, 164
meeting, image (receiving), 71f
owners, supply manufacture application, 55–56
pain points, elimination, 7
results, delivery, 9
running, 55
starting/static/scaling characteristic, 49
stepping stones, 48f

team, 56–64

transformation, 64

Business for Good (B1G1), 28, 68–70, 84

Business model, 21, 102–104, 119, 190

Business-to-business (B2B) environment, issues, 301

Business-to-business (B2B) expectations, 122

Business-to-business (B2B) focus, 7

Butler-Madden, Carolyn, 14

Buyer identification, 207

C

Cadence, establishment, 54–56

Call to action, 11

Cancellation, pushback, 195

Capitalism, impact, 329

Carnegie, Andrew, 246

Carrillo, Hilda, 64

Casey, Jim, 278

Cash flow, debate, 244

Castellano, Joseph f., 64

Castro, Fidel, 129–130

Catmull, Ed, 248, 289, 294

CFO Bookshelf (podcast), 175

Challenges, importance, 21

Change, 96

   handling, ability, 285

   speed, 31

Change Requests, determination, 113

Charging, level, 200–203

Checklist Manifesto, The (Gawande), 63

Chesterton, G.K., 146, 157

Chief Information Officers (CIOs), becoming, 28

Chinn, Mark, 137

Christensen, Clayton, 120, 134, 311, 315–317

Churn, 260, 264, 270, 301

Class with Drucker, A (Cohen), 320

Clear, James, 7–8

Client, definition, 163–164

Coaching firms, impact, 34

Coaching skills, 286

Code of Professional Conduct (AICPA), 223–224

Cohen, Ben, 187–188

Cohen, William, 320

Coincident indicators, 268–269

Collinshume, website (appearance), 33–34, 33f

Collins, Jim, 24, 293

Commitment, 39–40

   impact, 287

   lengthening, requirement, 224, 225–226

Commodity

   analysis, 157–159

   production, 329

   term, deletion, 160

   value, 181

Community, improvement, 66–67

Company

   customer recommendation, 274

   goals, review, 69

   owner exit, 24

   responses, 80–81

   social/environmental impact, measurement, 29

   triggers/goals, 68–69

Competence, derivation/ representation, 223–224

Competition, plagiarism (relationship), 157

Competitive differentiator, 173

Complexity tax, 145

Compulsory risk, 162

Concentric Circles (Marston), 222

Consultancy questioning sequence, 88f

Consumers
counting, ability, 249
surplus, 143
Contingencies, knowledge, 220, 222
Continuous innovation, 113, 157
Continuous learning, 285–286
Cook, Tim, 261
Core competency, 173
Corporate culture, definition, 138
Corporate financial statements,
analysis, 258–259
Corporate social responsibility (CSR)
initiative, 70
Cost
accounting, debate, 244, 247
determination, price (impact), 185
justification, 189, 245
minimization, obsession, 185–186
Cost-plus pricing, 124, 185
Covey, Stephen, 10
Covid, impact, 13, 252, 257
Creative destruction, 119, 125
Creativity, 154, 284
Creativity, Inc. (Catmull), 248, 289
Credence products, 191–192
Crosby, Philip, 242
Cross-selling metric (Wells Fargo
Bank), 250
Cross-subsidization situation, 219
Cult Status (Duggan), 68
Culture, importance, 61
Curtis, Carlton, 164
Customer
acceptance/nonacceptance, 10
acquisition, 274, 299
behavior, lagging indicator, 131
businesses, potential, 10
complaints, 304–306
complaints/defects, recovery
process, 305–306
connection, 67

contacts, recency/frequency/
quality, 276–277
effort score, 275
experience, 155, 227, 266
feedback, 201, 283
feelings, potential, 87
firm lifetime value, 302
hero, status, 172
improvement, subscriber
role, 64–66
innovation/transformation,
providing, 302
interaction, 176, 308
loss, reasons, 271
loyalty, 115, 273–275, 304
options, offering (effects), 205–206
outcomes, 71
perspectives, 14
price, 103
relationship, 115
retention, profitability, 299
risk, 192–196
segmentation, 205, 207–209
selection, 308
termination, 309
transformations, 167, 214
usage, payment, 218
Customer accounting service (CAS)
Smile Curve, 211–213, 212f
Customer acquisition cost (CAC),
264
Customer-centered outcomes, 34
Customer-driven organization charts,
65–66, 65f
"Customer-is-always-right"
philosophy, 10
Customer lifetime value (CLV), 125,
265–266, 269
Customer retention rate (CRR), 264
Customers for Life (Sewell), 305
Cyberchondria, 114

D

Dawson, Ross, 284

Deadlines, impact, 76

Dealers of Lighting (Hiltzik), 317

Decision-making process, 268

Default diary, usage, 54

Defects, absence, 298

Defensive medicine, 113

Deloitte, purpose, 25–26

Deming, W. Edwards, 180, 245–246, 278, 320

Derman, Emanuel, 120–121

Destruction (production), capitalism (impact), 329

Deteriorating paradigm, 259

Developing Knowledge-Based Client Relationships (Dawson), 284

Diamonds, expense (comparison), 183–187

Dijkstra, Edsger, 147

Director of joy (DJ), 54

Direct Primary Care (DPC), 111–112, 123, 132, 155

   disrupters, 107

   doctors, 115, 208, 218

   physicians, 156–157, 170

   practice, 315

   subscription model, 214

Direct-to-consumer (D2C) models, 122

Disney, Walt (company), 140, 152–153, 164, 221

Disrupters, 109–112, 312

Disruptive Strategy, 311–312

Dixon, Matthew, 275

Doctor's Expanded Guide to Concierge Medicine, The, 110, 112

Donkey strategy, 124

Double-entry bookkeeping, 174

Drucker, Peter, 131, 138, 146, 154, 281, 320

business management, ability, 246–247

customer value, question, 200

decision-making process, 268

knowledge worker perspective, 286

measurements, manageability, 248

opportunity, conversion, 171

path, discovery, 324

procrastination, avoidance, 273

risk classification, 162

Due care, 223–224

Dugan, David, 49, 51, 89

Duggan, Tim, 68

Dunn, Paul (script), 309

Dynamism, 254, 328–330

E

Earhart, Amelia, 333

Earned growth, components, 82

Earned new growth (ENG), 82

Ebeling, Richard, 322–323

Economics in One Lesson (Hazlitt), 269

Effective Executive, The (Drucker), 171, 268

Effectiveness, 145, 280–281

Efficiency, 241–242, 280

Einstein, Albert, 270, 290

Eisner, Michael, 303

Eliot, T.S., 292, 334

Embed, Social, Good (ESG), 79, 84

Emerson, Ralph Waldo, 141

Employees

   disengagement, 57–58

   empowerment, 27

   engagement, absence, 56f

Empowerment, 95–96

E-Myth (Gerber), 301

End of Accounting and the Path Forward for Investors and Managers, The (Lev/Gu), 258

Ends Game, The (Bertini/
 Koenigsberg), 102, 330
Engagement, 45, 56, 222–232, 234
Engine rooms, driving, 92f
Ensurance, 132
Enterprise choice, 224, 226–227
Enterprise resource planning
 (ERP), 209
Enterprise, soul (presence), 121
Entrepreneurship, 151–153, 161
Entrepreneurs, impact, 329
Environmental, Social, and
 Governance (ESG),
 25, 79, 81–83
Environment, performance
 (relationship), 74–77
Executive leadership team (ELT), 51
Expansion annual recurring revenue
 (EARR), 264
Experience Economy, The (Pine II/
 Gilmore), 130, 169, 178
Experience products, 191–192
Experience, theory (relationship),
 320
Explicit knowledge, 290–291

F

Facebook (FB) platforms, advertiser
 boycott, 19
Fader, Peter, 265
FairPay idea, 332
Fallacy of misplaced
 concreteness, 242–243
Fanning, Shawn, 119
Feedback
 delay, 293
 loop, creation, 15
 negative feedback, 231–232
Fee-for-service (FFS) business model,
 incentivization, 108
Fee-for-service competitor, 156–157
Fee-for-service mentality, 169

Fee-for-service (FFS)
 model, 314–315
Fender Play app, offering, 105
Feynman, Richard, 134, 153
Financial ratios, 159
Financial risk, 193
Financial statement reporting, GAAP
 (usage), 232
Fink, Larry, 22, 83
Firm, 144–147, 157–158
 creation, 313
 language, Williams test, 148–149
Firm of the Future 2.0, The, 123–129
Firm of the Future, The (Dunn/
 Baker), 42, 117, 124–126,
 134, 189
First-in, first-out (FIFO) valuation
 method, 243
First-in, still-here (FISH), 273
Fish model, 318
*Five Most Important Questions You
 Will Ever Ask About Your
 Organization, The*
 (Drucker), 138
Fixed-fee agreements, 319
Flow-on effect, impact, 15
FORD Consulting Model, 222
Ford, Henry, 143, 185–187, 245
Foresight, providing, 269
Forever Transaction, The (Kellman
 Baxter), 62
Framing effect, 148, 155–156, 206
Franklin, Aretha, 41
Fredericksen, Chris, 274
Freeman, Karen, 275
Friedman, Milton, 162, 267
Funnel, flywheel (relationship), 44f

G

Galford, Robert M., 271
Gamed (Smith), 262
Game plan, 74–75

Gandy, Mark, 175
Gates, Bill, 143
Gawande, Atul, 63–64
Geisse, John F., 312
Gellert, Ryan, 19
Generally accepted accounting
    principles (GAAP), 126–127,
    144, 232, 252, 258–259
Generic efficiency, absence, 124
Gerber, Michael, 301
Gibson, William, 326
Gilder, George, 131, 132, 142, 254
Gilmore, James H., 130,
    169–171, 177
Global Financial Crisis (2008), 13, 81
Global Goals, 36, 38
Goal, The (Goldratt), 245
Godin, Seth, 9–10, 16, 21, 45, 116
Goizueta, Robert, 129
Goldratt, Eliyahu, 245, 247
Goodhart's law, 249–250
Good to Great (Collins), 24
Gradual pivot, 314
Gratitude, impact, 75
Gray, Dave, 333
Great Depression, 249
Green, Charles H., 271
Greenfield, Jerry, 187
Gross churn, 264
Gross revenue retention
    (GRR), 263–264
Grove, Andy, 120
Growth costs, 260
Gu, Feng, 258
Guiding coalition, formation, 94

H
Hall, Scott, 109
Hammer, Michael, 104
Hard data, consideration, 242
Harnish, Verne, 59
Harper, Michael V., 292, 295

Hassle Free Home Services, Inc., 123
Hastings, Reed, 289
Havens, Joey, 175
Hayek, Friedrich A., 327
Hazlitt, Henry, 269
Health, assets, 116
Heisenberg's Uncertainty
    Principle, 249–250
Heraclitus, 172
Heymann, John, 288
High Satisfaction Day
    (HSD™), 288–289
Hilbert, David, 320
Hildenbrand, Robert, 313
Hiltzik, Michael, 317
Hindsight, providing, 269
Hoffer, Eric, 173
Holden, Reed, 207
Hollender, Jeffrey, 22, 62
Holmes, Oliver Wendell, 282
Hope Is Not a Method (Sullivan/
    Harper), 292
Horowitz, Andreessen, 263
Huddles, importance, 60–61
Human capital (HC), 127–129
Humans, physical/spiritual
    dimension, 121
Human-to-human relationships,
    enhancement, 6–7
Hume, David, 268

I
Impact-driven matters, 27, 44
Impact-driven purpose, 28–30, 34
Impact-driven results triangle,
    41–42, 42f
Impact, measurement, 34
Implementing Value Pricing (Baker),
    102, 125, 189, 222
Inadequacy marketing, 171–172
Income statement, 258, 261
Infinite value, 183

Information-graphic, impact, 34
Information technology (IT) firms,
    Smile Curve usage, 211f
Innovation, 151, 154, 294, 302
  continuation innovation, 113
  death, questions (usage), 319–326
  revenue, 273
  wealth creation, 254
Inputs, usage, 103
InspireCA, 59, 73f
Intellectual capital (IC),
    125–133, 199, 253
Intellectual property (IP)
Internet of Things (IOT), 177
Intuition/insight, measures
    (impact), 251
Inventory, valuation, 242
Invisible balance sheet, 253

J
Jackson, Jamere, 81
Janzer, Anne, 102
Jefferson, Thomas (questions), 323
Jevons, William Stanley, 182
Jiwa, Bernadette, 11
Jobs, Steve, 11–12, 119, 127,
    143, 261–262
Johnson, H. Thomas, 244–246, 251

K
Kaplan, Robert S., 244–246
Katzenbach, Jon, 287
Kellman Baxter, Robbie, 22, 62
Kennedy, Paul, 176
Keune, Timothy M., 64
Key performance indicators (KPIs),
    46, 126, 248, 257, 276
  accountability, equiva-
    lence, 277–278
  change, 133
  selection, 278
  shift, 43–44
  usage, 242, 262–267

Key predictive indicators, 267–277
Kierkegaard, Søren, 254
Kimball, Ward, 153
Kingdom of Speech, The (Wolfe), 163
King, Jr., Martin Luther, 282
Kitchen Confidential (Bourdain), 147
Kless, Ed, 79, 103, 121, 126, 134, 323
Knowledge, 6, 254
  elicitation, 284–285
  firms, asset-less organizations, 129
  lesson (US Army), 291–295
  producer/consumer, 285
Knowledge and Decisions
    (Sowell), 131
Knowledge-Creating Company, The
    (Nonaka/Takeuchi), 284, 291
Knowledge worker
  effectiveness, model, 280–282
  KPIs, 279, 282–287
Known knowns, 220
Known unknowns, 220, 301, 325
Koenigsberg, Oded, 102
Kotter, John, 93
Kuhn, Thomas, 267

L
Lagging indicators, 241, 266–269
Lagging KPIs, tracking, 270
Land, Edwind, 144
Language, innovation/invention,
    163–165, 165t, 173
Last-in, first-out (LIFO) valuation
    method, 243
Lawsuits, avoidance, 113
Lazanis, Ryan, 6, 62
Leadership, 59, 149–150
Leading indicators, 267, 268
Leading KPIs, development, 272
Lean programs, 297–298
Learning
  innovation, relationship, 131–132
  unlearning, difficulty, 318
Lee, Brody, 35

Lee, Reginald Tomas, 244, 255
Lee Segall's law, 243
Legacy
  change, 87
  living/leveraging/leaving, 91
Legal commitment, making, 29
Legal firms, necessities, 6
Lev, Baruch, 253, 258
Lies, Damned Lies, and Cost
    Accounting (Lee), 244
Liminal Thinking (Gray), 333
Liminal thinking, require-
    ment, 333–334
LinkedIn, user segmentation, 208
Listening/communication
    skills, 283–284
Lives
  changes, 6
  enrichment, goal, 4
  loss (WHO report), 14
  trust, 174–175
Loyalty, 38, 102
Loyalty Economics (Reichheld), 299
Loyalty Effect, The (Reichheld), 298

M
Macroeconomic environment,
    elements, 328
Macro pricing strategies, 196–197
Maister, David, 124, 155, 271
"Management by means" (Toyota
    usage), 245–246, 251
"Management by results,"
    245–246, 251
Management, focus, 52
Management thinking, advances, 328
Mandela, Nelson, 189
Marcus, Stanley, 142, 249
Marginalist Revolution
    (1871), 124, 182
Marketing, 151
  concept, 154
  problem, 119

Maron, Howard, 109, 197
Marston, Chris, 222
Martel, Dan, 54
Marx, Karl, 124, 181
Mattering, 21
McKinsey, maxim, 240–242, 248
MD^2, creation, 109–111, 197
Measurement
  change, 249–250
  content/usage, 239
  impossibility, 242
  moral hazards, 247–254
Measures, 249–251
  increase, comparison
    reduction, 252
  lag, 253–254
  metrics, contrast, 242–247
  reduction, 253
  unreliability, 251–252
Melancon, Barry, 6, 91
Menger, Carl, 182
Mercantilism, idea (discrediting), 127
Meta values, bank disappointment, 20
Metering, 208
Metrics, 242, 248, 262–267
  measures, contrast, 242–247
Micro-management, 93–94
Millennium Development Goals, 38
Mindset, 89, 314
Mind shift, difficulty, 315
Mintzberg, Henry, 253, 281–282
Misplaced concreteness,
    fallacy, 242–243
Mission, impact/statements, 25, 32
Models Behaving Badly
    (Derman), 120
Moment of truth (MOT), 303–304
Monitor Deloitte report,
    23–24, 23f, 58
Monthly recurring revenue (MRR),
    66, 263, 270
Moores Agreed Pricing (MAP), 237
Moral hazards, 239

Morris, Dan, 149
Mourkogiannis, Nikos, 138
Moving forward plans, 89–90
Munger, Michael C., 101
Musk, Elon, 157
My Life and Work (Ford), 185
Myths That Divide Us, The
    (Perazzo), 334

N
Nagle, Tom, 207
Negative experience, 303
Negative feedback, 231–232
Negative intellectual capital, 129–133
Net churn, 265
Net Positive (Polman/Winston), 47
Net Promoter Score™, 24, 45–46,
    273–275
Net recurring revenue (NRR), 82
Net retention rate (NRR), 264
Neuhofel, W. Ryan, 107
Neutral experience, 303
Neutral pricing, 199–200
New subscribers (fundamental
    KPI), 263
Newton, Isaac, 27
Nonaffordable risk, 162
Nonaka, Ikujiro, 284, 291
Nonfungible token (NFT), creation,
    180–181
Nonrival asset, 214
Nonrival good, 128
North Stars, 10, 38, 66
No Rules Rules (Hastings), 289
Novus, website (appearance), 34, 35f

O
Objective quality, 298
Objects and key results (OKRs), 243
O'Bryne, Paul, 309
O'Byrne, Paul (legacy), 176
Offerings, innovation, 236

Ogilvy, David, 146, 153
Onboarding, maximization, 301
One-and-done services, firm
    engagement, 171
One-firm business model, 103–104
One-off engagements, 222–232
Ongoing relationship, 63
Only the Paranoid Survive
    (Grove), 120
On-purpose company, employees
    (involvement), 58
Opportunity cost, 53, 241
Opportunity risk, 193
Organizational charts, 65f
Organizations, transformation, 93
Outcome-driven approach, 44
Outcomes, 7, 303, 304
    achievement, 230
    change, 11
    guarantee, absence, 330
    production, 18
Outside-in pricing, 233
Outward-focused business model,
    development, 115

P
Palo Alto Research Center (PARC),
    innovation develop-
    ment, 316–317
Passion, impact, 287
Patagonia, ad campaigns
    (withdrawal), 19–20
Patients
    doctor role, future, 114–117
    outcomes, 112–113
Payment commitment, 10
Payne, Ric, 42, 93, 176, 311
Peace-of-Mind models, 123
Penetration pricing, 198–199
Perazzo, John, 334
Perceived Value Curve, 176, 176f
Performance risk, 193

Personal development, 287
Personal medicine, power, 110
Personal transformations, 171
Pettengill, Samuel Barrett, 142
Physical risk, 193
Pine II, Joseph B., 130, 132,
    169–171, 177
Pivot Wealth, impacts (display), 85f
Platt, Lew, 128
Plussing, 155–157, 266
Polanyi, Michael, 290
Polman, Paul, 47
Popper, Karl, 267
Porsche Drive, 123, 219
Porter, Michael, 144
Portfolio pricing, 133, 217
Positioning, 137, 147–150, 217
Positioning for Professionals
    (Williams), 139
Positive experience, 303
Post-it Notes, usage, 60
Pragmamorphism, 121
Predictive indicators, tracking, 270
Price, 184–185
    contextuality, 180
    decline, 224, 226
    euphemisms, avoidance, 236
    increases, 235–237
    subtractive relationship, 184
    transparency, achievement,
        201–202
    upfront payment, 224, 225
    value, tradeoff, 206
Price, Dan, 27
Price, Harrison, 151
Price-led costing, usage (perceptions),
    186
Pricing
    branding, 237
    complex, 222–232
    flexibility, 236–237
    macro pricing strategies, 196–197

strategies, 196–200
tiers, 205–206
transparency, achievement, 202
Pricing on Purpose (Baker), 111
Pride, impact, 287
Problems, reframing, 87
Procrastination, avoidance, 273
Product
    bundling, 207
    classes, 191–192
    design, 207
Product, Place, Promotion, and Price
    (4 Ps), 186
Professional firm business model,
    history, 102–104
Professionals (role), payment
    (determination), 104–106
Profit, 142
    center, 154
    elimination, 161
    purpose, contrast, 141–144
Profitability
    equation, 125
    improvement, 66
Profit Beyond Measure (Johnson),
    245
Profit-led company, 22–26
Profit & loss (P&L) statement, 277
    income statement, contrast, 261
Profit-maximizing price,
        revenue-maximizing price
        (contrast), 197
Profits, source, 161–163
Progress, reporting, 37f
Project groups, 59
Propulsion (newsletter), 146
Psychological risk, 193
Purchase, location/time/quantity, 207
Purpose, 94–95, 137–144, 217
    measurement, 39
    power, 26
Purpose (Mourkogiannis), 138

Purpose-driven businesses,
drive, 39–40
Purpose-Driven Life, The
(Warren), 30
Purpose-led companies, 22–26
Purpose Triangle (Rajamannar), 39f

Q
QB CONNECT Conference
(Intuit), 61
Quantum Marketing (Rajamannar), 38

R
Rajamannar, Raja, 38–40
Purpose Triangle, 39f
Ravindran, Vijay, 102
Recurring costs, 260
Recurring profit margin, 260–261
Recurring revenue, 300
Reflections on the Human Condition
(Hoffer), 173
Reichheld, Fred, 10, 24, 82, 273–
275, 298–299
Reisman, Richard, 332
Relationships
pricing, 133, 189–190, 201
termination, 114
Relevance Lost (Johnson/
Kaplan), 244
Reoccurring revenue, 115, 307
Results
guarantee, absence, 330
influence, measurability (impos-
sibility), 246
Retainer medicine, 333
Retention, impact, 266
Retro, 59–64
Retrospective price, 229
Revealed preference, teaching, 104
Revenue, 102
equation, 124

fundamental KPI, 263
model, 200, 317
Revenue-maximizing price,
profit-maximizing price
(contrast), 197
Revenue/profits metric, 66
Reversal of flow, 43
Reverse auction, 251
Review, Align, Plan (RAP)
Sheets, usage, 90
Risk, 151
avoidance, 248
classification, 162–163
Risk-taking, 157, 284
Rumsfeld, Donald, 220

S
Sagan Fallacy, The, 240
Sales, attraction, 23
Salk, Jonas, 9, 183
Sato, Masami, 70
Scaling, 218, 219
Schmidt-Subramanian, Maxie, 82
Schmitt, William, 151
Schott, Ed, 151, 153
Schultz, Howard, 177
Schulze, Horst, 306
Schumpeter, Joseph, 119
Schutz, Peter, 145
Schwab, Charles R., 315–316
Scientific theories, formulation
method, 268
Scope creep, absence, 113
Search products, 191–192
Self
changes, 17
website, 36f
Serial transformations, providing, 168
Service quality, 297
Services
classes, 191–192

guarantee, 237
offerings, 213–214
satisfaction, 229–230
Sewell, Carl, 305
Shareholder theory, 141
Shifting-thinking, 7
Shift, making (requirement), 17f, 30f
Short-term wins, planning/
creating, 96
Sick leave, 77
Simon, Herbert A., 172
Simon, Julian, 251
Simplifier, The, 123
Simpson, Bruce, 20
Sinek, Simon, 24, 26, 29, 137
Six Sigma programs, 297–298
Skillsets, impact, 6, 43
Skim pricing, 197–198
Smile Curve. *See* Stan Shih
Smile Curve
Smith, Adam, 127
Smith, Bernie, 262
Social capital, 125, 128
Social/environmental performance,
demonstration, 29
Social good, embedding, 91
Social impact, 28
Social labour, crystallisation, 181
Social risk, 193
Society, leadership/stability, 15
Soft information, 241
Soft judgment, measurements
(relationship), 240
Software as a Service (SaaS),
7, 202–203
Soul of Enterprise, The (podcast),
108–109, 130, 134, 178
Southwest Airlines, pricing/
transparent approach, 198, 202
Sowell, Thomas, 131
Spooner, Fiona, 63

Stakeholder theory, 141
Stalin, Josef, 249
Standard, standout shift,
30–31, 31f, 33
Standard-Standout-Stand For, 84
Standing for, 31, 33f, 35f
Standing Team Huddle, 59
Stan Shih Smile Curve,
209–215, 210f
CAS usage, 211, 212f
frown curve, conversion, 212f
IT firm usage, 211f
Startup DPC (Thomas), 116
Start with Why (Sinek), 26, 29
Status quo, 77
maintenance, 325–326
Stearns, Gus, 232–234
Stein, Herbert, 249
Stengal, Jim, 158
Stiving, Mark, 265–266
Story arc, 12–13, 67f
Story creator, function, 12
Storyteller, vision/values/agenda, 12
Strategy, 137, 144–147, 217
Strategy and Tactics of Pricing, The
(Nagle/Holden), 207
Structural capital, 125, 128–129
Structures/processes, impact, 90
Subjective value, 298
Suboptimal pricing model, 116
Subscribed (Tzuo), 261
Subscription
adoption models/strategies,
313–319, 313f
architecture, 314
business, 190, 257
economy, 9–10, 99
impact, 330–331
pricing, adjustments, 236–237
revenues, growth (Subscription
Trade Association report), 100

Subscription-based service, building, 21
Subscription business model, 62–63, 99–100, 122–123, 155
  income statement, 259
  strategies, 224
  transition, decision, 324–325
Subscription Economy Index (SEI), 100
Subscription Marketing (Janzer), 102
Subscription model, 12, 21, 43, 299–300
  advantages, 190–191
  caring, importance, 80
  customer cancellation, 194–196
  customer risk, impact, 194
  dashboard, 262–267
  income statement, 258–262
  problem, 307–308
Success, measurement, 270
Success price, 229
Sullivan, Gordon R., 292, 295
Sunk cost, 241
Supply/demand, fundamentals, 55–56
Surrogation, 250
Sustainable Development Goals (SDGs), 6, 37f, 38
Sutherland, Rory, 156
Sveiby, Karl-Erik, 127
"Swallowing the fish," 318
Synsam Group, Synsam Lifestyle (launch), 105

T
Table stakes, 5
Tacit knowledge, 290–291, 295
Takeuchi, Hirotaka, 291
Taleb, Nassim, 268
Team
  improvement, 56–64
  members, business (connection), 62
Teams of Income, 43

Technical quality, 297
Teeming (Wooley-Barker), 25
Tesla, Nikola, 41
Testimonials, valuation, 17–18
Tetreault, Michael, 116
Thatcher, Margaret, 150
Theory, experience (relationship), 320
Thomas, Paul, 108, 116, 270, 315
Tie-ins, 208
Time, constraint, 116
Time-driven matters, 27, 44
Time loss risk, 193
Timesheets, usage (absence), 61
TIP clause, usage, 184, 224, 228–232, 234, 332
Toman, Nicholas, 275
Tomorrow 3.0 (Munger), 101
Total quality management (TQM), 297–298
Total quality service (TQS), 298, 320
Tower, Christopher, 82
Toyota, cost justification, 245
Transaction costs, 101, 174
Transfarency (Southwest Airlines), 202
Transfer (transaction cost type), 101
Transformation, 17–18, 45–46, 87, 93, 130–131
  customization, 99
  definition, 170, 314
  effectuation, 171
  focus, 168
  liminal thinking, requirement, 333–334
  opportunities, 173
  providing, 302
  revenue model, alignment, 201
  steps, 94–96
  value-creating projects, 177
Transformation as a Service (TaaS), 7
Transparency, exhibition, 29

Triangulation (transaction cost type), 101
True Professionalism (Maister), 155
True purpose, humanness, 26
Trust, 101, 173–174
Trusted advisor, table stake, 173–176
Trusted Advisor, The (Maister/Green/Galford), 271
Turnaround time, 272
Tzuo, Tien, 83, 100, 113, 201–203, 261–263, 313
   swallowing the fish, 318

U

Ukraine, Russian invasion (disruption), 13
Ultimate Question, The (Reichheld), 274
Uminger, Glenn, 245
Uncommon offerings/pricing, 200–203
Unconventional offerings, premium prices, 116
Underpricing, prevalence, 196
United Nations General Assembly (UN-GA) Resolution, 38
Unknowns unknowns, 222, 301, 325
Unlearning, difficulty, 318
Untrepreneur, 68
Upfront price, requirement, 224, 225
Upward spiral model, 87–89, 88f
Urgency, sense (establishment), 94
US Army, knowledge lessons, 291–295

V

Value
   axioms, 183–184
   capture, 143f, 190
   creation, 143f, 186
   customer perception, 200
   establishment, 233

   gap, 276
   highest level, 169–172
   labor theory, 181, 185, 220
   price, tradeoff, 206
   reframing, 155–157
   score, monitoring, 52–54
   stagnation, 173
   subjective theory, 10, 185, 187–189
   subtractive relationship, 184
   theories, comparison, 185
   trust, 224, 227–228
Value-creating projects, 177
Value Creation Score, 52
Value, Price, and Profit (Marx), 181
Value pricing, 221
   business model, 224
   principles, 318
   superiority, 125
   theory, comparison, 185
Value/values, 19–20
Vance, Ashlee, 157
Vision, 10, 25, 93
   creation/communication, 95
   representation, 50
   setting, 12, 15, 91
Volatility, uncertainty, complexity, and ambiguity (VUCA), 120
von Hayek, Friedrich, 280

W

Wall posters, example, 95f
Walras, Leon, 182
Warren, Rick, 30
Warrillow, John, 122, 300
Water, expense (comparison), 183–187
Wealth creation, 254
Webinar/web events, usage, 50
Welch, Jack, 146
Wells Fargo Bank, cross-selling metric, 250

*When You Come to a Fork in the
     Road, Take It!*
     (Berra), 230–231
Whitehead, Alfred North, 242
Whitney, George, 151, 153
Wickersham, Mark, 213, 218
Wicksell, Knut, 182
Wicksteed, Philip, 182
Williams, Tim, 139, 146, 148
Window on Main Street (Arsdale
     France), 140
Win, Keep, Grow (Stiving), 265
Winning on Purpose
     (Reichheld), 24, 82
Winston, Andrew, 47

Wolfe, Tom, 163
Wooley-Barker, Tamsin, 25,
     34, 45, 87
Work in progress (WIP),
     218, 260–261
World, understanding, 120–121
Wu, Eddy, 307–308

X
Xerox, problems, 316–317

Z
Zaid, Gabriel, 334
Zero defects/defections, 297,
     299